THE IMAGINARY AND ITS WORLDS

RE-MAPPING THE TRANSNATIONAL

A Dartmouth Series in American Studies
Series Editor
Donald E. Pease
Avalon Foundation Chair of Humanities
Founding Director of the Futures of American Studies Institute
Dartmouth College

The emergence of Transnational American Studies in the wake of the cold war marks the most significant reconfiguration of American Studies since its inception. The shock waves generated by a newly globalized world order demanded an understanding of America's embeddedness within global and local processes rather than scholarly reaffirmations of its splendid isolation. The series Re-Mapping the Transnational seeks to foster the cross-national dialogues needed to sustain the vitality of this emergent field. To advance a truly comparativist understanding of this scholarly endeavor, Dartmouth College Press welcomes monographs from scholars both inside and outside the United States.
For a complete list of books available in this series, see www.upne.com.

THE
IMAGINARY
AND ITS W●RLDS

American Studies after the
Transnational Turn

Edited by

Laura Bieger, Ramón Saldívar,
and Johannes Voelz

DARTMOUTH COLLEGE PRESS

Hanover, New Hampshire

DARTMOUTH COLLEGE PRESS

An imprint of University Press of New England

www.upne.com

© 2013 Trustees of Dartmouth College

All rights reserved

Manufactured in the United States of America

Designed by Katherine B. Kimball

Typeset in Sabon by Integrated Publishing Solutions

Library of Congress Cataloging-in-Publication Data

The imaginary and its worlds: American studies after the transnational turn / edited by Laura Bieger, Ramón Saldívar, and Johannes Voelz.

pages cm.—(Re-mapping the transnational: a Dartmouth series in American studies)

Based on papers originally presented at a 2009 conference hosted at the John-F.-Kennedy-Institut of the Freie Universität Berlin.

Includes bibliographical references and index.

ISBN 978-1-61168-418-6 (cloth: alk. paper)—ISBN 978-1-61168-407-0 (pbk.: alk. paper)—ISBN 978-1-61168-406-3 (ebook)

1. American literature—History and criticism—Congresses. 2. Transnationalism in literature—Congresses. 3. Culture in literature—Congresses. 4. Literature and transnationalism—United States—Congresses. 5. Transnationalism—United States—Congresses.

I. Bieger, Laura, editor of compilation. II. Saldívar, Ramón, 1949– editor of compilation. III. Voelz, Johannes, editor of compilation.

PS169.T73143 2013

810.9'355—dc23   2012046204

5 4 3 2 1

Contents

The Imaginary and Its Worlds
An Introduction

LAURA BIEGER, RAMÓN SALDÍVAR, AND JOHANNES VOELZ

This collection of essays is dedicated to conceptualizing the imaginary as a critical tool for the study of American literature and culture after the "transnational turn." Without a doubt, the "transnational turn" (a term coined by Shelley Fisher Fishkin) is here, and here to stay: the field of "transnational American studies" is growing with breathtaking rapidity, generating work on a wide range of cultural, political, and economic configurations that reach across national boundaries and change our views of what is situated within them. Even objects of study that once required a national frame of analysis now seem to demand a focus that does justice to regional, hemispheric, and global connectivities. The objective of this volume, however, is not to contribute to the scholarship of particular transnational formations, or to the mapping of the transnational turn. Rather, we are concerned with the concept of the imaginary, which the transnational turn newly urges us to recognize as a methodological and conceptual problem, and which takes different contours in a world conceived in transnational terms.

Transnational American Studies and the
Problem of the Imaginary

It is surely no coincidence that the concepts of the imagination and the imaginary have called forth a great level of renewed interest at the very moment when the transnational turn is transforming fields of inquiry once bound by national boundaries and exceptionalism. A wide range of scholars and activists, from David Graeber to Anthony Bogues and Robin G. Kelley, have invoked the "radical imagination" as the political act of thinking into existence alternative worlds that have not yet been granted social sanctioning or recognition. Indeed, the "radical imagination" has become something of a rallying cry for all kinds of political movements working toward social change. David Graeber, for instance, has praised the Occupy Wall Street activists of Zuccotti Park as creating a realistic chance for breaking "the 30-year stranglehold that has been placed on the human imagination" by the regime of free-market neoliberalism (Graeber). These appeals to the concept rest on what Arjun Appadurai has described as the "projective sense" of the imagination: "the sense of being a prelude to some sort of expression, whether aesthetic or otherwise" (Appadurai 7). The imagination (which is never quite identical with the term *imaginary:* we'll come to the distinction shortly) here refers to the appearance of new possibilities of social organization and political action, which are not yet spelled out as concrete utopias, and which—thanks to the vagueness of the pre-expressive—provide a source of hope for change.

But the imagination is also what creates the possibility for collective formations to recognize themselves as such, and it is here that the link between the transnational and the imagination/imaginary comes to the fore. The realm of the transnational is generally understood not as a set of stable social units spanning across national orders but rather as a constantly changing ensemble of formations-in-formation. The transnational is frequently described as a world that is in the process of becoming, and that shares with the imagination the sense of the preliminary. From the perspectives of transnational subjects, this means that the imagination takes on a more central role in everyday life, moving it out of its traditional, delimited cultural spaces like myth and ritual. With Appadurai we can argue that the transnational world, consisting of diasporas and spatially dispersed communities of all sorts, "bring[s] the force of the imagination, as both memory and desire, into the lives of many ordinary people, into mythographies different from the disciplines of myth and ritual of the classic sort. The key difference here is that these new mythographies are charters for new social projects, and not just a counterpoint to the certainties of daily life" (Appadurai 6).

The conceptualizing project undertaken in this volume stems from a particular conversation about the critical merits of the transnational turn, and about recent developments in American studies more generally. In this ongoing debate a group of Americanists from Europe (primarily Germany) and the United States have taken to heart Winfried Fluck's call to take the project of transnational studies truly seriously, which means "that scholars outside the U.S. do not just mimic the latest U.S.-American developments, but are self-confident and independent enough to develop their own perspective on them" (Fluck 2007a, 70). One such difference in perspective is the different intellectual traditions from which the contributors draw. We may broadly describe these traditions as "European" or "continental philosophy" on the one hand and "poststructuralist" or "postcolonial ideology critique" on the other. In staging acts and axes of this particular conversation, this volume does not return to the familiar cold war geography. Instead it seeks to capitalize on the confrontation of those different traditions, whose evolution resists being mapped onto national territories while being, at least in substantial part, traceable to particular locales and nodal points.

The immediate occasion out of which this book has grown was a conference hosted at the John-F.-Kennedy-Institut of the Freie Universität Berlin in the summer of 2009 in honor of Winfried Fluck. For over four decades Fluck has influentially intervened in international debates within the field, articulating disagreements between European and U.S. approaches to American studies. Having drawn on a range of philosophical and critical traditions, including reception aesthetics, pragmatism, phenomenology, and sociological theories of modernity, he has critically interrogated the plausibility of the premises suggested by what has become a largely unquestioned canon of poststructuralist and post-Marxist thought. Building on this critique, Fluck has also questioned dominant variants of the transnational reconceptualization of American studies. As he has argued repeatedly, transnational American studies should not do away with the nation-state but should contribute to the effort of theorizing American culture with the goal of gaining a more adequate understanding thereof. In his analysis, however, transnational American studies practitioners have fulfilled this task only implicitly—and, in fact, without much awareness of it. From his perspective, the impetus of many current Americanists to move their objects of inquiry beyond the borders of the nation is best described as the latest scholarly enterprise in a search for spaces of resistance. While Americanists of the myth-and-symbol school hoped to find a space of resistance in nonconformist aesthetics and values embodied in the masterpieces of the American Renaissance, later scholars described the aesthetic realm as thoroughly co-opted by ideology and instead believed themselves to have found spaces of resistance in the margins of a multicultural society. Seen in this light, transnationalism is a logical extension of this very trajectory, for now the potential spaces of resistance appear no longer at the social margins but beyond the nation's physical borders. In Fluck's reconstruction of the Americanist project, Americanists have increasingly described American culture as being controlled by various forms of ideological power, yet they have also continually construed the meaning of American culture as a function of its potential to resist (Fluck 2007a). Since World War II, the forces of power that were seen to demand resistance have quickly changed. What did not change was the goal of resistance itself.

A common way of evoking this potential to resist has recently offered itself by turning to the concept of the imaginary. As we outline momentarily, the concept of the imaginary is philosophically much too complex to be reduced to a longing for resistance. But much in line with the aforementioned appeal that the "radical imagination" has for political movements, the striking lure of the imaginary for Americanists may be attributed at least in part to the fact that as humanists we have been trained, and compelled, to search for spaces of resistance. Even the suggestive compounds in the titles and subtitles of several monographs by contributors to our immediate debate attest to this. To name just three, we point to the "transnational imaginary" (Ramón Saldívar), the "environmental imagination" (Lawrence Buell), and the "transatlantic imaginary" (Paul Giles).

At a closer look, the imaginaries invoked in the titles of these studies are of two kinds. In the more neutral version, the imaginary amounts to the widely shared common sense of a given society, or a "constellation of conflicting ideologies" (Moya and Saldívar 5). In its more emphatic variant, however, the imaginary brings forward a world that is less exclusionary and exceptionalist, more porous, overlapping, and cosmopolitan than traditional worldviews based on national boundaries had led us to presume. This notion of the imaginary does not present its "better worlds" as radically utopian; rather, it draws attention to the potentials— unrecognized by official discourses—slumbering in a given social formation. But if the imaginary is deemed crucial in both binding and transgressing social realities, its implicit or even unarticulated nature makes it not just an evocative but also a challenging object of study.

Literary and cultural studies are particularly drawn to the concept of the imaginary since it allows them to claim a privileged role for fiction, and cultural texts more generally, in the unfolding and assessing of these potential worlds. Fiction, according to the implied logic of this claim, is a forerunner in creating, articulating, and shaping these worlds; in giving them imaginary substance it can, in turn, affect the substance of the world beyond the text. Fiction thus becomes the province in which we can experience other versions of our actual world. This also means that the concept of the imaginary is immensely capable of lending relevance to the humanities, and literary studies in particular. Interpreting literature can, from this perspective, be conceived as an act of social and cultural criticism since it is in a privileged position to envision and articulate social alternatives. The imaginary thus becomes the touchstone of any political aspiration of literature and literary criticism. In ascribing this potential relevance to literature, literary studies implies a notion of the imaginary that highlights its generative capacities; it implies the imaginary as a productive force.

Even from such a rudimentary sketch it becomes clear that the imaginary is not separate from reality, an addendum or a surplus, somehow less important than the world "out there." Rather, the real itself depends on the existence of an imaginary. We cannot understand the *reality of the real* without mediating it through the imaginary. Whatever is real is accessible to us only if it is *imagined as real*. It *becomes* real not as an individual act or as the result of an individual faculty—the imagination—but by drawing on already existing forms and patterns—imaginaries—that have an important social function. Imaginaries provide communities with the glue that makes their members stick together. In their capacity of adjusting to changing social formations, these imaginaries not only give coherence to a collectivity but also enable and condition subjectivity. Imaginaries are thus structurally Janus-faced: they are generative processes that bring forth what does not yet have a social correlative, but they also have the power—indeed, it is their function—to fix, delimit, and reproduce collectively organized subjectivity.

Currently, this two-sidedness of the imaginary is in a process of complex readjustment. Globalization, in its recent intensification, exposes former modes of cultural cohesiveness to the centrifugal forces of disjunction and fragmentation. Yet at the same time it enables formations of imaginary belonging beyond the borders of the nation. A series of presidents of the American Studies Association, among them Amy Kaplan (in 2004), Shelley Fisher Fishkin (in 2005), and Emory Elliott (in 2007), have dedicated their presidential addresses to spelling out an agenda for an American studies that leaves behind the epistemic and methodological nationalism that has organized the study of American literature and culture since its inception.

If, however, the imaginary provides the forms and patterns that structure individual acts of imagining, a transnational turn in American studies urges us to explore a crucial complex of questions that has been neglected so far: How do the centrifugal forces of globalization affect the cultural and social productivity of the imaginary? Considering that transnational ways of belonging do not simply replicate the structures of collective imaginaries through which national communities cohere, nor have imaginaries been far from unmoored from the nation, how are we to reconceptualize the imaginary in a globalized world? More specifically, how do we theorize the function of the imaginary as a relay between the individual and its multi-scaled forms of social belonging, from the local to the global? How does the transnational framework alter the imaginary's work of interlacing interiority and exterior conditions? What are the effects of the transnational turn on the imaginary's interdependent constructions of mental and social space, as well as social space and social structure? Does transnationalism really give more prominence to the imagination in everyday life, and does that change the imaginary's role of relating the emergence of the as yet unsanctioned to the culturally prescripted? These questions provide the frame for this collection of essays as it sets out to consider the usefulness and potential of the imaginary in a globalized world. We want to use the remainder of this introduction to spell out some of the theoretical underpinnings of this endeavor.

Theoretical Perspectives on the Imaginary

Today, most literary scholars associate the imaginary with the work of Jacques Lacan, whose concept of the imaginary has, in fact, a highly productive dimension. At the very core of his notion of identity formation, its interplay with the symbolic order is instrumental in turning the individual into a social being. But the Lacanian imaginary gains its productive force by acts of misrepresentation: the individual identifies with its specular image in the mirror, though this image suggests a degree of coherence that the individual does not in fact possess. For Lacan, the specular image situates "the agency of the ego . . . in a fictional direction" (Lacan 2). Understood as fiction, this agency is more than a mere illusion: the ego begins to orient itself according to this fiction; it lives by it. Nonetheless, the specular image remains the basis of an alienating misrecognition: the self identifies with what it is not and cannot be.

Hal Foster has insightfully commented on the implicit yet rarely acknowledged historicity of this model of the self-alienated subject, pointing out that even though Lacan

> does not specify his theory of the subject as historical, and [it is] certainly . . .
> not limited to one period, this armored and aggressive subject is not just any
> being across history and culture: it is the modern subject as paranoid, even
> fascistic. Ghosted in his theory is a contemporary history of which fascism
> is the extreme symptom: a history of world war and military mutilation, of

industrial discipline and mechanical fragmentation, of mercenary murder and political terror. In relation to such events the modern subject becomes armored—against otherness from within (sexuality, the unconscious) and otherness without (for the fascists this can mean Jews, Communists, gays, women), all figures of this fear of the body in pieces come again, of the body given over to the fragmentary and the fluid. (Foster 226)

If the Lacanian model of the imaginary, in generalizing a subject not only split between self and image but also armored inside and out, prescribes a radical state of non-belonging out of historic circumstance, the many applications of this model tend to reiterate this state for the sake of its seemingly ahistorical premises about self-alienation as a sine qua non of subjecthood (and often at the risk of tautological argumentation, in which this "master condition" features as both premise and result). It seems to us, however, that matters of belonging adhere to different forms and patterns of imagining subjectivity and collectivity after the transnational turn—a social imaginary that pays tribute to both the lasting presence of the nation and the centrifugal forces of globalization. The Lacanian model, with its strong bias of the imaginary's productivity toward self-alienation, might not be the best model for the task at hand.

Lacan's enormous influence in cultural and literary criticism must in part be attributed to his reception by structuralist Marxists like Louis Althusser, who used the Lacanian notion of the imaginary to explain how ideology works. In the act that Althusser calls "ideological interpellation"— the transformation from individual to subject through hailing—the "I" is propelled by precisely the kind of imaginary misrecognition theorized by Lacan. Upon being hailed, the subject accepts the ruling ideologies of its society and does so in a particular manner: by imagining—and misrecognizing—itself as an autonomous subject, that is, by misrecognizing how it relates to "the conditions of existence." In Althusser's diction, "It is not their real conditions of existence, their real world, that 'men' 'represent to themselves' in ideology, but above all it is their relation to those conditions of existence which is represented to them there. It is this relation which is at the centre of every ideological, i.e. imaginary, representation of the real world" (Althusser 164). For Althusser, imaginary representations *are* ideological representations; what is present in the imaginary is an ideologically tinted (even inverted) version of the real conditions of existence. Misrepresenting "the relationship of individuals to their real conditions of existence" (162), the imaginary remains dependent on these conditions. In the tradition deriving from Lacan and Althusser, the imaginary is a category of reflection, and is thus incapable of producing anything new or socially unmarked. It ultimately stands in the service of reproducing existing power relations.

This point is relevant not simply because the Althusserian heritage has played a major role in shaping a theoretical common sense for U.S.-based literary and cultural studies. By providing a model for conceptualizing the imaginary as a force of social reproduction, the Althusserian tradition also intersects with approaches to the imaginary that may not be Marxist at all but that have become canonized points of reference in interdisciplinary discussions of the imaginary. The most striking example of this kind is the work on "social imaginaries" by Charles Taylor. Taylor's work has been taken up in literary and cultural studies in part because it ascribes to cultural texts the role of articulating what binds a given social entity together. Taylor draws explicitly on Benedict Anderson's theorem of "imagined communities" in order to trace historically the constituent elements of the "modern social imaginary." For the present discussion, these historically specific elements are of less interest than his conception of the social imaginary itself, which he conceives not as a specific set of ideas but rather as "what enables, through making sense of, the practices of a society" (Taylor 91). For Taylor, the term *imaginary* refers to "the ways in which people imagine their social existence, how they fit together with others, how things go on between them and their fellows, the expectations that are normally met, and the deeper normative notions and images that underlie these expectations. . . . I speak of *imaginary* because I'm talking about the way ordinary people 'imagine' their social surroundings, and this is often not expressed in theoretical terms; it is carried in images, stories, and legends" (106).

Taylor's definition seems very plausible; surely it must be the case that members of a social unit share some deep assumptions on the basis of which they come to an unspoken agreement on how to live together. Through this claim, however, Taylor's concept of the imaginary becomes a rather one-sided affair: this type of social imaginary is always already in place. While modernity develops its own distinct social imaginaries—in Taylor's analysis they center on the economy, the public sphere, and popular sovereignty—imaginaries have an integrative function and thus bind the individual to what is shared by a given society. For Taylor, the imaginary is the end result of a process of the popularization of theory. Explicit ideas are first introduced by philosophers; from there they stand a chance of seeping into images, stories, and legends of "ordinary people." Thus some theories become shared in imaginary rather than theoretical form by all members of a society. Taylor's imaginary is therefore not productive but derivative: it does not articulate the previously unimaginable but rather represents what has moved from theoretical and conscious deliberation to an uncontested consensus.

This allows us to spell out the often unacknowledged premise of literary and cultural scholarship that draws on Taylor: literary texts and other cultural artifacts are seen as materials worth studying insofar as they contain those elements that glue together a social body. In a manner not so different from the Althusserian tradition, reading for the imaginary under Taylor's precepts turns into a practice that treats texts as reflective mirrors for their social contexts. While for Althusser what is reflected (and imaginarily obscured) are the "real"—economic—conditions, for Taylor the social imaginary prestructures an individual's worldview so that this individual's expression (or an individual work of art) reflects the antecedent social structure of mind.

In his argument Taylor adopts central assumptions from Benedict Anderson's seminal *Imagined Communities* (1983), which, like Taylor's recent writings, has more to say about the historical specificity of the modern imaginary than about the concept itself. Anderson initially emphasizes its productive dimension: the imaginary brings forth communities, not as illusions but as realities. In order to emerge, collectives need to imagine themselves as such: "In fact, all communities other than primordial villages of face-to-face contact (and perhaps even these) are imagined" (Anderson 6). But because such imaginations are collective, the productivity is limited to the collective dimension. From the perspective of the individual, what is imagined is already shared and therefore given.

For Anderson, modern nations imagine themselves as limited (the imagination rests on a distinction between self and other), sovereign (it is the idea of freedom that sets the nation, in its self-understanding, apart from divinely ordained, dynastic rule), and communal (in the national imagination all members are equal, independent of actual power inequalities) (see Anderson 7). Taylor's key characteristics of the modern social imaginary (economy, popular sovereignty, and public sphere) refine and revise the dominant traits laid out by Anderson (limitation, sovereignty, and community). But while it is tempting to engage with Taylor and Anderson in a discussion over the usefulness of their suggested characteristics, it is perhaps even more central to turn to the consequences of their respective approaches. For both Anderson and Taylor, imaginaries correspond to finite social bodies that develop an imagination about themselves. Ultimately, a community that imagines itself appears as a community with clear-cut boundaries. For Anderson and Taylor, nations exist because the imagination changes at the national border (though social or national imaginaries will be structured along parallel lines).

As the anthropologist Claudia Strauss has aptly pointed out, Anderson's and Taylor's theories are a seamless fit for "cognitive anthropologists' conception of cultural models, which are similarly shared, implicit schemas of interpretation, rather than explicit ideologies" (Strauss 325). She writes despairingly about her own field that "the application [of these theories to anthropology often] is shallow, with 'imaginary' or 'the imagined' used . . . in a context where, 20 or more years ago, 'culture' or 'cultural beliefs' would have been used instead" (331). We have to wonder whether Strauss's dissatisfaction with these applications in her own field does not in part go back to a limitation within Anderson's and Taylor's concepts. Where the imaginary designates a shared corpus of background assumptions, it may indeed come close to reviving anthropological notions of "culture" that stand at the center of literary and cultural studies as well.

The most obvious problem of such a tacit exchange of *imaginary* for *culture* would be that while postcolonial studies, border studies, and, increasingly, American studies have worked hard to conceptualize cultures as fluid, hybrid, overlapping, and so on, the turn to the imaginary would reinstate, as a parallel discourse, a reified notion of culture once again. The imaginary, from this perspective, would appear as a concept strikingly unproductive for theorizing phenomena of a global or transnational reach. Even if, however, Anderson and particularly Taylor tend to overemphasize the imaginary's function of providing a common set of background assumptions for the members of a bounded collective, this should not lead us to give up on the potentials of the concept. As we pointed out before, the imaginary is inherently Janus-faced. It does not simply designate what binds us together; it also points to the generative work of the imagination. No theorist has been more intensely concerned with this productive dimension of the imaginary than Cornelius Castoriadis.

For Castoriadis, the imaginary does not represent but rather makes present. It is a radically creative force that brings forth ex nihilo the new and indeterminate. Castoriadis's study *The Imaginary Institution of Society* (1975) was leveled at both orthodox Marxism (to which he often referred as functionalism) and structuralism. From his own position, steeped in a nonstructuralist Marxist variant of psychoanalysis, "creation" is a process that happens on the level of individual and society. On the level of the psyche, what he calls the "radical imagination" gives presence and form to an undifferentiated undercurrent of being. Analogously, on the social level, the "radical imaginary" brings forth, in an indeterminate manner, meanings and significations that form the basis of institutions. Castoriadis calls this the "instituting imaginary." Despite this emphasis on creation, Castoriadis shares with Anderson and Taylor the view that societies need to establish a set of background assumptions that provide the grounds for the creation of new meanings. Castoriadis calls these background assumptions "imaginary significations." His favorite example of an imaginary signification is God: "God is perhaps, for each of the faithful, an 'image'—which can even be a 'precise' representation— but God, as an imaginary social signification, is neither the 'sum,' nor the 'common part,' nor the 'average' of these images; it is rather their condition of possibility and what makes these images images 'of God'" (Castoriadis 1987, 143).

In a broader sense, imaginary significations provide societies with both a self-image and an accompanying world-image. "World-image and self-image are obviously always related. Their unity, however, is in its turn borne by the definition each society gives of its needs, as this is inscribed in its activity, its actual social doing. The self-image a society gives itself includes as an essential moment the choice of objects and acts, etc., embodying that which, for it, has meaning and value" (Castoriadis 147). For Castoriadis, the imaginary thus encompasses two sides that initially may seem very much at odds with each other. On the one hand, societies are constantly in the process of constructing a self-image for themselves. This act of imaginary social self-construction can be understood as the social or collective version of the generative power of the individual imagination. In both cases, something without prior existence is posited imaginarily. But on the other hand, these social acts of imaginary creation also produce social meanings (imaginary significations) that are in turn the condition of possibility for social imaginary creation. In Castoriadis's theory, the imaginary thus refers both to the act of creation and to what has been created.

Castoriadis describes this two-sidedness through the terms "instituting imaginary" and "instituted imaginary." These contrasting terms may seem antagonists in an epic struggle of autonomy against heteronomy. But for Castoriadis, the instituting and instituted imaginaries are both essential to society's capacity of autonomous creation. Jeff Klooger explains how Castoriadis links instituting and instituted imaginary as two elements of autonomous social creation: "Since all determination is limitation, the self-determination of an autonomous subject is necessarily a self-limitation. . . . Self-creation inevitably involves both a striving for determination and against it, the establishment of boundaries as well as their rejection, the struggle to escape and transcend them. This dichotomy merely represents twin aspects of one and the same activity: self-creation as a perpetual mode of being" (Klooger 29). In other words, the background assumptions of the instituted imaginary are flexible and moreover functional for the process of perpetual imaginary creation. Their necessary presence presupposes their own decomposition.

From Castoriadis's perspective, acts of the imaginary are at once socially embedded and inherently transgressive. It is because of this transgressive force that the imaginary projects, on the basis of imaginary significations, what can be called a social avant-garde. According to Wolfgang Iser, whose work has been most substantial in thinking about literature's relation to the imaginary, the realm of the literary broadens the possible range in which the imagination can come into play. Building on Castoriadis's notion of the radical imaginary, he stresses the special importance of fictionalizing acts in mediating between the imaginary and the real. In drawing on the frames, discourses, and world pictures of the given world ("reality"), the fictionalizing acts of literature give the amorphous, inarticulate stream of the imaginary their *Gestalt*. Because they are not bound to pragmatic use, fictionalizing acts can go to extremes in articulating aspects of the imaginary. Iser's approach may be the strongest theoretical explanation for why literary studies is a particularly pertinent field for exploring the functions of the imaginary. If literature assumes a privileged role in making us understand particular imaginaries, critical readings can engender avant-garde movements by bringing to the fore meanings that are not yet within the realm of the sayable or thinkable of other social settings.

The Imaginary and the Spatial Turn

The "transnational imaginary" can be understood as precisely such an avant-garde intervention. "The transnational" is an act of imaginary *Gestalt*-giving. In making present something that could not be articulated before, the transnational imaginary engenders a creative rethinking of the relation between social structure and space. If transnationalism thinks in terms of networks, flows, and dynamic relations, such as the juxtaposed, the near and far, the side-by-side, or the dispersed (see Foucault 22), space is no longer a stable entity on which processes of historical change act. In this sense the transnational reminds us that our conceptions of the imaginary must begin to grapple with this recently "discovered" dynamism and productivity of space, and with the complex and contested ways in which it is *socially produced* (see Lefebvre, Soja, Massey). As Doreen Massey aptly stresses:

> Social relations always have a spatial form and spatial content. They exist, necessarily, both *in* space (i.e., in a locational relation to other social phenomena) and *across* space. And it is the vast complexity of the interlocking and articulating nets of social relations which is social space. Given that conception of space, a 'place' is formed out of the particular set of social relations which interact at a particular location. And the singularity of any individual place is formed in part out of the specificity of the interactions which occur at that location (nowhere else does this precise mixture occur) and in part out of the fact that the meeting of those social relations at that location (their partly happenstance juxtaposition) will in turn produce new social effects. (Massey 168)

But if we take space to be produced through social interaction, it also, inevitably, becomes subjected to the transformative maelstrom of the imaginary. The transnational, in encountering and reenvisioning modes of spatial production and social organization, urges us to rethink the relation between the imaginary as a transformative force and the imaginary as a spatiotemporal agent of fixity and institutionalization. Drawing substantially on Castoriadis and Iser, Winfried Fluck has dedicated much of his work to assessing the scope in which the productive force of the imaginary pervades and conditions social action and formation (Fluck 1996, 2002, 2003a, 2003b, 2005, 2007b). His reflections have also taken him to the issue of space. As Fluck points out, in order to assess one's surroundings, a recipient has to bind and make cohere the "physical particles and sense impressions [of a perceived space] by means of an ordering principle, that is, a principle that provides it with some kind of meaning (if only that of representing a 'chaotic' world). Or, to put it differently: in order to gain cultural meaning, physical space has to become mental space or, more precisely, *imaginary space*" (Fluck 2005, 25; emphasis added). Turning to literary and cultural representations of space, he goes on to argue that they too "create not only a mental but an imaginary space; even where this representation may appear life-like, truthful or authentic, its actual status is that of an aesthetic object that invites, in effect, necessitates a transfer by the spectator in order to provide meaning and to create an aesthetic experience" (34).

While we think that this point is perfectly apt in stressing the indispensible function of the imaginary in the creation of space, its impact on the social production of space can be pressed even further. On the one hand, literary and cultural representations of space have the effect of fictionally "doubling" the mechanisms and processes of their production since fictional world-making reenacts the reality-conditioning imagination of space. Within the fictional world of the text, this process thus becomes an object of aesthetic experience; beyond its borders, on the other hand, these representations become effective as a social practice that—through the fictional doubling that feeds the aesthetic experience—partakes in the productivity of Lefebvre's third pole of spatial production. It creates imaginary maps of the social relations that constitute space and thus vitally define—and challenge—the very frames in which this space is *used* and *lived* (Lefebvre 1991).

The Essays

Two main trajectories are opened up by these reflections that are to serve as our starting point. One is to explore the imaginary in relation to a number of dominant facets of globalization, among them transnational flows of ideas, practices, and goods; an increasingly mediated life; free trade economies; and de-territorialized state powers. The other takes globalization's challenge to the imaginary as an invitation to rethink the concept itself, generating new perspectives on the role of the imaginary as a crucial force in shaping modernity; on the very notion of collective cohesiveness; on the attempts of power to permeate the imaginary in order to set in place binding imperatives and foreclosures; and on the potential for the transgressions occurring at the interface of individual and collective imaginaries to effect the transformation of social orders.

The first section of this volume, "Literary Imaginaries," opens with the theme of transnational imaginaries and explores their articulation in U.S. literature through a sample of texts spanning three centuries: contemporary ethnic fiction, the tradition of the *Bildungsroman*, and literary modernism. Stressing the task of integrating formerly unacknowledged voices and collectives, Ramón Saldívar's essay, "Imagining Cultures: The Transnational Imaginary in Postrace America," approaches the imaginary from the perspective of critical race studies. Saldívar focuses on the topic of race and narrative theory in relation to the question of literary form and history in Junot Díaz's Pulitzer Prize–winning novel *The Brief and Wondrous Life of Oscar Wao* (2007). Saldívar addresses the poetics of genre and the generative power of generic hybridity in classic narrative forms in order to show how versions of aesthetics, as well as conceptions of history linked to the historical novel in their modern and postmodern versions, are being fundamentally reshaped by contemporary American writers of color. Exemplary in staging a collective imaginary that attempts to consolidate the geographically disparate and troubled sites of Dominican American identity by means of fiction, Díaz's novel becomes a test case for reframing and re-creating the shattered imaginaries of diasporic communities in the form of "imaginary history."

In "The Necessary Fragmentation of the (U.S.) Literary-Cultural Imaginary," Lawrence Buell explores fragmentation and cohesion as two opposite thrusts that work on national imaginaries in the age of transnationalism. In order to trace historically how these forces have operated in U.S. culture—and literature in particular—Buell focuses on what he describes as the "American dream narrative," which he places in the transnational context of the *Bildungsroman*. Concerning the U.S. national imaginary, these narratives of self-realization oscillate between reaffirming American exceptionalism and fragmenting the national imaginary for its imposed limits on the self, especially if they belong to the "ethnic *Bildungsroman*." In Buell's account, this history is not just indicative of the genre's function to mediate between the contradictory forces within the collective imaginary of U.S. national culture; it can also be used as a matrix to study the shifts, mostly induced by revisionist scholarship, within the "field imaginary" (Donald Pease) of American studies. In light of Buell's argument, transnationalism emerges as the particular field imaginary that can achieve both an affirmation of fragmentation and the necessary degree of disciplinary cohesion.

In "Imaginaries of American Modernism," Heinz Ickstadt breaks up the established linear account of American modernism that celebrated aesthetic innovation as America's modern coming of age. Instead he places American modernism in a hemispheric and transatlantic network of conflicting and overlapping imaginary worlds that articulated culturally wished-for and yet-to-be realized alternatives. Ickstadt makes out two dominant imaginaries among American modernists that can be distinguished despite their ultimately congruent goals. On the one hand, there are cultural nationalists, like Waldo Frank, Jean Toomer, and several members of the Stieglitz circle, who strove for organic wholeness on various levels of awareness—expressive, psychological, spiritual, and aesthetic. This type of cultural nationalism did not praise the U.S. nation-state but, as exemplified by Waldo Frank's embrace of "Our America," aligned itself with Rubén Darío's and José Martí's visions of pre-Columbian, pan–Latin

American transnationalism. Ickstadt contrasts the cultural nationalists' organicism with the particularism of William Carlos Williams, Gertrude Stein, Ezra Pound, and others, which emphasized an anti-symbolic literalism, yet ultimately also envisioned a transformation of the shattered modern world through the capacity of the letter to reach an experience of higher unity.

The second section of this volume, "Social Imaginaries," addresses matters of normativization, exclusion/inclusion, and space production through the lens of Jamesian pragmatism, figurational sociology, Castoriadis's notion of the imaginary, and systems theory. Herwig Friedl opens the section by critically interrogating the very notion of a social imaginary. His essay, "William James versus Charles Taylor: Philosophy of Religion and the Confines of the Social and Cultural Imaginaries," critiques sociocentric tendencies that he traces from nineteenth-century philosophers like Ludwig Feuerbach to twentieth-century theorists such as Émile Durkheim and Charles Taylor. For Friedl, Taylor's concept of "social imaginaries" epitomizes the neglect characteristic of sociocentrism of those dimensions of being that transgress what is already socially scripted. Friedl links the theoretical debate of the imaginary's social determination to the question of the religious. He contends that the religious, if it is not reduced to a Durkheimian functionalism, poses a challenge to the totalizing force attributed to the social and cultural imaginary. In order to stage a confrontation between the religious and the social imaginary, Friedl contrasts Charles Taylor's *Varieties of Religion Today* (2002) and *Modern Social Imaginaries* (2004) to the work to which Taylor paid critical homage: William James's *Varieties of Religious Experience* (1902). Friedl wholeheartedly defends James's insistence on a "*trans-human Logos*" that forms an inextricable part not just of religious experience but of experiencing per se.

Christa Buschendorf, in "The Shaping of We-Group Identities in the African American Community: A Perspective of Figurational Sociology on the Cultural Imaginary," traces the construction of African American collective imaginaries through Frederick Douglass's and W. E. B. Du Bois's writings and rhetoric. These imaginaries challenge Benedict Anderson's and Charles Taylor's models, according to which modern national imaginaries are built on ideas of fraternity and equality. Drawing on Norbert Elias, Buschendorf reconstructs African American imaginaries as growing out of figurations constitutively organized by power differentials. In Douglass's and Du Bois's writings, we witness how the condition of marginality and violence produced an African American imagined community that adds to the identification with the national community an identification with universal networks. African American "we-identities" thus transform their socially ascribed outsider position into imaginaries of global connectedness and thus significantly move beyond the self-limitations characteristic of the imaginaries of established groups.

While Buschendorf shows how African Americans' imagination of the global and universal grew out of their national domination by white Americans, Lene Johannessen, in "Russia's Californio Romance: The Other Shores of Whitman's Pacific," explores a different way in which collective imaginaries contributed to the "experience of globality" (Peter Hitchcock). She focuses on the encounter of Nikolai Petrovitch Rezanov, envoy of the Russian American Company, with José Joaquín de Arrillaga, governor of Nueva California, and Don Luis Darío Argüello, commander of the Presidio, in San Francisco in 1806. From her reconstruction emerges a process of transnationalization that is quintessentially palimpsestic. Transnationalization adds and overwrites layers of imaginaries—in her case study, Russian, Spanish, and American—each of which operates as an enabling frame. Johannessen, in effect, extends Charles Taylor's notion of the imaginary. Just as in Taylor's view, for Johannessen the imaginary enables a group to grasp and perform an understanding of its own practices. But in doing so, the imaginary also becomes a trace in a palimpsestic process of transnationalization, a process that tears open the seams and confines of the collective identity which the imaginary helps articulate.

Taking yet another approach to the pervasive operation of social imaginaries, Mark Seltzer addresses them from a perspective of game theory and the ways in which the structure and function of games make conceivable—and, one might add, compellingly experienceable—the self-reflexivity of modern social systems. In "Form Games: Staging Life in the Systems Epoch," Seltzer takes Niklas Luhmann's systems theory as his point of departure to elucidate how games generate realities that are staged for the sake of their observation. These game realities are "models of a self-modeling world" that serve modern society to monitor reflexively its self-created social realities. Seltzer aligns the imaginary with the distinction between game and world, thought of as an incessant feedback loop between the human senses and the media. Real and fictional reality, Seltzer argues, are continually copied into each other. Games can thus become models "both of the world and in it." Seltzer's systems-theoretical approach opens up a new and comprehensive way of drawing attention to the crucial role a medial genealogy of the modernizing world has to play in rethinking the imaginary as an overarching critical tool.

The third and final section, "Political Imaginaries," rounds off this volume by investigating two topics with special importance for the proliferation of the political imaginaries of the future: the challenges of neoliberalism and political romanticism. In his essay "Real Toads," Walter Benn Michaels examines the contemporary literary imagination, exemplified by the popularity of the neorealist and historical novel, from the perspective of neoliberalism. Michaels has been at the center of a fervent debate focusing on his argument that American multiculturalism has embraced identitarian difference at the cost of eclipsing economic inequality. In his contribution to this volume, he enforces this argument by proposing that this logic, which rests on an "epistemology of pluralism," is also at play in celebrated novels by Toni Morrison and Philip Roth, as well as younger writers such as Michael Chabon and Colson Whitehead. In embracing the promise of justice entailed in this epistemology's normativity of difference, these novels fail not just once but twice: in articulating the pressing realities of economic inequality and in foreclosing the possibility of imagining them. In doing so, Michaels asserts, they advance the ongoing process of cementing and legitimizing a neoliberalist rationale that tampers with the democratic foundations of U.S. society.

The two remaining contributions to this section turn to the candidacy and presidency of Barack Obama as generators of political imaginaries. Christopher Newfield, in "Obama Unwound: The Romanticism of Victory and the Defeat of Compromise," takes Obama's poor midterm results in 2010 as a point of departure to ask what caused this president so sweepingly elected into office to lose much of his popularity in only half a term. Newfield locates the answer in the political romanticism that drove the 2008 election: Obama's popularity rested on his ability to tap into the country's "wounded romanticism" and channel it into the collective longing for a world in which personal desire would be not rejected but realized in a common democratic vision. It began to falter when his "coalition of political sufferers," coerced by imagining "a non-agonizing common world constituted by political life," was confronted with a political reality of compromise that not only betrayed the psychic needs of his supporters but also threatened to foreclose the opportunity for laying the real and imaginary foundations of economic recovery in the near future.

In "Barack Obama's Orphic Mysteries," Donald Pease offers an alternative reading to this recurring dilemma of political romanticism versus *Realpolitik*, proposing that Obama succeeded in fabricating a racial counterimaginary that subtended his campaign and election and stabilized his presidency, most notably against the assault of the Tea Party and his controversial foreign policies. Equally rejecting the roles of civil rights leader and illegal alien/Muslim terrorist, this new imaginary "discerned the black messiah/black devil complex as the racist antinomy that underpinned the history of race relations in the United States," thus deregulating "what was considered possible and impossible for African American political leaders to desire." The resulting rift was effectively filled, and continuously refilled, by Obama's plea for "a more perfect union," the foundational fantasy of his success. This success (if one wants to call it that) is "orphic" in the sense that Obama discerned the structuring antinomy underpinning the United States' racial imaginary when viewing the film *Black Orpheus* but did not displace it during his presidency. Obama's desire for a "more perfect union," Pease thus concludes, may be—like that of the classical Orpheus—made up of "radical hope and audacious despair."

The volume closes with a contribution by Winfried Fluck that explores the imaginary through the lens of reception aesthetics. In his long-standing engagement with theories of American culture before and after the transnational turn, Fluck has been particularly invested in two projects: he has relentlessly scrutinized the underlying premises of the field of American studies and their impact on prefiguring their object of study; and he has spelled out the process of "imaginary transfer," which he conceives as foundational to aesthetic experience and as a touchstone for assessing both the field's metamorphosing object and its method of study. His chapter, "The Imaginary and the Second Narrative: Reading as Transfer," is the most comprehensive attempt to date to bring these two trajectories together. "Imaginary transfer" constitutes a state in between the fictional and the nonfictional world inhabited by the recipient, as this recipient, in an act of imaginary role play, realizes the fictional world on the basis of his or her experience. When engaging with fictional texts, this act of transfer can exceed and enhance the actual, lived experience of the reader. Expanding on this model, Fluck now introduces the notion of a "second narrative" to designate a chain of analogies drawn by the reader between the world of the text and that of the reader. Because the production of analogies can depart from any element within the fictional world, it radically widens the scope of imaginary transfer, thus helping explain why there are endlessly diverging interpretations of texts, and also why texts with little obvious resonance for our own time still matter to us. The "second narrative," Fluck contends, is not determinable by interpellation or discursively produced readers since it consists of multiple positions of identification, opening up ever-newer possibilities of analogy production.

The ramifications of Fluck's emphasis on "imaginary transfer" for the theoretical discussion of the imaginary are as remarkable as they are controversial: Just as his account of the necessary plurality of second narratives calls into question the assumed goal of communities of interpreters to reach a consensus about a text's meaning—disagreement, writes Fluck, is a "resource," not a "problem"—so does the imaginary as a whole appear less a communal or cultural consensus about values and ways of doing things and much more the act of individuals in finding analogies to cultural givens. Because they articulate what hitherto could not find expression, these analogies are never entirely foreseeable; instead they generate the new. This capacity, however, can be activated only in a dialogue with the given, and it is by no means certain that what is generated will or can transpire into a political or collective vision. If this conception of the imaginary is brought to bear on the transnational—a step Fluck leaves to his readers—one might conclude that the transnational as produced by the imaginary is less a site of preeminently political resistance than an aesthetic construct emerging from the analogizing interaction with the world of the everyday. In fact, if the transnational and imaginary interact in bringing forth uncharted worlds, this becomes possible only under the condition of a world that is thoroughly aestheticized.

What is called for, then, is a self-critical account of how Americanists and fellow humanists, in using transnationalism to add a chapter to the long story of the search for resistance, have instituted and mastered an aesthetics of resistance. Such a self-reflexive turn requires a conceptualization of the triangular relation between the imaginary, aesthetics, and politics, a relation that complicates Jacques Rancière's approach to the irreducibly political dimension of the aesthetic in interesting ways. While agreeing with Rancière that an aesthetics is, in fact, at the core of any politics in the sense that "politics revolves around what is seen and what can be said about it, around who has the ability to see and the talent to speak, around the properties of space and the possibilities of time," and aesthetic practices distribute the sensible in ways that enact the "delimitation of spaces and times, of the visible and the invisible, of speech and noise" (Rancière 12–13), the imaginary plays into these distributing processes—as a cohering force that is essential to consolidating patterns of distribution *and* as an articulating force that can substantially alter them. The imaginary is not political per se, just as the concept alone is not entirely adequate for conferring political relevance on the work of humanists. Yet it is also the case that there can be no politics that does not play on the field of the imaginary.

WORKS CITED

Althusser, Louis. *Lenin and Philosophy*. New York: Monthly Review Press, 1971.
Anderson, Benedict. *Imagined Communities*. New York: Verso, 1983.
Appadurai, Arjun. *Modernity at Large: Cultural Dimensions of Globalization*. Minneapolis: University of Minnesota Press, 1996.
Castoriadis, Cornelius. *The Imaginary Institution of Society* [1975]. Cambridge: Polity, 1987.
Elliott, Emory. "Diversity in the United States and Abroad: What Does It Mean When American Studies Is Transnational?" *American Quarterly* 59.1 (2007): 1–22.
Fishkin, Shelley Fisher. "Crossroads of Culture: The Transnational Turn in American Studies—Presidential Address to the American Studies Association, November 12, 2004." *American Quarterly* 57.1 (2005): 17–57.
Fluck, Winfried. "Theories of American Culture (and the Transnational Turn in American Studies)" [2007a]. In *Romance with America? Essays on Literature, Culture and American Studies*, ed. Laura Bieger and Johannes Voelz [hereafter *Romance with America?*]. Heidelberg: Winter, 2009. 69–85.
———. "Playing Indian Aesthetic Experience, Recognition, Identity" [2007b]. In *Romance with America?* 433–452.
———. "Imaginary Space; Or: Space as Aesthetic Object." In *Space in America: History, Theory, Culture*, ed. Klaus Benesch and Kerstin Schmidt. Amsterdam: Rodopi, 2005. 25–40.
———. "Fiction and Justice" [2003a]. In *Romance with America?* 358–408.
———. "Aesthetic Experience of the Image" [2003b]. In *Romance with America?* 409–432.
———. "The Role of the Reader and the Changing Functions of Literature" [2002]. Rev. and repr. as "Why We Need Fiction: Reception Aesthetics, Literary Anthropology, *Funktionsgeschichte*." In *Romance with America?* 365–384.
———. "'The American Romance' and the Changing Functions of the Imaginary" [1996]. In *Romance with America?* 139–177.
Foster, Hal. *The Return of the Real: Art and Theory at the End of the Century*. Cambridge: MIT Press, 1996.
Foucault, Michel. "Of Other Spaces" [1984]. *Diacritics* 16.1 (Spring 1986): 22–27.
Graeber, David. "Occupy Wall Street Rediscovers the Radical Imagination." *The Guardian*, 25 September 2011.

Iser, Wolfgang. *The Fictive and the Imaginary.* Baltimore: Johns Hopkins University Press, 1993.

Kaplan, Amy. "Violent Belongings and the Question of Empire Today: Presidential Address to the American Studies Association, Hartford, Connecticut, October 17, 2003." *American Quarterly* 56.1 (2004): 1–18.

Klooger, Jeff. *Castoriadis: Psyche, Society, Autonomy.* Leiden: Brill, 2009.

Lacan, Jacques. *Écrits: A Selection.* New York: Norton, 1977.

Lefebvre, Henri. *The Production of Space* [1974]. Trans. Donald Nicholson-Smith. Oxford: Blackwell, 1991.

Massey, Doreen. *Space, Place and Gender.* Cambridge: Polity Press, 1994.

Moya, Paula, and Ramón Saldívar. "Fictions of the Trans-American Imaginary." *Modern Fiction Studies* 49.1 (Spring 2003): 1–18.

Rancière, Jacques. *The Politics of the Aesthetics: The Distribution of the Sensible.* London: Continuum, 2004.

Soja, Edward. *Postmodern Geographies: The Reassertion of Space in Critical Social Theory.* London: Verso, 1989.

Strauss, Claudia. "The Imaginary." *Anthropological Theory* 6.3 (2006): 322–344.

Taylor, Charles. "Modern Social Imaginaries." *Public Culture* 14.1 (Winter 2002): 91–124.

PART I

LITERARY IMAGINARIES

RAMÓN SALDÍVAR

1 Imagining Cultures

The Transnational Imaginary in Postrace America

In this essay I address the matter of the "cultural imaginary" and of the significant contributions to our understanding of it in the work of Winfried Fluck in two contexts: in relation to the question of literary form and in relation to history. Doing so also allows me explain the reasons for what I take to be a radical turn in twenty-first-century fiction by ethnic writers to a new stage in the history of the novel.[1] I argue that since the turn of the millennium, a new generation of writers, born for the most part in the post–civil rights era, have come to prominence. I use the works of these new authors to illustrate the post–magical realism, post-postmodern, post-borderlands, and neo-fantasy transnational turn in the postrace era of American literature. Outlining a paradigm that I term "historical fantasy," I argue that in the twenty-first century, the relationship between race and social justice, race and identity, and indeed race and history requires the new generation of writers to invent a new "imaginary" for thinking about the nature of a just society.

At the outset I want to make one thing clear: race and racism, ethnicity and difference are nowhere near to becoming extinct in America. But to say that is not to proclaim that race and racism, ethnicity and diversity are today what they were during the climactic events of the civil rights era in the 1960s. They are not. W. E. B. Dubois's classic prediction in 1901 that "the problem of the twentieth century is the problem of the color line" (The Freedman's Bureau, March 1901), couldn't have been more accurate as an assessment of the fate of race during the twentieth century. In 1901 the color line represented the uncrossable barrier between white and black America. At the beginning of the twenty-first century, the color line remains the central problem of American modernity, but one not exclusively defined in shades of black and white alone. Nor is the direction of the impossible crossing as obvious as it was once upon a time. Of greater moment today is the redeployment of arguments and strategies for understanding anew the way that "race" is constructed by the power of white supremacy and deconstructed by the lived experience of contemporary people of color. The narrative of this redefinition posits race and racialization as a doing, a communal ongoing system of processes that, as Paula M. L. Moya and Hazel Markus have convincingly argued in the preface to their immensely significant work *Doing Race: 21 Essays for the 21st Century*, "always involves creating groups based on perceived physical and behavioral characteristics, associating differential power and privilege with these characteristics, and then justifying the resulting inequalities" (Moya and Marcus x).

In making my case about form and history in relation to the transnational imaginary and the redeployment of race in contemporary fiction, I must of necessity be acutely selective. But I trust that my comments will suggest possibilities for richer and larger conjectures.

The Postrace Generation

Since the turn of the millennium, and especially since 9/11, a new generation of writers, born for the most part in the post–civil rights era, has come to prominence. I refer to postrace, postblack, postethnic writers such as African Americans Colson Whitehead, Percival Everett, Darieck Scott, and Touré; Asian Americans Larissa Lai and Sesshu Foster; and Latino/Latina writers such as Marta Acosta, Michelle Serros, Salvador Plascencia, and Junot Díaz. The works of these and numerous other writers represent the post–magical realism, post-postmodern, post-borderlands, and neohistorical transnational turn in what one could call postethnic fiction in the postrace era of American literature.[2] In the case of Latino and Mexican American authors, the generations of pre- and postwar baby boomer precursors have begun to be supplanted by Latina/Latino Generations X and Y, whose novels now populate our "Hispanic" bookshelves. I focus on one of these authors: 2008 Pulitzer Prize and 2012 MacArthur Award winner Junot Díaz. I use Díaz's novel *The Brief Wondrous Life of Oscar Wao* (2007) to illustrate this development in American ethnic fiction and to consider how the work of the millennial generation of Black, Latino, Asian, and Native authors contributes to our understanding of American literature in the global context within which American literary studies is today increasingly being viewed. To this end, I am concerned with what is and should be the relationship between American literary studies and other internationalist or comparative methods of literary and cultural study, especially in the age of globalization. Is there a place today for nationally defined area studies of the United States and the Americas under conditions of the relentless internationalization of cultural and literary studies? What are the options? Because the work of Winfried Fluck has done much to illuminate the functioning of the imaginary in American culture, what I offer here is no more than a footnote and partial rejoinder to his great achievement.

Macondo Meets McOndo in the Transnational Imaginary

One easy, and in my view incorrect, way to see the current turn toward post-postmodern realism among U.S. ethnic writers is to view it as a wholesale acceptance of the poetics of postmodern metafiction. A point in favor of this argument is the fact that the Dominican American Junot Díaz is a product of the creative writing program at Cornell University. That biographical fact tells us something about the institutionalization of ethnic literature in the American academy and about its relationship to what Mark McGurl has called "the Program Era" of American literature.[3] As a product of the institutionalization of creativity within the university in the postwar period, Díaz's award-winning novel fits the pattern McGurl describes as creative programmed writing. In the case of *The Brief Wondrous Life of Oscar Wao*, however, it is not postmodern metafiction that is at stake in the realignments of American racial history and narrative form and the cultural imaginary but *historical fiction* as such. Like the Homeric rhapsode in Derek Walcott's *Omeros* and *The Odyssey*, in *Oscar Wao* Díaz is attempting to "stitch together" the lost histories and isolated communities of the Antilles, in both the home islands and the diasporic communities of the United States, by using an attenuated version of a classical form. In Díaz's case, the story of the dispossessed takes the form of what I call here "historical fantasy," to signify the odd amalgam of historical novel, *Bildungsroman*, post–magical realism, sci-fi, fantasy, and superhero comic romance that structures the transnational imaginary of *Oscar Wao*. I begin with some formal considerations of this novel to make my point about the functioning of the transnational imaginary in American postrace, postethnic fiction.

Oscar de León, the protagonist of the story, is a first-generation Dominican American, a product of two nations. This duality is, however, doubly fraught, not doubly comforting, as Oscar is not at home in either Santo Domingo or New Jersey. Perhaps this is what the second epigraph to the novel, from Derek Walcott's poem "The Schooner *Flight*," is getting at: "I had a sound colonial education / I Dutch, nigger, and English in me, / and either I'm nobody, or I'm a nation." At the beginning of the third section of the poem, Walcott's poetic voice, Shabine, says, "I had no nation now but the imagination."[4] "Shabine" is the Antillean creole word for *mulatto* or *mestizo*, so clearly in Walcott, as in Díaz, we begin in a condition of racial hybridity. For Oscar, what does it mean to be a *mestizo*, a latter-day "nobody," or even "a nation"? And what do the answers have to do with the "imagi-nation"? A hint to a possible answer lies in the first epigraph of the novel: "Of what import are brief, nameless lives . . . to Galactus?" (from *Fantastic Four* 1.49 [April 1966]).

The hint has to do with fantasy and the fantastic, especially as it refers to stories of "brief, nameless lives." As a genre and a form, fantasy is always linked to imagination and desire. Its value seems to reside "in its 'free-floating' and escapist qualities."[5] The products of fantasy gain power from appearing "to be 'free' from many of the conventions and restraints of more realistic texts: "they have refused to observe unities of time, space, and character, doing away with chronology, three-dimensionality and with rigid distinctions between animate and inanimate objects, self and other, life and death" (Jackson 1–2). From W. H. Auden, C. S. Lewis, J. R. R. Tolkien, T. H. White, and other modern fabulists of fantasy, a literary tradition has emerged that claims the transcending of reality, the possibility of escaping the human condition and constructing alternate realities that recapture and revivify a lost moral and social hierarchy (Jackson 2).

But since the last decades of the twentieth century, another kind of fantasy has emerged to vie with earlier forms of fantasy and the imagination. It too links desire and imagination, utopia and history, but with a more pronounced edge intended to redeem, or perhaps even create, a new moral and social hierarchy. Its realm is not modern literature but popular culture, in the genres of TV cartoons, action hero comic books and graphic novels, science-fiction romance and space opera, video role-playing games, anime films, and a whole range of other techno neo-fantasy genres, with sci-fi chief among them, wrapped up with adolescent daydreams, wish fulfillment, and desires for a better world.[6] The novelty of this other form of sci-fi fantasy has to do with its allegiance "to inter-actions of estrangement and cognition, and whose main formal device is an imaginative framework alternative to the author's empirical environment."[7] And so, respecting the generic predilections of our hero, Yunior, the novel's first narrator and "humble Watcher," can thus say: "It might have been a consequence of our being Antillean (who more sci-fi than us?) or of living in the DR . . . and then abruptly wrenchingly relocating to New Jersey. . . . You really want to know what being an X-Man feels like? Just be a smart bookish boy of color in a contemporary U.S. ghetto. Mamma mia! Like having bat wings or a pair of tentacles growing out of your chest" (*OW* 22, footnote 6).

The intersection here of three concepts—history, in the reference to the diasporic migrations from the Antilles to the United States; science fiction and the phenomenology of fantastic alien-ness, asking us to imagine what it feels like to have "bat wings or a pair of tentacles growing out of your chest"; and racial otherness, referring to the experience of being "a smart bookish boy of color in a contemporary U.S. ghetto"—forms the unwritten base of multiple referentiality that Díaz's novel is about to explore.[8]

The recurring motif of doom which structures the fantasy about this intersection of history, fantasy, and racial otherness is something the narrator terms "fukú." Its ground zero is not the one of atomic holocaust but that of the terminal visions inspired by the instantiating moment of American modernity, that is, Columbus's arrival in the Americas: "They say it came first from Africa, carried in the screams of the enslaved; that it was the death bane of the Tainos, uttered just as one world perished and another began; that it was a demon drawn into Creation through the nightmare door that was cracked open in the Antilles. *Fukú americanus*, more colloquially, fukú—generally a curse or a doom of some kind; specifically the Curse and Doom of the New World" (*OW* 1).

Its "midwife and one of its great European victims" was the "discoverer" of the New World. We are back in the Antillean islands, where first contact occurred, where cultures first clashed, where the wonder and magic of the new world first revealed itself. "No matter what its name or provenance, it is believed that the arrival of Europeans on Hispaniola unleashed the fukú on the world, and we've been in the shit ever since. Santo Domingo might be fukú's Kilometer Zero, its port of entry," says Yunior, "but we are all of us its children, whether we know it or not" (*OW* 2). As an aside, I should point out that the moment of contact between Europe and the Americas has become an astonishingly prevalent motif in contemporary fiction as the instantiating moment of our times, linking modernity, coloniality, and the emergence of world systems of commodity flows and imperial power.[9]

So at the beginning, we know that the story of the doomed life of Oscar, as the latter-day recipient of the curse of imperial conquest and colonization, will also be the story of how five hundred years of historical and personal fukú shape the destiny of our short-lived protagonist and his world. Fukú is carried into the present by homegrown monsters like

Rafael Trujillo, "one of the twentieth century's most infamous dictators" (OW 2, footnote 1), as the first of the novel's footnotes informs us.

Like the *vaudou* of the sister-nation on the island of Hispaniola, Haiti, fukú is a symbolic residue of the violence of conquest in the Antilles. In defense against its malevolence, the narrator offers this:

> Not surprisingly, it was a word. A simple word (followed by a vigorous crossing of index fingers).
>
> Zafa.
>
> It used to be more popular in the old days, bigger, so to speak, in Macondo than in McOndo. . . . Even now as I write these words I wonder if this book ain't a zafa of sorts. My very own counterspell. (OW 7)

This is a García Márquez moment of magical realism: the end of the book at the beginning, the story having come full circle. This time, however, the picturesque, exotic stereotypes the publishing world has come to expect of Latino writers, dealing with underdevelopment and exotic atmospheres, collective social injustices, spiritual or metaphysical phenomena, and rural settings, have been superseded by the transnational middle-class experiences of diasporic subjects in both the urban Caribbean and the United States.

Referring here to the literary movement initiated by the Chilean author Alberto Fuguet, Díaz aligns himself with "the great nation of McOndo . . . a place closely linked to the concept of the global village and the meganet"; "an overpopulated, polluted country of freeways, metros, and cable TV [and] MacDonald's, Mac computers, and condos, five-star hotels," a spoof of magical realism, to be sure.[10] "In our McOndo," writes Fuguet, "as in [the magical] Macondo, anything can happen, although granted when persons fly [in our McOndo] it is because they are in an airplane or because they are high on drugs." McOndo (that is, Latin America plus Spain and the Latino United States) "is as magical realist (surrealist, insane, contradictory, hallucinatory) as the imaginary land where people levitate, predict the future, and live eternally. . . . [In McOndo] climate changes, rivers salinate, the earth trembles, and Don Francisco [coffee] colonizes our unconscious."[11]

The novel's sense of doom, even if not quite the apocalyptic catastrophe of the end of *One Hundred Years of Solitude*, or the postmillennial anxieties of a whole slew of contemporary disaster narratives in the wake of 9/11, is still pretty scary, and is set off by the rich and playful language of its prose, shifting from English to Spanish to vernacular Spanglish and urban "Negropolitan" youth slang:

It's a well-documented fact that in Trujillo's DR if you were of a certain class and you put your cute daughter anywhere near El Jefe, within the week she'd be mamando his ripio like an old pro and *there would be nothing you could do about it!* . . . Hiding your doe-eyed, large-breasted daughter from Trujillo . . . was anything but easy. (Like keeping the Ring from Sauron.) If you think the average Dominican guy's bad, Trujillo was five thousand times worse. Dude had hundreds of spies whose entire job was to scour the provinces for his next piece of ass; if the procurement of ass had been any more central to the Trujillato the regime would have been the world's first culocracy (and maybe, in fact, it was). In this climate, hoarding your women was tantamount to treason; offenders who didn't cough up the muchachas could easily find themselves enjoying the invigorating charm of an eight-shark bath (OW 217–218).

Hypermachismo as an instrument of brutal repression, the hot-blooded Latin thug turned head of state, all under the U.S.-sanctioned policy of cold war anticommunism in the Americas. But the experiences Yunior narrates are not weird or fantastic, exotic, or based in a Third World divided from the metropolitan United States, a Macondo unrelated to McOndo. In the world of *Oscar Wao*, the simultaneity of modernization and dependency has become the new norm, indeed, the *paradigm* of the new norm in the Americas. The great achievement of *Oscar Wao* is, then, Díaz's ability to balance a coming-of-age story and a meditation on the history of horrors in the Americas since the first days of discovery with the sci-fi, role-playing comic book fantasy life in the imaginary of one of the least heroic of disappearing fantasy heroes one could imagine. This is a case where the *Bildungsroman* leads us inexorably to the realm of the transnational imaginary.

In the Realm of the Imaginary

Why the transnational imaginary? In previous work I have described the transnational imaginary as a special form of Charles Taylor's idea of the "social imaginary."[12] Following Taylor, if in an American context we conceive of the syntax of codes, images, and icons, as well as the tacit assumptions, convictions, and beliefs that seek to bind together the varieties of national discourses, as forming a social imaginary structure, then a *transnational imaginary* is the attempt to describe imaginary structures emerging from the social, cultural, and political intersections of multinational populations across nation-states. While I am in accord with views emphasizing the persistence of state national power, I maintain that the transnational spaces we see developing around the globe today also emphasize the *limits* of national power. They do so by exceeding the bounds of nationally prescribed versions of culture, economics, and politics. Current debates on the meaning of citizenship in its historical setting have focused on the ways in which processes of decolonization and migration as well as social identities based on ethnicity, race, and gender point to the existence of *other* than national identities as the basis for defining citizenship.

In understanding the power of the visualization of a transnational world beyond restrictive nationalisms, literary works exploring the nature of the transnational experience are laying the groundwork for an understanding of a contemporary staging of new versions of the self, activating the new forms of identity, and imagining the new cultural and political worlds that we see today emerging at the intersections of the global South and North.[13]

At the very least, this representation of a transnational reality that does not yet exist in fully realized form serves to enable the postethnic and postrace visions emerging since the turn of the millennium, and especially since 9/11, from a whole new generation of writers, born for the most part, as I have noted, in the post–civil rights era. The works of these writers represent the post–magical realism, post-postmodern, post-borderlands, and neo-fantasy transnational turn in what one could call postethnic fiction in the postrace era of American literature. Díaz's *Oscar Wao* requires us to consider the nature of nation and community formation, the ethos of justice, and the crossing of symbolic borders and inhabiting of the transnational imaginary, but all in the mode of multicultural fantasy and romance.

The Global South and the Transnational Imaginary

The idea of the "global South" first emerged in the postwar era from the fact that, with few exceptions, practically all of the world's industrially developed countries lay to the north of the so-called developing countries. According to the sociologist Saskia Sassen, in any configuration of the global South, geopolitics is more important than geography. At the beginning of the twenty-first century, the term "global South" really refers to a new phase of global capital. For Sassen, consequently, the global South designates primarily the territories that have been subjected to a post-Keynesian financial logic of land grabs, the imposition of debt as a disciplining regime, the extraction of value, and the massive expulsion of persons from middle-class status into abject poverty (Sassen 24). The key word here is "expulsion." The underdevelopment of countries at a peripheral remove from the core of metropolitan economic power did not just happen; underdevelopment occurred as the result of active forces shaping that underdevelopment. For this reason it is fair to say that the various Southern economies and cultures share comparable experiences of marginalization and unequal access to the resources of globalization which differentiate them from fully developed and hegemonic cultures in their respective locations.

The term "global South" does not imply that all developing countries are similar and can therefore be lumped together in one category. On the contrary, Sassen's definition usefully complicates what has sometimes been described as the "center-periphery model" for the study of globalization, a model that makes "power, commodities, and influence [flow] in one direction only, from the urban centers in the West to a peripheral developing world" (Jay 3). As Paul Jay correctly notes, globalization works differently, and is "characterized by complex back-and-forth flows of people and cultural forms in which the appropriation of things—music, film, food, fashion—raise questions about the rigidity of the center-periphery model" (Jay 3). The concept of the global South usefully suggests that although developing countries range across the spectrum in every economic, social, and political attribute one can imagine, they nevertheless share a set of vulnerabilities and challenges in relation to the circuit of flow with developed countries. These vulnerabilities and challenges constitute an identifiable category of shared sociopolitical realities and fates that make the notion of the "global South" more than an empty abstraction.

The significance of these other critical angles of vision is not simply hermeneutical. These new critical vocabularies convey social analyses of contemporary ruling structures with the end of formulating the possibility of social justice and understanding the intersections, overlaps, and contact points between the global North and South. The writings of intellectuals from the border between global North and South draw their power from their analyses of the subjection and immiseration to which I referred earlier. Their writings also help to give form to an understanding of that condition. This is what I term vernacular poetics—the creative impulse governed by the imagination shaped by borderland experience. It represents an exclusion from the domain of rationality and history. Moreover, if we recognize, as Winfried Fluck reminds us, that "fictional texts represent made-up worlds, even when they claim to be 'realistic,'" vernacular poetics allows us to see how it is possible for fiction to reveal something meaningful about history. This is the place where fantasy and the imaginary intersect with history, in what Fluck terms "negative aesthetics" in his discussion of Wolfgang Iser's reception aesthetics, referring to the potential of literature to "expose the limitations and unacknowledged deficiencies of accepted systems of thought" (Fluck, "Role of the Reader" 255, 256).[14]

In the case of postethnic fiction, "negative aesthetics" allows us to conceive how *fantasy* functions in relation to *history* to create an *imaginary* vision that goes beyond the formulations of realism, modernism, magical realism, and postmodern metafiction to articulate precisely what is absent in realism, magical realism, and metafiction. Formally, the role of the imaginary is thus crucial to the functioning of postrace fiction, for in allowing the experience of something not literally represented, it compels readers to "provide links" across the "blanks" created by the intentional "suspension of relations" between meaningful segments of the text (Fluck, "Role of the Reader" 258).[15] But beyond literary modernism's defamiliarizing function of compelling "the reader to become active in making sense of what often appears incomplete or incomprehensible" (Fluck, "Role of the Reader" 256), the literary works I refer to here as postrace, postethnic fictions do *something more* in linking fantasy, history, and the imaginary. Allow me to explain.

Fantasy, History, and the Imaginary

Playing the role of a "Watcher," an extraterrestrial being from the *Fantastic Four* comic book series, a being committed to observing and compiling knowledge on all aspects of the universe but prohibited from interfering in the course of its history, Yunior in the end, as Watcher, is the ultimate post–magical realist narrator, whose "cosmic duty" enjoins him from saving worlds poised at the abyss of destruction. As narrator, Yunior is incapable of either expressing the ending of history or altering its course. At best his role is to compose the "counterspell" to the unending effects of the fukú, the "Fuck you" (OW 304). For that reason, in the end, the counterspell to the fukú of the atrocities of the history of the Americas takes three distinct iterations to bring the narrative to conclusion.

Chapter 8, "The End of the Story," thus ends three times. First, with the aftermath of Oscar's murder at the hands of a brutal "jealous Third World cop" (291) with whose girlfriend, Ybón, Oscar has finally consummated something approaching decolonial love. It also reveals Yunior's ten-year struggle to write Oscar's story of geekiness, loneliness, and brutal death. Of this jealous boyfriend, Yunior tells us that he is "one of those tall, arrogant, acerbically handsome niggers that most of the planet feels inferior to. Also one of those very bad men that not even postmodernism can explain away" (294). For the ending of the novel to work, it must give us a sincere explanation for murder, cruelty, and evil without resorting to postmodern irony or metafictional play.

A second attempt at an ending also concerns Yunior, and offers his "hope" and "dream" (331) that Oscar's niece, Lola's daughter Isis, will escape the doom of fukú and of those condemned to repeat its curse by taking "all we've done and all we've learned and add her own insights and she'll put an end to it" (331). This utopian ending too is compromised when Yunior reads "the last horrifying chapter: 'A Stronger Loving World'" of Oscar's treasured, "dog-eared copy of *Watchmen*" (331) and finds the only panel that Oscar has circled: "After the mutant brain has destroyed New York City; . . . after [Adrian] Veidt's plan has succeeded in 'saving the world,'" Dr. Manhattan replies, "Nothing ends, Adrian. Nothing ever ends" (331).

In the third and final attempt at an ending, we get yet another diffracted view of Oscar and a catalogue of failed hopes. Yunior mimes Oscar speaking from the dead when, "almost eight months after he died, a package arrived. . . . Two manuscripts enclosed," including chapters from Oscar's "never-to-be-completed opus, a four-book E. E. 'Doc' Smith-esque space opera called *Starscourge*, and . . . a long letter to Lola, the last thing he wrote, apparently, before he was killed" (333). Another promised package, "everything I've written on this journey . . . the cure to what ails us, . . . The Cosmo DNA," never arrives (333). But Oscar's letter reports "some amazing news": "Guess what? Ybón actually *kissed* him. Guess what else? Ybón actually *fucked* him. Praise be to Jesus!" The letter continues: "He reported that he'd liked it . . . but what really got him was not the bam-bam-bam of sex—it was the little intimacies that he'd never in his whole life anticipated" (334). Oscar writes: "So this is what everybody's always talking about! Diablo! If only I'd known. The beauty! The beauty!" (335). The sentimental rhetorical power of this poignant ending is also undercut, in this case, by the echoes of Kurtz's "The horror! The horror!" from Joseph Conrad's *The Heart of Darkness*.

The three failed endings, coupled with Yunior's ventriloquism of the proverbial voice from the grave, together deny the efficacy of the classical plot of the love story, the heroic story of deferred success, and the story of triumphant emergence. If it is justice we seek in love, in life, and in the world, then justice, poetic or otherwise, is precisely what we do *not* get at the end of *Oscar Wao*. Our hero, murdered cruelly, mercilessly, is not redeemed by romance; the history of the Dominican Republic, forged in both imported and homegrown tyranny, is not atoned for by utopian desire.[16] And if we think we might be able to bracket the tyranny by seeing it as a product of distant Third World perversities, it turns out that Ybón's jealous boyfriend has full "First World" credentials, as an "American citizen" who was "naturalized in the city of Buffalo, in the state of New York" (295). Given the magnitude of the crimes assembled in the chronicle of Oscar's family's story, itself a synecdoche of trans-American hemispheric history, none of the three endings can even hope to account for, let alone blunt, the apocalyptic, world-destroying evil "that not even postmodernism can explain away."

Imaginary History or Historical Fantasy

In *The Sense of an Ending*, Frank Kermode writes, "It is not that we are connoisseurs of chaos, but that we are surrounded by it, and equipped for co-existence with it only by our fictive powers" (67). The powers of the imagination and the desire for the wholesale transformation of American history drive Junot Díaz to find a way to coexist with the chaos, not because one finds peace in chaos but because in the context of the brutal histories of conquest, colonization, exploitation, and oppression in the Americas, it is less duplicitous to stake an ending on chaos than on the teleologies of romance, realism, or emergence. While romanticism gives us fantasy coalescing with reality, and literary modernism gives us the defamiliarization of reality, and postmodernism gives us the ludic play of metafiction, *Oscar Wao* gives us something else: the mimetic representation of fantasy. Not fantasy as such but its imitation, at double and sometimes triple remove. Why? And where does the mimesis of fantasy, the staging of fantasy rather than the representation of fantasy itself, leave us within the realms of the imaginary? Without a comic book, sci-fi, fantasy ending, *Oscar Wao* requires us to read the story of the history of conquest, colonization, diaspora, and social injustice in the Americas by forging links between the *fantasy of the imaginary* and the *real of history*.

This connection between *fantasy* and *history*, bewildering in the continual oscillation of the narrative's multiple referentiality to both the *real* and the *imaginary*, cannot be formulated by the text but forms the unwritten base that conditions and transcends the literal meanings of both history and fantasy, in the process creating something new, something we might call *imaginary history* or *historical fantasy*. This is the condition that Fluck identifies as the "negativity" of texts, in discussing Iser's theory of reception aesthetics from *The Act of Reading*.[17] It is the aesthetic equivalent of what I have identified as the rhetorical function of *parabasis* and *irony* in other related contexts of American postrace fiction. It is a way of describing the "something more" that the literary works I refer to as postrace fictions do in linking fantasy, history, and the imaginary, the *imaginary history*, in order to remain true to ethnic literature's utopian allegiance to social justice.[18]

Paul Jay is certainly correct to argue that in *The Brief Wondrous Life of Oscar Wao*, Díaz "frames the novel as both a historical critique of colonialism and dictatorship in the Americas, systems linked to masculinity and storytelling, and as a kind of counterspell that uses the very narrative power it critiques to undo that power" (Jay 12). Doing so allows him to call "attention to the power of storytelling to both critique and reverse dominant narratives, to, in effect, begin to undo the curse of colonizing power" (193). Even so, it is crucial to see that critiques of historical and social injustice and the curse of colonizing power take an unusually distinctive shape in *Oscar Wao*. In the end, true to the forms of fantasy that the narrative uses to tell his story, Oscar remains invisible, absent, and pieced together only tenuously from fragments and absences, all in the mode of fantasy, science fiction, gothic, and horror, that is to say, in the form of all the "genres" in the service of history gone awry.[19] As a sexual being manqué, racialized, classed, and colonized by the long historical legacies of coloniality and modernity, at novel's end Oscar does not so much disappear as he continues to perform his disappearance as a subject of history from the story of his own emergence. In contrast to the fantasy of heroic individual sexual desire, figured by Yunior's compulsive and destructive hypermasculine sexuality, a sexuality for which Oscar always longs and by which he is finally destroyed, Oscar's historical fantasy leads elsewhere. It binds him more closely to Beli, Lola, Ybón, Abelard, and all of the women and men caught in the total terror of real dictatorial regimes such as the historical Trujillato, even if narrated in the form of "the more speculative genres," as Oscar at one point describes them (*OW* 43). The terror created by really bad men masks "the beauty," which is but another name for "life."

How could one possibly conceive of a narrativity to still this chaos? How to create romance from consciousness colonized by self-hate and self-doubt? What kind of "beauty" could we even imagine to counter the horror before and after the "beauty"? And to what end? What would a literature of *political* and *racial* romance, sensation, fantasy, gothic, marvels, and absolute otherness appropriate to transporting us to the margins of the imaginary and the real accomplish that earlier forms of U.S. ethnic literature have not? What would its referential world look like?

It is the nature of romantic literature to pose these kinds of questions. But when fantasy and metafiction come into contact with history and the racialized imagination, vernacular cultures, and the stories of figures from the American global South, they become something else again. And now we are back to the role of history. For a Latino/Latina writer in the United States, appropriating history and the concerns of the distinctively modern experience of the borderlands with the global South does not require orthodox narrative structures and realist codes of representation. Sharing the goal of most ethnic writers to imagine a state of achieved social justice, Díaz certainly employs all of the classical forms and themes available to ethnic writers to make his point. He draws from the traditions of vernacular narrative, popular culture, and the literary avant-garde, however, not simply to reiterate them, but precisely to show the *constant* and *complete* rupture between the redemptive course of American history and its origins in conquest.[20]

Overcoming the choice between history and modernity by entering into a realm of post-postmodern and post–magical realism twenty-first-century *fantasy*, Díaz's novel exemplifies a phase of the U.S. ethnic novel that shares formally more with the ironic irony of Mark Z. Danielewski, Dave Eggers, Michael Chabon, Jonathan Lethem, and Alex Shakar than with the critical aesthetics of García Márquez or Toni Morrison. In postrace fiction, neither postmodern play nor magical realist wonder can suffice as stand-ins for justice. Unlike the ironists, and even the magical realists, Díaz seeks to unmask, in all sincerity, without irony, the function of *ideological fantasy*, which can use "justice" as a perfect disguise for injustice. As Slavoj Žižek has argued, a truly post-ideological position would recognize the way that even "freedom" can mask forms of exploitation. Ideological fantasy is the overlooked, misrecognized, unconscious illusion beyond illusion.[21] It demarcates the realm of the imaginary beyond illusion, precisely the direction in which Díaz's fiction points us.

Going beyond the defamiliarizing strategies of avant-garde literature, postrace works like *The Brief Wondrous Life of Oscar Wao* attempt to articulate an imaginary fantasy to the second and third degrees that might, paradoxically, serve as the real basis for understanding our bewilderingly complex post-contemporary history. That is why, with the cruel murder of our hero, Díaz brings us pitilessly, as Oscar is brought at the moment of his brutal beating, "back to the Real" (*OW* 298), with a capital R. He compels us to see that in the age of free markets and globalization, the world has diminished and constricted so that we "Americans" now share with others around the globe a synthetic fantasy culture of television shows, animated films, space operas, graphic novels, and digital media, a synchrony of intersecting fantasies worthy of being considered "magical." The reality of this new world is not gratuitous nor virtual; but it might well be, perhaps, postmagical and postracial.

Coda

Whatever its full features might be, I offer, as a coda, this synoptic glimpse of a future history of postrace American ethnic fiction. Gathering my evidence from the instance of *The Brief Wondrous Life of Oscar Wao* and numerous other contemporary fictions by a new generation of authors of color, I propose that U.S. ethnic fiction of the postrace and post-postmodern turn offers these specific characteristics:

1. It is multi-perspectival, offering heterogeneous views of a life that is itself so dynamically full of wonder and magic that no one single point of view can have a prayer of encompassing it.
2. The multi-perspectival quality leads to a second characteristic, involving the relationship of individuals to communities. The challenge faced by West Indians, Central Americans, Mexicans, and U.S. Americans is to imagine and artistically render their common experience when they lack a communally shared sense of what constitutes their cultural distinctiveness. Díaz's version attempts to redefine culture performatively. We are what we do as a community, not as individuals. The flip side of this is also true: that we cannot be known, or understood, or loved as individuals in isolation from the history of our families and our nation.
3. The American post-postmodern novel will be racially undetermined in its reflection of American identities, requiring a blend of Anglo, Latino, Euro-Hispanic, African, and Indian identities, necessitating a move beyond the American racial binary of black and white.
4. It will require a transnational imaginary in order to express its cosmopolitan and international allegiances.
5. It will be diasporic, migratory, and transitory in its hemispheric reach. These are not stories about immigration and the American

immigrant experience. They are about *diaspora* and what that experience "feels" like: family dramas intertwined with those of at least two nations.

6. The post-postmodern American novel will require a dialogical tongue, a bi- or multilingual aesthetic.

These features separately characterize much American ethnic literature, but taken together they signify something else: the radical reconfiguration and recapitulation of the history of fictional genres and classical forms of the novel.

NOTES

1. Aristotle's distinction between *history* and *poetry* is relevant here. For Aristotle, "history" is a form that fails to be as philosophical or as serious as "poetry" (*Poetics*, chap. 10). As Catherine Gallagher points out, "formalism in literary studies over the last two centuries has . . . often claimed that striving for form is the distinguishing mark of the literary." Catherine Gallagher, "Formalism and Time," *Modern Language Quarterly* 61.1 (2000): 233.

2. See, for example, Marta Acosta, *Happy Hour at Casa Dracula* (New York: Pocket Star Books, 2006); Salvador Plascencia, *The People of Paper*, 1st ed. (San Francisco: McSweeney's Books, 2005); Michelle Serros, *Honey Blond Chica* (New York: Simon Pulse, 2007); Touré, *Soul City*, 1st ed. (New York: Picador, 2005); Colson Whitehead, *Sag Harbor* (New York: Doubleday, 2009); Sesshu Foster, *Atomik Aztex* (San Francisco: City Lights, 2005); Darieck Scott, *Hex: A Novel of Love Spells*, 1st ed. (New York: Carroll & Graf, 2007); Percival L. Everett, *Erasure: A Novel* (Hanover: University Press of New England, 2001); and Larissa Lai, *Salt Fish Girl: A Novel* (Toronto: T. Allen Publishers 2002).

3. Mark McGurl, "The Program Era: Pluralisms of Postwar American Fiction," *Critical Inquiry* 32.1 (2005): 102–129. McGurl requires us to take seriously the institution of the university and the processes of the democratization of education in the Unites States during the postwar period in order to understand fully the nature of contemporary literary writing. The crucial evaluative questions that follow from his observation about the institutionalization of creativity within the university are: How have creative writing programs reorganized postwar American writing, and how might this reorganization have affected our understanding of the writing itself? McGurl does not give the definitive answers to these questions, but in posing and beginning to answer them, he moves the field significantly toward a major new understanding of the nature of contemporary American fiction. His rewriting of the history of postwar American fiction also allows for a new way of considering the relationship be-

tween postmodern experimental high literary fiction and ethnic literatures. "The Program Era" offers an explanation for how these seemingly divergent strains of American literature could emerge at essentially the same moment, as well as for how we might make sense of the relationships in form and content between them. This argument is now fully extended in Mark McGurl, *The Program Era: Postwar Fiction and the Rise of Creative Writing* (Cambridge: Harvard University Press, 2009).

4. Derek Walcott, *Collected Poems 1948–1984* (New York: Farrar, Straus & Giroux, 1986), 350. Paul Breslin, *Nobody's Nation: Reading Derek Walcott* (Chicago: University of Chicago Press, 2001). "Shabine," as noted in the text, is the St. Lucian creole name for mulatto; his task is "to give voice to one people's grief." Breslin, *Nobody's Nation*, 190.

5. Rosemary Jackson, *Fantasy: The Literature of Subversion* (London: Methuen, 1981), 1.

6. Fredric Jameson, *Archaeologies of the Future: The Desire Called Utopia and Other Science Fictions* (London: Verso, 2005), 2.

7. Veronica Hollinger, "Contemporary Trends in Science Fiction Criticism, 1980–1999," *Science Fiction Studies* 26.2 (1999): 232–262.

8. See Winfried Fluck, "The Role of the Reader and the Changing Functions of Literature: Reception Aesthetics, Literary Anthropology, *Funktionsgeschichte*," *European Journal of English Studies* 6.3 (2002): 258.

9. See, for example, Orson Scott Card, *Pastwatch: The Redemption of Christopher Columbus* (New York: Tor, 1996); Foster, *Atomik Aztex*; Leslie Marmon Silko, *Almanac of the Dead: A Novel* (New York: Simon & Schuster, 1991); Yxta Maya Murray, *The Conquest: A Novel*, 1st ed. (New York: Rayo, 2002). These and other contemporary novels use the mode of "alternative history" to imagine anew a different, perhaps utopian possibility for the history of the Americas.

10. Alberto Fuguet and Sergio Gómez, *McOndo*, 1st ed. (Barcelona: Mondadori, 1996), 15; all translations from this source are my own.

11. Ibid. Fuguet adds, "Latin America is, irremediably, MTV América Latina, that luminous consensus, that wave that colonizes our consciousness by way of cable, and which is being converted, in the grandest version of Bolivar's dream imaginable, into a unity, more concretely and effectively than a hundred treaties or international forums ever could" (15–16).

12. Charles Taylor, *Modern Social Imaginaries* (Durham: Duke University Press, 2004).

13. See Thomas Brook, "The Fictive and the Imaginary: Charting Literary Anthropology, or, What's Literature Have to Do with It?" *American Literary History* 20.3 (2008): 622–631. Thomas's discussion of Wolfgang Iser's "reception aesthetics" and Fluck's notion of "the cultural imaginary" are immensely useful articulations of the functioning of literary texts to compel readers not to imagine an "existing reality" but to "realize something that does not yet exist" (625).

14. See also Winfried Fluck, "The Search for Distance: Negation and Negativity in Wolfgang Iser's Literary Theory," *New Literary History* 31.1 (2000): 175–210. Here, concerning Iser's notion of "negativity" as "an unlimited negating potential" in a text, Fluck argues that as an integral and foundational quality of a text, negativity "dislocates all norms, meanings, and forms of organization, not just those we would like to negate. This continuous invalidation is . . . the precondition for activating literature's special potential," allowing it to serve as a permanent and ongoing "negation of the negation" (186).

15. Fluck puts it this way: "Every text consists of segments that are determinate, and of blanks between them that are indeterminate. In order to establish consistency between these segments, the reader has to become active in providing links for that which is missing. A blank is thus not a mere gap, or an ideologically instructive omission. It is an intentional, often carefully crafted, suspension of relations in order to make us provide links for what is disconnected. The difference is significant: A mere gap allows readers to indulge in their own projections, a blank compels them to set up relations between their own imaginary constructs and the text" ("The Role of the Reader," 258).

16. On the relationship between "justice" and "literature," see Winfried Fluck, "Fiction and Justice," *New Literary History* 34.1 (2003) 19–42. See also Martha Nussbaum, *Poetic Justice: The Literary Imagination and Public Life* (Boston: Beacon Press, 1995).

17. Fluck adds that "negativity generates aesthetic experience by enticing us to articulate something that is absent." ("The Role of the Reader," 258). See Wolfgang Iser, *The Act of Reading: A Theory of Aesthetic Response* (Baltimore: Johns Hopkins University Press, 1978). See also Fluck, "The Search for Distance," 186.

18. On the representation of social justice, see Fluck, "Fiction and Justice," 20–21

19. See Caroline Roberts, "*Bostonist* Interview: Junot Díaz, Author," *Bostonist*, 10 September 2007, http://bostonist.com.

20. Paul Gilroy, *The Black Atlantic: Modernity and Double Consciousness* (Cambridge: Harvard University Press, 1993), 222.

21. On the "ideological fantasy," see Slavoj Žižek, *The Sublime Object of Ideology* (London: Verso, 1989), 30–33.

WORKS CITED

Acosta, Marta. *Happy Hour at Casa Dracula.* New York: Pocket Star Books, 2006.
Breslin, Paul. *Nobody's Nation: Reading Derek Walcott.* Chicago: University of Chicago Press, 2001.
Card, Orson Scott. *Pastwatch: The Redemption of Christopher Columbus.* New York: Tor, 1996.

Díaz, Junot. *The Brief Wondrous Life of Oscar Wao*. 1st ed. New York: Riverhead Books, 2007. Cited as OW.

DuBois, W. E. B. "The Freedman's Bureau." *The Atlantic Monthly* 87.519 (1901): 354.

Everett, Percival L. *Erasure: A Novel*. Hanover: University Press of New England, 2001.

Fluck, Winfried. "Fiction and Justice." *New Literary History* 34.1 (2003): 19–42.

———. "The Role of the Reader and the Changing Functions of Literature: Reception Aesthetics, Literary Anthropology, *Funktionsgeschichte*." *European Journal of English Studies* 6.3 (2002): 253–271.

———. "The Search for Distance: Negation and Negativity in Wolfgang Iser's Literary Theory." *New Literary History* 31.1 (2000): 175–210.

Foster, Sesshu. *Atomik Aztex*. San Francisco: City Lights, 2005.

Fuguet, Alberto, and Sergio Gómez. *McOndo*. 1st ed. Barcelona: Mondadori, 1996.

Gallagher, Catherine. "Formalism and Time." *Modern Language Quarterly* 61.1 (2000): 229–251.

Hollinger, Veronica. "Contemporary Trends in Science Fiction Criticism, 1980–1999. " *Science Fiction Studies* 26.2 (1999): 232–262.

Iser, Wolfgang. *The Act of Reading: A Theory of Aesthetic Response*. Baltimore: Johns Hopkins University Press, 1978.

Jackson, Rosemary. *Fantasy: The Literature of Subversion*. London: Methuen, 1981.

Jameson, Fredric. *Archaeologies of the Future: The Desire Called Utopia and Other Science Fictions*. London: Verso, 2005.

Jay, Paul. *Global Matters: The Transnational Turn in Literary Studies*. Ithaca: Cornell University Press, 2010.

Kermode, Frank. *The Sense of an Ending: Studies in the Theory of Fiction*. New York: Oxford University Press, 1967.

Lai, Larissa. *Salt Fish Girl: A Novel*. Toronto: T. Allen Publishers, 2002.

Margolis, Mac. "Is Magical Realism Dead?" *Newsweek*, 6 May 2002, 46.

McGurl, Mark. *The Program Era: Postwar Fiction and the Rise of Creative Writing*. Cambridge: Harvard University Press, 2009.

———. "The Program Era: Pluralisms of Postwar American Fiction. " *Critical Inquiry* 32.1 (2005): 102–129.

Michaels, Walter Benn. *The Shape of the Signifier: 1967 to the End of History*. Princeton: Princeton University Press, 2004.

Moya, Paula M. L., and Hazel Markus, eds. *Doing Race: 21 Essays for the 21st Century*. New York: W. W. Norton & Co., 2010.

Murray, Yxta Maya. *The Conquest: A Novel*. 1st ed. New York: Rayo, 2002.

Nussbaum, Martha. *Poetic Justice: The Literary Imagination and Public Life*. Boston: Beacon Press, 1995.

Plascencia, Salvador. *The People of Paper.* 1st ed. San Francisco: McSweeney's Books, 2005.

Sassen, Saskia. "A Savage Sorting of Winners and Losers: Contemporary Versions of Primitive Accumulation." *Globalizations* 7.1–2 (2010): 23–50.

Scott, Darieck. *Hex: A Novel of Love Spells.* 1st ed. New York: Carroll & Graf, 2007.

Serros, Michelle. *Honey Blond Chica.* New York: Simon Pulse, 2007.

Silko, Leslie Marmon. *Almanac of the Dead: A Novel.* New York: Simon & Schuster, 1991.

Taylor, Charles. *Modern Social Imaginaries.* Durham: Duke University Press, 2004.

Thomas, Brook. "The Fictive and the Imaginary: Charting Literary Anthropology, or, What's Literature Have to Do with It?" *American Literary History* 20.3 (2008): 622–631.

Touré. *Soul City.* 1st ed. New York: Picador, 2005.

Walcott, Derek. *Collected Poems 1948–1984.* New York: Farrar, Straus & Giroux, 1986.

Whitehead, Colson. *Sag Harbor.* New York: Doubleday, 2009.

Žižek, Slavoj. *The Sublime Object of Ideology.* New York: Verso, 1989.

LAWRENCE BUELL

2 The Necessary Fragmentation of the (U.S.) Literary-Cultural Imaginary

Insofar as the idea—or myth—of distinctive national cultures still maintains any credible explanatory power, to what extent does it reinforce a view of (U.S.) national literary history as distinctive and/or coherent? That is the basic question with which this essay wrestles. I argue that although the explanatory power is not trivial, neither does it guarantee national cultural distinctiveness or internal coherence—and that is just as well.

Two preliminary anecdotes before getting under way. The first relates to an undergraduate course in twentieth-century American fiction taught in the late 1980s that used William Boelhower's then recent study of "ethnic semiosis in American literature" as one of its critical texts. The choice was admittedly problematic given that book's allusive density, but the students rose to the challenge with this fascinating result: within a month, every person in our mostly white, middle-class group had found a way to conceive of himself or herself in minoritized terms, with a hyphenated identity: if not ethno-racial, then in terms of religion, sexual preference, regional outback upbringing, working-class roots, etc.—and for many students, multiply.

Anecdote number two relates to the discussion provoked by a lecture given in the summer of 2008 in Suzhou to Chinese professors of American literature, a state-of-the-field reconnaissance centering on different kinds of Americanist transnational inquiry—Atlantic world studies, hemispheric studies, and transpacific studies—with special emphasis on specific paths of critical intervention that I fancied this sophisticated group of bilingual or multilingual Asian-country-of-origin colleagues might especially be equipped to make. Although the audience seemed generally receptive, some of the more senior scholars chided me for not having concentrated on the national cultural "mainstream" rather than the margins thereof, and on literary history as a carrier of paradigmatic models of national culture (and acculturation) rather than on the diasporic and the interstitial.

Between those two opposite thrusts—of splitting versus lumping, of the longing for heuristic coherence versus the drive to particularize and thereby to fragment—my own thoughts about how best to characterize national cultural imaginaries continue to oscillate. As these anecdotes suggest, the oscillation effect seems ascribable partly to the observer's distance from or immersion in the thing observed, partly to whether one's preferred way of thinking about issues of national cultural coherence is old-fashioned or au courant. It may well be—I venture this as speculation rather than as dogma—that in the case of "America" (here meaning the United States specifically), this oscillation is characteristically accentuated by its centuries-old history as a dream space, meaning simultaneously also of course a potential nightmare space, first for Europeans and Euro-Americans, then increasingly for the rest of the world. But already I am getting ahead of myself in broaching this issue of exceptionalism. For it seems clear that the recent predilection among Americanists generally for thinking of the U.S. national cultural imaginary in terms of fissures and/or dispersal arises not merely from the quiddities of U.S. cultural history or Americanist tribalism but, beyond those, and more fundamentally, from the percolation of the concept of the imaginary within cultural theory. I start, then, with the latter and work back to the former.

Cultural Imaginary/Americanist Field-Imaginary

Theories of the or "a" "cultural" or "social" "imaginary" seem inherently, designedly unstable on several counts. First, the imputed non-identity between the imagined or the represented and the existent. Beyond this, the expression as a singular of what turns out to be an assemblage of sometimes wildly discrepant elements. Consider the British cultural critic Graham Dawson's handy thumbnail definition of the cultural imaginary as "those vast networks of interlinking discursive themes, images, motifs and narrative forms that are publicly available within a culture at any one time, and articulate its psychic and social dimensions," furnishing "public forms which both organize knowledge of the social world and give shape to phantasies within the apparently 'internal' domain of psychic life" (48). This postulates *a* culture and *a* "social world" as well as a certain mechanism for generating collective fantasies; but the vast networks of interlinked discursive fields at the input end guarantee a plethora of incommensurable outputs.

Matters become further complicated with the next step of establishing the primary domain of reference for those master terms *culture* and *social world*. Midway through his *Imaginary Institution of Society* (1975), when Cornelius Castoriadis pauses to ask just what *is* the society being referred to under the sign of the social imaginary, he grants that in principle, it simply "designates the collectivity in question," which might be religious (Judaic, Islamic), might be ethnic (Hellene or Slav, for instance), or might be otherwise organized, but which he insists for his purposes must mean national, for that is the form of collective imaginary that "proves more solid than any other reality, as two world wars and the survival of nationalism have shown" (148). Here Castoriadis anticipates Benedict Anderson's seminal *Imagined Communities* (1983).

Neither author presents himself as having fallen under the spell of the collective imaginary he describes, however. Both books anatomize the imagined fictions of nationness as immensely potent historical forces from which the analyst, however, stands apart, if not immune. By conceiving nations not as organismal growths but as historically contingent artifacts, each provokes more impetus than resistance to next-stage accounts of diasporic and border-blurring cultural imaginaries, such as Homi Bhabha's "DissemiNation," which critiques Anderson's insistence on geographical boundedness, and in American studies the three transnationalisms I tried to summarize for my Chinese colleagues.

These post-Andersonian initiatives have of course profoundly affected what Donald Pease has fruitfully called the Americanist "field-imaginary" (11). Since the early 1990s, nation-centripetal approaches have been losing luster, while postnationalism and transnationalism have been increasingly "in." Just think of all those books of the 1980s, his and mine among them, that constituted what Michael Colacurcio wittily called "the American Renaissance Renaissance," from John Irwin's *American Hieroglyphics* (1980) to David Leverenz's *Manhood and the American Renaissance* (1989). Several were inflected by recent, ongoing challenges to the received canon and/or limitedly open to transnationalism (almost wholly of a North Atlantic sort); but the main coordinates remained the "major" national authors of the epoch of U.S. literary emergence and the internal narratives of U.S. literary and cultural history seemingly disclosed by the constellations formed by their work. How long ago that seems! Projects like Sean Gowdie's *Creole America*, which won the MLA first book prize in 2006, or Wai Chee Dimock's *Through Other Continents*, runner-up for the MLA's James Russell Lowell Prize the same year, were scarcely yet imaginable.

Yet however much this shift may have challenged the primacy of thinking about cultural imaginaries at the level of the nation, it clearly hasn't
killed off such thinking. As the Caribbeanist Peter Hitchcock reluctantly
grants, "the community of Nations still demands obeisance to an idea
of a Nation" (10). This might be called the aversive defense of persistent
nation-think: you'd like to get rid of it but you can't. An example of an
offsetting supportive defense is Partha Chatterjee's outrage at fears ema-
nating from the developed world after the implosion of the Soviet Union
that the greatest "danger to world peace is now posed by the resurgence
of nationalism," which he takes as a ploy to keep the non-West in its
place, as if, "like drugs, terrorism, and illegal immigration, [nationalism
were] one more product of the Third World that the West dislikes but is
powerless to prohibit" (3–4). Chatterjee proceeds *à propos* India to make
his case by reinstating a considerably more traditional *Gemeinschaft*-
like understanding of imagined community than Anderson's: that is,
"people living in different, contextually defined, communities," peace-
fully coexisting "within large political units" (238).

To return now to the *Americanist* field-imaginary, despite its recent
transnational turns, there's also good reason to expect U.S. literature
scholars as a tribe to continue to play the national culture card if only
because there is no way to distinguish U.S. literature from any other except in terms of some culturally valenced argument, since the distinctions at the level of language and genre difference are on the whole so
feeble except for traditional Native American orature. If only for that
reason, David Shumway's prediction of the mid-1990s may prove more
right than wrong: that the New Americanist insurgency would produce
not the counter-hegemony it sought but rather an amended extension
whereby "the canon established over the course of the century will continue to be part of any new disciplinary object that might be constituted"
(352). Winfried Fluck's "American Literary History and the Romance
with America" brilliantly updates and sophisticates this line of thinking by construing "diversity" as a "counter-term to the prison-house of a
monolithic national identity" designed in effect if not in intent to save the
original project, insofar as "diversity studies continues an approach that
stands at the center of American exceptionalism"—and to assess the
transnational turn as offering more of the same: "liberation of the ex-
traterritorial" to the end of "reviving [literature's] adversarial function"
(11, 7, 14).

In this account, for the national cultural imaginary to present itself to
the humanistic intelligentsia as an assemblage of breakaway fragments is,

up to a point, a wholly logical if not downright predictable new stage of the original romance plot. Up to a point, this formulation of the way we Americanists live now may seem a kind of rechanneling of Bercovitchian cultural consensus theory—what looks like dissent proves consensual at last (see Bercovitch 1993, 353–376). But it's an argument that perhaps only Fluck could have made, as the fruit of previous reflection on the work of the cultural imaginary in premodern U.S. fiction in providing a "motor" for a "cultural dehierarchicalization process" that coordinately scripts new "individual possibilities for self-development" at the textual level and conduces to a "freeing of the reader from the guardianship [*Vormundschaft*]" of the text (Fluck 1997, 29). As Fluck's readings of Twain's *Huckleberry Finn* in *Das kulturelle Imaginäre* and elsewhere especially show, relative to (say) Bercovitch on Hawthorne (Bercovitch 1991; 1993, 194–245), this conceptual framework entails a much less normative view of how literary texts work as refractions of national ideologies and correspondingly greater receptivity to considering fragmentation effects as part and parcel of the American cultural imaginary. Here Fluck seems to have been inspired by Wolfgang Iser's understanding of "play" as an activator of the (aesthetic) imaginary that will "explode" into "plurivocity" when "actualized by the potential recipient" (Iser 227), even while containing the imaginary within the arena of the cultural.

Fluck's 2009 article entertains, in closing, the further possibility that the romance with America plot might unravel into nothing more than "a heterogeneous plurality of narratives" (18) and/or lose its savor if the special charisma of the United States itself were to fade. Had Toni Morrison's *A Mercy* (2009) been available, he might have cited it as an augury of that scenario of terminal deliquescence, insofar as Morrison's project is to reimagine late-seventeenth-century America as a scattered assemblage of starkly isolated, embattled communal and individual life worlds representing disconnected bits of psychosocial space and trajectories of dislocation separated by barriers of race, class, language, and geography, pulverizing the whole array of traditional mythic larger-than-life sagas. The Puritan errand, Quaker communitarianism, planter dynastics, the dream of really making it big or even just finding a new lease on life in the new world get disenchanted into squalidly reduced versions of themselves. Despite its patches of enticing descriptivism, haunting pathos, and guarded empathy, *A Mercy* seems resolved not to be read, as *Beloved* was in some quarters, as eventuating in a sentimental melodrama of exorcism, with family values reaffirmed and Denver headed for a brighter future at Oberlin College. So it may not be too much of a stretch for the field-imaginary to correlate this transit in the career of the nation's most illustrious novelist with Fluck's futurism, especially considering how sensitively *A Mercy* registers the thrust of recent early Americanist revisionary scholarship since the 1980s toward concentration on the unheroic messiness of cross-national, cross-racial interactions in the contact zone.

But rather than continue with such speculations, I want to make three more specific observations about the fragmentation and dispersal of the Americanist field-imaginary per se inspired by Fluck's analysis.

1. Its degree of (in)coherence looks different at different levels. Coherence at a macro-level can comport with extreme fissiparousness at the micro-level. That is more or less the way we are living now, professionally speaking. Within American literature studies today there seems to be a fair degree of consensus, though certainly not unanimity, that our historicizations need to reckon seriously with even if not fully accept what I like to call the new Americanist grand narrative of settler culture history as a transit from genocidal conquest to Manifest Destiny to would-be new imperium—along the lines, in other words, of Amy Kaplan and Donald Pease's *Cultures of U.S. Imperialism*. But that doesn't by any means imply that the contributors to that collection constitute anything like a tightly coherent school or that all of them have taken a lasting interest in one another's work. Nor does it even guarantee that more than a very few self-identified "New Americanists" are going to hold themselves responsible for absorbing this or that particular new intervention that directly engages their work. Take, for example, the scrupulous historico-ethnographic analysis of the spiritual narrative of the first Hawaiian Christian convert offered in Rob Wilson's *Be Always Converting, Be Always Converted* (25–58), published just as I was drafting this essay. This book is a strong example of an illuminating ramification of the regnant paradigm that also presses inventively and revealingly against its limits, and yet no less striking an instance of the dispersal effect that follows from the dividing up of the huge archive of premodern vernacular life-narrative that bears in one degree or another on U.S. cultural history among specialists in black studies, hemispheric American studies, Pacificana, religion and culture studies, history of the book studies, and so forth. To put it crudely, there is simply too much worthy stuff of an intensely specialized nature coming out these days for even the most alertly responsive scholar to keep track even of all the "relevant" contributions, at least if he or she is pursuing a research program of moderately ambitious scope.

2. Centrifugalism within American literature studies is multicausal. It hasn't been wholly driven by the allure of the marginal position. One needs also, for openers, to reckon with what Fluck (2002) calls "expressive individualism"—the strain within the culture of humanistic professionalism, not limited to Americanists, though perhaps more prevalent within U.S. academe than elsewhere, that would attach preeminent importance to the original critical voice and countenance a highly selective, sometimes even amnesiac, (dis)regard for scholarly precursors. Doubtless related to this factor of pragmatic professionalism, American literature studies has been balkanized by multiple interpretative communities driven more by principled socio-methodological commitments of one sort or another than by investment in exploring any national imaginary. The one I myself know best, ecocriticism, is an instructive case in point, having gathered much of its original force from revisionist work on two different national archives—British romantic poetry on the one hand and American nature writing on the other—but since then increasingly applied to all epochs and genres of literary history from antiquity to the present and increasingly seen as transnational, having to do with such cross-cutting phenomena as place-attachment, aboriginality, toxification, ecological refugeeism, climate change, and so forth. So in Ursula Heise's *Sense of Place and Sense of Planet* (2008), for instance, national variations get taken into account but are deemed of secondary importance for the project at hand.

3. The impression of a fragmented or entropic field-imaginary is exaggerated when measured, as it customarily is, by the standard of Americanist work during the half-century from the 1940s through the late 1980s—from Matthiessen and Trilling through the Myth-Symbol era through the Americanist phase of New Historicism, during which time the emphasis was greater than ever before or since on defining and ramifying the internal coordinates of U.S. literary and cultural history in terms of which everything else would be mapped. Taking a longer view of things, during the century and a half between the American Revolution and the co-emergence of American literature and American studies as specialized fields, the conception (or rather the dream) of defining a distinctive literary-historical heritage did certainly exist, but in competition on the one hand with the felt reality of fragmentation—especially, during these years, the solidity of subnational regional culture relative to the federal—and on the other hand with the sense of U.S. culture as a peripheral outpost of the Anglo-European cultural imaginary. So the sense of a fragmented cultural imaginary is hardly unique to our moment. No

doubt that goes a long way toward explaining why there's never been a first-rate single-authored literary history of the United States, and why all the collaborative histories from the 1917–1921 Cambridge to the 2009 Harvard fission into the sum of their parts.

None of these considerations undermine Fluck's view that critiques of bad exceptionalism may work more to perpetuate the romance with America than to quash it, as in the British journalist Godfrey Hodgson's *Myth of American Exceptionalism* (2009), which reads like the lament of a disappointed lover. This, however, is quite a different project from (say) Thomas Bender's much more even-tempered and far-reaching comparative history, *A Nation among Nations*, which denies anything notably exceptional about U.S. culture whatever among major Europhone cultures since the age of empire began. "On the spectrum of difference," Bender concludes, the United States is one of many, and there is no single norm from which it deviates—or that it establishes" (296–297). If this were true, then by all rights the romance with America *should* dissipate. Of course it's not really true: in many ways the United States *is* distinctly an outlier in the developed world, or has become so—some of them bad (its percentage of incarcerated people, its reluctance to bind itself to international accords), some good (the invention of the first large-scale postcolonial republican democracy), some good or bad depending on how you see the matter (for example, the percentage of poll respondents who profess to believe in an afterlife or in Satan), some ethically neutral (the range of time zones and latitudes across which its territory stretches). But then again there's nothing exceptional about exceptionalism either; such lists could be drawn up for Japan, China, India, Indonesia, Germany, and Brazil. So the phenomenon of national exceptionalism is, *contra* Bender, not so much a chimera as a tossed salad of disparate motifs by no means equally important to the formation of a national cultural imaginary— Confucianism being, for instance, more fundamental to the Chinese cultural imaginary than giant pandas.

With all these considerations in mind, I direct the rest of this essay toward one particular ingredient of U.S. exceptionalism as traditionally imagined that seems incontestably as responsible as any other for producing the schizophrenic effect of the romance with America as luminous holism on the one hand versus fragmentation of the cultural imaginary on the other, and the narrative matrices refracting that: namely, the so-called American dream of individual transformation from modest beginnings and the array of narratives to which this has given rise.

American Dream Narrative(s) and/against
the National Cultural Imaginary

Obviously the "American dream" is precisely that: its imagined sagas don't "reflect statistical realities as much as they tell of possibilities," as the sociologist Robert Wuthnow sums up a turn-of-the-twenty-first-century study of "new elites" of non–European immigrant background that dramatizes both the dream's ongoing vigor and some of the characteristic frustrations and disillusionments that haunt those who are driven by it (108–109). Surely it's no accident that the phrase itself, "the American dream," was coined in the depths of the Great Depression, as Gordon Hutner reminds us in his study of middlebrow fiction between 1920 and 1960 (109–110). Also, obviously, this so-called dream, singular, is in practice pluriform, with differing avatars. It may tilt either toward the materialistic or the idealistic, with different weightings attached to character and luck, or to self-generated initiative as against luck and collaboration, to untrammeled individual autonomy as goal as against communal participation as goal. And so on. One could haggle about matters of taxonomic precision for a very long time. Most, though not all, of the relevant ambiguities are already embedded in the first and historically most influential canonical narrative of the prototypical saga, Benjamin Franklin's *Autobiography*. But I limit concentration only to these specific points: the durability of the land-of-opportunity dream (or fetish) as a crucial driver of America's perceived charisma despite whatever empirical evidence to the contrary, and the link between that perceived distinctiveness and the fragmentation of the cultural imaginary in U.S. literary history and, especially, in critical practice.

American dream narratives, whether told affirmatively or debunkingly, entail fragmentation of cultural imaginaries in various characteristic ways. One is the "forgetful nation" syndrome defined by Ali Behdad. The immigrant forsakes the culture of origin as the price of Americanization. Crèvecoeur's Andrew, the Hebridean, emerges from the middle-states melting pot of European ethnics as prosperous farmer, but good-bye, Scottishness (Behdad 32–47). Franklin's good-bye, Boston, and Gatsby's good-bye, North Dakota, are "native" counterparts. Another characteristic form of imagined fragmentation is personal isolation as the price of individual fulfillment, entrapment in the dungeon of your own heart, as Tocqueville mordantly wrote (2:106). One among many worst-case scenarios is the fictional saga of Van Harrington in Robert Herrick's *Memoirs of an American Citizen*, who starts as a fairly decent if wayward lad from the provinces and through increasing addiction to success in the marketplace becomes a moral monster.

Such fragmentation effects can also be at least partially offset. An immigration narrative project can trigger reminiscences that reinstate the culture nominally left behind, as with Mary Antin's autobiography *Promised Land*, which, even as it attaches supreme importance to being utterly remade by the new world, entangles the reader if not herself in its evocation of her early childhood in the old world shtetl. As to fragmentation type two, against Herrick's cautionary tale of lone-wolf ruthlessness could be set the two ultimate Gilded Age rags-to-riches stories, Andrew Carnegie's *Autobiography* and (in fiction) Lew Wallace's novel *Ben-Hur* (the best-selling novel between *Uncle Tom's Cabin* and *Gone with the Wind*), which go to great pains to qualify their stories of vertiginous ascent to fabulous wealth by insistence on the protagonist's principled turn to philanthropy and communitarian stewardship.

But the fragmentation effects that I want to discuss at greatest length, and that bring me back more closely to the Fluck critique, pertain more to different but related kinds of *critical* foreshortening when engaging this archive of what I have lumpingly called American dream narrative. On the one hand, American protagonist-centric stories of attempted self-realization might be framed more expansively as part of an expanding modern transnational imaginary, broadly Eurocentric in the first instance, within which the *Bildungsroman* is the representative fictional genre. On the other hand, the evolution of what is increasingly called the "ethnic *Bildungsroman*" might be framed more pointedly as one of U.S. literary history's most distinctive success stories—which is not, of course, to say that the texts themselves are always or even usually upbeat narratives of "making it." By *Bildungsroman* I mean here a person-centric narrative, whether or not fictitious, that follows the lifeline of a protagonist seen as more or less socially representative, with special attention to his or her maturation, or "coming of age." Much obviously depends on the strictness with which one defines *Bildungsroman*, which in some critical representations shrinks down to a few German novels. But if we accept Bakhtin's more elastic understanding of *Bildungsromane* as narratives of protagonist "emergence," then the field of possibilities becomes much more capacious.

Traditional Americanist opinion, seconded by Franco Moretti's influential reading of the Anglo-European *Bildungsroman*, deemed U.S. literary history exceptional for the paucity of the genre in so-called classic American fiction. That is true enough of the dramatis personae on whom D. H. Lawrence and F. O. Matthiessen concentrate. Indeed, among pre-realist fictions by canonical U.S. novelists, only James Fenimore Cooper's *Satanstoe* snugly fits the template. Hence Leslie Fiedler, following Lawrence, and also reacting to the intense fascination with protracted adolescence in post–World War II U.S. fiction from J. D. Salinger to Jack Kerouac and Philip Roth, defined "American" literary distinctiveness in terms of willful resistance to maturity, a refusal to grow up—a line of thinking given new life and placed in broader transnational-modernist context by Ross Posnock's arresting book on Roth. But with the elasticization of the Americanist field-imaginary to include women's fiction à la Maria Cummins's novel *The Lamplighter*, African American autobiography from slave narrative onward, other strains of "ethnic" narrative both autobiographical and fictive, as well as writing by white males formerly cordoned off as merely "popular" such as the Horatio Alger novels, the quest for mature social identity and agency looks considerably more central; the supposed national fascination with perpetual immaturity looks suspiciously like a white middle-class male affair; and the now expanded field of what counts as U.S. literary history looks less autonomous, or aberrant, if you will. The transatlantic Richardsonian continuum that Fiedler relentlessly consigned to the aesthetic substrate looms much larger; slave narrative becomes part of a larger Afro-Atlantic field; family resemblances between Dickensian and Melvillian versions of young male naïfs begin to emerge.

The full implications of these and other such shifts still remain to be absorbed fully even though they started to gather momentum several decades ago. I want to pursue some of them here more concretely through what may seem—so I hope!—a somewhat unexpected pairing from the first half of the twentieth century: Willa Cather and Carlos Bulosan. Cather's novel *The Song of the Lark* (1912) follows the metamorphosis of a second-generation Swedish immigrant girl from a backwater childhood in Moonstone, Colorado, to international opera stardom. Immigrant activist and man of letters Carlos Bulosan's autobiographical fiction *America Is in the Heart* (1946) follows its protagonist from early boyhood in the Philippines as the child of an impoverished farming family, through his ordeals as an exploited economic refugee in depression America, to his beginnings as a published writer and the onset of World War II. Among countless possible dyads that might be chosen, I select this pair of texts as being in multiple ways analogous yet positioning themselves in notably different ways vis-à-vis the romance with America that, ironically, have conduced to an almost diametrically opposite categorization by the Americanist field-imaginary that now prevails.

Here are some pertinent common threads. Both texts are ethnic *Bildungsromane*, the pivotal parts of which could have happened only in the United States, and what's more, in an unstably multiethnic American West. Both narratives also migrate about in space to the end of evoking their respective different transnational imaginaries; and both take pains to problematize the identification of the protagonist with America. Synchronously with their peripateia, both protagonists are emotionally driven figures, repeatedly misunderstood, who wrestle throughout their narratives with the challenges of self-understanding and articulacy, owing partly to language of family origin but in the long run more for reasons of culture and class.

These analogies might be offset by a still longer list of disparities, but the particular contrast I would stress here has to do with critical framing. *Song of the Lark* has seemed an unproblematically American text, however problematic its treatment of gender, sexual preference, and aboriginalism—a solid midlevel achievement by a writer always deemed at least borderline canonical, though briefly out of fashion under high modernism. Yet not only does it evince zero interest in thematizing Americanness as such, but also its plotline enacts an almost complete disaffiliation from the national. There's no romance with America whatever in this text, unless you count the romance of Mesa Verde, this being the first of Cather's fictions to deploy the vanished Indian motif. Virtually no one in the United States, even those most sympathetic to the heroine Thea Kronberg, more than gropingly understands what makes her tick except for foreigners: her Mexican neighbors in the local *barrio* and various European expatriates of similarly aesthetic bent who also feel like fish out of water in the United States. In respect to genre affiliations, the stakes of *Song of the Lark* are better understood when we divest ourselves of the assumption that it somehow belongs in the first instance to an American imaginary and reposition it within the atlas of modern fiction on the geographical periphery of the *Künstlerroman*, with texts like Mann's *Tonio Kröger* and Rilke's *Notebooks of Laurids Malte Brigge* at the center, Joyce's *Portrait of the Artist* on the semi-periphery, and Stella Miles Franklin's *My Brilliant Career* and Olive Schreiner's *Story of an African Farm* fellow denizens of the Anglophone outback. That isn't to say one can't identify a cohort of other national narratives that pursue comparable plotlines: Fanny Fern's *Ruth Hall*, Dreiser's *The Genius*, Richard Wright's *Black Boy*, and for that matter (in some critical accounts) *America Is in the Heart* (see Gonzalez). The point is simply the need to disenchant the assumption that *Song of the Lark* strongly attaches itself to a transnational cultural imaginary however much it seems to enact a storybook American dream–style rags-to-riches plot.

By contrast, the explicit thematic center of Bulosan's *America Is in the Heart* is precisely the romance with America, and yet those most drawn toward it seem to want to distance it as far as possible from that romance. Here I am not thinking simply or even primarily of arguments to the effect that the appearance of flag-waving patriotism in some of the most often quoted passages means the opposite of what the casual mainstream reader might think, i.e., that Bulosan's actual emphasis is on the scandal of the country's failure so far to deliver the equality it promises, as Ramón Saldívar has shown with subtlety and erudition in his analysis of the ironies (including circumstances of composition) of Bulosan's essay for the *Saturday Evening Post* to accompany the third of Norman Rockwell's four wildly popular illustrations of FDR's four American freedoms—all four of them iconic images of lily-white communities or families (205–214). Still more striking from my standpoint is the extent to which critical discussion of how to situate Bulosan in literary history has gravitated toward the resistance of *America Is in the Heart* to inclusion within a national cultural imaginary. Is it part of Asian American literature? Is it a Filipino-diasporic text whose particularity is betrayed by such agglomeration, as Epifanio San Juan holds (234)? Or is it misrecognized when coded "ethnic" as against "proletarian," as Michael Denning contends (238)? Such are the grounds on which the taxonomic discussions usually take place. Lisa Lowe, who reads the novel as a foundational Asian American text, shrewdly notes this rabbit/duck paradox: "Taught as an ethnic bildungsroman, as a tale of the subject's journey from foreign estrangement to integrated citizenship," it "responds to the reconciliatory and universalizing functions of canonization; taught with attention to social and historical, as well as formal and thematic, contradictions," it "thematize[s] how the demand for canonization simultaneously produces a critique of canonization itself" (57, 55). Yet this statement stops short of suggesting, as well it might, that these opposite readings are inherent to the project of the text itself—that they stand behind its signature passage, evidently first written during the war in a letter to the wife of a Filipino journalist in the resistance whom Bulosan believed had been killed, and then rewritten for the novel as a prewar speech by his older brother Macario: "America is not merely a land or an institution" but "the prophecy of a new society," "a system that knows no sorrow or strife or suffering"; it's also "the nameless foreigner, the homeless refugee. . . . We are all that nameless foreigner, that homeless refugee, that hungry boy, that illiterate immigrant and that lynched black body. . . . from the first Adams to the last Filipino, native born or alien, educated or illiterate—*We are America!*" (Bulosan 1943, 213; 1945,189). Anticipating Martin Luther King's "I Have a Dream" speech of the 1960s, the romance with America here seems to stand as a prolepsis of a still unfulfilled promise of a truly inclusive social order that would uplift the marginal and downtrodden without erasing the particularities of remembered suffering. As such, it frames American ethnic *Bildungsromane* as sagas of struggle rather than of clear success, whose protagonists remain accountable to community if, however, sometimes alien to it.

Two-thirds of a century later, after a series of ethnic literary renaissances and the advent of critical whiteness studies—such that for the critical intelligentsia if not the general public no longer is there any such thing as an unmarked ethnicity—Bulosan's template looks at least as representative of the U.S. cultural imaginary as Cather's. That is, within the expanded matrix that now counts as the database for the Americanist field-imaginary, the narrative of fraught minoritarian passage toward a social recognition that might promote or augur social change appears a more distinctive carrier of the national cultural imaginary than Franklin's saga of the transformation of runaway apprentice into founding father; and the success story of the American *Bildungsroman*—the marker that arguably distinguishes it most from its increasingly global look-alikes in the age of Obama—is its incremental proliferation of socially diverse sagas of personal emergence and the complexities thereof. Yet all this hardly guarantees either the sustainability of national cultural distinctiveness or the durability of the romance with America as a distinctively charismatic place. Both Cather's and Bulosan's narratives should alert one to the amenability of the *Bildungsroman* form, including the ethnic *Bildungsroman*, to both national and transnational imaginaries. Bruce Robbins has called attention to the attraction of upward mobility narratives for the developing world as well as Euro-America. Pheng Cheah argues for the importance of *Bildungsroman* as a defining postcolonial genre, one of his pivotal actors being also one of Bulosan's own heroes, the Philippine nationalist martyr José Rigal—Rigal's life story for Bulosan, his novelistic masterpiece of a young returnee's political awakening, *Noli Me Tangere*, for Cheah. Joseph Slaughter's *Human Rights, Inc.* argues, by contrast, in neo-Foucaultian terms for the *Bildungsroman* as the distinctive literary carrier of human rights discourse, namely that it works like the mainstream Victorian novel according to Nancy Armstrong's *How Novels Think*, as an apparatus of cultural production aimed at producing individuated liberal subjects who exercise social agency within strictly regulated bounds.

These various accounts of *Bildungsroman*'s cultural-historical import are obviously somewhat at odds, then. Pheng Cheah would radicalize the genre, whereas Armstrong and Slaughter see it as an engine of bourgeoisi-fication. But the aggregate effect of their combined interventions must be to qualify if not utterly to disenchant the impression of anything intractably exceptional about U.S. narratives of individual emergence, including the ethnic *Bildungsromane* formerly deemed subcanonical or marginal but now de facto paradigmatic. The same arguably holds even for the more traditional, Lawrentian-Fiedleresque-Posnockian view of narrative distinctiveness resting on refusal of cultural maturity—although some of the critics just named, notably Armstrong and Slaughter, would rule this out. For built into the genre itself, as far back as the most cited seminal text, Goethe's *Wilhelm Meister's Lehrjahre*, has been the counter-theme of resistance to maturity, in the classic touchstone English examples finally repressed but almost always present as an undercurrent and in some cases deliberately not overcome, as with Rilke's Malte. So Malte surfaces as an important reference point for Maxine Hong Kingston's perpetual post-1960s Chinese American male adolescent hippie Wittman Ah Sing in *Tripmaster Monkey*.

If, then, American dream narratives are understood as avatars of in-dividual emergence narratives increasingly distributed worldwide, albeit Eurocentric in the first instance, then there is no reason to expect that this aspect of the romance with America—that is, of supposed American cultural exceptionalism—should persist into the infinite future; indeed, quite the contrary. Yet neither should one expect it to vanish within the lifetimes even of our very youngest students. For one thing, the American dream will surely persist as an imagined field of possibility so long as the impression persists that the country is unusually hospitable to liberal individualism, and thereafter into the indefinite future as a historical memory. That the paradigm case for U.S. emergence narrative has become the minoritarian passage and not the Franklinian passage of white male youth will undoubtedly promote its durability, at least so long as the upper echelons of U.S. society continue to seem increasingly penetrable by minorities and Wuthnow's new immigrant elites. Meanwhile, however, for the Americanist field-imaginary to continue to question the coherence and distinctiveness of national culture and national literary history and to continue to concentrate more of its energies on the connecting links between national culture and the rest of the world seems fruitful, pragmatic, proper—and also, one might add, safe. It will make the Americanist field-imaginary increasingly more complex and less amenable to generalization, let alone control, by any one superscholar or camp; but it is certainly not going to put Americanists out of business anytime soon.

The foregoing paragraph doubtless gives the impression of siding with the forces of dispersal that Fluck skeptically anatomizes in "The Romance with America," not to mention my Boelhower-instigated undergraduate class of yore, rather than with the earnest senior Chinese professors who objected to my exegesis of "trans-" approaches and also with Fluck's own conviction, stated more pointedly in his 2007 "Theories of American Culture," that "the original goal of the American Studies movement—the analysis of the cultural sources of American power—continues to be as urgent as ever, and the dissolution of this project in transnational studies would be a major mistake" (73). Fluck's view of the importance of (American) nationness as frame of examination and historical force clearly lies somewhere between those of Hitchcock and Chatterjee cited earlier. Pragmatic rather than patriotic but certainly not aversive, Fluck calls for continued focus not on some "mythic national identity" but on the "particular set of economic, social or cultural conditions that, for historical and other reasons, are different from those of other countries and nations" (among which he cites "a strong transnational dimension") (74). The sense of urgency here evidently arises from the conviction that the special "historical constellations that have been developed by the United States" that have produced unique "forms of international dominance" still await adequate explanation (73). The risk of American-Studies-as-Deliquescence-of-America-through-Transnationalism (or runaway multiculturalism) is that it ignores the elephant in the international boardroom. I am actually much more sympathetic to this concern than this essay as a whole probably makes it seem. The extent to which I differ arises chiefly from these two convictions: First, a general conviction as to the potential importance of literary-intellectual work as a fringe activity that more or less systemically questions the ethical legitimacy of whatever forms of social dominance even while usually operating within them (e.g., for openers, the very choice to become a writer or a professor of humanities in the United States has always for the most part been a choice not to pursue a more socially acceptable path). And second, a more particular conviction as to the importance of national literary-cultural history as a barometric indicator of what is ethically legitimate as against what is politically-economically-militarily powerful about the present, long-standing—though since 1989 also increasingly embattled and endangered—prestige of the United States in the eyes of the world, a legitimacy intimately bound up with its gradual, often maddeningly slow and two-faced groping to make good on the founding promise—cruelly deceptive at the start—of social inclusiveness within and across borders.

WORKS CITED

Anderson, Benedict. *Imagined Communities* [1983]. Rev. ed. London: Verso, 2006.
Armstrong, Nancy. How Novels Think: The Limits of British Individualism from 1719–1900. New York: Columbia University Press, 2005.
Bakhtin, M. M. "The *Bildungsroman* and Its Significance in the History of Realism (Toward a Historical Typology of the Novel)." In *Speech Genres and Other Late Essays*. Trans. Vern W. McGee. Ed. Caryl Emerson and Michael Holquist. Austin: University of Texas Press, 1986. 10–59.
Behdad, Ali. *A Forgetful Nation: On Immigration and Cultural Identity in the United States*. Durham: Duke University Press, 2005.
Bender, Thomas. *A Nation among Nations: America's Place in World History*. New York: Hill & Wang, 2006.
Bercovitch, Sacvan. *The Office of the Scarlet Letter*. Baltimore: Johns Hopkins University Press, 1991.
———. *The Rites of Assent*. New York: Routledge, 1993.
Bhabha, Homi K. "DissemiNation: Time, Narrative, and the Margins of the Modern Nation." In *Nation and Narration*, ed. Homi K. Bhabha. London: Routledge, 1990. 291–322.
Boelhower, William. *Through a Glass Darkly: Ethnic Semiosis in American Literature* [1984]. New York: Oxford University Press, 1987.
Bulosan, Carlos. *America Is in the Heart* [1946]. Seattle: University of Washington Press, 1973.
———. "Letter to a Filipino Woman" [1943]. In *On Becoming Filipino: Selected Writings of Carlos Bulosan*. Ed. Epifanio San Juan Jr. Philadelphia: Temple University Press, 1995. 210–214.
Castoriadis, Cornelius. *The Imaginary Institution of Society* [1975. Trans. Kathleen Blamey. Cambridge: MIT Press, 1987.
Chatterjee, Partha. *The Nation and Its Fragments*. Princeton: Princeton University Press, 1993.
Cheah, Pheng. *Spectral Nationality: Passages of Freedom from Kant to Postcolonial Literatures of Liberation*. New York: Columbia University Press, 2003.
Colacurcio, Michael. "The American Renaissance Renaissance." *New England Quarterly* 64 (1991): 445–495.
Dawson, Graham. *Soldier Heroes: British Adventure, Empire and the Imagining of Masculinities*. London: Routledge, 1994.

Denning, Michael. *The Cultural Front: The Laboring of American Culture in the Twentieth Century*. London: Verso, 1997.

Dimock, Wai Chee. *Through Other Continents: American Literature across Deep Time*. Princeton: Princeton University Press, 2006.

Fiedler, Leslie. *Love and Death in the American Novel*. New York: Criterion, 1960.

Fluck, Winfried. "American Literary History and the Romance with America." *American Literary History* 24.1 (Spring 2009): 1–18.

———. "The Humanities in the Age of Expressive Individualism and Cultural Radicalism." In *The Futures of American Studies*, ed. Robyn Wiegman and Donald E. Pease. Durham: Duke University Press, 2002. 211–247.

———. *Das kulturelle Imaginäre: Eine Funktionsgeschichte des amerikanischen Romans, 1790–1860*. Frankfurt: Suhrkamp, 1997.

———. "Theories of American Culture (and the Transnational Turn in American Studies)." *REAL: Yearbook of Research in English and American Literature* 23 (2007): 59–77.

Gonzalez, Gabriel José. "*America Is in the Heart* as a Colonial-Immigrant Novel: Engaging the Bildungsroman." *Kritika Kultura* 8 (February 2007): 99–110.

Gowdie, Sean. *Creole America: The West Indies and the Formation of Literature and Culture in the New Republic*. Philadelphia: University of Pennsylvania Press, 2006.

Heise, Ursula. *Sense of Place and Sense of Planet: The Environmental Imagination of the Global*. New York: Oxford University Press, 2008.

Hitchcock, Peter. *Imaginary States: Studies in Cultural Transnationalism*. Urbana: University of Illinois Press, 2003.

Hodgson, Godfrey. *The Myth of American Exceptionalism*. New Haven: Yale University Press, 2009.

Hutner, Gordon. *What America Read: Taste, Class, and the Novel*. Chapel Hill: University of North Carolina Press, 2009.

Irwin, John. *American Hieroglyphics: The Symbol of the Egyptian Hieroglyphics in the American Renaissance*. Baltimore: Johns Hopkins University Press, 1980.

Iser, Wolfgang. *The Fictive and the Imaginary: Charting Literary Anthropology*. Baltimore: Johns Hopkins University Press, 1993.

Kaplan, Amy, and Donald E. Pease, eds. *The Cultures of U.S. Imperialism*. Durham: Duke University Press, 1993.

Lawrence, D. H. *Studies in Classic American Literature* [1923]. Ed. Ezra Greenspan, Lindeth Vasey, and John Worthen. Cambridge: Cambridge University Press, 2003.

Leverenz, David. *Manhood and the American Renaissance*. Ithaca: Cornell University Press, 1989.

Lowe, Lisa. "Canon, Institutionalization, Identity: Contradictions for Asian

American Studies." In *The Ethnic Canon: Histories, Institutions, and Interventions*, ed. David Palumbo-Liu. Minneapolis: University of Minnesota Press, 1995. 48–68.

Matthiessen, F. O. *American Renaissance: Art and Expression in the Age of Emerson and Whitman*. London: Oxford University Press, 1941.

Moretti, Franco. *The Way of the World: The Bildungsroman in European Culture*. London: Verso, 1987.

Pease, Donald E. "New American Revisionist Inter-ventions into the Canon." *boundary 2* 17.1 (1990): 1–37.

Posnock, Ross. *Philip Roth's Rude Truth: The Art of Immaturity*. Princeton: Princeton University Press, 2006.

Robbins, Bruce. *Upward Mobility and the Common Good: Toward a Literary History of the Welfare State*. Princeton: Princeton University Press, 2007.

Saldívar, Ramón. *The Borderlands of Culture: Amérigo Paredes and the Transnational Imaginary*. Durham: Duke University Press, 2006.

San Juan, E., Jr. "In Search of Filipino Writing: Reclaiming Whose 'America'?" In *The Ethnic Canon: Histories, Institutions, and Interventions*, ed. David Palumbi-Liu. Minneapolis: University of Minnesota Press, 1995. 213–240.

Shumway, David. *Creating American Civilization: A Genealogy of American Literature as an Academic Discipline*. Minneapolis: University of Minnesota Press, 1994.

Slaughter, Joseph R. *Human Rights, Inc.: The World Novel, Narrative Form, and International Law*. New York: Fordham University Press, 2007.

Tocqueville, Alexis de. *Democracy in America*. Trans. Henry Reeve. Ed. Phillips Bradley. 2 vols. New York: Vintage, 1954.

Wilson, Rob. *Be Always Converting, Be Always Converted*. Cambridge: Harvard University Press, 2009.

Wuthnow, Robert. *American Mythos: Why Our Best Efforts to Be a Better Nation Fall Short*. Princeton: Princeton University Press, 2006.

3 Imaginaries of American Modernism

In American literary and cultural history, "modernism" has been considered a phenomenon of uncertain status—even after it was academically institutionalized by the New Criticism of the 1950s. On the one hand, it had long been considered a provincial extension of European developments, since even its leading protagonists—Eliot, Faulkner, Pound, Stein—could be easily integrated into the larger European context.[1] On the other hand, not least through America's political, economic, and cultural assertion as a global power after World War II, insistence on its national particularity, if not uniqueness, entered the discourse especially of American studies when it finally began to deal with American modernism (after having been almost exclusively focused on the "classic" texts of the "American Renaissance"). Some twenty years ago it seemed plausible to conceive of American modernism and its history in linear terms, that is, as part of a progressivist/pragmatist attempt to dissolve, and yet maintain, an obsolete cultural order by adjusting it to the flow of experience as much as to the modernizing impulse of American society—first, by making the fluidity of life the object of representation (as, for example, in Dreiser's *Sister Carrie*), later by translating experiential instantaneousness and fluidity into increasingly abstract forms of linguistic or artistic expression (as in Dos Passos's *Manhattan Transfer*).[2]

"European modernism arrived at the threshold of a not yet fully modernized world in which old and new were violently knocked against each other, striking the sparks of that astonishing eruption of creativity that came to be known only much later as 'modernism,'" Andreas Huyssen has argued (Huyssen 2007, 190).[3] In contrast, American modernism, by attempting to create an art expressive of an already modernizing nation, seemed more in alignment with its technological environment—even though it did encounter resistance from a restrictive and still powerful genteel cultural tradition that modeled itself on European, especially on English high culture. Centered mostly in New York, American modernism integrated elements of a thriving metropolitan, popular, and commercial culture of modernity, at the same time that it reached back to what was considered the beginnings of a national culture centered in Emerson and Whitman. In doing so, it absorbed and modified the iconoclastic innovations of various European avant-gardes, leveling the differences among them in the process. It was thus possible to see American modernism as part of an international movement and yet also, as Hugh Kenner once phrased it, as a distinct "homemade world"—as a box within a box which contained, as yet another box, the counter-modernism of the Harlem Renaissance and its attempt "to beat barbaric beauty out of a white frame," in Claude McKay's words.[4]

This storyline became increasingly vulnerable to attacks from many sides. When its self-celebratory ideology of aesthetic innovation was analyzed within contexts of race, class, and gender, modernism lost its quasi-mythological status as a cultural counterforce. In the wake of the cultural upheaval of the early seventies and its long poststructuralist aftermath, it was generally regarded as a "politically retrograde phenomenon" (DeKoven 1991, 12), its transgressional tendencies only masking its undiminished commitment to "totality" as well as to a logocentric and patriarchal order in which the aesthetically revolutionary and the politically reactionary merged. Its turn toward the creative forces of the "primitive" and atavistic now seemed nothing but a white masquerade in blackface that thrived on the undiminished racism of American society; and its effort to give its discovery of the New a distinctly American face now appeared analogous to (or even complicit with) an all-pervasive nativism that identified the Anglo-Saxon with the truly, the essentially American.

Michael North's *Dialect of Modernism* (1994) and Walter Benn Michaels's *Our America* (1995) are surely the most brilliant examples of this deconstructive onslaught. Both critics have changed our view of American modernism once and for all by revealing its secret desires as well as its, in some cases, rather distasteful bedfellows. In thus uncovering the covered parts of modernism, however, they only replaced one image of it with another. In what follows, I try to look at modernism through *their* eyes and yet *beyond* their perception of it, because, in its craving for essentials or for universals (however modernistically redefined), the American variant of modernism was neither primarily about race (although it could not escape racism) nor about nativism (although it did raise the question of what America was all about). Its achievements are inseparable from its ideological and psychological entanglements. But in its dedication to the New (at a historic moment when the world seemed as much in decay as in revolutionary commotion), it explored cultural and linguistic possibilities *within* as well as *beyond* national boundaries— possibilities whose implications may have regained relevance only now, in a postmodern and transnational context.

In this attempt, the concept of a "cultural imaginary" that has recently entered the discourse of cultural theory via Cornelius Castoriadis and Josué Harari (among others) has been helpful. In his *Scenarios of the Imaginary* Harari argued:

> The imaginary world is always with us, as a parallel to our world, there is not a single moment of our existence which is not imbued with the imaginary. Yet, even if all its "markers" refer back to reality, the imaginary does not belong to reality proper. The imaginary is neither a lie nor an illusion that distracts us from the real (as dreams do); it is neither reality's "negative" nor the "unreal" of reality. The closest one can get to describing how the imaginary stands in relation to the real is to refer to the familiar Saussurian image of the sheet of paper whose front cannot be cut without its back being cut at the same time. In like manner, the real cannot be separated from the imaginary or the imaginary from the real: any such division could be accomplished only abstractly, and the result would be either pure representation or reality in its raw state—imageless and therefore meaningless. Thus if we were to define the imaginary according to clear-cut categories, we would reach a dead end, for the imaginary is always ambiguous; it functions as an ever-present "otherness," persistently soliciting the real. (Harari 57)

Accordingly, I base my argument on the assumption that the imaginary of American modernism is its culturally wished-for other and not-yet "Real,"[5] its cultural pre- or unconscious. I propose, however, that it consists in fact of several imaginaries: I visualize it as a mesh of conflicting but also overlapping dreams, fantasies, desires. Here I construct several frames—based on contrast and analogy—within which I imagine this network of modernist imaginaries as suspended. One could also conceive of such frames as consisting of lines connecting opposite positions along which imaginaries fluctuate: between the cosmopolitan or global and the local or nativist; between the universal or holistic and the particular or fragmentary; between a utopian, race-transcending humanism and racial essentialism; between the religious or mystical and the secular or materialist; between nostalgia for an absent (yet somehow still present) "Divine" and insistence on its revelation in the flesh.

"Our America": Hispanic Connections and European Projections

I start the outline of my imaginary web (as well as of my web of imaginaries) with a premodernist historical event: the imperial moment of Admiral Dewey's victory at the battle of Manila in 1898, which inspired Ernest Fenollosa, the famous orientalist scholar (and an American of Catalan origin), to write an exuberant essay for *Harper's Monthly* magazine, called "The Coming Fusion of East and West." It ends with an appeal to his countrymen to awake to a higher, world-embracing consciousness:

> But last night we were . . . content with our local issues, our private curse of slavery, intent to erect a little island of silver coinage. How could we unify our scattered aims with no centrality of focus on the needs of a common humanity? This morning we have waked to find ourselves citizens of a new world, full of Drakes, and Sidneys, and Philips, and Armadas; rich in immeasurable colonies, investments, adventures; of an unlimited mind-expansion; of a race sympathy new in human annals. Columbus and his discovery are but a four-century stepping stone to it; for we were obstacles in his western path that had to be first mastered: Today we enter literally into his dream, and carry the Aryan banner of his caravels where he aimed to plant it—on the heights of an awakened East. (Fenollosa 122)

Fenollosa's expansive imagination conceives of America's imperial venture as a long-hoped-for liberation from the nation's narrow provincialisms, as a cultural wakeup call from its colonial sleep. His vision is at once cosmopolitan and nationalist, humanist and racist; it connects the new military and economic assertion of the United States with "the needs of a common humanity" and the mythologized past of European empire building; but then also forward, by acts of "unlimited mind-expansion," to a universalism that will constitute the cultural empire of a global future. Material conquest finds its transcendent legitimation in spiritual conquest, and the progress of Western civilization unfolds—via America—as a process of territorial expansion and cultural integration. Columbus's discovery of the new empire is continued in the conquest of the American continent, which is continued in the conquest of the Philippines, which is prefigured in Whitman's metaphorical conquest of space in "Passage to India," which in turn anticipates the linguistic empire of Ezra Pound's *Cantos*. Pound would conceive of this empire as his, the American poet's, aesthetic appropriation of the world's cultural traditions whose fragments he would assemble and connect by an ideogrammatic method of collage—a method he developed from the same Fenollosa's study of Chinese characters.

A few years later, but in reaction to the same war, the Nicaraguan poet Rubén Darío wrote his poem "To Roosevelt," in which he rejects American expansionism with an emphatic "No": "You think that life is a fire, / that progress is an irruption, / that the future is wherever / your bullet strikes. / No." In a countermove he then evokes "our America, which has had poets / since the ancient times of Nezahualcóyotl; / . . . O men with Saxon eyes and barbarous souls, / our America lives. And dreams. And loves." No doubt, Darío uses the phrase "our America" ("nuestra America") consciously—in commemoration of his friend José Martí, whom he had met in New York more than a decade before and who had died in Cuba in 1895 fighting for its liberation.[6]

Martí's concept of "Our America"—as developed in an essay of 1891 that has become a major text in recent redefinitions of American studies—wavers between Cuban nationalism and pan–Latin American transnationalism, since the national can be achieved only from a transnational consciousness.[7] Martí's project is in any case dedicated to the creation of a political structure that does not yet exist, but is distinctly different in its spirituality and cultural substance from the America that is *not* ours—from that materialist Northern "giant in seven-mile-boots," that Anglo-Saxon "Caliban" (as Darío called the United States) against whose power "Our America" had still to be created in defensive self-assertion.[8]

"What 'Our' means," writes Doris Sommer, "is a promising problem, because the discriminating possessive pronoun is so shifty, so available for competing positionalities and equivocal meanings" (in Belnap and Fernández, 83). What happens, for example, when it is used in reference to the United States, as is the case with Waldo Frank's cultural critique of 1919 called *Our America*. Frank insisted that, when he wrote it, he had no knowledge of Martí's essay,[9] but rather that his book was written in response to the demands of his French friends to explain America to them: "My dear Jacques Copeau and Gaston Gallimard," he writes in his introductory remarks, "in a real sense this is your book." "America" was substance buried, a hidden "secret treasure" yet to be discovered, and a national concept that transcended nationalism. It was, in any case, not congruent with Anglo-Saxon America but—not unlike the vision of Darío, of Martí, or, somewhat later, of William Carlos Williams—pre-Columbian and continental, part of the avant-garde's attempt to define America as "something other than a white nation" (Hutchinson 1995, 446).

The continental dimension of Frank's vision became more evident during the 1920s, when he, in several books about Latin America, not only saw himself as allied in prophetic spirit to Simon Bolívar and Jose Martí but also assumed the role of cultural mediator between different "our" Americas—analogous to and yet vehemently against the reactionary and essentializing visions of people like Lothrop Stoddard that Walter Benn Michaels reflects in the ironic mirror of his own *Our America*, his deconstructive study of American modernism.

Although it is certainly true that the modernist turn to "Our America" was part of a general shift toward cultural self-definition during the twenties (a shift that was at least partially provoked by the United States' entering the league of imperialist nations), it is yet worthwhile to remember that it was also the result of a continuous dialogue across national and cultural borders. This is certainly true in the case of European (especially French) demands and expectations. Frank's *Our America* is one example, Williams's *In the American Grain* another—a book that was written in response to Valérie Larbaud and enthusiastically reviewed by D. H. Lawrence. In the first volume of the short-lived journal *The Seven Arts*, Frank's friend and mentor Romain Rolland—the celebrated author of the novel *Jean Cristophe* (published a few years before World War I)—had appealed to American artists not only to express their as yet unexplored cultural resources but also to become agents of a global integration of cultures. In fact, Rolland's appeal seems very much in line with Fenollosa's vision that I quoted earlier:

> The hour has struck for mankind to begin its march toward the ideal simply of Humanity:—to begin it with conscious fervor, to suffer no exclusion. . . . The Asiatic cultures—China, India—are being born anew. The Old and the New Worlds must bring forth the treasures of their souls, and place them in common with these equal treasures. For all great expressions of mankind . . . complement each other. And the Thought of the future must be a synthesis of all the great thoughts of the world. To achieve this fertile union should be the work of Americans. . . . It is they who live at the center of the life of the world! This is my dream.[10]

It has also been a persistent Western dream of progressive Enlightenment: this vision of a new world, emergent yet still to be created, led by an "America" to which Europe had passed the torch in mankind's evolutionary movement toward unity.

In several books written during the 1920s, Frank very much follows the line of Rolland's holistic vision. *Our America* (as well as his later

Re-Discovery of America) primarily aimed at the creation of a national culture but also referred to a continental America whose Hispanic parts were least modernized, least "Americanized," as he put it, and therefore a latent resource of spirituality.[11] In the peoples of Latin America, Frank writes, "mystic America has become . . . an organic undertaking. . . . Upon the side of our hope, there is first and last the peculiar energy of the American world—the forming life of our land which makes us all, Nordic and Negro, American; and which relates us more essentially with the Indian or the Peruvian, than with our blood-brothers of Europe. . . . It is so wondrously atune with our mystic tradition that one is almost ready to believe in an Atlantis, whence the Egyptian, Mediterranean, and Amerindian all emerged" (Frank 1929, 268, 229–230).

The four cultural histories Frank published between 1919 and 1931— *Our America* (1919), *Virgin Spain* (1926), *The Re-Discovery of America* (1929), and *America Hispana* (1931)—explore this "mystic tradition" that potentially united these cultures despite their apparent cultural differences: "two half-worlds" destined eventually to become "not a homogeneity (God forbid!), not an identity (God forbid!) but a complex multiple organism" (Frank 1943, 380). Accordingly, he dedicated *Virgin Spain* "To those brother Americans / whose tongues are Spanish and Portuguese / . . . but whose America like mine / stretches from the Arctic to the Horn" (Frank 1926, dedication page). Those friends and spiritual "brothers" belonged to Latin America's intellectual elite—the Mexican artists Alfonso Reyes, Diego Rivera, and José Clemente Orozco, or the Peruvian philosopher José Carlos Mariátegui, to whom Frank dedicated his *South American Journey* (1943).

In blending Marx with Spinoza, a critique of capitalism with a transnational concept of unity and mystic immanence, Frank assumed the role of a modern Jewish prophet. He thus found himself in competitive vicinity with other prophets of the day, most notably with Georges Gurdjieff and his disciple Piotr Ouspensky, whose mysticism of self-transcendence and consciousness expansion was brought to New York and taught there in the mid-twenties by Alfred Orage,[12] the former editor of *The New Age*, whose Social Credit theories exerted influence especially on Ezra Pound but also on William Carlos Williams and the critic Gorham Munson—all this confirming Leon Surette's thesis that modernism was born in alternative visions that included the esoteric and occult.

His prophetic claims and posturing make Frank difficult reading today. And yet, for a brief historical moment, he was a central figure on the margins of the intellectual life of both Americas, his vision of "wholeness" responding to the period's intense utopian longing. In the United States, *Our America*, Gorham Munson remembered, "dazzled my immediate generation."[13] It affected a group of artists and intellectuals commonly labeled "cultural nationalists"—although for them, the national and the transnational were two sides of the same humanist/modernist coin. Frank's notion of "wholeness" embraced the particular in order to transcend it. To reach a higher level of cultural synthesis, the regionally, racially, or nationally different first had to find and assert itself culturally in aesthetic self-expression. Frank's conceptual image for such a concordance *in* and *through* difference was that of the symphony—a metaphor he took from Romain Rolland, however, and *not* from Horace Kallen, whose symphonic multiculturalism he emphatically rejected (Frank 1929, 260–261 footnote).

His dialectics nevertheless involved him in a number of seemingly contradictory positions: Frank vehemently rejected industrialism and the Machine, but he also accepted both as necessary historical conditions for their eventual transformation into facts of consciousness. He was caught in a similar contradiction when it came to the matter of race. From a higher perspective of anticipated synthesis, race—though a painful reality in American life—did not exist. But it had to be creatively accepted, its hidden potential expressed, so that it could become the agent of a spiritual collective life. He therefore encouraged his friend and disciple Jean Toomer to explore his racial heritage at the same time that he tried to respect Toomer's anti-essentialist, transracial position. After having read drafts of *Cane*, he assured Toomer, "You do not write as a Negro" (O'Daniel, 87); but then, in his preface to the published book, he praised him as a remarkable Negro writer.

Toomer had originally accepted this double role as the inevitable part of his own racial in-betweenness and at one point pleaded for a literary journal devoted entirely to the artistic expression of African Americans.[14] After *Cane* had come out, however, he increasingly resented the pressure—exerted by his publisher Boni & Liveright, but also by Sherwood Anderson, Alain Locke, and by Frank himself—to accept being a Negro writer as his true identity and to continue writing "his Negro stuff."[15] Instead, he chose to abandon the black folk material he had so effectively made use of in *Cane* and committed himself to teaching Gurdjieff's ideas to the Harlem intelligentsia (among them Nella Larsen) in order to promote the "spiritual evolution of a new American race" (that is, of a race beyond race and color),[16] whose arrival he anticipated in his poem "The Blue Meridian"—while, as Walter Benn Michaels has demonstrated, the culture itself, by confirming racial difference as cultural difference, moved in the opposite direction.[17]

The Whole, the Fragmented, and the Particular

"Wholeness"—"personal, mystic, compact, myriad-formed, imperious," as Frank phrased it in *The Re-Discovery of America* (260)—operates on several interconnected levels of awareness. As expressive of the holiness of life and its creative energies, it is directed toward a more communal existence and against the fragmenting, the life-destroying impact of capitalism. As a psychologically integrative concept attempting to engage the creative energies of the unconscious, it is directed against the repressive coalition of rationalism and Puritanism. As a spiritual concept, it ultimately aims at achieving a higher, more inclusive stage of human consciousness. Therefore it also implied a specific aesthetic—those distinct strategies of organicist expressiveness that mark Frank's writings as well as the poetry, fictions, and paintings of those associated with the circles of "cultural nationalists" around Frank and the photographer Alfred Stieglitz: primarily the poets Jean Toomer and Hart Crane, the painters Arthur Dove and Marsden Hartley as well as Stieglitz himself; but also, if at a farther remove, the Mexican muralists Diego Rivera and Clemente Orozco, whom Frank counted among a continental brotherhood of creative spirits. (Orozco's great mural painting *The Epic of American Civilization* at Dartmouth College is very much in the spirit of Frank's mythopoetic concept of history.)

Frank considered his cultural-anthropological histories of Latin America and Spain aesthetic constructions: they sought to give organic expression to a people's spiritual essence and were thus focused macrocosmically. But in form and substance they were no different from his microcosmically conceived stories focused "on a person or group of persons" (Frank 1931, ix). The corporeal world—the landscape a people lived in, the objects it produced, its customs and rituals, its history, literature, and art: these all gave expression to that people's inner being, just as, inversely, a person's lack of spirituality, his or her psychological grotesqueness or distortion would symbolically express, as Mark Whalan writes in his introduction to Toomer's *Letters*, "the energy and turmoil of the prevailing social order," but also *in* and *through* them moments of spiritual transcendence "embedded in everyday life" (Toomer 2006, xxix).

The stories of Frank's short story cycle *City Block* (1922), for instance, give evidence of the modern city's disruptive and dispersive force at the same time that they reveal the individual mind, in its very longing, to be an "agent of coherence"—the very symptoms of its absence suggesting the presence of "wholeness" in what Toomer called the text's "spiritual entity." Frank's figures, just like those of Toomer's *Cane* and, in some measure, also of Sherwood Anderson's *Winesburg, Ohio*, are therefore not characters in any realistic sense but types or ciphers, symbolic agents representing states of emotional intensity or consciousness, not advancing plot but revealing a hidden structure of experience. Toomer called Frank "the only modern writer who has immediately influenced me" (Toomer 2006, 90–91) and saw in his strategies of essentializing, of spiritualizing everyday experience, of wringing "a measure of eternal beauty from the world's suffering," a "religious function" of art "in our day" that also informed his own aesthetic practice (99, 102). Searching for "aesthetic wholeness" in *Cane*, writes Werner Sollors, Toomer "espoused the fragmentary as the necessary part of larger totalities."[18] By mixing several literary genres and by combining strategies of European expressionism with elements of black oral culture, he went further than Frank in creating fragmented yet integrated texts, "lyrical crystallizations," as he called them, that would bring "a piece to a sudden, brilliant integration."[19]

Pressing spirituality from raw experience was not just a mode of life for Hart Crane; he also made it a formal pattern of organic transformation in his poetry. Like Frank and Toomer, Crane struggled hard to make the environment of city and machine part of a dialectics of visionary wholeness. In a letter to Lola Ridge, the editor of the avant-garde magazine *Broom*, Toomer had written, "The machine, its motion, mass, and precision is at last significant not because of the pain it inflicts upon sensitive maladjusted spirits, but for the reason that its elements are the starting point of creative form" (Toomer 2006, 111). In a related manner Crane tried to absorb the wound-inflicting context of the new urban-industrial culture and distill from the intensities of his queer experience the symbolic structure of an objective and timeless cosmic unity. If in this process the poem became the concrete evidence of an achieved state of higher consciousness (the "Word" revealed and become flesh in the word), the poet's "incarnate word" could also find material confirmation in the Brooklyn Bridge, whose beauty, for Crane, embodied the spiritual possibilities and aspirations latent in his culture. In analogy to Alfred Stieglitz's photographs of clouds and trees at Lake George, which made visible an invisible universe of energy and motion, Crane experienced the bridge as movement caught, as "moment made eternal": the vision of divinity revealed as visual and material presence at the same time that it was also caught and made present in the condensed dynamics of Crane's metaphors. If, with Stieglitz, the machine as camera had become an instrument of vision, with Crane, the Brooklyn Bridge—that supreme product of the industrial age—was not simply a tool or path to vision but its mythic incarnation.[20]

The Bridge—as symbolic expression of Divinity—thus constitutes the most evident link between an "aesthetic of wholeness" and that group of artists around Frank and Stieglitz dedicated to creating a national yet spiritually transformed culture in the sign of the modern. It is interesting, however, that William Carlos Williams—whose *In the American Grain* would seem to show him as clearly belonging to that group—vehemently rejected Crane's visionary poetry on aesthetic grounds: "His eyes seem to me often to have been blurred by 'vision' when they should have been held hard, as hard as he could hold them, on the object."[21] For Williams, the poem was not "a moment made eternal," not a timeless moment of revealed totality, but part of a world in constant transition: timelessness *was* process; not presence in the word made flesh but an ever-changing Now of perception that, for each moment, had to be caught and represented anew.

Therefore Frank, on the one hand, acknowledged his spiritual affinity with Williams, who, like Crane, had been "trying to forge a new aesthetic image of our past" (Frank 1929, 324). By imagining a counter-history beyond the Anglo-Saxon whose origins included pre-Columbian, Spanish, and French engagements with a primordial wilderness, Williams's project indeed appeared to run on a parallel track with Frank's. And yet, on the other hand, his alternative concept of America's past was different in that it was concerned not with a vision of organic unity but with what Williams called America's "inability before the new" (Williams 1954, 152). Williams was in fact obsessed with reimagining past moments of encounter with the continent's savage newness, now lost or buried under the rubble of an imported English culture. It was this fascination with the savage that made Frank call Williams "an anarch" and "a victim rather than a victor of our chaos" (Frank 1929, 324).[22] It seemed to prove Williams's affinity for Dada—a movement whose antiholistic and irreverent tendencies Frank abhorred and Williams sympathized with since, as he wrote in his defense of Gertrude Stein, the whole house of language had to come down before it could be reconstructed (Williams 1954, 163). Williams collaborated with Frank on a volume that paid tribute to Alfred Stieglitz (a central agent of American modernism, who had also been Gertrude Stein's first publisher), yet he was more strongly drawn to a circle of New York avant-gardists that included Marcel Duchamp and Francis Picabia—artists who felt attracted to America and were also instrumental in the shaping of American modernism.[23]

For Williams, doing the "American thing" meant moving "away from the word as symbol toward the word as reality," toward language "as an essential and primary experience."[24] His aesthetic of the fragmentary and particular is linked to the experimentalism of the European avant-garde, with whom Williams never ceased to be in dialogue. Emphasis of the particular also connected him with cosmopolitan expatriates such as Pound and, perhaps even more, with Gertrude Stein, who, like Williams, saw herself as immersed in a continuous present, in a fluid "now" of perceiving, thinking, writing—of words set in motion that transformed the perceived object as well as the perceiving self.

Despite these aesthetic affinities, however, Stein's as much as Pound's disdain for the provincial appears to run counter to Williams's passionate commitment to the local and American. Yet, although he fervently embraced the notion that, culturally, America was still a European colony and that finding his own voice meant finding a voice that was most of all American, he was not a stubborn nativist; nor did Stein (or, for that matter, Pound) represent unrelenting cosmopolitan disdain for the local or the national.

In his review of *In the American Grain*, D. H. Lawrence insisted: "Nationality in letters is deplorable, whereas the local is essential. All creative art must rise out of a specific soil and flicker with a spirit of place. The local, of course, in Mr. Williams' sense, is the very opposite of the parochial" (Lawrence 334). The "'new,'" as Williams defined it, was "a relation to the immediate conditions of the matter at hand, and a determination to assert them in all opposition to all intermediate authority" (Williams 1954, 143). It is thus closely connected with the local but also with the democratic, whose rhetoric enters Williams's (and Stein's) aesthetic as a metaphor of non-hierarchic structure as well as an ideological underpinning. The local is potentially everywhere and thus universal. (In fact, the universal could be grasped only in the local and particular.) Therefore, if the new as local is also the "American," that latter term cannot be confined to a strictly national(ist) meaning. Williams seems to waver between a concept of the modern that is specifically American and a concept of the American that is part or an aspect of the modern, is metonymically related to it. On the one hand, he thus argues that the drive toward the new is not a phenomenon "distinctively confined to America: it is the growing edge in every culture"; but on the other, he maintains that, by having to settle new ground, the Americans labor under different conditions than do the Europeans: "The effort to appraise the real through the maze of a cut-off and imposed culture from Europe has been a vivid task, if very often too great for their realizations. Thus the new and the real, hard to come at, are synonymous" (Williams 1954, 143). In other words, even if the new cannot be considered exclusively American, the American real and the really American always connote the new. It is essence and yet always in motion—to be realized in the act of expressing a continuously unfolding Now *and* New of experience.

Frank's, Toomer's, or Crane's "aesthetic of wholeness" was focused on a hidden mythic presence, a divine presence, revealed in moments of heightened experience; yet it was also utopian, anticipating a world that was still actively to be created. In contrast, Williams's "aesthetic of the particular" was decidedly non-teleological and secular. "The only human value of anything, writing included, is intense vision of the facts. God—sure if it means sense," Williams wrote. "'God' is poetic for the unattainable. Sense is hard to get but it can be got. Certainly that destroys 'God,' it destroys everything that interferes with simple clarity of apprehension" (Williams 1954, 71). He thus replaces the "divine"—so prominent in Crane—with the notion of the "real" that, "hard to come at," also is the "new"; or rather, for Williams the "divine" *is* the real *as* the new—to be continuously perceived and caught in a language of sensuous, especially of visual, perception. If, however, according to Williams, the expression of the new is the very definition of the modern, then modernism was—not unlike John Dewey's pragmatist concept of democracy—a continuous task, an unending process, never a state of achievement; and therefore, one might add, it could never connote either a closed aesthetic form nor a closed historical period.

The Local and the Cosmopolitan

Williams gives this continuous process its foundation in the local particular: in the locally perceived, or in the locally spoken. Stein often playfully refers to a national frame for her linguistic experiments—as when she acknowledges the abstractness of American space as well as the abstract modes of American industrial production as related to her own penchant for abstraction. "Henry Ford's perfection of the assembly line, and with it of a distinctly American capitalism, successfully completed the abstraction of the finished product from the individual assembly work," Steven Meyer writes. "The worker, no less than the Model T, was interchangeable; and Stein would insist this form of abstraction was even more fundamentally American than it was capitalist." Yet she dissolves this rather abstract national frame of her work in the ultimate, the supremely real space of writing, which, as Meyer suggests with reference to William James, is a space of "radical experience"; that is, it is timeless and open-ended consciousness, an agent in "the world's 'creative advance' into novelty" (Meyer 137, 215).

In the following passage from *The Geographical History of America: or the Relation of Human Nature to the Human Mind* (1936), Stein seems nevertheless to articulate, according to Marianne DeKoven, "a version of the theory of manifest destiny" (DeKoven 1988, 77); even if, at the same time, she appears to deny such a concrete historical and/or geographical frame to her writing:

Some people like a big country and some people like a little one but it all depends it depends whether you can wander around a big one or a little one. Wandering around a country has something to do with the geographical history of that country and the way one piece of it is not separated from any other one. Can one say too often just as loving or tears in one's eyes that the straight lines on the map of the United States of America make wandering a mission and an everything and can it only be a big country that can be like that or even a little one. Anyway it has a great deal to do with the relation between human nature and the human mind and not remembering and not forgetting and not as much as much having tears in one's eyes. No no tears in one's eyes, whatever any one else can say. In wandering around a big country some people who live in a big country do not wander. What has wandering to do with the human mind or religion. But really wandering has something to do with the human mind. A big or a little country. Wandering in a big or a little country. (Stein 1973, 84–85)

The enormous dimension of American space seems to invite movement and abstraction, freedom from past and memory (plus the tears that go with the memory of the past) and thus openness toward the modern and the new. But national geography is primarily connected with the limits of human nature, whereas the human mind becomes free in the space of writing. There it wanders where it pleases and takes its ultimate pleasure in moving in and through space—space that is a conceptual more than a geographical category. Whatever human nature may or may not do, in a country that is either big or little, the human mind's pleasure lies in breaking through "the prison of framing," be it the confinements of linguistic order, of literary tradition, or of other manifestations of what DeKoven calls "patriarchal cultural hegemony" (DeKoven 1988, 76).

And yet on other occasions Stein seems to place the freedom of the mind's movement as practiced in the various phases of her experimental writings quite firmly within the historical frame of America's "imperial" expansion. In a late essay, "American Language and Literature" (1944), she writes:

> Then came the Spanish American war . . . and that was another big step in making Americans American. We then knew that we could do what we wanted to do and we did not need Europe to tell us to do what we wanted to do, we did not any longer feel that we were attached to Europe at all except of course pleasantly not at all as anything to dominate us. It was a decided liberation, that was when I began to write, and I found myself plunged into a water of words, having words choosing words liberating words feeling words and the words were all ours and it was enough that we held them in our hands to play with them whatever you can play with is yours and this was the beginning of knowing of all America knowing that it could play and play and play with words and the words were all ours all ours. (Stein 1988, 231)

Stein's empire of writing is appositional (yet quite evidently not oppositional) to America's metamorphosis from a "provincial" to an imperial nation—a change that, in 1901, Secretary of State John Hay had metaphorically equated, in a memorable speech after President McKinley's assassination, with the butterfly's breaking of its chrysalis.[25] In that sense Frank's or Williams's call for a national culture and Stein's or Pound's cosmopolitanism are aspects of the same cultural effort. If, on the axis connecting the cosmopolitan and the national, Stein and Frank are placed at opposite poles (Frank representing the cosmopolitan within the national and Stein the national within the cosmopolitan), then Pound is somewhere in between. Although he rejected America's imperial expansion, it is difficult *not* to see *The Cantos* as a parallel venture of cultural imperialism (however antagonistically that work may be related to it). The new American imperialism provided both Stein and Pound with a feeling of cultural empowerment which Stein enacted as linguistic liberation, as an immersion "in a water of words," and Pound as establishing poetic mastery over a vast cultural territory.

With Stein, but especially with Williams, Pound shared a passion for exactness and a delight in particularity. Like them, he was trying to connect words tightly to things, "concentrated upon achieving a direct and primitive contact with the world." Through the dynamics of the image, he argued, we know the reality of the world with "a subtle and instantaneous perception . . . such as savages and wild animals have of the necessities and dangers of the forest" (quoted in Materer 278). And not unlike both Stein and Williams, Pound practiced an anti-symbolic literalism of the imagination—what Max Schneidau called a "pagan fundamentalism" whereby words have the sacredness of objects and objects are perceived with sensuous immediacy, "as if"—wrote Pound in an essay of 1918—"the gods were standing behind us" (Pound 1973, 48). "Knowledge," Schneidau elaborates, quoting Pound, "even mystical knowledge of the gods, is in the particulars of the world. . . . 'Art does not avoid universals, it strikes at them all the harder in that it strikes through particulars'" (Schneidau 221).

Yet despite his fascination with the factual and the particular, with polyphonic composition and the dynamics of the fragmentary in his method of collage, it is not implausible to see Pound as also connected to Waldo Frank by a belief in synergetic "wholeness." "*The Cantos*," Leon Surette writes, "are designed to announce the birth of a new age" (Surette 36); and in this they seem very much in accordance with Romain Rolland's holistic vision of assembling the best of the world's cultures by linking West and East, the old world and the new. They were meant to juxtapose yet also to connect—like pearls distributed on a string of continuity—the sensuous presence of the gods (as represented in the myths of the Greeks), the struggle for a just society against the forces of greed and *usura* throughout the Middle Ages, the Italian Renaissance, the long history of imperial China, and the experience of the modern age. They were to document a heretical, countercultural, and anticapitalist tradition, "a conspiracy of intelligence" (Hesse 293) that Pound also believed he recognized in the values of the early American republic (as represented once by Adams and Jefferson and now by Mussolini), as well as in the teachings of Confucius.

While both Pound and Frank thus attempted to link spiritual vision and social practice, Frank's yearning for wholeness drove him to the Left during the thirties (and later into total isolation and neglect), as Pound, during the same period, moved further to the paranoid Right. He had stated in a letter to his father that he had modeled *The Cantos* on Dante's *Divina Commedia*, that they would (not unlike Crane's *The Bridge*) lead from Hades and Purgatory to a vision of Paradise: to an ideal city, Ecbatan (Pound's version of what Frank and Crane had called Atlantis), whose latent presence could be glimpsed throughout the ages yet whose fulfillment was still to come. He was able to sustain his faith, however, only by embracing the unholy holism of Italian fascism, whose collapse made him eventually fear that his *Cantos*, far from suggesting wholeness, might be nothing but an accumulation of scattered fragments—"Though my errors and wrecks lie about me . . . I cannot make it cohere" (Pound 1996, 816).

Yet as late as 1954 he tried to convince himself that there *was* a system to his *Cantos*—that, as Massimo Bacigalupo writes, "America and China would be its historical poles, and these would be as it were connected by Europe and Italy" (Bacigalupo 232). Throughout his last years, Pound seems to have wavered between acknowledging his failure to create a poetic order suggestive of a hidden unity and an acceptance of the ultimate randomness and fragmentariness of life. If anything, *The Cantos* thus represent another universalist dream in ruins. On the one hand, they are, as Bacigalupo puts it, "the sacred poem of the Nazi-Fascist millennium which mercifully never eventuated" (Bacigalupo x); on the other, they anticipate, as a modernist collage of diverse cultural forms and traditions, a global postmodern culture in which things increasingly hang together, although nothing essentially coheres.

• • •

My imagined web of imaginaries has allowed me to see American modernism as a field fluctuating between contradictory desires and diverse expressive forms that was held together by a shared dream of an alternative or "other" Real. In this field, seemingly irreconcilable opposites (between subjective and objective vision, between the whole or universal and the particular or local, between the cosmopolitan or transnational and the provincial or nativist, between the religious and the secular) were distinct yet never absolute, since even the insistence on the particular (as in Williams, Stein, or Pound) was linked to a pervasive desire for organic coherence. In each case, the modernist writer saw himself or herself as an agent in a process of cultural transformation: by accepting the shattering experience of the modern as the very basis of his or her calling, he or she hoped to liberate its latent possibilities (however differently these might be defined) through the unity-evoking power of the Word.

NOTES

1. Faulkner via Joyce and his *Ulysses;* Eliot, Pound, or Stein since they apparently needed the aesthetic ambiance of Europe to find their modernist voice.

2. See, e.g., the special issue of *American Studies* 39.1 (Spring 1987), "Modernist Culture in America"; and Werner Sollors, "Ethnic Modernism"; as well

as my own contributions to the discussion, "Deconstructing/Reconstructing Order: The Faces of Trans-atlantic Modernism," in *Transatlantic Modernism*, ed. Martin Klepper and Joseph Schöpp (Heidelberg: Winter, 2001), 15–34; "Die amerikanische Moderne," in *Amerikanische Literaturgeschichte*, ed. Hubert Zapf (Stuttgart: Metzler, 1997), 218–280; and, earlier, "Modernisierung und die Tradition des Neuen: Aspekte der amerikanischen Moderne 1900–1920," *Amerikastudien* 35 (1990): 175–188. I admit that the ambivalent status of American modernism has held a great fascination for me throughout my academic life so that I have returned to it time and again.

3. "Indeed, modernism as an adversary culture (Lionel Trilling) cannot be discussed without introducing the concept of alternative modernities to which the multiple modernisms and their different trajectories remain tied in complex mediated ways" (Huyssen 2007, 191). In this connection, see also Djelal Kadir and Dorothea Löbbermann, eds., *Other Modernisms in an Age of Globalization* (Heidelberg: Winter, 2002).

4. Hugh Kenner, *A Homemade World* (New York: William Morrow, 1975). Claude McKay's phrase is taken from his novel *Home to Harlem* (1928; Boston: Northeastern University Press, 1987), 94. For an interpretation of the Harlem Renaissance as a form of subversive counter-modernism that answered white mastery of form with the black deformation of mastery, see Houston Baker Jr., *Modernism and the Harlem Renaissance* (Chicago: University of Chicago Press, 1987).

5. In his preface to a collection of essays, *Other Cities, Other Worlds: Urban Imaginaries in a Globalizing Age*, Andreas Huyssen adopts the concept of the imaginary for his own purpose: "An urban imaginary marks first and foremost the way city dwellers imagine their own city as the place of everyday life, the site of inspiring traditions and continuities as well as the scene of histories of destruction, crime, and conflicts of all kinds. Urban space is always and inevitably social space involving subjectivities and identities differentiated by class and race, gender and age, education and religion. An urban imaginary is the cognitive and somatic image which we carry within us of the places where we live, work, and play. It is an embodied material fact. Urban imaginaries are thus part of any city's reality, rather than being only figments of the imagination. What we think about a city and how we perceive it informs the ways we act in it" (Huyssen 2008, 3). In my case, "imaginary" is, to be sure, also applied to the experience of metropolitan space, specifically of New York (the locus of American modern culture par excellence), but also to the experience, the felt impact, of cultural modernity itself—responding to it but also creatively shaping it.

6. Rubén Darío, "To Roosevelt," in *Selected Poems by Rubén Darío*, trans. Lysander Kemp (Austin: University of Texas Press, 1988); in Spanish in Rubén Darío, *Poesía* (Caracas: Bibliotheca Aayacucho, n.d.), 255–256.

7. José Martí, "Our America." For the subsequent discussion, see also Jeffrey Belnap and Raúl Fernández, eds., *José Martí's "Our America."*

8. "The ideals of these Calibans are none but the stock market and the factory. They eat and eat, and calculate, and drink whisky, and make millions. They sing 'Home, Sweet Home' and their home is a checking account, a banjo, a black man, and a pipe. Enemies of all idealism, in their progress they are apoplectic, perpetual mirrors of expansion, but their Emerson, rightly classified, is like the moon to Carlyle's sun; their Whitman with his hatchet-hewn verses is a democratic prophet in the service of Uncle Sam; and their Poe, their great Poe, a poor swan drunk on alcohol and pain, was the martyr to his dream in a land where he will never be understood." Rubén Darío, "The Triumph of Caliban," in *Selected Writings*, 507–508.

9. In 1930, however, he commented extensively on Martí's concept of a Cuban nation in *America Hispana*, 265–272.

10. Romain Rolland, "America and the Arts," *The Seven Arts* 1 (November 1916–April 1917): 47–51.

11. "Did I know what Our America was really? Not an objective portrait of a real land, but an appeal to it to be?" he retrospectively reflected in his memoirs; and "I had come to tell the Mexicans my plans for a cultural union of the Americas through the minorities of each. . . . In the decades ahead, I would come down many times to Mexico and visit every part of it; multiverse and potential cosmos" (Frank, *Memoirs*, 99, 157).

12. See Gorham Munson's account in *Orage in America* (1940), http://www .docstoc.com. To the group around Orage belonged Waldo Frank and his wife, Margaret Naumberg; Herbert Croly, the editor of the *New Republic;* Mabel Dodge Luhan; Jane Heap, co-editor of the *Little Review;* and Jean Toomer.

13. From Gorham Munson, *The Awakening Twenties;* Van Wyck Brooks called it "the Bible of our generation"; both quoted in George Hutchinson, *The Harlem Renaissance in Black and White*, 106–107. See also Mark Whalan's introduction to his edition of *The Letters of Jean Toomer*, especially xxix.

14. "My art will aid in giving the Negro to himself. In this connection, I have thought of a magazine. A magazine, American, but concentrating on the significant contributions . . . of the Negro to the western world. A magazine that would consciously hoist, and perhaps at first a trifle over emphasize a negroid ideal. A magazine that would function organically for what I feel to be the building of the Negro's consciousness. The need is great" (Toomer, *Letters*, 106).

15. On the complex relationship between Negro artists and the white American avant-garde, see Michael North, *The Dialect of Modernism*, especially chaps. 6 and 7. With reference to Toomer's reaction to the pressures of stereotyping, Whalan argues: "Toomer's annoyance at being racially labeled sprung not only from representations of his own racial position; it also arose from critics misreading or missing altogether the fluidity and liminality of racial identity that marks *Cane* as such a fascinating piece of writing in the first place" (introduction to Toomer, *Letters*, xxii).

16. "I am at once no one of the races and I am all of them. I belong to no

one of them and I belong to all. I am, in a strict racial sense, a member of a new race. This new race, of which I happen to be one of the first articulate members, is now forming perhaps everywhere on the Earth, but its formation is more rapid and marked in certain countries, one of which is America." Jean Toomer, "The Crock of Problems," in *A Jean Toomer Reader*, 58.

17. "And it is precisely this pluralism that transforms the substitution of culture for race into the preservation of race. . . . [A]lthough the move from racial identity to cultural identity appears to replace essentialist criteria of identity (who we are) with performative criteria (what we do), the commitment to pluralism requires in fact that the question of who we are continue to be understood as prior to questions about what we do" (Michaels, *Our America*, 14–15).

18. Sollors, "Ethnic Modernism," 445.

19. Quoted in George Hutchinson, "Identity in Motion," 49.

20. Crane to Stieglitz, in *The Letters of Hart Crane*, ed. Brom Weber (Berkeley: University of California Press, 1965), 132; also see Hart Crane, "Modern Poetry," in *The Complete Poems of Hart Crane*, ed. Waldo Frank (New York: Doubleday, 1958), 175–179; and Paul Strand, "Photography and the New God," *Broom* 5 (1922): 252–258.

21. William Carlos Williams, "Hart Crane, 1899–1932," *Contempo* 2 (July 5, 1932): 1, 4.

22. How averse Frank was to any idea of fragmentation is apparent in a letter he wrote to Jean Toomer: "The one impossibility of the human mind is incoherence, since mind is above all an active agent of coherence. The word experience should be confined to the form of that fusion of the initial reality of a man's life with the unitary synthesis of what he knows his life, at every instant and every act, to be." Quoted in Mark Helbling, "Jean Toomer and Waldo Frank: A Creative Friendship," in O'Daniel, *Jean Toomer*, 89.

23. See Waldo Frank et al., *America and Alfred Stieglitz*, with contributions by Crane and Williams. On William Carlos Williams and the modernist art scene in New York, see Bram Dijkstra, *The Hieroglyphics of a New Speech: Cubism, Stieglitz, and the Early Poetry of William Carlos Williams* (Princeton: Princeton University Press, 1969); Dickran Tashjian, *William Carlos Williams and the American Scene, 1920–1940* (New York: Whitney Museum, 1978); Francis Naumann, *New York Dada, 1915–1923* (New York: Harry N. Abrams, 1994); and Wanda Corn, *The Great American Thing: Modern Art and National Identity, 1915–1935* (Berkeley: University of California Press, 1999), especially the introductory chapter, "Spiritual America."

24. Lyn Hejinian, "Language and Realism," in *Two Stein Talks* (Santa Fe: Weaselsleeves Press, 1995), 10. The phrase is in fact taken from an essay on Gertrude Stein, yet it applies to Williams as well and underlines the linguistic affinity between the two writers. But although for both, language is a reality in itself, reality is not (yet) subsumed in language, as Jennifer Ashton argues in her subtle analysis of modernist poetry, *From Modernism to Postmodernism:*

American Poetry and Theory in the Twentieth Century (Cambridge: Cambridge University Press, 2005), in which she sees Stein as anticipating a postmodernist linguistic turn.

25. "It finds itself floating on wings which had not existed before, whose strength it had never tested. . . . The past gives no clue to the future. The fathers where are they? And the prophets, do they live forever? We are ourselves the fathers! We are ourselves the prophets!" *Addresses of John Hay* (New York, 1906), 173.

WORKS CITED

Bacigalupo, Massimo. *The Forméd Trace. The Later Poetry of Ezra Pound.* New York: Columbia University Press, 1980.
Belnap, Jeffrey, and Raúl Fernández, eds. *José Martí's "Our America": From National to Hemispheric Cultural Studies.* Durham: Duke University Press, 1998.
Darío, Rubén. *Selected Writings.* New York: Penguin, 2007.
DeKoven, Marianne. "Half in and Half Out of Doors: Gertrude Stein and Literary Tradition." In *A Gertrude Stein Companion*, ed. Bruce Kellner. New York: Greenwood Press, 1988. 75–83.
———. *Rich and Strange: Gender, History, Modernism.* Princeton: Princeton University Press, 1991.
Fenollosa, Ernest Francisco. "The Coming Fusion of East and West." *Harper's Monthly* 98 (December 1898): 115–122.
Frank, Waldo. *Our America.* New York: Boni & Liveright, 1919.
———. *Virgin Spain.* New York: Boni & Liveright, 1926.
———. *The Re-Discovery of America.* New York: Scribner's, 1929.
———. *America Hispana.* New York: Scribner's, 1931.
———. *South American Journey.* New York: Duell, Sloan & Pearce, 1943.
———. *The Memoirs of Waldo Frank.* Ed. Alan Trachtenberg. Amherst: University of Massachusetts Press, 1973.
Frank, Waldo, et al. *America and Alfred Stieglitz: A Collective Portrait.* New York: Doubleday, 1934.
Harari, Josué. *Scenarios of the Imaginary.* Ithaca: Cornell University Press, 1987.
Hesse, Eva. *"Ich liebe, also bin ich": Der unbekannte Ezra Pound.* Berlin: Osburg Verlag, 2008.
Hutchinson, George. *The Harlem Renaissance in Black and White.* Cambridge: Harvard University Press, 1995.
———. "Identity in Motion: Placing Cane." In *Jean Toomer and the Harlem Renaissance*, ed. Geneviève Fabre and Michel Fleiss. New Brunswick: Rutgers University Press, 2001. 38–56.
Huyssen, Andreas. "Geographies of Modernism in a Globalizing World." *New German Critique* 100 (2007): 189–207.

———, ed. *Other Cities, Other Worlds: Urban Imaginaries in a Globalizing Age*. Durham: Duke University Press, 2008.

Lawrence, D. H. "William Carlos Williams's 'In the American Grain.'" In *Phoenix: The Posthumous Papers of D. H. Lawrence* [1936]. Vol. 1. Ed. N. H. Revve and John Worthen. Reprint. London: Heineman, 1961. 334–336.

Martí, José. "Our America." In *José Martí Reader: Writings on the Americas*. Ed. Deborah Shnookal and Mirta Muñiz. New York: Ocean Press, 1999. 118–127.

Materer, Timothy. *Vortex: Pound, Eliot, and Lewis*. Ithaca: Cornell University Press, 1979.

Meyer, Steven. *Irresistible Dictation: Gertrude Stein and the Correlations of Writing and Science*. Stanford: Stanford University Press, 2001.

Michaels, Walter Benn. *Our America: Nativism, Modernism, and Pluralism*. Durham: Duke University Press, 1995.

North, Michael. *The Dialect of Modernism: Race, Language, and Twentieth-Century Literature*. New York: Oxford University Press, 1994.

O'Daniel, Therman, ed. *Jean Toomer: A Critical Evaluation*. Washington, D.C.: Howard University Press, 1988.

Pound, Ezra. "Religio, or, The Child's Guide to Knowledge." In *Selected Prose, 1909–1965*. Ed. William Cookson. New York: New Directions, 1973. 47–48.

———. *The Cantos of Ezra Pound*. New York: New Directions, 1996.

Schneidau, Max. *Waking Giants: The Presence of the Past in Modernism*. New York: Oxford University Press, 1991.

Sollors, Werner. "Ethnic Modernism." In *The Cambridge History of American Literature*. Gen. ed. Sacvan Bercovitch. Vol. 6. Cambridge: Cambridge University Press, 2002. 355–556.

Stein, Gertrude. *The Geographic History of America* [1936]. Baltimore: Johns Hopkins University Press, 1973.

———. "American Language and Literature." In *Gertrude Stein and the Making of Literature*. Ed. Shirley Neuman and Ira B. Nadel. Boston: Northeastern University Press, 1988. 226–231.

Surette, Leon. *The Birth of Modernism: Ezra Pound, T. S. Eliot, W. B. Yeats and the Occult*. Montreal: McGill University Press, 1993.

Toomer, Jean. *A Jean Toomer Reader: Selected Unpublished Writings*. Ed. Frederick Rusch. New York: Oxford University Press, 1991.

———. *The Letters of Jean Toomer*. Ed. Mark Whalan. Knoxville: University of Tennessee Press, 2006.

Williams, William Carlos. *Selected Essays*. New York: New Directions, 1954.

———. *In the American Grain* [1925]. New York: New Directions, 1956.

PART II

SOCIAL IMAGINARIES

4 William James versus Charles Taylor

Philosophy of Religion and the Confines of the Social and Cultural Imaginaries

Nietzsche's diagnosis of the modern existential condition as a continuous loss of the once cosmic centrality of human existence appears to be accompanied by a complementary and opposing tendency of growing anthropocentrism and sociocentrism. The anthropocentric reductionism in the nineteenth-century interpretation of religious phenomena and especially of religious experience by Ludwig Feuerbach is expanded to, among others, the sociocentric functionalism in reading religions in Émile Durkheim. Twentieth- and twenty-first-century cultural studies have, in various ways, continued this tendency of subjecting all significant realities, all signification, all experience pregnant with meaning, to the regime of human potential and interest, be that interest individual or collective. The dispensation of Being which insinuates that reality is fundamentally and exclusively ready for and defined as the realm of human appropriation, as the space and site of feasibility and machination, as the predominance of what Heidegger called the *Machenschaft*, this dispensation has facilitated and grounded conceptions of cultural and social reality as "fields of cultural production," as in Pierre Bourdieu, or as social and cultural imaginaries in the complex and sophisticated studies of Cornelius Castoriadis and in the more simplified contemporary analyses of, among many others, Charles Taylor. What these readings of reality have in common is that they do not allow for any (meaningful) outsides of their fields or imaginaries. According to Bourdieu, even radical challenges, say, in philosophy, to established positions in the field of cultural production, will always be defined and delimited by the very field they question (Bourdieu, *Distinction* 496). Speaking of literary production as another example of human meaning-making, Bourdieu dogmatically asserts that "every position-taking is defined in relation to the *space of possibles*. . . .

[I]t receives its distinctive *value* from its negative relationship with the co-existent position-takings to which it is objectively related and which determine it by delimiting it" (Bourdieu, *Field* 30). There is no escaping from and no breathing space outside the always already humanly appropriated and defined, the solipsistic worlds of sense-making. In terms of the imaginary, Castoriadis argues in similar fashion: "Society brings into being a world of significations and itself exists in reference to such a world. Correlatively *nothing can exist* for society if it is not related to the world of significations; everything that appears is immediately caught up in this world—and can *even come to appear only* by being caught up in this world" (Castoriadis 359; emphasis added).

The totalizing features of the social (or, for that matter, cultural) imaginary which negate any outside to its domination are even more starkly asserted by Charles Taylor: "our social imaginary . . . constitutes a horizon we are virtually incapable of thinking beyond" (Taylor, *Imaginaries* 185). Thinking in the sense of an awareness of a beyond which transgresses the always already defined reality, however, is, ever so simply, that realm of the transcendent, of unforeseen newness as revelation, which we may designate as the space, site, realm, or spreading extension of the religious. Once the religious is functionally subjected to the dominion of the individual or collective subject, once it is absorbed by the all-pervasive presence of fields of cultural production or of imaginaries, once this happens, the religious is in danger of disappearing or of remaining as a mere vestige of its former identity, as an epiphenomenon. The awareness of the religious, of religious experience as a spread, to use a term of William James's, which extends, by definition, beyond the control of its subjective pole, this awareness in thinkers as different as James, Dewey, Heidegger, or Levinas poses a continuous and serious challenge for the proponents of the dominance of the cultural field or the social and cultural imaginary. The ensuing tension is a particularly fruitful and challenging subject for critical philosophical analysis when it manifests itself as a debate between two thinkers.

In the wider context of this historical tension I present in three parts my thoughts on the significant debate concerning religion in which the Canadian philosopher Charles Taylor engages William James's study *The Varieties of Religious Experience*. I begin by, first and briefly, introducing Taylor's book *Varieties of Religion Today* and its basic attitude toward James. In a second part I critically reconstruct and evaluate what Taylor calls his "conversation/confrontation with William James" (Taylor, *Varieties* vi). I read this occasionally belligerent conversation as Taylor's argument in favor of the power and significance of, especially, *social* imaginaries. The third and last part is primarily devoted to William James's conception of the philosophy of religion in *The Varieties of Religious Experience*. This final part is intended as an apology, a defense of the Jamesian vision, and a critical description of the boundaries or limitations of imaginaries as Taylor understands them.

Taylor's Varieties of Religion Today: *William James Revisited*

In 1902 William James's 1901 Gifford Lectures at Edinburgh University became his best-known and commercially most successful publication, under the title *The Varieties of Religious Experience: A Study in Human Nature*. The literary appeal and the theological as well as the philosophical actuality of the work seem not to have diminished during the first one hundred years after its initial appearance. In 2000 Charles Taylor presented several lectures devoted to a critical appreciation of James's *Varieties* in the Institute for Human Sciences' Vienna Lecture Series. Appropriately and fittingly, these lectures were published by Harvard University Press in 2002, exactly one hundred years after James's *Varieties of Religious Experience*, with the title *Varieties of Religion Today: William James Revisited*. The change from "religious experience" in James's title to "religion" in Taylor's marks, for me, one of the central philosophical problems, concerns, and difficulties posed by Taylor's "conversation/ confrontation with James." The question arises: What happens once the philosophical inquiry shifts its focus from the live events or processes of experiencing to a substantive entity called religion? Do we still deal with the same matter of thinking, with the identical *Sache*, phenomenologically speaking, or does this shift imply a major ontological difference, or maybe even a fundamental reversal?

Taylor begins and ends his critical discussions of James's *Varieties* with deeply respectful, often conciliatory, occasionally genuinely appreciative, and sometimes even admiring statements. He commences by noting that James's position today seems "entirely understandable, even axiomatic, to lots of people . . . [and] central to Western modernity" (Taylor, *Varieties* 13). One of James's great methodological achievements is the application of "wide sympathy, coupled with unparalleled phenomenological insight" (Taylor, *Varieties* 22). The book ends with this compliment for James: "[He sees] so deeply into an essential feature of our divided age. In some sense religious 'experience,' the beginning intimations and intuitions that we feel bound to follow up, is crucial as never before, wherever we end up taking them in our divergent spiritual lives. It is because he saw this with such intensity, and could articulate it with such force, that James's book lives on so strongly in our world" (Taylor, *Varieties* 116).

Taylor's repeated positive evaluations of James's study of religious experience are intimately and almost exclusively tied to the seemingly indisputable fact of the ongoing and still impressive contemporaneity or modernity of James's phenomenological descriptions. If, however, one considers Taylor's deeply critical assessment of central features of contemporary society and culture, the praise accorded to James tends to take on a decidedly ambiguous hue and character. In his *Ethics of Authenticity* Taylor diagnoses the fundamental ills of contemporary existential and social reality. He speaks of the three malaises of untrammeled individualism, the pervasive and almost exclusive presence of instrumental reason, and the "alienation from the public sphere and consequent loss of political control" (Taylor, *Ethics* 10). For Taylor these features indicate seemingly inescapable and yet decidedly negative side effects and after-effects of the originally positive achievement of individual emancipation in the contexts of the Enlightenment and early modernity. One may therefore wonder whether, in Taylor's overall view, James's *Varieties* is, first and foremost, a profound philosophical assessment of at least one of the only potentially ambivalent traits of modern society and culture in the realm of religion—namely, individualism—or whether the book is not, rather, part and parcel of the latter-day problematic or malaise itself which includes the separation of the individually religious and the public spheres. This is a condition that Taylor calls the post-Durkheimian dispensation, because, according to Taylor, James obviously does *not* consider, or *no longer* considers, religious phenomena as functional aspects *of* or *within* social realities (Taylor, *Varieties* 75–107, 95, 111–116). In addition to that, religious experience is qualified by Taylor as *only* "the beginning intimations and intuitions" of a—so one may surmise—fuller spiritual life (Taylor, *Varieties* 116); the fuller spiritual life would then, Taylor implies, have to transcend personal, individual experience. This and the seemingly innocuous fact that the term "experience" is set in quotation marks are politely subdued indicators of a fundamental unease in Taylor's encounter with James's vision.

There are ways, Taylor proposes in his preface, in which James's "take on religion could perhaps be considered too narrow and restrictive" (Taylor, *Varieties* vi). The opening of the first chapter, which presents the case against James most concisely, puts the critical charge "slightly more polemically: one could argue that James has certain blind spots in his view of religion" (Taylor, *Varieties* 3). James's approach to religion as a matter of thinking is thus seen as not comprehensive enough, as limited in scope, and as marred by fundamental oversights within the very field of vision (blind spots)—a serious charge especially against a phenomenological thinker. For Taylor the basic problem with James's thinking is simply and essentially the priority, the preeminence, and the valuation of experience: "James sees religion primarily as something that individuals experience. He makes a distinction between living religious experience, which is that of the individual, and religious life, which is derivative because it is taken over from a community or church. . . . [C]hurches play at best a secondary role, in transmitting and communicating the original inspiration" (Taylor, *Varieties* 4–5).

Taylor questions the legitimacy of distinguishing between religious experience as an existentially privileged, as an authentic personal event and the, from James's point of view, merely formalized participation in various socially organized, politically institutionalized, collectivized, and more or less public forms of religious practice. Taylor asks, "How are the phenomena of religion distorted or narrowed through being conceived in terms of religious 'experience'?" (Taylor, *Varieties* 20). The charges of distortion and narrowing imply a serious deviation in James from a true and comprehensive, an undistorted and exhaustive, that is, a philosophically fully competent vision. I now move from Taylor's value judgments concerning James's work to his substantial philosophical criticism.

Taylor's Conversation/Confrontation with James and the Power of Social Imaginaries

Taylor understands James's interpretation of the validity of (religious) experience as closely and problematically related to the role and potential of language and ideas: "So the *real* locus of religion is in individual experience, and not in corporate life. That is one facet of the Jamesian thesis. But the other is that the real locus is in *experience*, that is, in feeling, as against the formulations by which people define, justify, rationalize their feelings (operations that are, of course, frequently undertaken by churches). . . . These two are clearly connected in James's mind. Feelings occur, he holds, in individuals; and in turn 'individuality is founded in feeling'" (Taylor, *Varieties* 7).

A very basic disagreement emerges here: Taylor doubts whether it is ontologically legitimate to confine the reality, the existence of religion to individual experience and not to extend its true being into what he calls the "corporate" realm. Taylor defines James's notion of experience primarily and exclusively as preverbal and preconceptual, as a matter of feeling in a generalized fashion. This does not do justice to James's sophisticated understanding of the fundamental existential dispositions that he calls feelings. Feelings as inescapable existential dispositions in James do not simply *not* exclude rationalizations; like moods in Emerson, feelings in James importantly and inescapably color and inflect all perceptual and conceptual appropriations of experience, they convey knowledge, they are "noetic."[1] Taylor, however, indirectly advances the idea that an adequate analysis of the ontological status of religion demands that it significantly manifest itself primarily in conceptualizations, in "rationalizations," in communally entertained ideas as the basis of conduct. Conduct, socially viable and recognizable and valuable behavior, a behavior based on and mediated by ideas and concepts, conduct embedded in a social imaginary and articulated in language, becomes an indispensable aspect or ingredient of Taylor's understanding of religion, a view that James supposedly does not adequately provide for (Taylor, *Varieties* 23–29). In addition, Taylor deepens his critical objections by exploring James's problematic insistence on felt experience as the only true and authentic site of religious awareness by way of a more detailed meditation on the, as he sees it, necessary interrelations between individuality, experience, and language:

> ... one might make the more radical conceptual or transcendental point, that
> the very idea of an experience that is in no way formulated is impossible. ...
> experience can have no content at all if you can't say *anything* about it. ...
> A similar set of considerations might be deployed to question the sense in
> which one can really have an individual experience. All experiences require
> some vocabulary, and these are inevitably in large part handed to us in the
> first place by our society. ... The ideas, the understanding with which we
> live our lives, shape directly what we could call religious experience; and
> these languages, these vocabularies, are never those simply of an individual.
> (Taylor, *Varieties* 26, 27–28)

Not only mystics, Buddhist or Christian or Muslim, could and would seriously and legitimately challenge the validity of the dogmatic statement that experiences *must* lend themselves to some kind of rendering in language. In order to be valid experiences, mystical experiences as quintessential religious experiences, as James plausibly maintains in chapters 16 and 17 of *Varieties*, do not need, they even have to dispense with, *proper* linguistic expression in order to remain true to themselves (James,

Varieties 301–339, 302). Taylor also ignores and does not critically engage James's anticonceptualist stance, his radical linguistic skepticism, which he succinctly expressed in *The Principles of Psychology*, stating, "Language works against our perception of the truth" (James, *Principles* 234). Any perception, as the foundational mode of experiential awareness, James insisted in his last great, unfinished work, *Some Problems of Philosophy*, any perception in the fullness of its present givenness always exceeds the capability of any language to do it justice: "The deeper features of reality are found *only* in perceptual experience" (James, *Some Problems* 53–54; emphasis added). In refuting or ignoring this stance, Taylor obviously believes in some version of the prison-house of language. Neo-pragmatist critics like Richard Poirier have questioned the validity of the metaphor of a prison-house by insisting on the fact that an existing language may and must always be *individually* inflected, changed, and even radically reconceptualized, that is, troped (Poirier 13–19). Religious experience for Taylor, however, reveals itself as conditioned by, as dependent on the always already preestablished, the vast and total cultural, the inescapably communal network of signs and significations called language. I repeat two of Taylor's defining statements, with added emphasis: "*All* experiences require some vocabulary, and these are *inevitably* in large part handed to us *in the first place* by our society. . . . The ideas, the understanding with which we live our lives, *shape directly* what we could call religious experience." This is a primacy of the word certainly not intended by the famous opening sentence of the Gospel According to Saint John. *Human society* and *its* cultural meanings are a first for Taylor. What he calls the "wider whole" in *Ethics of Authenticity* is the very foundation of true selfhood and individuality; the self is truly a self only if it is grounded in the encompassing other of collective existence. The "wider whole" in *Ethics of Authenticity* becomes the social imaginary in Taylor's later writings. This is defined or described in his book *Modern Social Imaginaries* as a "wider grasp [that] has no clear limits. . . . It is in fact that large unstructured and inarticulate understanding of our whole situation, within which particular features of our world show up for us in the sense they have. It can never be adequately expressed in the form of explicit doctrines because of its unlimited and indefinite nature. That is another reason for speaking here of an imaginary and not a theory" (Taylor, *Imaginaries* 25).

This—it seems to me—somewhat simplified and vague resuscitation of Castoriadis's conception of the social imaginary as a totalizing realm of signification has nothing to say about its ontological status (Castoriadis pt. 1, chap. 3, and pt. 2, chap. 7). Taylor presents an ontologically dubious, all-embracing entity without specific location which is supposed to provide the foundation, the orientation, and the possibility of "particular" features" and "the sense they have" for our social worlds and thus for its articulation in a communal language and vocabulary which is subsequently, as Taylor maintains, handed to individuals. Because the individual has *no* say, or only a severely limited say, in determining *what or how* her or his religious experience *is*, this experience can never be either primarily individual *or*, as an alternative, momentous and significant in its silence. Religious experience, the individual awareness of the transcendent, tends to become a culturally and socially conditioned and mediated epiphenomenon. It seems ironic, however, that a philosopher who, as we saw, argues so vehemently against the possibility of an "idea of an experience that is *in no way formulated*" should nevertheless ground all communal meaning and cultural formations of modernity in a determining, constraining, and socially as well as individually empowering totality called the "social imaginary," which is characterized as a "large unstructured and *inarticulate* understanding of our whole situation." This obvious inconsistency does make sense, however, within Taylor's overall vision of modernity as a "long march" (his metaphor [Taylor, *Imaginaries* 17]) toward a truly emancipated, secular, liberal democratic society. The numinous, the core of religious experience, has been shifted away from the individual to find a (is it a secularized?) refuge in the transcendental sphere and horizon of the collective social imaginary and its vaguely defined but unlimited power to ground, frame, direct, and provide possibilities of meaning for any and all individual experiences. Taylor's social imaginary, it appears, offers a new version of the Durkheimian social functionalism in reading religion: "*A religion,*" Durkheim argued, "*is a unified system of beliefs and practices relative to sacred things . . .* [that is,] *beliefs and practices which unite into one single moral community called a Church, all those who adhere to them*"; or, more abstractly and even closer to Taylor's vision and terminology, religion is "before all, . . . a system of ideas with which the individuals represent to themselves the society of which they are members, and the obscure but intimate relations which they have with it" (Durkheim 47, 225).[2]

The power of the social imaginary in Taylor's sense similarly provides the possibility of social cohesion through faith and its communal language. The validity of religious experience as an existential dimension is in turn communally sanctioned and grounded and articulated. This is what in *Modern Social Imaginaries* he describes as the "space for religion in the modern state, for God can figure strongly in the political identity" (Taylor, *Imaginaries* 193). Instead "of an ontic dependence [of human society] on something higher," the sacred, the divine "can still be present to us in the design of things, in cosmos, state, and personal life" and as "the inescapable source for our power to impart order to our lives, both individually and socially" (Taylor, *Imaginaries* 193). Taylor's position in *Varieties of Religion Today* and in *Modern Social Imaginaries* does in this way raise the question whether he is really dealing with religion or with religious experience or whether his ultimately reductionist grounding of religious phenomena in social imaginaries implies jeopardizing the religious as a *Sache*, as a *phenomenon* in the philosophical sense of the term. The social imaginary which is at the basis of the long march toward the fulfillment of "the ideal of order as mutual benefit" (Taylor, *Imaginaries* 3, 3–22) in a secular, liberal democratic condition appears in Taylor problematically as total—one hesitates to call it totalitarian—conditioning. This is ominously foreshadowed in *Varieties of Religion Today* when Taylor uses two somewhat haphazardly chosen examples to demonstrate the emergence of religion as a phenomenon of privacy and interiority as dictated, as enforced, by constraints of the social imaginary. Amazingly, already in the late Middle Ages he sees the spread of the "inward form of religion" as the result of "pressure . . . through the preaching of mendicant friars and others" (Taylor, *Varieties* 9); similarly, the prevalence of private religious experience in France in the nineteenth century "stood at the end of a long process in which ordinary believers had been preached at, organized, sometimes *bullied*, into patterns of practice that reflected more personal commitment.—They had been pressed, we might be tempted to say, into 'taking their religion seriously'" (Taylor, *Varieties* 11; emphasis added).

The total usurpation of the religious by and through the social imaginary in the present is then unmistakably pronounced as dogma in *Modern Social Imaginaries:* "Our social imaginary . . . constitutes a horizon we are virtually incapable of thinking beyond" (Taylor, *Imaginaries* 185). In this way the all-encompassing social imaginary dissolves religious experiencing into the functional historical processes of social, political, and cultural formation.

*James's Philosophy of Religion and the
Boundaries of Social Imaginaries: An Apology*

A study of religious experience was for James, however, not a historical or social, let alone a political or even a cultural concern. The subtitle of

Varieties reminds one that the book is a study of human nature, that is, a philosophical inquiry, presentation, and meditation concerning an essential and indispensable *existential* and thus an ontological feature of being human. An apology, a defense of William James's thinking on religion, will therefore have to go beyond the implied assumption of Charles Taylor that all entities and *all* meaningful aspects of experience, belief, and conduct are primarily and ultimately embedded in and mediated by significations that arise out of the social imaginary as an inescapably antecedent transcendental horizon. I focus here on two major areas of contention in Taylor's "conversation/confrontation" with William James's view of the religious that are apt to show the limits of the social imaginary as soon as fundamental ontological and existential questions are raised. The two areas are the interpretations of experience and of the human self. I occasionally enlist the help of what appears at a first and very superficial glance a highly unlikely ally in the project of defending William James, namely, Martin Heidegger. In his 1920–21 lecture on the phenomenology of the religious life, however, Heidegger not only agrees with Ernst Troeltsch's evaluation of James's *Varieties* as the best description of religious phenomena extant (Heidegger 20) but also reads the meanings of *Existenziale* (foundational aspects of Being, such as experience and selfhood) in an unquestionably radical empiricist—that is, Jamesian—mode (Heidegger 75–86).

The first area of contention is experience. Experience in James, as Taylor interprets it, is essentially characterized by feeling, and in terms of its validity as an aspect of the religious life, it belongs, as we saw, only with the "beginning intimations and intuitions," that is, not with the fully unfolded reality of religious existence. More fundamental even, and more important, however, in diagnosing the underlying philosophical reasons for their oppositional stances is this seemingly innocuous statement by Taylor on experience, which will help me to open the apologia proper: "James sees religion primarily as something that individuals experience" (Taylor, *Varieties* 4). In this statement religion is an object, a *Sachverhalt*, encountered and appropriated by a subject in an act or event called experience. This, however, is not at all what James means by experience. We find what is probably James's most concise and most profound definition or, more appropriately, interpretation of "experience" in his entry "Experience" for J. M. Baldwin's *Dictionary of Philosophy and Psychology* (1902), which thus appeared in the same year as James's *Varieties*. James states that the term indicates "the entire process of phenomena, of present data considered in their raw immediacy, before reflective thought has analysed them into subjective or objective aspects or ingredients. It is the summum genus of which everything must have been a part before we can speak of it at all. . . . If philosophy insists on keeping this term indeterminate, she can refer to her subject-matter without committing herself as to certain questions in dispute. But if experience be used with either an objective or a subjective shade of meaning, then question-begging occurs, and discussion grows impossible" (James, "Experience" 95).

Experience designates the "summum genus of which everything must have been a part before we can speak of it at all." This means that for James, experience is a name for Being in general. As such it necessarily and logically precedes all verbal articulation and the constraints, for example, of social imaginaries. Being as experience occurs before the subject-object split so dear to traditional metaphysical and epistemological modes of thinking. James's postmetaphysical, radical empiricist thinking therefore demands—in a wonderful pun—that the *term* experience be kept inde-*term*-inate, that is, that it be both spoken and unspoken. Experience is the togetherness of an awareness and its "contents," contents or objects that emerge as such only once "reflective thought" approaches the simple *this* or *there* of the really real, the experiential event. Strictly speaking, experience as such in its immediacy cannot be talked about; it issues in nameable aspects and elements only once it has been retrospectively focused in the context of a new event of experience called reflection; in this way a prior experience manifests itself in the form of a testimony. Experience is or provides or shows as what James called "knowledge by direct acquaintance," as distinguished from retrospective, reflexive knowledge or "knowledge about." Knowledge by acquaintance is quintessentially religious knowledge for James. One might say and clarify that experience as the *summum genus*, as Being, as *pure experience* in the way James defined it in *Essays in Radical Experience*, is religious experience in a comprehensive sense of the word. It is experience not controlled (as yet) by a human subject-center. It is the openness to the unforeseen, the radically and always revelatory new. Religious experience in a narrower sense of the term, then, would imply tentative appropriations, tentative naming, ascriptions of meaning that are ultimately always at the mercy of those primary reaches of the field of experiencing not subject to human a posteriori appropriation. In this *religionsphilosophische* position James, however, is neither a modernist nor a mere liberal Protestant contemporary, as Taylor keeps arguing throughout his study of James's *Varieties*. The non-social, the individual, the preverbal and immediate, the socially and culturally unmediated character of knowledge by acquaintance has been universally attested to as the true mark of religious experience in its fullness. Religious experience in its fullness may thus also be understood as the fountainhead of all subsequent, predominantly nonreligious modes of conceptual appropriation of the events of experiencing. In *Varieties* William James has simply and consistently reaffirmed the testimony of the world's heritage of sincere religious awareness from the Buddha to Teresa of Avila, Jonathan Edwards, Emerson, and Whitman. Religious experience in its primary integrity is, however, not initial as Taylor maintains; it has no necessary telos beyond itself—even though, of course and trivially, it may have all sorts of consequences, primarily nonreligious. Like perceptual awareness, it is, before any appropriation in the context of socially created significations, simply itself. This is what Heidegger calls "faktische Erfahrung," the concretely specific primary *here and now* in its ontological authority: in it the self and that which is experienced are not yet, as Heidegger says, "torn apart" (Heidegger 10–14, 9).

One would, however, overlook the true significance of the Jamesian vision of religious experience if he did not sufficiently stress its specific noetic character, which has often been discussed in connection with the gnostic or mystical implications and connotations of such intimate moments of awareness. James himself has given us this summary appreciation of the noetic dimension of mystical experiences and states of the intimate presence of divine existence or the numinous in mystical moments: "They break down the authority of the non-mystical or rationalistic consciousness, based upon the understanding and the senses alone. They show it to be only one kind of consciousness. They open out the possibility of other orders of truth, in which, so far as anything in us vitally responds to them, we may freely continue to have faith. . . . It must always remain an open question whether mystical states may not possibly be . . . superior points of view, windows through which the mind looks out upon a more extensive and inclusive world" (James, *Varieties* 335, 338–339).

The characteristic openness and generosity of James's views, his readiness to accommodate and appreciate *other* modes of experiential awareness than those generally or socially or culturally or scientifically approved within imaginaries, this genuine fairness not only demands that he allow the possibility and even superiority of the noetic dimensions of religious experience, but also makes him energetically fight and refute the exclusive, the severely reductive, and for him always totalitarian and predominantly modern claims of rational and conceptual or scientific interpretations of experience and the world. Heidegger argues for a similar refutation of what he calls the theoretical or scientific stance in dealing with religious experience (Heidegger 6 and passim). In his focusing exclusively on the whatness or thing-character of a phenomenon, in this case of religious experience transformed to the status of a mere object called religion, thus in his focusing on the whatness of religion, as does Taylor, the basic meaning and significance of its factual enactment in and as experience defined in a radical empiricist mode is abandoned. In Heidegger's terminology, the *Vollzugssinn* is lost; that is, the manifest meaning of the factual presence and event of religious experiencing, which is not attributed to any subject, is jeopardized (Heidegger 62–65). Both James and Heidegger allow the *Vollzugssinn* of religious experience as a unified moment of authentic awareness to show itself in methodogically identical ways: in *Varieties*, James presents an abundance of testimonies of religious experiences; he allows the verbal traces of silent noetic experience to manifest themselves without evaluating their truth claims; their existential importance is highlighted simply by his way of gathering the religious heritage within plausible categories testifying to certain family likenesses. Heidegger argues for a similar restraint and aversion to objectification. The phenomenologist of religion will have to be content with a "formale Anzeige"—a formal indication or indexing—of the religious testimony (Heidegger 62–63). Philosophy of religion will present textual manifestations of moments of actual, existentially pregnant experiential presence. In Heidegger's lecture course the testimony is that of the New Testament: the philosopher of religion allows it to speak of and for itself. He forgoes any ascription of truth value and meaning in the sense of its possible social or cultural or philosophical or even theological function.

At this point I want to move toward the second part of this apology, which deals with James's philosophical *vision of the self* as it emerges from his interpretation of experience. This discussion may help refute the strictures in Taylor's reading of James which focus on his seemingly too subjectivist interpretation of religious experience and practice.

In his book *Experience and God*, the neo-pragmatist philosopher of religion John E. Smith pointedly asks whether the traditional conceptions of "experience" as "private" are adequate in general and in particular in cases of religious experience. Smith shows convincingly that "the dogma of experience as private, mental content" has to be "challenged as a non-empirical and erroneous view of experience" that leads to "an impoverishment of experience" (Smith 24, 21–45). This critique is legitimate and plausible because the relational character of experiencing established by William James's radical empiricism evinces the primary, the intimate and aboriginal co-presence of the so-called subject and the so-called objective content of experience. There is no subject or separate self to begin with, no self that then or later appropriates experiential objects. Selves *are* experiential; that is, in James's thinking they belong with and arise out of their worlds of ongoing experience, as Jonathan Levin has shown with impressive subtlety (Levin 61–62). In Heidegger's phenomenological discussion of religious experience this vision may be paraphrased thus: In the factual enactment of life I do not even experience an ego-object as a separate entity; this is so because experiencing itself always already possesses the character and features of a world, because my self-world is factually indistinguishable from my environing world (Heidegger 13).

Experience, Smith insinuates, is not a matter of subjective inwardness; rather it is a mode in which all of Being, and not only social reality, truly is and manifests itself; this would necessarily and prominently include what experiences identify as the most significant, essential, or the highest mode of "encounter": the *real*-ization, the becoming real, in and as experience, of the numinous.

James called the most fundamental mode of experience "pure experience." Pure experience designates anything that shows itself, or makes itself felt or might be thought of as real in its sheer *thisness*. In one of his *Essays in Radical Empiricism*, "The Thing and Its Relations," James makes it clear that pure experience as the "immediate flux of life," as the process of Being itself, precedes all "conceptual categories" (including subject and object) and that its purity means "the . . . amount of un-verbalized sensation which it . . . embodies" (James, "Thing" 46). In "Does 'Consciousness' Exist?" James described this silent yet dynamic reservoir of possibilities in this way: "The instant field of the present is at all times what I call the "pure" experience. It is only virtually or potentially either object or subject as yet. For the time being, it is plain, unqualified actuality or existence, a simple *that*. In this *naif* immediacy it is of course *valid;* it is *there*, we *act* upon it" (James, "Consciousness" 13).

The field of experiencing is therefore neither primarily nor necessarily subjective. This means that for James—and here one must radically challenge Taylor's reading of James—(religious) experience in its preverbal intensity, as the field of *thereness*, is exactly *not* a private or subjective affair, as Taylor insinuates and charges, nor is it a mere socially or culturally determined epiphenomenon. Pure experience, pure religious awareness, for James is an open field of realization within which what we later call the self or subject and the "content" or object of his or her experiencing, the numinous or the holy, are continuous with each other, and do indeed form a homogeneous spatial realm which *may* issue in a personal identity and his or her beliefs. First and foremost, however, religious experience as pure experience is a vast *this* or *there* which goes beyond any conceptual or subjectivist de-limitations or de-finitions and thus exceeds what may be thought of as existing within the social imaginary. In *Varieties* James calls this aspect of religious experiencing the *More* out of which humans may feel themselves addressed (James, *Varieties* 381–408, esp. 401). This *More* is, ontologically speaking, radically different from Taylor's "wider whole" or "corporate life" or "social imaginary," which he thinks of as determining the language and existence of individuals. James's *More* is a realm "into which our beings plunge" (James, *Varieties* 406), as he says; it is a space at the further reaches of experiencing which we encounter only when we allow for self-surrender, the abandonment of the socially, the historically realized and culturally mediated selfhood, or rather subjectivity, which is constrained by the mandates of social imaginaries. Experience as existential spread without any privileged subject-position, as I have tried to argue, is religious experience proper; it resides before and beyond the confines of social imaginaries, beyond any humanly social or subjectivist concerns whatever. Differing again from Taylor's reading of James, one has to insist: it is not without language. James says of the *More* within the primary event of experiencing that it contains "ontological messages" which arrive on the horizons of our experiential sites; he speaks of communications not about reality but of the articulate presence of reality within the event of experiencing itself: "There is a verge of the mind which these things haunt; and whispers therefrom mingle with the operations of our understanding, even as the waters of the infinite ocean send their waves to break among the pebbles that lie upon our shores" (James, *Varieties* 334).

Religious experience in James, then, is prior to all the determinations we may ever think of as belonging to our real or imagined, our concrete or desired collective existence. The social imaginary is always already transcended here. The expansive spread of religious experiencing does not, as James maintains, show without language; it is not the kind of socially conditioned language Charles Taylor insists on so much in his critique of James. The "ontological messages" or the "whispers" James addresses in the last quotation are his way of modestly and undogmatically reminding his readers of the primacy of a trans-human *Logos* which speaks within the vast reaches of experiencing and to which we may respond or not, depending on how far we feel ourselves determined, defined, or possibly even hemmed in by the con-fines of our imaginaries.

1. James's early essay "The Sentiment of Rationality" (1879), a precursor of important aspects of *Pragmatism* (1907), presents a thorough and strong argument supporting the idea of the suffusion of all perceptual and conceptual activities with overtones of feeling which help direct rational thinking and which may also support and establish the truth value of new insights in connecting them with their individually or collectively validated antecedents.

2. Durkheim argues against William James's conception of religious experience as primary in a way that foreshadows aspects of Taylor's strictures. Durkheim maintains that interpretations of religious experience, "ideas which believers have of it [i.e., religious experience]," are, more often than not, inadequate. In this way he dismisses religious experience as the inarticulate foreshadowing of later, socially relevant and socially conditioned rationalizations (Durkheim 417), as does Taylor.

WORKS CITED

Bourdieu, Pierre. *Distinction: A Social Critique of the Judgement of Taste.* Trans. Richard Nice. Cambridge: Harvard University Press, 1984.
———. *The Field of Cultural Production: Essays on Art and Literature.* Ed. Randal Johnson. New York: Columbia University Press, 1993.
Castoriadis, Cornelius. *The Imaginary Institution of Society.* Reprint. Cambridge: Polity Press, 2005.
Durkheim, Émile. *The Elementary Forms of the Religious Life.* Trans. Joseph Ward Swain. Glencoe, Ill.: Free Press, n.d.
Heidegger, Martin. *Phänomenologie des religiösen Lebens.* Vol. 60 of *Gesamtausgabe.* Frankfurt am Main: Vittorio Klostermann, 1995.
James, William. "The Thing and Its Relations." In *Essays in Radical Empiricism.* Cambridge: Harvard University Press, 1976. 45–59.
———. "Does Consciousness Exist?" In *Essays in Radical Empiricism.* Cambridge: Harvard University Press, 1976. 3–19.
———. "Experience." In *Essays in Philosophy.* Cambridge: Harvard University Press, 1978. 95.
———. *Some Problems of Philosophy.* Cambridge: Harvard University Press, 1979.
———. *The Principles of Psychology.* Vol. 1. Cambridge: Harvard University Press, 1981.
———. *The Varieties of Religious Experience: A Study in Human Nature.* Cambridge: Harvard University Press, 1985.
Levin, Jonathan. *The Poetics of Transition: Emerson, Pragmatism, and American Literary Modernism.* Durham: Duke University Press, 1999.

Poirier, Richard. *The Renewal of Literature: Emersonian Reflections.* New York: Random House, 1987.

Smith, John E. *Experience and God.* New York: Fordham University Press, 1995.

Taylor, Charles. *The Ethics of Authenticity.* Cambridge: Harvard University Press, 1991.

———. *Varieties of Religion Today: William James Revisited.* Cambridge: Harvard University Press, 2002.

———. *Modern Social Imaginaries.* Durham: Duke University Press, 2004.

5 The Shaping of We-Group Identities in the African American Community

A Perspective of Figurational Sociology on the Cultural Imaginary

If *we* can't cry for the Nation, then who? Because who else draws their grief and consternation from a larger knowledge or from a deeper and more desperate hope? And who've paid more in trying to achieve their better promise?

RALPH ELLISON, THREE DAYS BEFORE THE SHOOTING . . .

The Concept of Collective Identity in Figurational Sociology

Benedict Anderson's concept of the nation as "imagined community" is based on an understanding of the relation of society and individual which has been very common in Western thinking since the Renaissance. As the sociologist Norbert Elias explains in his study *The Society of Individuals*, we have come to refer "to the single human being as if he or she were an entity existing in complete isolation," while society "is understood either as a mere accumulation, an additive and unstructured collection of many individual people, or as an object existing beyond individuals" (vii). In contrast, Elias doubts the adequacy of "this form of I-identity, the perception of one's own person as a we-less I" (198). On the basis of a figurational theory of sociology, Elias even claims that there is no I-identity without a we-identity. Yet as a sociologist who analyzes long-term processes, he draws attention to historical changes in the we-I balance, and shows that in the course of the last centuries the we-I balance has tilted more and more toward I-identity. To Elias, Descartes's famous formula *cogito, ergo sum* turns the philosopher into a pioneer of this shift toward individualization and the humanists of the Renaissance into "one of the earliest groups of people whose personal achievements and character traits gave them opportunities to rise to respected social positions" (197). In addition to such historical changes that are indicative of changes in the social structure, there are also national differences in the we-I balance. As Stephen Mennell puts it in his study *The American Civilizing Process*, in which he explores Elias's theory of the civilizing process by applying it to the development of the United States: "Tocqueville employed the concept of 'individualism' for the purpose of characterizing the Americans . . . , but this statement of Tocqueville's elegantly captures an American proneness to what Elias calls the *homo clausus* conception of human beings—a mode of self-experience as a 'closed person,' as a single isolated individual separate from other individuals" (302). In fact, one of the reasons why figurational sociology has received less attention in the United States than in Europe may be its insistence on the interdependence of society and individual.[1]

In *The Civilizing Process*, Elias defined "figuration" as "the web of interdependences formed among human beings and which connects them: that is to say, a structure of mutually oriented and dependent persons" (249). Elias's concept of figuration can be compared to Pierre Bourdieu's "thoroughgoing *relationalism* which grasps both objective and subjective reality in the form of mutually interpenetrating systems of relations" (Wacquant 320). While it seems obvious that such overcoming of the dualisms of micro/macro and agency/structure provides a useful methodological tool for the debate of group-identities, there is yet another essential feature of figurational and relational sociology that offers valuable insights into the structure of (imagined) communities: it is important to note that figurational sociology always takes into account relations of competition and power between groups. According to Elias, the driving forces of the development that he investigated in *The Civilizing Process* are competition and the ensuing power struggles between interdependent groups. Likewise, the social figuration he came to define as "the established" and "the outsiders" is determined by the power differential that, in turn, is shaped by factors such as group cohesion, which the long-term inhabitants use to protect their privileges against the newcomers. Thus when Elias—a German Jew who had been driven into exile—tried to understand the "barbarization" of German society (*Civilizing Process* 302), he did so by analyzing the German national habitus emerging in the nineteenth and twentieth centuries as a result of fierce power struggles between Germany's gate-keeping "good society" and the lower middle class, which aspired to a share of the elite's social distinction of being capable of satisfaction while also trying to shield itself against the rising working class.[2]

In contrast to figurational sociology's focus on power struggles, theories based on the concept of the *homo clausus* tend to emphasize the equality of individuals. Thus according to Charles Taylor, individualism and equality are at the core of modern nation-states. In an essay titled "Nationalism and Modernity," Taylor refers to "modern nation-states" as "'imagined communities' in Benedict Anderson's celebrated phrase." Taylor sees a "shift from hierarchical, mediated-access societies to horizontal, direct-access societies" (196). Consequently, he characterizes the relation of the individual to the nation-state from the perspective of the individual as follows: "My fundamental way of belonging to the state is not dependent on, or mediated by any of these other belongings. I stand alongside all my fellow citizens, in direct relationship to the state which is the object of our common allegiance" (196). Taylor further maintains that "these modes of imagined direct access are linked to, indeed are just different facets of, modern equality and individualism. Directness of access abolishes the heterogeneity of hierarchical belonging. It makes us uniform, and that is one way of becoming equal" (197). Anderson and Taylor then perceive the relation between the I of the individual and the we of the nation as one between a we-less individual who feels bound to the idea of the nation, a feeling that is thought to be independent of the individual's relation to other individuals. Furthermore, the bond to the nation connects the individual to all other national subjects as if they were all equal, disregarding social differences of class and race. "Finally," Anderson claims, a nation "is imagined as a *community*, because, regardless of the actual inequality and exploitation that may prevail in each, the nation is always conceived as a deep, horizontal comradeship. Ultimately it is this fraternity that makes it possible, over the past two centuries, for so many millions of people, not so much to kill, as willingly to die for such limited imaginings" (16). In contrast, Cas Wouters stresses the other side of the coin of fraternity, namely, a lack of value attributed to the life of an individual. Distinguishing between we-identity proper and an idealized we-identity that he calls "we-ideal," Wouters expounds: "Vehement nationalism usually indicates a strong we-ideal in combination with a contested and insecure we-identity, a combination that usually blocks a deeper sense of mortality, for in defence of both we-identity and we-ideals, I-ideals are subordinated, sacrificed, and the use of violence is accepted more easily. At the same time, the value of an individual human life is impeded from rising" (153–154). The interrelation Wouters postulates between the strength of the bond with which the individual is linked to the imagined community and the weakness of social cohesion among the individuals in the respective nation differs from Anderson's model in that it considers both the dynamic nature of the figuration of the nation as well as its inherent power structure.

In *The Society of Individuals*, Elias points out that owing to "the complexity of humanity at its present stage of development" (202)—by which he means the development of modern societies since the Renaissance—the concept of the we-I balance has to be modified. It is no longer sufficient to consider just "one level or plane of integration in relation to which people can say 'we.'" Thus, in accordance with the "plurality of interlocking integration planes" characteristic of societies today, we have to bear in mind "this multi-layered aspect of we-concepts" (202). Such "we-relations" include people's families or friends, their hometowns, nation-states, and even mankind. Obviously "the intensity of identification varies with these different integration planes" (202), and while "involvement or commitment expressed by the use of the pronoun 'we' is probably usually strongest in relation to family," Elias thinks that "it is probably not an exaggeration to say that for most people mankind as a frame of reference for we-identity is a blank area on their emotional maps" (203). With regard to the increasing integration of humanity, Taylor seems to agree with Elias when he defines "modern individualism" as "imagining oneself as belonging to ever wider and more impersonal entities: the state, the movement, the community of mankind." And Taylor points out that "this is the same change—seen from another angle—that [can be] described . . . in terms borrowed from Craig Calhoun: the shift from 'network' or 'relational' identities to 'categorical' ones" (198).

In an article titled "Nationalism and Identity," Calhoun defines "ethnic groups" "in relation to the nation-state as subordinate internal and/or cross-cutting identities" (220). He quotes Max Weber's definition of an ethnic group as one whose members "entertain a subjective belief in their common descent because of similarities of physical type or of customs or both, or because of memories of colonization and migration" (231). Obviously these factors are highly relevant aspects in the shaping of African American we-identities. Like Elias, Calhoun emphasizes the instability of collective identities with regard both to competing meanings of a particular ethnic identity and to the negotiations between ethnic and national identities: "Ethnic solidarities and identities are claimed most often where groups do not seek 'national' autonomy but rather recognition internal to or cross-cutting national or state boundaries. The possibility of a closer link to nationalism is seldom altogether absent from such ethnic claims, however, and the two sorts of categorical identities are often invoked in similar ways" (235). One of the causes of the tensions between ethnic identity and national identity derives from the fact that "nationalism demands internal homogeneity" so that "nationalists commonly claim that national identities 'trump' other personal or group identities (such as gender, family, or ethnicity) and link individuals directly to the nation as a whole. This is sharply contrary to the way in which most ethnic identities flow from family membership, kinship, and membership in intermediate groups" (229). The reason why the we-feeling of ethnic identity changes very slowly has to do with the manner in which traditions are transmitted, namely, as Calhoun points out in reference to Pierre Bourdieu's *Logic of Practice* (1990), not by the mere passing on of contents but by the reproduction of "a 'habitus' or orientation to social action" (222).

Like Elias, Calhoun criticizes the notion of a "self-contained individual" because this concept of the self has "made it common to understand social groupings as sets of equivalent persons . . . rather than webs of relationships among persons or hierarchies of positions" (230). Such a neglect of the continuous and inevitable interweaving of individual beings leads to an overemphasis on equality that does not do justice to the situation of minorities.

The Instability of the African American We-Identity

Since the founding of the American nation, African Americans have been exposed to strategies of exclusion that according to Wouters are correlative to the strength of the national we-ideal and the corresponding insecurity of the we-identity. The fact that African Americans were considered outsiders necessarily shaped their own we-group identities and we-ideals. Given their marginality, what kinds of communities did they imagine, and how were they negotiated? Under what conditions were African Americans susceptible to the notion of the nation as imagined community despite their continuous experience of exploitation and exclusion? Not surprisingly, African Americans often expressed an ambivalence toward the American nation. In reaction to the history of slavery and segregation, they developed two complementary strategies of resistance: integrationism and nationalism. Moreover, their attitudes were prone to shift depending on the willingness or unwillingness of whites to integrate the outsiders into the "fraternity" of the nation.[3] In a statement on black nationalism, Cornel West stresses the interdependence of nationalism and ostracism: "Any kind of nationalism, for the most part, will be used in a way that ends up dehumanizing folks. We all need recognition and some form of protection, but usually in these dominant forms the quest for group unity results in attacking someone else" (525). Asked whether he felt he could be an integral part of American society, West expressed an ambivalence not untypical of black intellectuals and referred explicitly to W. E. B. Du Bois's famous notion of "double consciousness," responding: "Yes and no. After 244 years of slavery and 87 years of Jim Crow, I think black people in America will always have some sense of being outsiders. Yet there's a sense in which I am part of it, because the nation is unimaginable without black people in the culture, either past or present. It's the tension between being an outsider and being more integral to America than 90 percent of Americans. It's what Du Bois called 'double consciousness.' I'm thirteenth-generation American! That's about as integral as you can get" (525).

While the locus classicus of Du Bois's concept of "double consciousness" is, of course, his early essay collection *The Souls of Black Folk*, he further elaborated on the notion of the "twoness of the black American" in his essay "The Conservation of Races": "What, after all, am I? Am I an American or am I a Negro? Can I be both? Or is it my duty to cease to be a Negro as soon as possible and be an American? If I strive as a Negro, am I not perpetuating the very cleft that threatens and separates black and white America? Is not my only possible practical aim the subduction of all that is Negro in me to the American?" (5). In this passage Du Bois poses the question as a theoretical one, as if the choice between the national and the ethnic identity could be resolved once and for all. In practice, however, concepts of integrationism and black nationalism often competed with each other, not only in the form of various programmatic movements but also in the shifting attitudes of African American intellectuals and activists. As mentioned before, more often than not, these changing positions depended on the degree of inclusion in, or respectively exclusion from, the national community imagined by whites. Figurational sociology turns this experience into the following theoretical statement: "It is a general principle that one group's '*we-image*' is defined in large measure in relation to its '*they-image*' of another group or groups" (Mennell 19).

What is important to realize—and what is usually not discussed in non-figurational theories—is the fact that the relation between "we-image" and "they-image" is not neutral but depends on power imbalances between the established and the outsiders. Not surprisingly, then, African Americans tend to express an awareness of the structural inequality that is at the basis of the relationship between blacks and whites. In a study that looks at imagined black communities from the perspective of African American thinkers, Richard Johnson addresses "the pernicious dilemma" by pointing out that "African-Americans yearn for an imagined community that is *yet to be* while existing as subaltern[s] in actual communities that privilege majority normativity. . . . I argue that this is a form of conceptual political violence" (19).[4]

In the discussion that follows, I trace major manifestations of skepticism toward belonging to the national community as well as affirmations of belonging to other imagined communities in the writings of two seminal black intellectuals and activists of the past, Frederick Douglass and W. E. B. Du Bois. Not only are they considered the most prominent black intellectuals of their time, but also they are both examples of activists who—unlike black leaders who strove for a separate black nation—were willing to probe various measures of integrationism. For this reason their struggles with alternative we-identities are more complex than those of radical nationalists who have given up on the United States as a homeland for African Americans. The relation of the African American we-I balance is often negotiated in autobiographies, since in the case of black subjects the act of evoking the individual past necessarily involves grappling with the collective history of slavery and Jim Crow segregation and the effects that white supremacy have had on the we-identity of African Americans. Consequently, more often than not, African American writers interweave the narrative of their life story with reflections on the social situation of the African American people. While Douglass included some of his speeches in his two autobiographies, Du Bois, in *Dusk of Dawn*, intended to interrelate the development of his own intellectual and political strivings with the events of global history and their consequences for himself and "many millions, who with me have had their lives shaped and directed by this course of events" (3). The centrality of the interweaving of individual and collective experience to Du Bois's book already becomes obvious from its subtitle: *An Essay toward an Autobiography of a Race Concept.*

"Wounded in the House of His Friends": Frederick Douglass's Negotiations of African American We-Identities

In the case of Frederick Douglass, his changing position as to the relation between the "we" of the nation-state and the "we" of the ethnic community of the Negro has been a contested issue among critics. I cannot possibly do justice to this long-standing and complex debate. For the purposes of this essay it may suffice to discuss a few examples of his shifting ideas of African American we-identities. The classic expression of the exclusion of African Americans from the American nation is Douglass's famous 1852 speech "What to the Slave Is the Fourth of July?" an extract of which he included in his autobiography, *My Bondage and My Freedom*, published in 1855. In this speech Douglass articulates in unequivocal terms the sense of exclusion vis-à-vis the imagined community of the nation-state. He rhetorically asks, "What have I, or those I represent, to do with your national independence?" (*Autobiographies* 431). He assures his "fellow-citizens" that he would gladly join them in the celebration; "but," he adds, "with a sad sense of the disparity between us. I am not included within the pale of this glorious anniversary! . . . The rich inheritance of justice, liberty, prosperity, and independence, bequeathed by your fathers, is shared by you, not by me. . . . This Fourth of July is *yours*, not *mine*" (431). And in the final passage of his speech, he attacks the false we-ideal of Americans in a most powerful sequence of reproaches: "To him [the slave], your celebration is a sham; your boasted liberty, an unholy license; your national greatness, swelling vanity; your sounds of rejoicing are empty and heartless; your denunciations of tyrants, brass-fronted impudence; your shouts of liberty and equality, hollow mockery, your prayers and hymns, your sermons and thanksgivings, with all your religious parade and solemnity, are to him mere bombast, fraud, deception, impiety, and hypocrisy—a thin veil to cover up crimes which would disgrace a nation of savages" (434).[5]

This speech, rich in implications about vital political and moral issues such as the United States Constitution, the framers' "original intent," and natural law doctrine, has been widely examined.[6] Within the context of African American we-identities, it is relevant because of the rhetorical devices Douglass employs to stress the crucial difference between the national—that is, "white"—view of the celebration of liberty and the slave's outsider position. He makes extensive use of the juxtaposition of personal and possessive pronouns, and he shifts the meaning of "we," sometimes identifying with the citizens of the nation, sometimes distancing himself from his "fellow citizens" as well as from the slave by referring to the latter in the third-person singular.[7]

In a lecture on the antislavery movement Douglass gave in 1855, he sets his hope on a we-group that transcends the nation: the abolitionist movement. In enumerating its allies, Douglass claims that "in addition to authors, poets, and scholars at home, the moral sense of the civilized world is with us" (450), and he refers to England, France, and Germany as "the three great lights of modern civilization" that support the cause. "But," he points out, "there is a deeper and truer method of measuring the power of our cause, and of comprehending its vitality. This is to be found in its accordance with the best elements of human nature.... The slave is bound to mankind by the powerful and inextricable net-work of human brotherhood" (449). It is interesting to note that in transgressing the national toward the international and from there even moving toward the most comprehensive level of integration, namely, humankind, Douglass phrases his appeal to universalism in terms of an imagined community, or as he calls it, the "net-work of human brotherhood."

After Emancipation, Douglass develops the concept of what in his well-known speech of 1869 he calls "Our Composite Nationality."[8] Here he expresses his hope that the United States will come up to its mission and mold the various races and ethnicities represented in its population into Americans in order to become "the perfect national illustration of the unity and dignity of the human family that the world has ever seen" (*Papers* 253). Again, Douglass conceptualizes what according to Calhoun is a "categorical identity," as if it were a network identity analogous to the family. As Robert S. Levine argues in his informative study *Dislocating Race and Nation*, Douglass insisted that his support of the Santo Domingo annexation plan differed from American imperialism: "For Douglass, Santo Domingo annexation was about a hemispheric nationalism in which various peoples of the Americas recognize their common aspirations and shared humanity.... Douglass thus invokes the cosmopolitanism that throughout his career would have such a pronounced impact on his views of race and nation, appealing to 'that side which allies man to the Infinite, which in some sense leads him to view the broad world as his country and all mankind as his countrymen'" (217).[9]

As naïve and bizarre as Douglass's position may appear to us, given the political context of imperialism (see Levine 218), his attempt to forge an imagined community by cross-cutting national boundaries while at the same time extending the U.S. black imagined community is a significant step in Douglass's various efforts to shape new we-identities that would ultimately lead to a genuinely cosmopolitan American community. Moreover, the example highlights the importance of print media in the development of the imagined community of the nation. After all, it is "the novel and the newspaper" that "provided the technical means for 're-presenting' the *kind* of imagined community that is the nation" (Anderson 30). At the time Douglass became involved in the Santo Domingo annexation plan, he was also the publisher and editor of the

African American newspaper the *New National Era*. In the first issue under his editorship, Douglass justified the renaming of the newspaper, formerly known as the *New Era*, by "stating that it now aspires to be a 'national journal in its truest and broadest sense'" (Levine 205). True to his "nationalist" agenda, Douglass politicizes the newspaper by shifting its focus from literary contributions to the questions of nation and race (see Levine chap. 4).

Nevertheless, Douglass's vision of the complete assimilation of race within a we-ideal of a cosmopolitan nation would fade whenever he was confronted with versions of the imagined national community of his white fellow citizens that depended on the ostracizing of African Americans. The *Dred Scott* decision was one of these moments to which Douglass reacted by contemplating emigration to the black republic of Haiti. Yet Douglass saw the "most flagrant example of . . . national deterioration" in the 1883 decision of the United States Supreme Court that declared unconstitutional the Civil Rights Act of 1875, which had been intended to enforce the Fourteenth Amendment. He devotes a whole chapter to the discussion of the Supreme Court ruling in his autobiography, *Life and Times*, in which he sharply accuses the Court of being "wholly under the influence of the slave power" and "placing itself on the side of prejudice, proscription, and persecution" (*Autobiographies* 966). In his depiction of the reaction of blacks to this decision, Douglass uses the image of the American nation as a house with a twist, for in this house African Americans live as guests whose hosts have violated the universal law of hospitality by failing to protect them: "The colored citizen . . . was wounded in the house of his friends. He felt that this decision drove him from the doors of the great temple of American justice. The nation that he had served against its enemies had thus turned him over naked to those enemies" (987). In contrast to the integrationist vision of a nation that would merge all its various peoples into a perfect union which Douglass fostered in the promising early years of Reconstruction, the image of the betrayed black citizen conveys a reservation vis-à-vis the possibility of full integration. And yet, rather than giving up the concept of integration altogether, Douglass reveals a deep ambivalence, which again is significantly expressed in the changing meaning of the pronoun "we." The greater part of the chapter consists of the speech Douglass gave in protest to the Supreme Court decision at Lincoln Hall in Washington, D.C. In this speech he had used the metaphor of the house of friends with a slight variation: "We have been, as a class, grievously wounded, wounded in the house of our friends, and this wound is too deep and too painful for ordinary and measured speech" (968). In this sentence the personal pronoun "we" refers to the group of black citizens with whom the speaker identifies, while in a later passage of the speech Douglass changes the meaning of "we" to signify "we, the nation." Appealing to his "fellow-citizens," Douglass speaks for the whole nation: "We want no black Ireland in America. We want no aggrieved class in America. Strong as we are without the negro, we are stronger with him than without him. The power and friendship of seven millions of people, however scattered all over the country, are not to be despised" (973–974). By shifting the meaning of "we," Douglass stresses the fact that there is more than a single we-identity, and he emphasizes the perspective of the marginalized ethnic group that does not necessarily identify with the imagined community of the nation.

The World's Columbian Exposition in 1893, a spectacular moment in American history, when the nation staged itself as an idealized community and the epitome of civilization, caused Douglass to reflect on a missed opportunity. As he put it in his last great speech, "Why Is the Negro Lynched?" (1892): "As nowhere in the world, it was hoped that here the idea of human brotherhood would have been grandly recognized and most gloriously illustrated. It should have been thus, had it been what it professed to be, a World's Exposition. It was not such, however, in its spirit at this point; it was only an American Exposition. The spirit of American caste against the educated Negro was conspicuously seen from start to finish" (*Speeches* 763). Indeed, African Americans were systematically excluded from all U.S. exhibits, and it was only due to the president of Haiti, who invited Douglass to represent Haiti at the World's Columbian Exposition, that African Americans became part of the exhibition. Douglass turned the Haitian pavilion into a meeting place of African American intellectuals. In sharp protest to the politics of the government, Douglass claimed: "The negro exclusion . . . says to the world that the colored people of America are not deemed by Americans within the compass of American law, progress and civilization. It says to the lynchers and mobocrats of the South, go on in your hellish work of Negro persecution. You kill their bodies, we kill their souls" (764).

In this address Douglass demonstrates once more his deep understanding of structural power imbalances. In fact he seems to be fully aware of a decisive mechanism of established-outsider relations, which allows the group of the established to feel superior. At the core of the claim of superiority is the interrelation of group charisma and complementary group disgrace, as theorized by Elias in *The Established and the Outsiders*

(1965): "One can observe again and again that members of groups which are, in terms of *power*, stronger than other interdependent groups, think of themselves in human terms as *better* than the others" (1).[10] More specifically, Elias emphasizes the structural regularity of established-outsider relations: "An established group tends to attribute to its outsider group as a whole the 'bad' characteristics of that group's 'worst' section—of its anomic minority. In contrast, the self-image of the established group tends to be modelled on its exemplary, most 'nomic' or norm-setting section, on the minority of its 'best' members. This *pars pro toto* distortion in opposite directions enables an established group to prove their point to themselves as well as to others" (5).

Douglass clearly recognizes the principle underlying the injustice and cruelty of the social ritual of lynching, namely, the identification of black individuals with the outsiders' "worst" section: "When a white man steals, robs or murders, his crime is visited upon his own head alone. But not so with the black man. When he commits a crime, the whole race is made responsible. The case before us [lynching in the South] is an example" (*Speeches* 763). Douglass also realizes that the "*pars pro toto* distortion in opposite directions" is enforced by representations of the two groups in visual art: "Even when American art undertakes to picture the types of the two races, it invariably places in comparison, not the best of both races as common fairness would dictate, but it puts side by side and in glaring contrast, the lowest type of the Negro with the highest type of the white man and then calls upon the world to 'look upon this picture, then upon that'" (763). As Elias points out, "there is always some evidence to show that one's group is 'good' and the other is 'bad'" (5).

Elias insisted on a figurative conception of "prejudices," according to which they have to be understood as a result of the sociodynamics of stigmatization deriving from group processes: "Thus one misses the key to the problem usually discussed under headings such as 'social prejudice,' if one looks for it solely in the personality structure of individual people. One can find it only if one considers the figuration formed by the two (or more) groups concerned or, in other words, the nature of their interdependence. The centrepiece of that figuration is an uneven balance of power and the tensions inherent in it. . . . Unmitigated contempt and one-sided stigmatisation of outsiders without redress . . . signal a very uneven balance of power. Attaching the label of 'lower human value' to another group is one of the weapons used in a power struggle by superior groups as a means of maintaining their social superiority" (6).

The high level of American status insecurity "as a function of both class and nationality" (Wouters) enhances the anxiety of "social contamination," that is, the fear of losing one's we- and I-identity by close contact with members of the group of outsiders (Wouters 43). As long as this basic social fear remains widespread among the established, a more even balance of power is unlikely to emerge. As the insecurity of their own we- and I-identity grows, whites display a tendency to increase physical and symbolic violence toward blacks. This creates a mounting distance among African Americans toward the imagined community of the nation. Consequently, even Douglass, who in general favors an integrationist model of American society, is forced repeatedly to distance himself from the national layer of we-identity and to resume the rhetoric of resistance. Rather than replacing the national we-identity with the we-identity of a separate black community, however, he resorts to the transnational level and the ideals of universalism. By evoking the idea of human brotherhood, he admonishes the American nation to fulfill the promises of its own Constitution.

"Looking Out from a Dark Cave": W. E. B. Du Bois's Struggle against Provincialism

Like Douglass, W. E. B. Du Bois was aware of "the pattern of group charisma and complementary group disgrace" in established-outsider relations. In *Dusk of Dawn* he states: "The Negro group is spoken of continually as one undifferentiated low-class mass. The culture of the higher whites is often considered as typical of all the whites" (93). In his case, the insight into this mechanism that helps sustain power imbalances between whites and blacks is not surprising. After all, he was one of the earliest representatives of the discipline of sociology. He had heard Max Weber in Berlin and later corresponded with him on his sociological investigation *The Philadelphia Negro* (1899). About his studies at Harvard Du Bois writes: "It was at Harvard that my education, turning from philosophy, centered in history and then gradually in economics and social problems. Today [1940] my course of study would have been called sociology; but in that day Harvard did not recognize any such science" (*Dusk* 20).

Du Bois thought that his life had "deep significance [only] because it was a part of a problem," and thus in his autobiography *Dusk of Dawn* he set out to analyze the "race problem . . . in the terms of the one human life I know best" (xxx–xxxi). In taking a sociological perspective on his own life, he focuses on the nation's division along the color line, linking the internal segregation of, discrimination against, and exploitation of the Negro to the oppression of colored peoples of the world. In fact, in the very first paragraph of *Dusk of Dawn*, Du Bois establishes the connection between national and global history as it evolved over the seven decades of his life: "From 1868 to 1940 stretch seventy-two mighty years, which are incidentally the years of my own life but more especially years of cosmic significance, when one remembers that they rush from the American Civil War to the reign of the second Roosevelt; from Victoria to the sixth George; from the Franco-Prussian to the two World Wars. They contain the rise and fall of the Hohenzollerns, the shadowy emergence, magnificence and miracle of Russia; the turmoil of Asia in China, India and Japan, and the world-wide domination of white Europe" (1).

Yet writing about his early upbringing, he also emphasizes the local and regional. Raised in Great Barrington, a small town in western Massachusetts, Du Bois "in general thought and conduct" became "quite thoroughly New England" (9)—so much so, he writes, that "the Negroes in the South, when I came to know them, could never understand why I did not naturally greet everyone I passed on the street or slap my friends on the back" (9). He also stresses his early indebtedness to the Protestant work ethic: "My general attitude toward property and income was that all who were willing to work could easily earn a living; that those who had property had earned it and deserved it and could use it as they wished; that poverty was the shadow of crime and connoted lack of thrift and shiftlessness. These were the current patterns of economic thought of the town of my boyhood" (9). He thinks that there was but one consideration that saved him "from complete conformity with the thoughts and confusions of then current social trends; and that was the problems of racial and cultural contacts" (13). And yet in the beginning he was still caught in a parochial point of view, he writes, limiting "the struggle for which I was preparing . . . primarily to the plight of the comparatively small group of American Negroes with which I was identified, and theoretically to the larger Negro race. I did not face the general plight and conditions of all humankind" (13). During the three years Du Bois spent studying at Fisk University, his awareness of the color line deepened. For the fist time in his life he was confronted, he recalls, "with a sort of violence that I had never realized in New England" (15). It was in reaction to his experiences of more violent forms of discrimination and racial segregation that he started his career as a public speaker. For his graduation speech, Du Bois chose a topic related to nation-building, namely, Bismarck: "Bismarck was my hero. He had made a nation out of a mass of bickering peoples. He had dominated the whole development with his strength until he crowned an emperor at Versailles. This foreshadowed in my mind the kind of thing that American Negroes must do, marching forth with strength and determination under trained leadership" (16). Looking back, Du Bois is very critical of his choice which "showed the abyss between my education and the truth in the world" (16), and he calls himself "blithely European and imperialist in outlook; democratic as democracy was conceived in America" (17). It is only later, when he studied at the University of Berlin (1892–1894), that he "began to see the race problem in America, the problem of the peoples of Africa and Asia, and the development of Europe as one" (23–24).[11]

What, then, is Du Bois's we-identity? The tensions in his loyalties are obvious. Having absorbed New England cultural patterns and speech, he writes, "my African racial feeling was then purely a matter of my own later learning and reaction. . . . But it was none the less real and a large determinant of my life and character. I felt myself African by 'race' and by that token was African and an integral member of the group of dark Americans who were called Negroes. At the same time I was firm in asserting that these Negroes were Americans" (58). Referring to his own family history, he produces excellent anecdotal evidence of the fragile status of his group's membership in the imagined community of the nation: "On the basis of my great-great-grandfather's Revolutionary record I was accepted as a member of the Massachusetts Society of the Sons of the American Revolution, in 1908. When, however, the notice of this election reached the headquarters in Washington and was emphasized by my requesting a national certificate, the secretary, A. Howard Clark of the Smithsonian Institution, wrote to Massachusetts and demanded 'proof of marriage of the ancestor of Tom Burghardt and record of birth of the son.' He knew, of course, that the birth record of a stolen African slave could not possibly be produced. My membership was, therefore, suspended" (58).

As to his ethnic identity, Du Bois agrees with Weber's definition by claiming: "The badge of color [was] relatively unimportant save as a badge; the real essence of this kinship is its social heritage of slavery; the discrimination and insult; and this heritage binds together not simply the children of Africa, but extends through yellow Asia and into the South Seas. It is this unity that draws me to Africa" (59). His transnational, global perspective is based, then, on the we-identity of African Americans forged both from the knowledge of the heritage of bondage and from the experience of the continuing consequences of slavery. In a fictional conversation about race between a persona of Du Bois's and a white supremacist, Roger Van Dieman, the latter reacts in bewilderment to Du Bois's statement that race "is a cultural, sometimes an historical fact," and finally asks:

> "But what is this group; and how do you differentiate it; and how can you call it 'black' when you admit it is not black?"
>
> "I recognize it quite easily and with full legal sanction; the black man is a person who must ride 'Jim Crow' in Georgia." (77)

Less often discussed than the metaphor of the veil and the concept of double consciousness is Du Bois's much darker image of the "full psychological meaning of caste segregation" that he paints in *Dusk of Dawn:* "It is as though one, looking out from a dark cave in a side of an impending mountain, sees the world passing and speaks to it" (66). He imagines himself as someone who tries to explain to the outer world "how these entombed souls are hindered in their natural movement, expression, and development." But those who pass by do not take notice of the prisoners. Owing to "some thick sheet of invisible but horribly tangible plate glass . . . between them and the world," communication fails. Du Bois stresses the growing despair of the prisoners when they realize that the outer world does not hear them even when they start screaming and tends to react in amusement at their frantic gesticulations. And when "here and there" the prisoners manage to "break through in blood and disfigurement," they are confronted by "a horrified . . . mob of people frightened for their own very existence" (66). This "group imprisonment" in a cave, while resonant of Plato's allegory of the cave, is all the more dismal for deconstructing Platonic idealism. Furthermore, in contrast to the image of the veil, the metaphor of the "wall of glass" (66) stresses the pain and the suffering of the victimized outsiders and both the indifference of the established and the fear that erupts when the glass wall is broken by violence and they feel threatened. Apart from the emotional tribute paid by both groups, Du Bois emphasizes the negative effects that the "group imprisonment within a group" (67) has on the prisoner. Focusing exclusively on the problems of his own group, the prisoner becomes provincial and "tends to neglect the wider aspects of national life and human existence" (67). This leads on the one hand to an almost unlimited loyalty to his group and on the other hand to a deeply ingrained resentment, if not hatred, toward the white world, which in turn enhances the difficulties of communication between the two "castes" (66). According to Du Bois, then, the we-identity of the Negro trumps his we-identity as an American, not for reasons inherent in race or cultural tradition, however, but rather in reaction to the we-ideal of Americans that does not allow for the inclusion of the "uncivilized" Negro in the fraternity of the nation.

Although Du Bois calls this parable "the race concept which has dominated my life" (67), it should not be misunderstood as a static model. The social scientist Du Bois himself adds this methodological caveat: "Perhaps it is wrong to speak of it as a 'concept' rather than as a group of contradictory forces, facts and tendencies" (67). With regard to Du Bois's individual we-identity, it is not a fixed position either. First, as an African American intellectual and activist, he sees himself in the difficult position of an interpreter and mediator whose fundamental limitations he candidly discloses. Although he can communicate with his fellows from the position outside the glass wall and is able to "assume a facile championship of the entombed, and gain the enthusiastic and even gushing thanks of the victims" (66), this "outside leadership," as Du Bois calls it, will always be in danger of misinterpreting experiences and feelings not shared. More important, "the outside advocacy . . . remains impotent and unsuccessful until it actually succeeds in freeing and making articulate the submerged caste" (67). Second, the same pattern that is typical of Douglass reoccurs in Du Bois, namely, a shifting between the we-identities of "Negro" and "American." For example, Du Bois recalls during World War I becoming "nearer to feeling myself a real and full American than ever before or since" (128).[12] And in 1919 Du Bois experienced the conflict of his feelings of national pride and disillusionment. He had planned "a national Negro celebration of the Tercentenary" in memory of the landing of a group of twenty Africans in Virginia, in August 1619. But "alas, almost exactly three hundred years later there occurred race riots in Chicago and Washington which were among the worst in their significance that the Negro had encountered during his three hundred years of slavery and emancipation" (131–132). In addition to the economic reasons (above all, growing competition between black and white workers due to the migration of southern blacks to the northern industrial cities) that triggered hostilities against African Americans, which in turn caused the riots, there were increasing incidents of lynching. A considerable number of victims were black soldiers, and, according to Du Bois, the resentment behind the violence was based on "the recognition and kudos which Negroes received in the World War; and particularly their treatment in France" (132).

The tension between inclusion and exclusion as described by Du Bois in *Dusk of Dawn* is, of course, not limited to his experiences in the postwar era, nor is it restricted to his autobiographical narratives. What

Glenda Carpio convincingly suggests with regard to Du Bois's book *The Gift of Black Folk* is true of his grappling with the "problem of the color line" throughout his life, namely, that he "walks a tightrope between a patriotic embrace of an America in which African American culture has become an inextricable part and an exhortation of the rebellion and struggle out of which that culture arose" (xxiii).

After World War I, Du Bois pursued three complementary strategies to improve the situation of African Americans, one cultural, one political, and one economic. The first "represented an old ideal and ambition, the development of literature and art among Negroes"; the second consisted of the further development of the Pan-African movement; and the third was about "the economic rehabilitation and defense of the American Negro" (*Dusk* 134). Du Bois considered the third the most fundamental. It was about the establishment of cooperative forms of the economy. Not only did Du Bois question capitalism, but also he tried to devise new organizations, such as the Negro Co-operative Guild. Interestingly, the "Citizens Co-operative stores" were quite successful, and so was a program of teaching basic theories of co-operation at a black state school in West Virginia—until it was outlawed by the state (*Dusk* 140).

Inspired by a socialist view of the forces of global capitalism, Du Bois came to understand the interrelation between the exploitation of the peoples of Africa and Asia by Europe and the United States and the "expulsion of black men from American democracy, their subjection to caste control and wage slavery" (*Dusk* 48). He himself had overcome what he considered the provincial outlook derived from fostering the narrow racial we-identity of the black community, shaped by the glass wall of segregation. As Henry Louis Gates Jr. points out in the series introduction to the Oxford edition of Du Bois, the image Du Bois creates for the community that transcends national boundaries in *Worlds of Color* (1961)—book 3 of the Black Flame trilogy—is "the world as one unified dwelling place" (Gates xix).[13]

• • •

As I hope I have shown, the conflicts and tensions between the ethnic we-identity and the national we-identity can be severe in outsider groups. They suffer from the physical or symbolic violence exerted by the group of the established in reaction to the weakness of their own we-identity. Because of long-standing experiences of exclusion and suppression—or in Du Bois's harsh words, the "imprisonment of a human group with chains in hands of an environing group" (*Dusk* 69)—African Americans usually forge a strong we-identity with their ethnic group, which is constructed as a relational group identity whose members are considered extended family, that is, "brothers and sisters." At the same time, the concept of race suggests a reaching out beyond the imagined community of the nation by identifying instead with international or global communities. Douglass, who was very much influenced by the tradition of the Enlightenment, took resort in the universalistic network of brotherhood and, temporarily, in "hemispheric nationalism." Du Bois favored the Pan-African movement and the international movement of socialism. Although these types of group identities may be defined as categorical, both thinkers succeeded in investing them with great fervor, that is, with considerable we-feelings, which in turn strengthened their commitment. Thus in contrast to the general long-term development of the we-I balance tilting toward the I-identity, the we-I balance of African Americans seems to have maintained a relatively strong we-identity component. According to figurational sociology, this could change only with a weakening of the we-ideal of the established (see Wouters 154). A weakening of nationalism could result from the ongoing processes toward an increasing social integration of mankind. As Elias pointed out, the majority of human beings are emotionally not yet ready to identify with the we-identity of mankind (*Society* 203). But as the example of African Americans has shown, the willingness to identify with the "network of human brotherhood" is dependent on the violence exerted on social groups. Rather than falling back to lower levels of integration, such as the family or the clan, political parties, or religious groups, they may choose to reach out for the solidarity of human beings on the highest level of integration.

NOTES

1. For a discussion of the reception of Elias's figurational and Pierre Bourdieu's relational sociology in the United States and a brief survey of similarities between the theories and concepts of the two sociologists, see Buschendorf, Franke, and Voelz 1–7; for further impediments to the reception of Elias in the United States, see Mennell; for an assessment of the historical and systematical obstacles to the American reception of Bourdieu's relational sociology, see Wacquant; see also Susen and Turner. Until recently, sociologists have disregarded the conceptual similarities between Elias and Bourdieu; see Paulle, van Heerikhuzen, and Emirbayer.

2. While it is universally known that Bourdieu's concepts of field and capital are based on the assumption that power struggles are an integral part of human

societies, the importance of his concept of "symbolic violence" as an essential tool of analyzing the "gentle and often invisible violence" (Bourdieu 35) has only fairly recently been recognized.

3. Cf. James H. Cone on the interrelatedness of both traditions in the section titles "Integrationism and Nationalism in African-American Intellectual History" in his introduction to *Martin & Malcolm & America*, 3–17. Cone argues: "The ebb and flow of black nationalism, during the nineteenth century and thereafter, was influenced by the decline and rise of black expectations of equality in the United States. When blacks felt that the achievement of equality was impossible, the nationalist sentiment among them always increased" (11).

4. Johnson explicitly draws on Anderson's term "imagined communities," but "with the stipulation that [in contrast to the nineteenth century] there are no government authorities currently using media to promote positive visions of African-American community" (2). Johnson probes African American visions appropriate for a post-nationalistic age. He analyzes concepts of Black Nationalism as well as Martin Luther King Jr.'s ideal of the "beloved community" and then investigates the postmodern black condition from the point of view of Cornel West and Lucius Outlaw.

5. Cf. this passage from Douglass's autobiography *My Bondage and My Freedom*, in which he quotes from one of a series of letters written to William Lloyd Garrison during his stay in Great Britain on January 1, 1846: "As to nation, I belong to none. . . . I am an outcast from the society of my childhood, and an outlaw in the land of my birth. . . . That men should be patriotic, is to me perfectly natural; and as a philosophical fact, I am able to give it an *intellectual* recognition. But no further can I go. If ever I had any patriotism, or any capacity for the feeling, it was whipped out of me long since, by the lash of the American soul-drivers" (*Autobiographies* 372).

6. Cf. Colaiaco's monograph on Douglass's speech, which also discusses earlier debates.

7. Cf. Elias's observations on the interconnectedness of personal pronouns reflecting the correlation between macro- and micro-sociological investigations in his essay "The Personal Pronouns as a Figurational Model," in *What Is Sociology?* 122–127.

8. Douglass, "Our Composite Nationality: An Address Delivered in Boston, Massachusetts, on 7 December 1869," in *The Frederick Douglass Papers*, 240–259.

9. Levine refers here to a stump speech, "Santo Domingo," that Douglass would give between 1871 and 1873; he quotes from a version of the speech Douglass presented in St. Louis in January 1873, which was reprinted in the *New National Era* in January 1873.

10. *The Established and the Outsiders* is based on extensive fieldwork undertaken near Leicester, England, in the course of which Elias and John Scotson discovered that this statistically homogeneous community, whose population did not differ with regard to nationality, ethnicity, class, education, or religion,

displayed a sharp dividing line between an old-established group who had lived in Winston Parva (the fictive name for South Wigston) for about three generations and a group of residents who had only recently moved to a newly developed site. The longer duration of residence correlating with a high degree of group cohesion was sufficient to exclude the newcomers from the older residents' social networks and important positions. In short, the study revealed an unexpected power differential and, as a consequence, a certain pattern of group behavior that Elias theorized as the established-outsider relationship.

11. In the light of today's emphasis on interdisciplinarity, it is interesting to note that Du Bois, by studying a discipline called "Staatswissenschaften" under the renowned Professor Gustav Schmoller, was introduced to genuinely interdisciplinary research based on statistics, economics, (economic) history, and sociology, an approach that was highly influential on his own work; see Wortham 3.

12. Cf. Du Bois's later emphasis on patriotism: "I felt for a moment as the war progressed that I could be without reservation a patriotic American" (*Autobiography* 274). Yet Du Bois expresses deep skepticism at the type of fervent patriotism he—with scathing sarcasm—ascribes to a white friend: "We must put patriotism before everything—make'em salute the flag, stop radical treason, keep out the dirty foreigners, disfranchise niggers and make America a Power!" (*Dusk* 84).

13. Cf. the similar image Martin Luther King Jr. proposed in his last book, *Where Do We Go from Here?* He writes: "However deeply American Negroes are caught in the struggle to be at last at home in our homeland of the United States, we cannot ignore the larger world house in which we are also dwellers. Equality with whites will not solve the problems of either whites or Negroes if it means equality in a world society stricken by poverty and in a universe doomed to extinction by war" (177).

WORKS CITED

Anderson, Benedict. *Imagined Communities: Reflections on the Origin and Spread of Nationalism*. London: Verso, 1983.

Bourdieu, Pierre. *Masculine Domination*. Trans. Richard Nice. Stanford: Stanford University Press, 2001.

Buschendorf, Christa, Astrid Franke, and Johannes Voelz. Introduction. In *Civilizing and Decivilizing Processes: Figurational Approaches to American Culture*, ed. Christa Buschendorf, Astrid Franke, and Johannes Voelz. Newcastle upon Tyne: Cambridge Scholars Publishing, 2011. 1–16.

Calhoun, Craig. "Nationalism and Ethnicity." *Annual Review of Sociology* 19 (1993): 211–239.

Carpio, Glenda. Introduction. In *The Gift of Black Folk: The Oxford W. E. B. Du Bois*. Ed. Henry Louis Gates Jr. New York: Oxford University Press, 2007. xxiii–xxvi.

Colaiaco, James A. *Frederick Douglass and the Fourth of July Oration*. New York: Palgrave Macmillan, 2006.

Cone, James H. *Martin & Malcolm & America: A Dream or a Nightmare*. New York: Orbis Books, 1991.

Douglass, Frederick. *Autobiographies*. New York: Library of America, 1994.

———. *The Frederick Douglass Papers*. Series 1. *Speeches, Debates, and Interviews*. Vol. 4. *1864–80*. Ed. John W. Blassingame and John R. McKivigan. New Haven: Yale University Press, 1991.

———. *Selected Speeches and Writings*. Ed. Philip S. Foner. Abridged and adapted by Yuval Taylor. Chicago: Lawrence Hill, 1999.

Du Bois, W. E. B. *The Autobiography of W. E. B. Du Bois: A Soliloquy on Viewing My Life from the Last Decade of Its First Century*. New York: International Publishers, 1968.

———. "The Conservation of Races." In *Pamphlets and Leaflets by W. E. B. Du Bois*. Ed. Herbert Aptheker. White Plains, N.Y: Kraus-Thomson, 1986. 1–8.

———. *Dusk of Dawn: An Essay toward an Autobiography of a Race Concept*. *The Oxford W. E. B. Du Bois*. Ed. Henry Louis Gates Jr. New York: Oxford University Press, 2007.

Elias, Norbert. *The Civilizing Process: Sociogenetic and Psychogenetic Investigations* [1939]. Ed. Eric Dunning, Johan Goudsblom, and Stephen Mennell. Trans. Edmund Jephcott. Oxford: Blackwell, 2000.

———. *The Germans: Power Struggles and the Development of Habitus in the Nineteenth and Twentieth Centuries* [1989]. Ed. Michael Schroeter. Trans. Eric Dunning and Stephen Mennell. New York: Columbia University Press, 1996.

———. *The Society of Individuals*. Ed. Michael Schröter. Trans. Edmund Jephcott. New York: Continuum, 1991.

———. *What Is Sociology?* [1970]. Trans. Stephen Mennell and Grace Morrissey. New York: Columbia University Press, 1978.

Elias, Norbert, and John L. Scotson. *The Established and the Outsiders*. Vol. 4 of *The Collected Works of Norbert Elias*. Ed. Cas Wouters. Dublin: University College Dublin Press, 2008.

Gates, Henry Louis, Jr. "The Black Letters on the Sign: W. E. B. Du Bois and the Canon." Series introduction. In *The Oxford W. E. B. Du Bois*. Ed. Henry Louis Gates Jr. New York: Oxford University Press, 2007. xi–xxiv.

Johnson, Richard A. *African-American Sociopolitical Philosophy: Imagining Black Communities*. Lewiston, N.Y.: Edwin Mellen Press, 2004.

King, Martin Luther, Jr. *Where Do We Go from Here: Chaos or Community?* Boston: Beacon Press, 2010.

Levine, Robert S. *Dislocating Race and Nation: Episodes in Nineteenth-Century American Literary Nationalism*. Chapel Hill: University of North Carolina Press, 2008.

Mennell, Stephen. *The American Civilizing Process*. Cambridge: Polity Press, 2007.

Paulle, Bowen, Bart van Heerikhuizen, and Mustafa Emirbayer. "Elias and Bourdieu." In *The Legacy of Pierre Bourdieu: Critical Essays*. Ed. Simon Susen and Bryan S. Turner. London: Anthem, 2011. 145–172.

Susen, Simon, and Bryan S. Turner. Introduction. In *The Legacy of Pierre Bourdieu: Critical Essays*. Ed. Simon Susen and Bryan S. Turner. London: Anthem, 2011. xiii–xxix.

Taylor, Charles. "Nationalism and Modernity." In *The State of the Nation: Ernest Gellner and the Theory of Nationalism*. Ed. John A. Hall. Cambridge: Cambridge University Press, 1998. 191–218.

Wacquant, Loïc. "Bourdieu in America: Notes on the Transatlantic Importation of Social Theory." In *Bourdieu: Critical Perspectives*. Ed. Craig Calhoun, Edward LiPuma, and Moishe Postone. Chicago: University of Chicago Press, 1993. 235–262.

West, Cornel. "On Black Nationalism" [1989]. In *The Cornel West Reader*. New York: Basic Civitas Books, 1999. 521–529.

Wortham, Robert A., ed. *W. E. B. Du Bois and the Sociological Imagination: A Reader, 1897–1914*. Waco, Tex.: Baylor University Press, 2009.

Wouters, Cas. *Informalization: Manners and Emotions since 1890*. London: Sage, 2007.

6 Russia's Californio Romance

The Other Shores of Whitman's Pacific

See how the metaphor of the West dissolves into foam at our feet.
—RICHARD RODRIGUEZ, BROWN: *The Last Discovery of America*

On the morning of March 28, 1806, an envoy of the Russian American Company, Nikolai Petrovitch Rezanov, decided to ignore the Spanish ban on trade with foreign ships and sailed right into the harbor of San Francisco. "Knowing the suspicious nature of the Spanish government," he wrote, "I thought it best to go straight through the gate and by the fort . . . and decided that two or three cannonballs would make less difference to us than refusal" (*Voyage* 11). The journey that had brought Rezanov to San Francisco was the first Russian circumnavigation, begun in St. Petersburg in 1803. He had sailed south along the coast of western Africa, around the Cape, and east across the Indian Ocean, then northbound past the Japanese coast to the Bering Strait. Arriving in Sitka three years later, Rezanov found this outpost of the Russian Empire near starvation after an unusually severe winter. He took a handful of reasonably able men with him and proceeded south to Spanish Nueva California and the settlement in San Francisco to try to buy much-needed "breadstuffs" for the starving colony.

A more long-term concern also motivated the trip south, namely, to test the northern boundaries of the Spanish Empire in the Americas and bring Russia into the marketplace of the new world. In his reports back to St. Petersburg, Rezanov would optimistically prophesy that "the industries of interior Russia will receive a new impulse when the number of factories will have to be increased on account of the California trade alone, and in the mean time ways will be found for trade with India by way of Siberia" (*Voyage* 42). The confidence these lines exude speaks of many things, among them the transnational, indeed trans-imperial character of California in the early nineteenth century, and the multiplicity of differently originated points of view, imaginations, and imaginaries it already played host to. While it may not have been one of the more momentous historical events in American history, the account of Rezanov's visit with the commander of the San Francisco Presidio and the governor of Nueva California during those few spring weeks of 1806 meaningfully echoes with what Peter Hitchcock calls "the experience of globality" (7).

In her essay "Place in Fiction" Eudora Welty observes that "to the writer at work, [place] is seen in a frame. Not an empty frame, a brimming one. Point of view is a sort of burning-glass, a product of personal experience and time; it is burnished with feelings and sensibilities, charged from moment to moment with the sun-points of imagination" (114). Welty's conceptualization of the locale's import may serve well as an entry point to the relatively little-known encounter between Russian and Spanish plenipotentiaries in what is today the Bay Area. For what she calls a "brimming frame" applies not merely to the artist at work; it is a lens through which other kinds of perspectives can also see. To expand this into the sphere of culture, we may borrow from Bakhtin his conceptualization of situatedness, of (culturological) consciousness as always configured by the specifics of temporal and spatial circumstance and circumscription. Such situatedness consequently generates unique points of view and corresponds to what in Bakhtin is knotted into the chronotope—the organizing principle for narrative, always carried in relation to other, also unique, points of view (*Dialogic*). Transposed onto the culturological scene where the Russian-Spanish meeting was staged, such chronotopic perspective must, however, be perceived, and tentatively gauged, within the broader framework of the "feelings and sensibilities" that charge the cultural, social imaginaries and thus authorize their "frame," their unique way of seeing.

I use the concept of social imaginaries here according to what the philosopher Charles Taylor in general terms describes as "the ways people imagine their social existence, how they fit together with others, how things go on between them and their fellows, the expectations that are normally met, and the deeper normative notions and images that underlie these expectations" (23). Underpinning this seemingly straightforward explication, however, is a wealth of intricate contingencies.[1] The imaginary, Taylor continues, is "carried in images, stories, legends," "is shared by large groups of people," and constitutes "that common understanding that makes possible common practices and a widely shared sense of legitimacy" (23). Taylor's "sense of legitimacy" aligns closely with Welty's description of point of view in a collective context as the "product of personal experience and time," for we cannot conceive of legitimacy without also inferring a situated consciousness, communal or individual, which provides the "background understanding" necessary in order for the social imaginary to make sense, to be precisely legitimate.

This brings us to the next, crucial node in Taylor's thesis, that "if the [background] understanding makes the practice possible, it is also true that it is the practice that largely carries the understanding. At any given time, we can speak of the 'repertory' of collective actions at the disposal of a given group of society" (25). The social imaginary can consequently be conceived of as a kind of enabling—and enabled—frame, or filter, through which a group, community, or society sees, grasps, and performs an understanding of its own practices. To elaborate a little further on the frame or filter, it may be useful to turn to another thinker whose calibrations of the imaginary interestingly complement those of Taylor. Cornelius Castoriadis talks not about the modern social imaginary but about the more general and always present "*instituted* social imaginary." This is specifically "a constitutive faculty of human collectivities, and more generally of the social-historical sphere," among whose work are institutions, "quickened by—and bearers of—significations." These significations, Castoriadis continues, "refer neither to reality nor to logic, which is why I call them social imaginary significations" ("Imaginary" 73). The accent on the less tangible elements is more clearly explicated in his suggestion that the imaginary has to "use the symbolic not only to 'express' itself (this is self-evident), but to 'exist,' to pass from the virtual to anything more than this" (*Institution* 127). This latter observation is particularly relevant to the focus of this essay: one could argue that it was precisely the varying instantiations and institutions of the symbolic that at least in part would determine the future of Russia's and Spain's roles on the Pacific coast. For there is a third party present in the scenario briefly sketched earlier but not yet explicitly mentioned, and that is the newly constituted Americans and *their* sense of legitimacy, their understanding and practices, and subsequent enabling and enabled (chronotopic) frame. In Rezanov's reports, however, references to this imaginary are largely absent.

With these conceptual scaffolding preliminaries in mind, I want to explore the Russian-Spanish encounter in northern California along the following itinerary. First, as I show, the exchanges resulting from the visit serve to illustrate the already existing characteristics of the California coast as a node of economic and political transnational matrixes on a global scale. Second, I want to suggest that this lesser-known relation both exemplifies and, more important, anticipates other social imaginaries' encounters with the newcomer, which in 1806 was still mostly confined at some distance from the west coast. Finally, "Russia's Californio romance" speaks to the kind of palimpsesting that processes of transnationalization inevitably bring with them. Key here is, again, perspective and place, and the enabling frames and senses of legitimacy that at any given point lay claim to the overwriting of the frames already present.

California Songs

Let me begin with the voice that in the nineteenth century would sing the American imaginary more than any other, and would celebrate *post factum* the locale that once had framed the Russian-Spanish encounter. For, depending of course on the artist, any location can potentially transpire with the promise and wealth Welty speaks of, but when the artist is Walt Whitman and the place is California, "brimming" and "charge" reach particularly intense levels:

> I see in you, certain to come, the promise of thousands of years,
> till now deferr'd,
> Promis'd to be fulfill'd, our common kind, the race.
> The new society at last, proportionate to Nature,
> In man of you, more than your mountain peaks or stalwart trees imperial,
> In woman more, far more, than all your gold or vines, or even vital air.
> Fresh come, to a new world indeed, yet long prepared,
> I see the genius of the modern, child of the real and ideal,
> Clearing the ground for broad humanity, the true America, heir of
> the past so grand,
> To build a grander future. ("Song of the Redwood-Tree" 465)

"Song of the Redwood-Tree," from 1874, articulates a vision of the past yielding to the future under the auspices of progress and democracy in familiar Whitmanesque style. The closing lines of the poem capture a sensibility to and a conviction of advancement that suggest the California coast as more than just an emblem of national significance. As we shall see later, it comes to stand as a singular trope of modernity in the "new world," a harbinger of "a grander future" and "the promise of thousands of years," thus imagining and inscribing, as happened in so much of Whitman's work, this new cultural imaginary.

He was of course not the first to imagine and frame California in triumphant and near-fantastical terms, and neither was he the first (nor the last, for that matter) to prophesy the role it would, or should, have. Centuries before Whitman saw "the genius of the modern" in California, the coast had been host to what James Clifford describes as "the mix of human times we call history: the long span of indigenous traditions and folk histories; the waxing and waning of tribes and nations, of empires; the struggles and ruses of conquest, adaptation, survival; the movements of natives, explorers, and immigrants, with their distinct relations to land, place, and memory; the changing rhythm of markets, commodities, communications, capital—organizing and disorganizing everything" (302) .

The twenty or more Indian tribes who lived between what is today Oregon and the Mexican border when Juan Cabrillo made landfall in San Diego in 1542 covered among them six different language families. All the tribes had different names for the places where they dwelled, and hence, "in the tribal mind and in the tribal world, [California] did not exist" (Hicks et al. 2). Indeed, the very name California is, as we know, itself the result of fiction, conjured up in Garcí Ordoñez Rodriguez de Motalvo's romance *Las Sergas de Esplandián* (The Adventures of Esplandián), published in Madrid in 1510. Herein is described an island populated by Amazon women who are led by their Queen Calafia, and so, "long before the name appeared on maps, California had a place in the European mind" (Hicks et al. 76–77). Much, much later, in 1850, Marx and Engels would assess the discovery of gold in California:

> The Californian gold mines were only discovered eighteen months ago and the Yankees have already set about building a railway, a great overland road and a canal from the Gulf of Mexico, steamships are already sailing regularly from New York to Chagres, from Panama to San Francisco, Pacific trade is already concentrating in Panama and the journey around Cape Horn has become obsolete. A coastline which stretches across thirty degrees of latitude, one of the most beautiful and fertile in the world and hitherto more or less unpopulated, is now being visibly transformed into a rich, civilized land thickly populated by men of all races, from the Yankee to the Chinese, from the Negro to the Indian and Malay, from the Creole and Mestizo to the European. (8)

The emphases on the trade routes that open up, and on the prospect of confluence, prosperity, and movement of peoples and commodities that follow, already define the dynamics of a globalization of economies and cultures at a rather early point. As in Whitman's "California Song," as the "Redwood" poem is also called, Marx and Engel's reflections do not significantly question the direction of the "transformation" of "the most beautiful and fertile" land into one that is "civilized" and "thickly populated." And as in Whitman, the direction of the modern, what he calls the "chant of the future," is not problematized: the lines "Ships coming in from the whole round world, and going out to / the whole world, / To India and China and Australia, and the thousand island / paradises of the Pacific" refract the sentiment celebrating the transnational in strangely similar tenors (465).

These are only a few samples from the vast repository of the chronicles of encounters, sojourns, interpellations, real as well as fictional and mythical, that have furnished the California coast with its complex and rich history. Whether they are actual historical events or the stuff of imagination, they can all be deciphered according to temporal and spatial circumstances. Hence this short list of presences and perspectives already exemplifies the argument Arjun Appadurai makes in relation to area studies generally: "We need to recognize that histories produce geographies and not vice versa. We must get away from the notion that there is some kind of spatial landscape against which time writes its story. Instead, it is historical agents, institutions, actors, powers that make the geography" (9).

One such historical agent on the Pacific coast was the Russian Empire, albeit admittedly not one that would go on to "produce locality" quite as notably as would other agents and powers. This lesser-known history of the encounter and exchanges between the representatives of the Spanish and Russian empires' outposts at the beginning of the nineteenth century is, however, worth attention, not only, as we will see, because of its dramatic and romantic patina, but also because it is one of those seemingly immaterial accounts that turn out to encapsulate and refract in miniature version larger narratives that more obviously and crucially serve history. One of the lessons we may draw from the story is, as Hitchcock puts it, the way that cultural transnationalism is "first and foremost about the experience of globality"—and "whose imagination?" (7). Russia's "experience of globality" began in earnest with that first journey around the world in 1803, and it had, as mentioned, several objectives: one was to inspect the Russian Empire's farthest reaches in today's Alaska, another to explore trans-Pacific supply routes and the possibilities of opening up trade with China and Japan. According to the tsar's designs, the northwestern Pacific could be annexed into the Russian Basin, and in this way strengthen the easternmost boundaries of his reign.

The commander of the Presidio, Don Luis Dário Argüello, was away at the time Rezanov and his party entered the port of San Fransciso in full sail, but his son, Don Luis Antonio Argüello, had been notified of the arrival and welcomed the Russians in a most gracious and hospitable manner. There were some initial language problems; Rezanov's personal doctor, the naturalist Georg von Langsdorff, notes in his journal that "[as] neither Lieutenant Davidov nor myself understood Spanish, the conversation was carried on in Latin, between me and the Franciscan padre, this being the only medium by which either one could make himself intelligible to the other" (*Langdorff's Narrative* 38). Rezanov's own account of the visit is heartfelt and enthusiastic, and the renderings in his reports of the exchanges between the two government representatives in these outposts of each one's empire are almost touching. They speak far away from cosmopolitan and administrative centers in old as well as in new lands, and come across today as strangely unmoored from these other realities, which would come to determine the future of much of the world.

In his letters Rezanov cites several dialogues that wonderfully illustrate this. For instance, on his way to see the recently arrived governor of Nueva California, José Joaquín de Arrillaga, Rezanov asks his companion, one of the mission's padres, if he has been granted permission yet to buy "breadstuffs" from the Spaniards. The padre, a little uneasily, tells him of ominous reports: "I must answer you in confidence. Previous to his leaving Monterey the Gobernador received news from Mexico to the effect that if we are not at war with you now we soon shall be. 'What blunder!' said I, laughingly. 'Would I have come here at such a time?' 'That is what we said,' the Padre replied" (21).

As news of the Napoleonic Wars in Europe begins reaching San Francisco shortly after this exchange, the disjuncture between local, peripheral bonhomie and the rising hostilities among the imperial centers becomes more pressing. The governor is acutely aware of this, and in a very open address to Rezanov in connection with a trade agreement they are negotiating, he tells him very directly: "I acknowledge that I wish you success with all my heart, but I cannot conceal the fact that I hourly expect a report of a total breach of concord between our governments. I do not know how to meet and consider your project, and I must tell you frankly that it would be very agreeable to me if you would hasten your departure in a friendly manner before the arrival of the courier expected by me" (30).

The deliberations between Governor Arrillaga and Rezanov, who would become close friends during the latter's stay, refract interesting references to the conceptions of global trade routes, international foreign policy, and, for the purposes of this essay, their relationship to the United States and the future destiny of the coast. We should bear in mind that Rezanov's reports were written only three years after Jefferson had secured the Louisiana Territory, and while Jefferson harbored no immediate plan for pushing the boundaries of the new territory farther west at the time, the sentiments that would be collapsed into the powerful trope of Manifest Destiny were already circulating. Several years earlier Jefferson had noted, "Our Confederacy must be viewed as the nest from which all America, North and South, is to be peopled" (quoted in Horsman 86). His Lewis and Clark expedition was in progress while Rezanov was staying in San Francisco, and was completed in the fall of 1806. We may now wonder how these movements could be so absent from the dialogues of Arrillaga and Rezanov, but they seem to have found events in Europe far more relevant than whatever was going on more immediately to the east. The reports Rezanov sent home abound with the exchanges he has with the Spanish governor and commander about European relations, Bonaparte's forays, trade agreements, and their respective imperial administrations' unwillingness to bolster their peripheries. The last is a recurring topic of conversation. An exasperated Arrillaga tells Rezanov that quite often when he solicits assistance from Mexico, the answer he receives is a Mexicans cursing of California as "causing nothing but problems and expenses!"—as if the problems were *his* fault (*Voyage* 55).

This complaint is connected to the few times their conversations touch on the American states. On a couple of occasions Arrillaga refers to the problems the "Bostonians" are giving Nueva California, confiding that "the audacity of the Bostonians has alarmed us, but the ministers have promised to dispatch a frigate this year to watch the vessels from the American states" (56). Rezanov on his part expresses confidence in the workings of diplomacy, and in reassuring tones reports back to St. Petersburg that the Americans "claim the right to [the northern Pacific] shore, as the headwaters of the Columbia River are in their territory, but, upon the same principle, they could extend their possessions to all the country wherein there are no European settlements. But they will, I think, discontinue making settlements there, for the Spaniards have opened to them four ports on the Eastern coast of America, and they are excluded from touching the western coasts of America by a commercial agreement" (72).

In his account Rezanov thus appears oblivious to the significance of the Pacific in the designs of the newcomer to the east. For as we know, the "audacity" of the "Bostonians" (so called because the majority of early American sea merchants hailed from Boston) would only forty years later be carried out on a military and ideological scale that realized the mythological quality of California as, the explorer Charles Wilkes noted in 1839, the controller "of the destinies of the Pacific" (McDougall 93). Mexico would gain independence from Spain in 1821, and in 1842 the Russians would withdraw to Alaska. Shortly after, the commander of Northern California, Don Mariano Guadalupe Vallejo, would be ousted from his home in Sonoma and imprisoned at Fort Sutter in Sacramento. Two years later Vallejo and his fellow Californios were American citizens; then, in 1849, gold was found, and this, as we saw, would be assessed by Marx and Engels as "the most important thing which has happened in America" (7). The prosperity they prophesied would sure enough come true, but not the coexistence of disparate peoples. The determination of Anglo-American forty-niners overran that of other groups, and Marx's interracial "rich, civilized" land was soon in the hands of only some. I come back to all of this a little later; for now I want to return to Rezanov, for his visit to San Francisco was not all business.

Rezanov had quite early on fallen head over heels in love with the commander's daughter, Maria Concepción Argüello. The romance is mentioned briefly in his reports; a little abashedly he tells the minister in St. Petersburg that he apologizes for divulging such personal affairs but that after "associating daily with and paying his address to the beautiful Spanish senorita," he at last "proffered his hand, and she accepted," agreeing to move to Russia after the marriage (37). The romance is immortalized in Bret Harte's long poem "Concepcion de Arguello":

Count von Resanoff, the Russian, envoy of the mighty Czar,
Stood beside the deep embrasures, where the brazen
cannon are.
He with grave provincial magnates long had held serene
debate
On the Treaty of Alliance and the high affairs of state;
He from grave provincial magnates oft had turned to talk
apart
With the Commandante's daughter on the questions of the
heart,
Until points of gravest import yielded slowly one by one,
And by Love was consummated what Diplomacy begun. (sec. 2)

When Rezanov left the Presidio in the late spring of 1806 it was with the promise of a speedy return to his future wife once the tsar and the pope had blessed the mixed marriage, and a pledge to continue working on the plans for these fringes of his empire. This was, however, not to be. On the way back to St. Petersburg, traveling across Siberia on horseback, Rezanov suffered from three bouts of pneumonia and died at the beginning of March 1807. Various accounts tell the story differently, but most sources maintain that the news did not reach Doña Concepcion until two years later. She then joined a Dominican order and spent the rest of her life in the monastery, dedicating her life to helping others until her death in 1857. She is, incidentally, buried in the least known of California's several early capitals, Benicia.

The last stanzas of Harte's poem tell of the end of the romance. The voice we hear inquiring about the couple is Sir George Simpson, governor of the Hudson's Bay Company, who visited Santa Barbara early in 1842. These concluding lines also serve to end this part of my discussion:

> "Died while speeding home to Russia, falling from a fractious
> horse.
> Left a sweetheart, too, they tell me. Married, I suppose,
> of course!
> "Lives she yet?" A deathlike silence fell on banquet, guests,
> and hall,
> And a trembling figure rising fixed the awestruck gaze of all.
> Two black eyes in darkened orbits gleamed beneath the
> nun's white hood;
> Black serge hid the wasted figure, bowed and stricken
> where it stood.
> "Lives she yet?" Sir George repeated. All were hushed as
> Concha drew
> Closer yet her nun's attire. "Señor, pardon, she died, too!"

"To You, the Empire New"

The Rezanov story has come down to us as one of California's great love stories; indeed it is part of California's "romantic history." The inscription in *The Rezanov Voyage to Nueva California*, published by the Private Press of Thomas C. Russell in 1926, reads: "To C.O.G. Miller, Esq. of San Francisco, who, amid his multifarious business interests, is never-failing in his interest in the romantic history of California." The kind of historiography that casts things past and gone in the Golden State as romantic speaks to an ideologically "soft" overwriting that certainly finds worthy outlets in fictionalized accounts such as Harte's poem, Gertrude

Atherton's *Rezanov* (1906), and Alexey Rybnikov's opera *Juno and Avos* (1981). But if we look at the story as embedded precisely in ideologically circumscribed circumstances premised on Hitchcock's "experience of globality," as underlying the geography made by "historical agents," other and harder lessons may be learned. For it has something to tell us about temporal and spatial realities, and should consequently be considered the material of what Susan Friedman calls "locational 'thick descriptions' of historically and geographically specific situations'" (90). This approach, she argues, "stresses mutual agencies on all sides, though not necessarily equally unencumbered agencies," and privileges the multi-temporal and multi-spatial complexities of colonial, postcolonial, and indeed neocolonial practices and stories (90). Thus, the particular situatedness of "Russia's Californio romance" also details the extent to which the new world served as a stage for the European powers' scrambling for primacy, at home as well as abroad. It tells us how differently the actors conceived of their geographical and cultural destinations and the routes leading there, and of the kinds of imaginaries in which their expansionist designs were embedded as they encountered one another on California's shores.

We may begin by noting that for the Russians as well as the Spanish, the California coast was merely a north-south/south-north axis, and the new world simply that, a "new" world, a market to claim. We hear Rezanov cautioning his government, "There is still left an unoccupied intervening territory fully as rich, and if we allow it to slip through our fingers, what will succeeding generations say?" (*Voyage* 45), a warning first and foremost referring to the threat posed by Spain to Russian expansion, not by the United States. This leads to a second consideration, namely, that to Europeans posted in the Americas in the early nineteenth century, the activities of other Europeans were far more critical than anybody else's. The United States had not yet made much of a dent in foreign policy; Rezanov's visit is still two decades or so before Monroe declares the Americas to be off limits to European influence. And still, as we have seen, there is evidence of certain worries about the Bostonians in Rezanov's conversations which direct our attention to problems possibly existing already in 1806. Walter McDougall observes that as early as 1801, Jefferson had marked the continent for his own purposes: "Our rapid multiplication will . . . cover the whole northern if not southern continent, with people speaking the same language, governed by similar forms, and by similar laws" (quoted in McDougall 78). Commenting on John L. O'Sullivan's coining of the phrase "Manifest Destiny" in 1845, McDougall furthermore points to the much earlier beginnings of what he calls its tradition:

"If the United States was to remain free and independent—the first tradition[,] . . . then it must pursue a unilateral foreign policy—the second tradition. If Unilateralism was to survive, then it must promote an American System of states—the third tradition. But . . . it must preempt European bids for influence over the vast unsettled lands that remained in North America—the fourth tradition" (77–78).

On the one hand, clearly neither Rezanov nor Arrillaga can be blamed for not having spotted this connection; but on the other hand, the foundation of absolute principles that McDougall identifies also lets us see how, and why, the presence of these other nations on the California coast could not last; how, as Whitman would put it in his "Redwood" poem later on, "the New arriving, assuming, taking possession, / A swarming and busy race settling and organizing everything" was not about to be stopped ("Song" 465). Nevertheless, Californio and Russian obliviousness to the particular energy in the East may ultimately also be caused by more elusive rationales, rooted in the imaginaries that embedded their understandings and practices as slightly different from those of the newcomer.

On a basic level, Spain and Russia of course had their own countries and centers elsewhere to worry about, and did not absolutely have to make a go at it in the new world. More crucially, though, they lacked a coherent vision founded in symbolic conceptions of California and the coast as an area providing the newness necessary to a new experiment, a project in the world. This was, after all, what underlay the point of view from the East, what as early as 1786 can be detected in Jefferson's aforementioned prophecy about the "Confederacy as the nest from which all America, North and South, is to be peopled."

Distinguishing the instantiation of the American imaginary is consequently a kind of symbolic coherence that already at this stage launches purpose, presence, and perspective radically differently from that of the Spanish and the Russians. Among the central elements of this variable are differing understandings of temporality, as Richard Rodriguez poignantly observes:

The two groups (Spanish and English) had different ambitions. Spaniards dreamt of gold. Spanish settlement was also, of course, Roman Catholic and connected the United States with Mexico, and through Mexico to the court of Madrid and the Church of Rome—a continuous line uniting past with present.Low-church English Puritans tended to be in rebellion against English memory; everything was focused on the future. (20)

A similar link from past to present via religion could be posited in Russia's case, and, as Gwenn Miller notes, the teaching of Orthodoxy to colonial subjects in the Kodiak Islands was explicitly endorsed by, among others, Rezanov himself (112–113).

Anchoring the future of new worlds in spiritual centers in the old thus forges a kind of continuity that, as Rodriguez notes, envelops the actors of the present in a backward-looking gaze. Related to this temporal enactment of continuity is a spatial one: the overextended Spanish and Russian empires both had rather uncertain edges. By that I have in mind the way centers' relation to peripheries proceeded along principles of gradation rather than breach. In Russia's case this was a function of the overland routes early explorers traversed before the circumnavigations started in 1803. Ilya Vinkovetsky notes that "the Russian crossings of Siberia were greatly assisted by the indigenous Siberians who lived along the way. The diversity among [these] cultures is impressive, but what is particularly salient is that some of these cultures . . . bore striking similarities to the indigenous cultures that the Russians would find on the North American side of the Pacific. . . . In a very real sense, in the eighteenth century, for the *sibiriaki* (the Russians of Siberia) the line between the so-called Old World and New World remained blurred and fuzzy" (196).

Somewhat in the same vein, when Spanish explorers traveled north from today's Mexico City into the present American Southwest, they, too, traveled through a space of cultural gradation: Native American peoples in New Mexico, for instance, had much in common with peoples farther south. One might also add here that the rate of intermarriage between ethnic Russians and indigenous Aleuts led to the introduction of the term *kreoly*, and it was in fact Rezanov himself who was the first to use the term, if only informally (Vinkovetsky 201). In the Spanish colonies, of course, the corresponding term was from early on *mestizo*, the first generation of whom were born in Peru around the mid-sixteenth century. In several ways, then, the routes from the centers of the two empires into the new world marked not a definite breach (with the periphery as inherently and irreconcilably Other, different, and past), but a more blurred and continuous trail that may also have posited frontiers that were more porous.

They were certainly different from the route leading from Virginia to the California coast; that trail blazes through the lands of numerous Others until those lands are collapsed into the nation's own fold, a "rolling westward" that sets out to erase or accommodate all difference into its own specific vision. In it are the callings of the Exemplary and Destiny, the future-oriented gaze of, as Whitman puts it, "the Genius of the Modern, child of the Real and Ideal," posed to "build a grander future" ("Song" 465). In the same way that O'Sullivan simply packed a composite of already existing principles into Manifest Destiny, so Whitman gives poetic voice to an energy that long preceded his "Redwood" poem. The history of that energy, if we may call it that, is certainly complex, but in relation to social-imaginary significations and the trajectory of its symbolic institutions, an important trace reaches back to what David Lowenthal locates thus: "In severing imperial bonds, Americans discarded not only the mother country but many of its traditions. Three interrelated ideas helped justify dismissal of the past: a belief that autonomy was the birthright of each successive generation; an organic analogy that assigned America to a place of youth in history; and a faith that the new nation was divinely exempt from decay and decline" (105). Coming to the "new" sense of temporality from a slightly different angle, Lowenthal nevertheless echoes the emphasis on breach rather than continuity, pointing at a frame or a filter predicated on future orientation rather than the previously mentioned backward-looking gaze.

We can tune this perspective further by turning to what Sacvan Bercovitch in a related vein calls the "America game." "America" is a "language game of malleable beginnings and possible futures," he says, quite different from its "old world" relatives, where nationality "remains an endgame puzzle: identity to be resolved in three or four moves" (54–55). Instead what we have in the America game, a middle game, Bercovitch continues, is newness as a "continual movement toward endings that issue in an endless affirmation of beginnings" (54). This returns us squarely to a spatial and temporal orientation that sees ahead, unhampered by ties to a past, released from old world imaginaries and their sway. Whitman's redwoods in northern California thus "leave the field for them / For a superber Race—they too to grandly fill their time" and abdicate "To the new Culminating Man—to you, the Empire New" ("Song" 463). In a game that was begun before the beginning of the nineteenth century, California's multiple presences and perspectives had little to offer. As we have seen, only four decades after Rezanov's visit, the space of California was thoroughly rearranged according to "the New arriving, assuming, taking possession."

The "genius of the modern" thus names a layer in the California transnational cultural palimpsest that would erase most of the presences that had come before. In his time, Rezanov had great plans for Russia in America. "Your excellency perhaps may laugh at my far-reaching plans," he tells the minister in St. Petersburg, "but I am certain that they will prove exceedingly profitable ventures, and if we had men and means, even without any great sacrifice on the part of the treasury, all this country could be made a corporeal part of the Russian empire" (*Voyage* 44). In retrospect, one suspects that more than "men and means" would have been required, and of the Russian presence only a small memento is left. About four hours' drive north of San Francisco there is a settlement called Fort Ross, the direct result of Rezanov's negotiations in 1806, and the place that for a short while marked the southernmost point of the Russian Empire in America.[2] About twenty weather-beaten Russian Orthodox crosses overlook the little fort and the Pacific. Today it is a state park, with volunteers looking after it and tending to the orchards that in their time helped supply the Russian colonists in Alaska with the much-needed "breadstuffs" Rezanov finally was allowed to buy from Governor Arrillaga.

The other layer, the Spanish one, is far more noticeable, and is allowed to be "read" in service to tourism and the romantic Californio history mentioned earlier. The twenty-one missions remain where they were built, and they must be taken care of, not only for the sake of the mythical past they have been relegated to but also in service to the very real present. At least half of them still serve their parishes. Among these is the Misión San Francisco de Asís in San Francisco, or Mission Dolores as it is better known, and this would have been the home of the padres Rezanov conversed with. So Spain and Russia are all but relegated to myth, and it is the "Bostonians' audacity," constituted in and by the frame of a "grander future," that seems to have prevailed in the reality of the present, which has passed from the symbolic into the instituted imaginary. And yet, as with most erasures and overlayerings, the underlying scripts, as Sarah Dillon notes, remain. All palimpsests imply the inscription and superimposition of new, emerging worlds and ideas, but built in to the dynamics of this very domination is the observation that palimpsests "paradoxically preserved [ancient texts] for posterity" (Dillon 7). In other words, intended absence becomes unintended presence, and the dual nature of the missions, as simultaneously serving the Spanish mythical past and the very real parishes of the present, is a compelling illustration.

These missions are central tropes now in the *Mexican* presence on the coast, a presence that surfaced from underneath New Spain's coating, and even if the American rush toward the Pacific intended to erase this layer, it is there. It does not matter that Senator John C. Calhoun, before his government declared war on Mexico in 1846, predicted that Mexicans would fade away: "We do not want the people of Mexico either as citizens or subjects. All we want is a portion of territory, which they nominally hold, generally uninhabited, or, where at all, sparsely so, and with a population, which would soon recede, or identify itself with ours" (quoted in Horsman 241). For all the subsequent erasures after 1848 (breaches of treaties, border policing, fences, deportations), the population would not quite recede, and neither would it identify entirely with the Anglo. Instead, Mexico in the transnational California palimpsest has been preserved despite and because of its overwriting first by Spanish, then by American layers. Imaginaries, therefore, as carriers of background understandings and their practices, as bearers of significations, do not simply supersede and replace, once and for all. Rather, as frames or filters they linger, they overlay one another with various spatial anchorings, testimonies to Bakhtin's often quoted comment that "at any moment in the development there are immense, boundless masses of forgotten contextual meanings, but at certain moments of the dialogue's subsequent development along the way they are recalled and invigorated in renewed form (in a new context). Nothing is absolutely dead: every meaning will have its homecoming festival" (*Speech Genres* 170).

And consequently, in what Norma Klahn calls the "Mexican social imaginary," the West poses as North, "offering a re/membering," as she says, "that re-imagines, recalls and unifies" (167). I want to fasten on to reimagining, and the way that the Mexican imaginary also in a sense interrupts the tropological sway that California as trope of national significance and project of modernity has held and continues to hold in the American imaginary. For if Whitman had it right—and I believe it is fair to say that, from within the imaginary and the vantage point of the Anglo-American rush across the continent from which he spoke, he had it exactly right—California was indeed to be the land of "a swarming and busy race settling and organizing everything." Both then and later that particular energy can be attributed to what Richard Rodriguez with reference to our own time calls the "Quest for I." He suggests that one reason why voices are raised in protest against the Hispanification of America is the fear "of losing the individualistic culture . . .—the 'I' civilization." Rodriguez further suggests that "even if most Mexican immigrants coming to the United States, legally or illegally, are in quest of the 'I,' though they do not say it, they of course also bring with them aspects of their 'we' culture" (Interview 21). Thus the sometimes ironic way of history brushes off some of the veneer from the most recent layer in the transnational California palimpsest and recalls other imaginaries that came before.

Another irony: as a result of the recent financial crisis and numerous cutbacks in the early years of the twenty-first century, the Russians are back in Fort Ross. In 2009 word reached Moscow that Governor Arnold Schwarzenegger intended to drop the funding for Fort Ross as one of many California state parks. The Russian government promptly sent Ambassador Sergey Kislyak to save the little fort, and on his visit with the California governor, Kislyak "pleaded [with him] to spare the site," saying it "holds significant cultural, historic and sentimental value for the Kremlin, Russians and Russian Americans" ("Russians Urge Governor"). Although the governor could not make any such promise at the time, a year later the president of the Renova Group, a Russian conglomerate interested in expanding its markets, signed a three-year agreement to sponsor Fort Ross as it was nearing its bicentennial in 2012. While these renewed relations did not mean all that much in the everyday lives of either Californians or Russians, this chapter added to the story of Russia's California romance, and to the nature of the transnational palimpsest of imaginaries of which it was a part.

• • •

By way of conclusion I return to Whitman, singing the nation, the self, and California, but also, as he famously proclaims in "Song of Myself," contradicting himself. It may be that deep down there was a kind of unease with the canvassing progress he catalogued, for in another of his California poems, "Facing West from California's Shores" (1860), which was written more than a decade before the "Redwood" poem, he strikes a very different tone. It is a fairly short poem, so I include the whole of it:

FACING west, from California's shores,
Inquiring, tireless, seeking what is yet unfound,
I, a child, very old, over waves, towards the house of maternity,
the land of migrations, look afar,
Look off the shores of my Western sea—the circle almost
circled;
For, starting westward from Hindustan, from the vales of Kash-
mere,
From Asia—from the north—from the God, the sage, and the
hero,
From the south—from the flowery peninsulas and the spice
islands;
Long having wander'd since—round the earth having wander'd,
Now I face home again—very pleas'd and joyous;

(But where is what I started for, so long ago?
And why is it yet unfound?) (114-15)

This final note of doubt and hesitancy, placed in parentheses in the poem, raises some interesting issues pertaining specifically to Whitman's own vision as well as to more general perspectives on the spatial configurations of California in the American imaginary. It certainly challenges the praise of progress and modernity in his "Song of the Redwood-Tree." Perhaps Whitman asked, as in this driven paradigm someone at some point would have to ask, where are we going? The perspective facing west casts the "it" that the persona searches for somehow uncertainly in a register of perpetual journey forward.

A very basic fact bears remembering, of course. In the traditional frame, America, as Rodriguez comments, moves from east to west: "Californians have been trying to tell Eastern Americans for decades that our nation is finite" (*Brown* 174). From east to west, California signifies the end of the land, and consequently, and traditionally, of possibility, and of further quest, as the tentativeness in Whitman's poem signals. But this is only one perspective, for this space, and any space inflected by heterochronic itineraries of projections, movements and encounters, conquests and quests, will present different views depending on which frames, perspectives, and variously originated "burning glasses" and imaginaries we see through and with. Rezanov's visit to San Francisco consequently epitomizes only one of multiple geography-making (his)stories and imaginaries that contribute to the ever-shifting space of, in this case, California. In this sense perhaps we should approach the study of any area as through a kaleidoscope, only instead of seeing a succession of phases and forms, we see them as coterminous and co-constitutive, and always shifting.

NOTES

1. Taylor's argument in his *Modern Social Imaginaries* is far more complex and rich than the quotes I extract here do justice to. The main thrust of his book focuses on what he calls the "long march of modernity," the delineation of which ends in a profound assessment of Western modernity, an imaginary, a way of being, that solidly breaks with the enchanted embedding of archaic systems. I have written more extensively on Taylor's specifically modern social imaginary in relation to the American imaginary and what I call its "magic" elsewhere; see Lene Johannessen, *Horizons of Enchantment: Essays in the American Imaginary* (Hanover: Dartmouth College Press/University Press of New England, 2011).

2. For a marvelous history of Fort Ross and sea otter hunting along the northern California coast, see James Clifford, "Fort Ross Meditation," in *Routes: Travel and Translation in the Late Twentieth Century*, 299–348. Here he traces the history of the Russians and their relations to indigenous peoples in California as well as Alaska.

WORKS CITED

Appadurai, Arjun. "How Histories Make Geographies: Circulation and Context in a Global Perspective." *Transcultural Studies* 1 (2010): 4–12.

Bakhtin, Mikhail. *The Dialogic Imagination: Four Essays*. Ed. Michael Holquist. Trans. Caryl Emerson and Michael Holquist. Austin: University of Texas Press, 1991.

———. *Speech Genres and Other Late Essays*. Ed. Michael Holquist and Caryl Emerson. Trans. Vern W. McGee. Austin: University of Texas Press, 1986.

Bercovitch, Sacvan. "Games of Chess: A Model of Literary and Cultural Studies." In *Centuries' Ends, Narrative Means*. Ed. Robert Newman. Stanford: Stanford University Press, 1996. 54–55.

Castoriadis, Cornelius. "Imaginary and Imagination at the Crossroads." In *Figures of the Thinkable*. Stanford: Stanford University Press, 2007. 71–101.

———. *The Imaginary Institution of Society*. Cambridge: Polity Press, 2005.

Clifford, James. *Routes: Travel and Translation in the Late Twentieth Century*. Cambridge: Harvard University Press, 1997.

Dillon, Sarah. *The Palimpsest: Literature, Criticism, Theory*. London: Continuum, 2007.

Friedman, Susan Stanford. *Mappings: Feminism and the Cultural Geographies of Encounter*. Princeton: Princeton University Press, 1998.

Harte, Bret. "Concepcion de Arguello." *The Literature Network*. . http://www .online-literature.com/bret-harte/complete-poetical-works/27/ (accessed 20 September 2010).

Hicks, Jack, James D. Houston, Maxine Hong Kingston, and Al Young, eds. *The Literature of California: Writings from the Golden State*. Berkeley: University of California Press, 2000.

Hitchcock, Peter. *Imaginary States: Studies in Cultural Transnationalism*. Urbana: University of Illinois Press, 2003.

Horsman, Reginald. *Race and Manifest Destiny: The Origins of American Racial Anglo-Saxonism*. Cambridge: Harvard University Press, 1981.

Klahn, Norma. "Chicana and Mexicana Feminist Practises: De/Linking Cultural Imaginaries." In *Genealogies of Displacement: Diaspora/Exile/Migration and Chicana/o/Latina/o/Latin American/Peninsular Literary and Cultural Studies*, ed. Jordi Aladro, Norma Klahn, Lourdes Martínez-Echazábal, and Juan Poblete. Nuevo Texto Critico 29–32 (2002–3): 163–174.

Lowenthal, David. *The Past Is a Foreign Country*. Cambridge: Cambridge University Press, 1990.

Marx, Karl, and Friedrich Engels. Review. *Neue Rheinische Zeitung: Politisch-Ökonomische Revue* (January–February 1850). http://www.marxists.org/archive/marx/works/1850/01/31.htm#1 (accessed 20 May 2010).

McDougall, Walter. *Promised Land, Crusader State: The American Encounter with the World since 1776*. Boston: Houghton Mifflin, 1997.

Miller, Gwenn. Kodiak Kreol: *Communities of Empire in Early Russian America*. Ithaca: Cornell University Press, 2010.

Rezanov, Nikolai Petrovitch. *The Rezanov Voyage to Nueva California in 1806: The Report of Count Nikolai Petrovich Rezanov of His Voyage to That Provincia of Nueva Espana from New Archangel*. Trans. Thomas C. Russell. San Francisco: Private Press of Thomas C. Russell, 1926.

Rodriguez, Richard. *Brown: The Last Discovery of America*. New York: Viking Press, 2002.

———. Interview. Lene Johannessen. "Amerikas Historier på Langs" [America's Stories: Perpendicular]. *Replikk* 26 (2008): 16–23.

"Russians Urge Governor to Save Fort Ross." *SFGate*, 28 August 2009. http://www.sfgate.com (accessed 1 December 2011).

Taylor, Charles. *Modern Social Imaginaries*. Durham: Duke University Press, 2002.

Vinkovetsky, Ilya. "Circumnavigation, Empire, Modernity, Race: The Impact of Round-the-World Voyages on Russia's Imperial Consciousness." *Ab Imperio: Studies of New Imperial History and Nationalism in the Post-Soviet Space* 1–2 (2001): 191–209.

Von Langsdorff, Georg H. "Langsdorff's Narrative of the Rezanov Voyage to Nueva California in 1806." *Voyages and Travels in Various Parts of the World: The Years 1803, 1804, 1805, 1806, and 1807*. Part 2. London: Henry Colburn, 1814. 3–145.

Welty, Eudora. "Place in Fiction." In *The Eye of the Story: Selected Essays and Reviews*. New York: Random House, 1978. 116–133.

Whitman, Walt. "Song of the Redwood-Tree" and "Facing West from California's Shores." In *Leaves of Grass*. Ed. David Kaye. Philadelphia: Sherman & Co., 1900. 114–115, 462–465.

MARK SELTZER

7 Form Games

Staging Life in the Systems Epoch

A modern society comes to itself by staging its own conditions. A modern world is a self-conditioning and self-reporting one. If, prior to the nineteenth century, society could not describe itself, now it cannot stop describing itself. Or, as the great science-fiction writer Stanislaw Lem neatly put it, "In the Eolithic age there were no seminars on whether to invent the Paleolithic." If a modernizing society is what Durkheim described as an "almost sui generis" society, then the self-inducing and self-evaluative character of that world—its drive toward autonomy—makes up what Durkheim also would call a social fact.[1]

Put a bit differently, a modern world imagines itself: it consists of itself plus its registration. One way of understanding reflexive modernity, then, is precisely in terms of a shift in the status of imagined, or counterfactual, worlds. Contemporary society—what I call here the official world—everywhere launches models of a self-modeling world. In doing so, it curates a world.

In this way, real reality and fictional reality are copied into each other. In this way, too, the official world takes note of itself, and so (as Niklas Luhmann puts it) makes the world appear in the world. Hence the official world is game-like—in its autonomy, its contingency, and its artificiality. And it is art-like—in its self-reflexive, autogenic, and stand-alone character. The form of the official world—and the game-like and the artificial, or art-like (*künstlich*), way of that world in imagining, and realizing, itself—are what I want to set out here. The form games of the official world epitomize, it will be seen, the situation of the work of art in the epoch of social systems. These forms games, for starters, are nowhere clearer, or better epitomized, than in the small, sequestered, and closely observed worlds of a forensic realism—the modern crime story and its forms of death and life.

• • •

"'There's no such thing as a perfect murder,' Tom [Ripley] said to Reeves," opening Patricia Highsmith's remarkable novel *Ripley's Game* (1974). "That's just a parlour game."[2] Yet it's not hard to see that the relation between murder and game—between real worlds and parlor games—is a good deal more complicated here. And not least in that the modern scene of the crime always resembles a gamespace.[3] Three questions: What does it mean to talk about murder as a parlor game? What does it tell us about modern forms of both violence and games? And what does it tell us about their place in making up modern social systems, what they look like, and how they work?

In these pages I take up these questions about game and world through a sampling of several very different scenes—initially, Highsmith's crime novel *Ripley's Game;* next, a more recent best seller that is in effect a popularization of systems thinking, Malcolm Gladwell's *Blink: Thinking without Thinking;* and, briefly, Kazuo Ishiguro's 2005 novel *Never Let Me Go*, about a newly normal form of death and life and the social ecologies of ignorance that go with it. The focus across these scenes is, first, via Highsmith, parlor games; second, via Gladwell, war games; and third, via Ishiguro, form games. These are, I mean to suggest, scenes that remain remarkably stable across their different scenographies. Each appears as the subset of a structure that persists through its variations: encounters of a performance and a syntax—or, more exactly, *the emergence of comparable conditions in diverse systems, which is a defining attribute of modernity*. These scenes then make it possible to map these games, their rules, and their media—and the social territory they at once model and realize.

Parlor Games

> Can we get certain pathological phenomena as well-defined games? . . . I don't believe any game that can't be played as a parlor game.
> —MARTIN SHUBIK, RAND Corporation

Why perfect murders and parlor games, then?

For one thing, modern game theory, and the game-theoretical worldview that goes with it, takes off from John von Neumann's 1928 paper "Zur Theorie der Gesellschaftsspiele," "On the Theory of Parlor Games." The attempt, in von Neumann's account, is to put on a mathematical basis the little games in which (unlike, say, playing dice) one is not merely playing against the odds but playing against others. This is a game, like poker or chess, in which we move against opponents whose intentions, or what look like them (bluffs), enter into the form of the game. This is a complex game in that one must observe and measure and misinform self-observing observers who are doing the same: that is, one must observe what and how the observed observer can't observe—and whether he can observe that or not.

In short, the effects of playing the game must be included in it. It is (on von Neumann's account) "the game as played by perfectly intelligent, perfectly ruthless operators," like oneself.[4] It is a game, then, like the *Kriegsspiele*, or war games, that von Neumann (a prototype for Stanley Kubrick's Dr. Strangelove) will go on to model. It is then something like a play-at-home version of the fog of war, or a dress rehearsal for what has come to be called the military-entertainment complex.[5]

This is to suggest that parlor games, games played for leisure and that contain their own outcome—"social games," as the literal sense of the idiomatic *Gesellschaftsspiele* indicates—are already and from the start more than that. "The problem," as von Neumann puts it, "is well known," and "there is hardly a situation in daily life into which this problem does not enter. . . . A great many different things come under this heading [the theory of parlor games], anything from roulette to chess, from baccarat to bridge. And after all, any event—given the external conditions and the participants in the situation (provided the latter are acting of their own free will)—may be regarded as a game of strategy if one looks at the effect it has on the participants."[6] The theory of parlor games (the mathematicization of games of strategy) becomes, in von Neumann's and Oskar Morgenstern's *Theory of Games and Economic Behavior* (1947), the basis for the game-theoretical modeling of economic and other real-world behavior.[7]

We might say that *deficiency of the game model* (at least as popularly understood) comes into view from the start: the presumption of the rationality of actors or operators, the perfectly rational and perfectly ruthless; the reliance of the model on the assumption of decisive information, on the self-conditioned efficiency of the markets, on the tendency toward self-correcting equilibrium, and so on.[8] Or we can reverse the picture. Then we might say that the *deficiency of the world*, and hence the attraction of the game world, here immediately comes into view—not least for gamers looking for a better or more perfect world, or at least one that plays by the rules.

We might say too, then, that this game outlook on life amounts to "expanding the game to the whole world" (Wark), or that a world that's like a game is thus part rules and part fiction—or "half-real" (Juul)—as two influential accounts of gamer theory have it.[9] But both notions—the notion of the expansion of the game to the whole world, and the division of real life by halves—are too crude to do much work with. For one thing, the unity of the difference between game and world is left uninterpreted in both. For another, so are the social conditions that make for the form of the distinction in the first place.[10]

Consider, for example, the film *Avalon* (2001), directed by Mamoru Oshii (director too of the anime film *Ghost in the Shell*). *Avalon* is familiar enough in the canon of recent reality game films. The plot involves a potentially lethal virtual-reality war game played by addicted combatants—with the goal, it turns out, to arrive at the game stage "Class Real." There is no doubt a canonicity to the subset of such films—and their rehearsal, or retesting, of the distinction between the game world and the real one. But the film inquires into the very problem of this distinction and the conditions that enable it from the start.

It does so in part by doubling it at the level of form—the form of the cinematic medium. That is to say, in *Avalon*, the virtual reality of the film medium—the mechanized doubling of observation and act that cinema posits as its condition and mode of operation and that makes up the reality of motion pictures—here arrives as its own theme.[11] It is not merely that we view the world viewed—the observed observer in the act of observation and so the continual reproduction of the act via its observation (what might be described as the modalization of the world). And it is not merely that this doubling continually reproduces itself via the technical process that implies a second order of vision. The afterimage, for early film theorists, was taken to emit to viewers their own processes of perception. The transformation of stills into motion appears as the special effect of a cultural technique: in effect, a becoming-medial of the psychophysiology of vision. Form and medium feed back into each other.

These feedback loops between the human senses and the media, and between observation and act, thus take on the theme of the game/world distinction. The difference between the film world and the game world looks like the difference between the real world and a fictional one. The difference between real and fictional reality then oscillates—between discourse and story, fabula and sjuzhet. And the point not to be missed is that the unity of the difference becomes visible precisely via an oscillation between media.

Reality—"real life"—can be spoken of only by contrasting it to something else from which it is distinguished, say, fictional (or statistical, or mathematical) reality.[12] (And it's worth remembering that the term "real life" itself comes to us from eighteenth-century fiction.) The internal articulation of reality in the film makes it possible, or necessary, to distinguish real and fictional reality: they are copied into each other. Hence the paradoxical determination of "class real" (the real as one classification among others) itself becomes visible. And given what appears here as the preference for violence over paradox, it is not surprising that it becomes visible in the film as war game. That is to say, the choice of the game enters into it: "Which is the better game? Which would you choose given the choice? The sort of game that you think you can win but can't. Or, alternatively, one that seems to be impossible, but isn't. Maintaining a delicate balance somewhere in between throughout every level of the game, that's what keeps it going."[13] The balancing between the necessary and the possible defines the self-defining space of the game. In short, what defines the game form is its contingency, its self-conditioning, and its deliberate self-complication.[14] It's *contingent* in the sense that the rules of the game are neither necessary nor impossible. It's *self-conditioned* in that rules, measure, and outcome are defined by the "sort of game" chosen and by what's possible, or impossible, in it. It's *deliberately complicated* to relieve the boredom of that self-conditioning. These are the "sandbox elements" that prolong the play—the gratuitous difficulties that "keep it going," that seduce players to continue to play. This is (as Roger Caillois expresses it, in his account of play and games) "the pleasure experienced in solving a problem arbitrarily designed for this purpose"—like probing a toothache with one's tongue, playing with one's own pain.[15]

"We lead," as the microsociologist of these little worlds, Erving Goffman, puts it, "an indoor social life."[16] It is in this sense that the parlor game is a scale model of the modern social field—or, more exactly, of its small and sequestered, discrete but comparable worlds. These small worlds are themselves working models of the "sequestration" of modern life—to the extent that it is modern.[17] And games such as these—parlor games, crime games, war games, and the rest—are, in short, *models of a self-modeling world.* They are scale models of the modern social field, which is then, in effect, a life-size model of itself.

This is not the place to rehearse the large topic of the social differentiation of modern society, set out in variant detail from Weber to Schmitt, from Foucault to Luhmann. Suffice it to say that if, from the late eighteenth century on, prisons come to resemble hospitals which come to resemble factories which come to resemble schools which come to resemble prisons, this is not merely because they share in common a grand theme such as discipline. These social microworlds—at once differentiated and fractally self-similar—are the genre forms of a self-realizing society: one that is "almost-completely self-reliant,"[18] one that more and more generates and dispels uncertainties itself, and "almost" on its own terms (Durkheim's sui generis society on the way to recognizing itself).

These training, educating, correcting, grading, and self-realizing institutions are the small worlds that calibrate and compare and measure and individualize individuals, and socially distribute the possibilities of personally attributable reflection, action, and evaluation. They lend incremental form to the lifestyle called a career. (And only academic field-observers, proliferating new microfields in the name of the opposite, the *inter* and the *trans*—that is, dreaming of a general world in which they do not exist—still seem awed by this fact.) That is to say—and there will be more to say about this in a moment—the self-reference system of modern society, like the self-reference system of modern literature, gives itself priority over all external reference.[19] But, like the modern art system, it does so knowing that. It at every point reflexively monitors its own self-created reality—and so makes visible all the paradoxes of that self-implication.

It would not be difficult to enumerate these recursive social systems and their media, and the shift to the observation of observation—second-order observation—that each turns on. Here I can do little more than itemize what social systems analysis has already more or less detailed: the political system (and its media of self-observation called public opinion); the legal system (which makes texts from texts); the scientific system (and the medium of publications, such that observations—experiments—can be observed); the art system (which leaves the determination of what counts as art to the art system itself); the erotic system (with its love and intimacy media: hothouse circuits communicating the uncommunicable); the education system (which discovers, or posits, the child in order to demonstrate that persons are things that can be made and measured); the economic system (the real in the final instance, which, to the extent that it is a social system—social and a system—never finds out what real needs or real values might be, or needs to); the crime system (which, via the mass media, generalizes the scene of the crime as the boundaries of the modern world). And so on.[20]

In short, modernity, to the extent that it is modern, trends toward tautology. It more and more realizes a nullification, or denudation, of extrinsic determinations. (That's one reason why the weather—from Third

World disasters to global warming—becomes the test case of relative modernization, of a "greenhouse effect" self-determination.) This general trending toward tautology is, as it were, re-reflected in these small worlds, this indoor social life. And it is here that the game, in its contingency, self-conditioning, and purposive complication, shows itself as a working model of the self-modeling modern world—and so makes the world appear in the world.

The Rules of Irrelevance

The game strategist of the perfect murder in Highsmith's *Ripley's Game* is Reeves Minot, who plans the crime, as Tom Ripley puts it, "just to start the ball rolling" (62). In short, "he plays games" (128). Reeves, we are told, is "like a small boy playing a game he had invented himself, a rather obsessive game with severe rules—for other people" (112). The point, however, is not quite that Reeves exempts himself from the rules by determining them and so seeing through them. The real point is that seeing through the game and obsessively playing the game are not at all at odds here. For if one does not see, and see through, the rules, one cannot play by the rules: seeing through the game is part of it. That is to say, in order for self-determinations to count as self-determinations, they have to be seen as such. And in a self-validating world, the crime story, its prolonged suspense and its surprising outcome, must work the same way: it requires *suspense in the sense of a self-generated uncertainty* and *surprise in the sense of a self-dispelled mystery*. The paradox, catch, or trick of the expected surprise is its form game.

One thing the novel allows, then, is for this circular causality to take the form of form. "Word did get around, he realized" (23). This is how the circuits of communication and realization continually reproduce (and reenter) each other. "I'm just telling you what Jonathan told me" (223). This is how the novel conveys information, or news of difference. It continually switches back and forth between act and observation, story and discourse—such that, as with the news today, the reporting on the news becomes the news reported on. "It was a matter of protecting—what had gone before" (227). The sentence's short circuit is the syntax of recursive causal systems, feeding back outcomes into intentions, effects into causes.[21]

This is simply to observe, once again, that second-order observation is first tested in novels, which become the models for trying out the modalization of the world, with serious consequences. That makes for the generic preference for characters (as modal terms: self-observing observers). It makes, too, for the novelistic preference for affects that include their self-reflection as part of their operation: sympathy (or envy), for example, which posits the social reflection of pleasure (or pain) in the pain (or pleasure) of others, via a reciprocity of observation and self-observation.[22]

The formality of the game is in part what looks like its suspension of external reference—or what Erving Goffman calls its *rules of irrelevance*. Games, for Goffman, "illustrate how participants are willing to forswear for the duration of the play any apparent interest in the aesthetic, sentimental, or monetary value of the equipment employed, adhering to what might be called *rules of irrelevance*." In this way the real-world conditions of the game or the material that the game is made of—for example, "whether checkers are played with bottle tops on a piece of squared linoleum, with gold figures on inlaid marble, or with uniformed men standing on colored flagstones"—can be suspended. Hence the "same sequence of strategic moves and countermoves" can be made nevertheless—and still "generate the same contour of excitement."[23]

Yet from another point of view the rules of the game are scarcely a suspension of the way of the world, in that the same sequestration, and so the same rules of irrelevance, mark both. The first sentence of the first chapter of *Ripley's Game* is about murder and parlor games. The last sentences of that opening chapter are about the game Reeves is playing—if, that is, he's playing a game at all. It's not at all clear that Reeves's actions, or play actions, are more than strictly gratuitous. "Toying" with things is the novel's repeated term for this. That is, it's not at all clear that Reeves has anything classed real to get out of it—beyond, of course, just prolonging the play.

Here, then, is the astonishing passage with which the initial chapter of the novel closes:

> Reeves might gain—according to Reeves, but let Reeves figure that out, because what Reeves wanted seemed as vague to Tom as Reeves' microfilm activities, which presumably had to do with international spying. Were governments aware of the insane antics of some of their spies? Or those whimsical, half-demented men flitting from Bucharest to Moscow and Washington with guns and microfilm—men who might with the same enthusiasm have put their energies to international warfare in stamp-collecting, or in acquiring secrets of miniature electric trains? (11–12)

The first chapter of *Ripley's Game* begins, then, with parlor games and ends with medial systems. But what links this antic series of activities? What draws into relation stamps, model trains, photography, information, spies, and war by other means? What makes it possible for these miniature systems of information and body-and-message transport (electric trains, stamp collections, microfilm, and so on) to make up a world? What makes it possible for these little medial systems to work as conditions and techniques of existence? To operate via scale models and working models that are models both of the world and in it?

When, that is, did the communication of words and things become the modern medial system before our very eyes? 1839, the annus mirabilis of the network of modern matter and message transport systems (and the criteria of speed, regularity, predictability, and reproducibility). The first commercial electric telegraph, in 1839, constructed by Wheatstone and Cooke for the Great Western Railway; the first Baedeker guide (to the Rhine), 1839; and the first national railway timetable (Bradshaw's), in 1839; the invention of photography—and its use in guidebooks, among other things—in 1839 (by Daguerre in France and, in 1840, by Fox Talbot in England); and the first national postal system, Rowland Hill's Penny Post (based on the invention of the prepaid stamp), in Britain, in 1840.[24] What spreads throughout the social field, what makes up the infrastructure of the modernizing social field, is the intensified self-organization of a system of self-organizing systems, what the author of an article in the *Spectator* (February 1839) titled "Self-Operating Processes of Fine Art: The Daguerreotype" calls "self-acting machines of mechanical operation."[25]

This begins to indicate the medial genealogy of a modernizing world, one tending toward, and more and more conditioned by, speed and repeatability, and by a permanent and asymptotically continuous connectedness—a media union. It's possible to fill out this genealogy a bit more: first, by way of specifying how what might be called the *apriorization of the media* in these operations is bound to forms of observation and self-observation, and their systemic and reciprocal conditioning; second, by way of locating how the differences of medium and form, model and scale, fundamentally structure these operations; and third and finally, by way of sorting out what we might then make of the whimsical, half-demented, insane links—"International warfare in stamp-collecting"! "Acquiring secrets of miniature electric trains"!—that make up Ripley's game: that is, both modern parlor games and modern crime games.

Stamp collecting. The "closing of the postal system as a system" occurs with the shift from the individual registration of letters (and their rates) to postal standards (and the mass reproducibility of stamps); with the shift from names of places to street numbers; with the appearance across the social field of systems-integral standards at every level—a working diagram for the conveyance of communications (from place to place, on time). The postal system is no longer person to person: "The postage stamp made the sender's presence at the postal counter just as superfluous as the recipient's presence at delivery"; the mailboxes and mail slots that are the standard inputs and outputs for sending and delivery processes, irrespective of persons.[26] The standardized post—its collection, sending, delivery—neutralizes the idea of distance (within standardized zones), just as the railroad annihilates time (standardizing those zones).

The very existence of prepaid and mass-produced stamps implies a media union: a postal system. *Ripley's Game:* "He dropped the letter in a yellow box *en route* to his shop. It would probably be a week before he heard from Alan. . . . He thought of his letter, making its progress to Orly airport, maybe by this evening, maybe by tomorrow morning" (20). The purpose of letter writing, we know, is to mark absences, absent writers for absent readers. With the advent of a postal system, the significance of a theory of communication, and its deferrals, can then be formulated (and so deconstructed).[27] With the advent of telegraphy and then telephony, and systems of communication that do not depend on the sending of things or bodies, the transportation of people and the transportation of information divide—which allows for a period in which they (functionally or nostalgically) track each other, as for a period telegraph lines ran alongside railway lines.

Spies and secrets. By then we are in the zone of the detective story, its encrypted secrets and purloined letters. "From the point of view of the cryptanalyst," as one of the founders of communications systems theory, Claude Shannon, observed, "a secrecy system is almost identical with a noisy communication system."[28] It is not merely that the modeling, in Shannon's theory of communication, of transmitter and receiver as *encoder* and *decoder* explicitly identifies "communication with cryptanalysis."[29] Or that there are the tight couplings between the take-off point of communication theory and computational analysis, on the one side, and espionage and code breaking, on the other, during the Second World War.[30] The inverse relation between the probability of the message and the information it gives means that "the uncertainty about the value of individual bits that is called forth by interference on the channel is more or less indistinguishable from the uncertainty produced by enemy codes."[31] On that logic the problem of modern literary interpretation— the uncertainty as to whether something is an intended/coded message or simply interference on the line (noise)—is tightly coupled to the form of the secrecy system too.

And in that the model of the new media—without as yet a credible account of either the media or the new—has come to look like the magical solution to the two cultures problem, we might recall what that solution looked like at the beginning of the cold war. Warren Weaver, for example, observes in his review of Shannon's work in *Scientific American* that the analysis of communicative systems as a series of probabilistic events might be applied to "*all of the procedures by which one mind may affect another.* . . . This . . . involves not only written and oral speech, but also music, the pictorial arts, the theater, the ballet, and in fact all human behavior. In some connections it may be desirable to use a still broader definition of communication . . . [including] the procedures by means of which (say automatic equipment to track an airplane and to compute its probable future positions) affects another mechanism (say a guided missile chasing this airplane)."[32] Here guns and information—Norbert Wiener's groundbreaking work in recursive systems analysis via the design of anti-aircraft predictors and, via that, cybernetics in general—meet and fuse.[33]

Miniatures and models. No doubt the mechanical toy may excite the thrill and panic of the "self-invoking fiction." And the miniature—the miniature railway, for example—may be "nostalgic in a fundamental sense," a movement "from work to play, from utility to aesthetics." But that fiction now provides, too, a working model of the self-steering and self-modeling social field. The collection—stamps or trains or toys—may "replace history with *classification*" and present a "hermetic world" that is "self-sufficient and self-generating"; and it may provide a "narrative of interiority," one made up of the "complete number of elements necessary for an autonomous world."[34]

But for precisely these reasons its formalism appears not as the alternative to the modern social field but the form of the modern social field, and its small worlds. The form of the scale model is a matter both of modeling and of scale. It makes visible the relation of observation to itself—and so its contingent and self-referential structure.[35] And in the search for America's next top model, it may then be well worth taking into account the way of the modern world as a self-mapping and self-modeling one.

The Medium in Person

The doubling of the object or world in the model—the doubling that allows the world to appear in the world—means that the world can be observed in different (rival or correspondent) ways, and so recast by the existence of alternatives. There are three basic consequences to this. First, it marks the relativity of the observer, who observes himself as an observer among others. Second, one is then asked to distinguish "real" reality from other kinds (fictional or statistical, for example). Third, the matter of scale makes observation itself visible: seeing itself seen, albeit out of the corner of the eye. The photographic—which, it seems, "permits a blow-up any scale"—epitomizes that, from the microfilmic to the big close-up of the human face; the filmic close-up is a solicitation to observe what the observed observer observes.[36] What the photographic brings into view are scales of viewing: modernity ready for its close-up. And that induces a second-nature reflexivity, installing it as a medium and framework of perception, or cultural technique.[37]

The little models that proliferate in, and as, the world of *Ripley's Game*, for example, show the self-modeling of that world and how it operates. Here the *historia rerum gestarum* coincides with the *res gestae*, the story of events with the events themselves (if we recall that the *res gestae* is not exactly the event itself but instead in itself the coincidence of the event and its observation). The novel is in effect nothing but this self-modeling and self-sampling, and for that reason, several small and rapid examples can suffice here.

1. "His hobby was naval history, and he made model nineteenth-century and eighteenth-century frigates in which he installed miniature electric lights that he could put completely or partially on by a switch in his living room. Gerard himself laughed at the anachronism of electric lights in his frigates, but the effect was beautiful when all the other lights in the house were turned out" (47). History and model, war and game, hesitate each other here, not least via the anachronism of electric lights. (And the notion of anachronism itself is media-dependent, an effect of the "typographical persistence" of print.)[38]

2. So the scale can be reversed: "Little boats bobbed gaily at anchor, and two or three boats were sailing about, simple and clean as brand-new toys" (67). These little boats are life-size and miniature at once, shifting in scale from one to the other.

3. Or, again, since the act takes shape in its recording or registration, making for the relays between game and world in the modern crime story: "He'd done little jobs for Reeves Minot, like posting on small, stolen items, or recovering from toothpaste tubes . . . tiny objects like microfilm rolls" (6). In passages such as this, scale itself becomes thick and palpable—an element in the concreteness of the medium of representation.

4. Or, yet again, consider what living life and living space look like in *Ripley's Game:* "Jonathan carried a second cup of coffee into the small square living room where Georges was now sprawled on the floor with his cut-outs. Jonathan sat down at the writing desk, which always made him feel like a giant" (19). The geometry, the small square, of real space; the boy and his cut-out models; the writing desk that scales between writing and world: all are graphs of a self-graphing world. And the writing desk, like the light switch in the living room that turns the lights of the model on and off, is a switch point between two worlds.

The model for that is the switch itself:

> We do not notice that the concept "switch" is of quite a different order than the concepts "stone," "table," and the like. Closer examination shows that the switch, considered as a part of an electric circuit, *does not exist* when it is in the on position. From the point of view of the circuit, it is not different from the conducting wire which leads to it and the wire which leads away from it. It is merely "more conductor." Conversely, but similarly, when the switch is off, it does not exist from the point of view of the circuit. It is nothing, a gap between two conductors which themselves exist only as conductors when the switch is on. In other words, the switch is *not* except at the moments of its change of setting.[39]

We do not notice that the switch is an object of a different order: a quasi-object. That is, we do not notice the switch—the medium is anaesthetic and disappears—if it works; it appears only if it fails: "If the relation succeeds, if it is perfect, optimum, and immediate, it disappears as a relation. If it is there, if it exists, that means that it failed. It is only mediation."[40] This is the unity of the difference between the channel and its breakdowns—its interceptions and its accidents, the waves and shocks along the line. There is of course a paradox in our insistence that the media determine our situation but do so to the extent that we do not cease not registering that; and one can then either abide in the deconstruction of this paradox or see how it works.[41] It works via the doubling of form and medium—the form games—by which the world intermittently appears in the world, and does so by way of *a suspension or cancellation of the distinction between map and territory to which it at the same time appeals.*

One finds, across all these examples, an oscillation between form and medium, between model and world, between map and territory. The closing or cancellation of the distinction between map and territory is centrally here the denudation of the distinction between game and world, a self-invented game with its own canons of credibility. ("Or was it even a game that Tom was playing? Jonathan couldn't believe it was entirely a game" [189]). This is what Poe, early on, called the "half-credences" that make believable parlor games, like the murder story.[42] In short: We know, first, that the map is not the territory (the effect is not the cause). We know that, second, because it's always the map and never the territory that we deal with (there's no doing without codes and transforms). But then, third, what of the media ensembles, distributed across virtual and real landscapes, making up the material and formal infrastructure of modern society? Is the medial system (in a territory full of maps) map or territory?

The object of media theory "is then not an object but a difference"— the difference between medium and form (with all the paradoxes that involves). The difference between medium and form "oscillates from one side to the other [but] is never univocally defined, because each side depends on the other"—and can be observed only through the other.[43] In *Ripley's Game*, a novel and game world so relentlessly given over to observing media of observation and self-observation, and to the conditions of what can be seen and what can't, it is not at all surprising that the medium of visibility—light itself—reenters as its own theme. It would be possible to point to its arrivals again and again across the novel. But the becoming-medial of the medium occurs late in the story, after Ripley has entered into the game and made it his own. Here Ripley and Jonathan, the pawn in Reeves's game, have just murdered a couple of murderers and are about to do away with the bodies: "Tom's car stopped. They had gone perhaps two hundred yards from the main road in a great curve. Tom had cut his lights, but the interior of the car lit when he opened the door. Tom left the door open, and walked towards Jonathan, waving his arms cheerfully. Jonathan was at that instant cutting his own motor and his lights. The image of Tom's figure in the baggy trousers, green suede jacket, stayed in Jonathan's eyes for a moment as if Tom had been composed of light. Jonathan blinked" (210). "Composed of light": this is the *puncta inflata* of the novel's optics. The term "composed"—in its terminological change of state, or indifference, between matter and form—could not be more exact, in turn form and medium, oscillating (blinking) between them.[44] Put simply, here "light and matter are on an equal basis" (which is the modernist turn in physics).[45]

Ripley is identified through and through with medial techniques and transformations in the series of novels that carry his name. These novels operate entirely by way of cultural technologies of body and message transport, their commutability and their self-reflection. And they double the world via Ripley's self-observed observation.[46] Here Ripley becomes the medium in person. In that light and matter are on an equal basis, observation becomes its own object (a quasi-object, or materialized *theoria*). The motorized world stops for a moment, such that the medium apriorizes itself (and in doing so marks its own blind spot). The scene is in effect Ripley's transubstantiation, or transfiguration (into "figure" or "image" or artwork): the moment at which the channel refers to itself. If light and matter are mutually contingent, there is no alternative to the modalization of the world. That modalization of the world introduces the observer at every point. And it's "impossible to introduce the observer without also introducing the idea of message."[47] That means that the world and its communication are on an equal basis too.

Under the conditions of a modernizing and technogenic age, anthropological grounds are transposed into historical ones, and historical grounds into media techniques. This can also be played in reverse: media self-reflexivity can be taken, or mistaken, for self-reflection or subjectification. It's played in reverse via characters in novels, for example—not least via Highsmith's epochal character Tom Ripley. Ripley (like other serial killers, fictional and factual) is a sort of nonperson, a *man without content*. He is not merely one among an indeterminate number of others, but the third person in person—one who does not exist apart from the conditions of existence provided by the technical media and union of cultural techniques.[48] The character without qualities gives those techniques a proper name—albeit the name of a reality game, *Ripley's Believe It or Not!*

The Systems Turn

There's another toy in *Ripley's Game:* "The gyroscope Jonathan bought for Georges in Munich turned out to be the most appreciated toy Jonathan had ever given his son. Its magic remained, every time Georges pulled it from its square box where Jonathan insisted that he keep it." The "delicate instrument" is a scale, and working, model of "a larger gyroscope" that "keeps ships from rolling on the sea." And "to illustrate what he meant," Jonathan "rolled over on the floor, propped on his elbows" (139).

The embodiment, or anthropomorphization, of the little self-correcting machine is clear enough, and not merely in the tendency toward self-illustration (the tendency for acts to trace their own diagram) at work in this scene. The sociologist David Riesman, for example, in his 1960s best seller *The Lonely Crowd*, had identified the gyroscope as the analogue of what he calls the "inner-directed" person: "A new psychological mechanism is 'invented': it is what I like to describe as a psychological gyroscope. This instrument, once it is set in motion by the parents and other authorities, keeps the inner-directed person, as we shall see, 'on course' even when tradition, as responded to by his character, no longer dictates his moves."[49] Something more, then, is at stake than the bid for scientific aura implicit in a loose coupling of sociology and mechanics.

The gyroscope here is both a toy and a worldview: the gyroscope thus might be seen as a *Gedenken*-experiment, or better a *Gedenken*-machine, with many forms of life. If Ripley, composed of light, is the channel or medium reflecting on itself, in this scene self-reflection is itself reflected on—via one of the defining instruments of the second machine age.

The gyroscope, put simply, is a mechanism that links self-governing to self-observing—and mechanizes both. The term meaning literally "to view the turning," the gyroscope is introduced in 1852 by the physicist Léon Foucault (finding its first notable use in the device to demonstrate the earth's rotation, Foucault's pendulum). Its application to steering mechanisms takes a half-century (Elmer Sperry's development of the gyrostabilizer and gyrocompass for the U.S. Navy).[50]

That application is, then, one of the delays of the second machine age.[51] The "principle of feedback" remained like a fish out of water for a period, unable as yet to find a place to breathe. That is, the self-observing and self-steering instrument; the reciprocal flow of information back into a controller; the "control of a machine on the basis of its *actual* performance rather than its *expected* performance" (Wiener); the need to take into account what the machine has already said, such that effects of events can be carried all around to produce changes at the point of origin (Bateson)—these escalating or vicious circles remained for a period unthinkable.[52] It was not yet possible to arrive at a theory of self-reflection that was not also a theory of subjectification. (And both literary theory, and a new media studies eager to repeat the mistakes of phenomenology all over again, continue to complete the same short circuit between reflexivity and self-consciousness.)[53]

It was not yet possible, put simply, to inhabit the conditions of second-order observation: that, first, whatever is said is said by an observer; that, second, whatever is said is said to an observer; and hence that, third, reflexivity (observing the turn) is not the logical paradox on which the operation of the system founders but instead the temporal condition of possibility that founds it.[54] The modalization of the world is part of that—and the move to periodization via observing modes of seeing. Epochs appear as "turns" (in turn, the linguistic turn, the cultural turn, the affective turn), and thus bound to the distinct forms of media that steer them (from print culture to the age of technical reproducibility to digital culture). This is what it looks like to become acclimated to systems that feed outcomes back into inputs and do so by observing the turn and observing themselves doing so—hence entering into the sequestered, contingent, and self-conditioned form of *Gesellschaftsspiele* and other social games.

These are the conditions of Highsmith's murder games—and what might be called Highsmith's cold war. If there is any doubt about this, Highsmith makes the connection as explicit as possible. In this novel about artificial, forged, and self-reliant worlds, with all its train and air and postal schedules; all its little regimes of body and message transport and assessment, from readouts of blood counts to the feedback of news reports on the murders (command and control via communication); all its maps and "paper places" and art shops and frame stores, italicizations of the cultural techniques of the media (its necessary self-framing of what it maps and frames); all its "endless corridors" administered by "omniscient specialists" in life and death management, the little life support systems of an indoor social life; and, in sum, all its observations on these modes of observing and reflection—given all this, here then is the description of Gauthier, "the art supply man" with an artificial eye, and what his way of seeing looks like: "Gauthier's shiny glass eye did not laugh but looked out from his head with a bold stare, as if there were a different brain from Gauthier's behind that eye, a computer kind of brain that at once could know everything, if someone just set the programming" (31). These are the technics of a second order of vision, a seeing and knowing via the protocols of a program; a form of binocular vision that provides the feedback links between the human senses and media, a complex system of discrete processes that is also a differential relation of observation to itself.

The doubling back of seeing and knowing on itself could not be more emphatic than in the later part of the novel, when, for example, "a bomb through that window" is called "Unthinkable"! (189), and when the observation of what cannot be observed—"double-think" (233)—is named. We know that observing and observing what cannot be observed—"thinking the unthinkable"—emerges as the very form of cold war thinking ("the bomb," brinkmanship, and its war games). These are the code words for the cold war world. The looping of thinking back on itself, such that effects feed back into causes, so that the effects of events can be carried all around to produce changes at the point of origin: this thinking the unthinkable is of course epitomized and renamed by a cold war novel, *Catch-22* (with "22" as the ordinance of double-think—along with the trick, or catch, of the continuous reentry of the outcome into the intent). We might call that literary reflection on the form of a modernity exasperated with the failure of its own self-description "postmodern"; or we might say that it represents something like the R & D phase of R & D.[55]

World of Warcraft

At this point it becomes possible to set out, with a bit more detail, the ties between these violence games and what I earlier referred to as form games (literary and otherwise). I want to do so by way of another account of the war game strategy for thinking the unthinkable, this time drawn from the *New Yorker* writer Malcolm Gladwell's 2005 best seller, *Blink: The Power of Thinking without Thinking*. Gladwell presents a series of case studies that amount to something like a "gee-whiz" version of systems theory. In this, the book is directly in line with something like "the *New Yorker* uncanny." The same could be said about another *New Yorker* book, *The Wisdom of Crowds* by James Surowiecki—which might have been titled "the wisdom of systems." These adept case studies proceed via a toggling between close-ups (little anecdotes) and pattern (the big picture), and by way of these shifts in scale, the first, as if spontaneously, seems to give the second. That is to say, the narrative form of that process arrives as its subject (the power of thinking without thinking; the wisdom of crowds). In both, a recursive and systemic ecology of ignorance (unthinking or nonknowing) yields wisdom, or at least allows for the appearance of a knowledge a bit more trivial than wisdom: information. It allows, that is, for what Gladwell defines as "creating structure for spontaneity," the paradox of a meaning that appears without intention, and its implications.[56]

It is the art of war that comes into focus in Gladwell's centering chapter, "Paul Van Riper's Big Victory." More precisely, what comes into view is the war gamer's way of creating form for improvisation: the surprise of thinking without thinking that makes for blink-of-an-eye "pattern recognition," and so decision, in games of strategy. Van Riper, a veteran Vietnam War battalion commander and former head of the Marine Corps

University at Quantico, was recruited to play the "rogue commander" in the most expensive war game in history: Millennium Challenge 2002. It cost a quarter of a billion dollars to play out and amounted to a "full dress rehearsal for war" (104)—that is to say, for the invasion of Iraq in 2003.

Here is the way one of his soldiers described Van Riper in action: "He was always out in the field . . . figuring out what to do next. If he had an idea and he had a scrap of paper in his pocket, he would write that idea on the scrap, and then, when we had a meeting, he would pull out seven or eight pieces of paper. Once he and I were in the jungle a few yards from a river, and he wanted to reconnoiter over certain areas, but he couldn't get the view he wanted. . . . Damned if he didn't take off his shoes, dive into the river, swim out to the middle, and tread water so he could see" (100). There is something of a resemblance between this double-entry system of observation and act, seeing and recording, and Gauthier's computer eye or *Time*'s animate war computer. But there is something of a resemblance as well to the patients whom the psychiatrist Charcot, in his account of fin-de-siècle maladies of energy and will ("fatigue amnesia"), described as "l'homme du petit papier": men with little pieces of paper, who arrived for sessions "with slips of paper endlessly listing their ailments"—as they knew how they felt and what they saw only by reading about it. The recording of the act enters into the act, such that the act consists of both itself and its registration. What appears in Charcot as a modern malady of agency here appears as the art of thinking without thinking, and a selective adaptation to the second machine age.[57]

One observes by recording, which makes the act and its recording two sides of a single formation. There is a live transfer between them. There is, therefore, a routinized nondistinction between training and fighting (*"believe it or not* . . . we would practice platoon and squad tactics or bayonet training in the bush. And we did it on a routine basis" [104; emphasis added]). That is, there is a routine coming down of the distinction between dress rehearsal and act—or between war game and war: "Sometimes when Blue Team fired a missile or launched a plane, a missile actually fired or a plane actually took off, and whenever it didn't, one of forty-two separate computer models simulated each of those actions so precisely that the people in the war room often couldn't tell it wasn't real" (104).

This doubling of observation and act (and so the doubling of reality) structures these war game scenarios.[58] The games themselves migrate between military and entertainment industries, as part of what has been described as the military-entertainment complex. (And Millennium Challenge was not just a run-up to the war in Iraq; its engineered outcome scripted the war plan—and its marketing.) Familiar too by now is the sequestration, or self-suspension, of game worlds and their rules of irrelevance: the war gamers set up shop in "huge, windowless rooms known as test bays" (103) in the Joint Forces Command building—windowless black-boxed monads. Thus Van Riper discovers that the "only difference" between stock traders on Wall Street and those who "played war games on computer" is that "one group bet on money and the other bet on lives" (108).

The war game, in short, is a "management system" (119) mixing "complexity theory and military strategy" (106). It operates via a predictive and recursive guide system—but one without "specific guidance," intents, or effects: "I mean that the overall guidance and the intent were provided by me and the senior leadership . . . but the forces in the field wouldn't depend on . . . orders coming from the top. . . . I never wanted to hear the word 'effects' . . . We would not get caught up in any of these mechanistic processes" (118). The war game is then one of the parlor games (*Gesellschaftsspiele*) in which one must observe what the opponent observes or can't observe, and whether or not he can observe that: "What my brother always says is, 'hey, say you are looking at a chess board. Is there anything you can't see? No. But are you guaranteed to win? Not at all, because you can't see what the other guy is thinking'" (144).[59]

It's not hard to see, then, how parlor games enter into social games and war games. But it is the form of these games—these form games—that concerns us for the moment. To understand the "internal computer" that creates structure for improvisation or spontaneity (the power of thinking without thinking) is, for Gladwell, to understand that improvisation "is an art form governed by a series of rules" (113). And here "art form" comes to mean, then, the paradox of improvised form: the ongoing reproduction of action out of action.

This art form governed by serialized rules is part of an aesthetic of cold war modernism. One historian of brinkmanship (or blinkmanship) in the "intuitive science" of thermonuclear war, Sharon Ghamari-Tabrizi, lucidly sets out the terms of analysis sponsored by the RAND corporation: "Setting the terms for gaming and man-machine simulations in the 1950s and later, RAND analysts commended these techniques for sharpening intuition, stimulating creativity, offering insight into complex fields of interaction, exploring intersubjective exchanges in an interdisciplinary research setting, instilling tolerance for ambiguity and uncertainties, and heightening sensitivity to the practitioners' own blind spots and rigidities."[60] That setting of the terms puts R & D in the orbit of an aesthetic modernism premised on art as paradox: the paradox of structure and spontaneity, which one can call "art" (or the paradox of "form and intent in the American new criticism," which one can then deconstruct).[61]

We might see this, I've suggested, as another of the delays of the second machine age. That's to see modern literature (or literature from the standpoint of modernity) as something of a preadaptive advance on the social systems of reflexive modernity (an advance that can then be played out with real social consequences). And I am referring again as well, then, to the delays in its recognition or theorization, that is, why it takes until the development of cybernetics—and New Critical formalism (and its deconstruction) alongside that—for the self-evidence of autopoietic and recursive literary form to become evident. In this way the little game world of the poem or novel (like the little game worlds of the world) realize modern society—as an *exceptional* and at the same time *exemplary* case. We know that literature was always already and from the start a form game, such that the nonrecognition of that seems as strange as the inability (in the paradox of Maxwell's demon) to understand information processing as real work, or, correlatively, as strange as the inability (in the paradox of feedback) to understand that the effect is not the cause (and so the form is not the intent).[62]

Here one moves from dice games to games of strategy; from the calculus of probabilities to recursive systems theory; from the great probability salesman of the nineteenth century, Laplace, to the great cybernetics booster of the twentieth, Wiener. I have tracked elsewhere the first, via Poe and his advent crime story about the death of a beautiful woman— "The Mystery of Marie Roget"—and, along the way, about structure and motive in modern crime; the second, in these pages, via Highsmith. The crime story, with its dependence on the topoi of motive and surprise, is of course the happy hunting ground of intention (the motive of the crime) and outcome (the form of its surprise). Hence it provides an economical way of dramatizing (or overdramatizing) the feedback loops between structure and spontaneity—and the tautological repetition that secures the genre as genre. For Poe, for example, "accident forms part of the substructure." And the reinhabiting of intentions is a way of apprehending the criminal by reverse-engineering the plot. But this from the start appears as a trick or paradox (not least the paradox of waiting to be surprised). In "The Murders in the Rue Morgue," for example, the doubling of motive and act means entering into the motives of an actor who cannot properly have motives or perform acts (an orangutan, providing a version of what Poe elsewhere calls "motive not motivirt").[63]

One can start either from the form side or from the intent side, and either way keep discovering that structure and motivation, form and intent keep shifting sides. This is (I've elsewhere suggested) something like another game about intent and outcome: the very young child who plays hide-and-seek by saying, "I'm going to hide here, now you try to find me." Or it is like the looping effects of a historical interpretation by which persons and acts illustrate the conditions that make up the persons who act that way. Or it is like the paradox of the work of art as at once exceptional and exemplary, with respect to reflexive modernity.

"In explaining the work of art," as Niklas Luhmann frames it, "one frequently draws on the artist's *intention* in producing the work, but this is trivial, a tautological explanation, because the intent must be feigned, while its psychological correlates remain inaccessible." Since the artwork, and its production, can only be comprehended as intentional, "this raises the issue of how to dissolve the tautological construct of productive intent and unfold this tautology in ways that yield intelligible representations." The work's "artificiality provokes the question of purpose" in that it displays "something unexpected, something inexplicable, or as it is often put, something new," and so creates structure *for* spontaneity.[64]

The unfolding of the tautology of purpose or intent, and all the paradoxes it provokes, raise further questions, some of which I have taken up here. What, then, is the status of these form games in modern social systems? Or, more exactly, what is the status of the work of art in the age of reflexive social systems—systems marked by the apriorization of the media?

For one thing, the unfolding of that tautology then means that, in understanding "art as a social system," one understands that "the art system realizes society in it own realm as an exemplary case."[65] But for another, if the art system (and its form games) then reflects reflexive modernity, the notion of the autonomy of art and the notion of the exemplarity of art enter into each other at every point. Luhmann expresses that paradoxical reentry in these terms: "The theme of reflection does not define the meaning of the autonomy of art, but the meaning of the doubling of reality (*Realitätsverdoppelung*) in which this autonomy established itself."[66] That is to say, the theme of reflection arrives as its own theme—and, collaterally, the medium appears (or stages itself) as its own object. Put as simply as possible, this means it's not that art explains society or that society explains art. If one takes seriously the form of recursive causal systems (form games), then the explanation is precisely that, an explanation, and not what is explained. The effect is not the cause—which is to say, the artwork works like a black box.

Imaginary Animals; or, 2 + 2 = 5

The black box is a conceptual machine that makes possible "that most magical of tricks, a way of acting confidently with/from the unknown/unknowable."[67] Consider, for example, a simple version of black box theory, this one from Ross Ashby's *Introduction to Cybernetics* (1956): "The child who tries to open a door has to manipulate the handle (the input) so as to produce the desired movement at the latch (the output); and he has to learn how to control the one by the other without being able to see the internal mechanism that links them. In our daily lives we are confronted at every turn with systems whose internal mechanisms are not fully open to inspection, and which must be treated by the methods appropriate to the Black Box."[68] The difference between input and output means that there is a before and an after, and that this is a difference that makes a difference. The job is then to find a causal connection between them. (Thus the centrality of the notion of regularities in behavior and pattern recognition—and the shift from discourses governed by meaning and sense to those driven by pattern and code.)[69] It means, too, that whitening the black box (to see how it really works) or eliminating it (by positing the identity of intention and outcome) sidelines, it will be seen, the problem of form in these form games today, and not least in terms of the contemporary conception of the work of art.[70]

These form games enter into the official world at every point. For one thing, the contemporary differentiation of knowledges and their rival media of communication (from the conflict of the faculties to the extreme narrowness of inter- or trans disciplinary citation circles) make that clear enough. The owl of Minerva may still take flight at dusk, but now there are a lot of them (and, as in the Harry Potter stories, they just deliver the mail). These ecologies of ignorance are black boxes—ways of acting confidently, and building descriptions of the world out of the unknown and out of "knowing about non-knowing," since there is no alternative anyway.[71]

For another, we might reconsider the question of observation in the formation of knowledge (and self-knowledge)—and, too, in the formation of social systems that rely on internal mechanisms of knowing and self-knowing, and the ways in which these are copied into each. For example, Foucault's communication-and-control systems may be seen to instance perfectly the internal mechanisms of these black-boxed cybernetic systems (mechanisms more denoted than explicated via the term "power").[72]

For example, one way of making use of the seeing-machine, or panopticon, set out in Foucault's account of Bentham's architectural mechanism might be to "try out pedagogical experiments":

> In particular to take up once again the well-debated problem of secluded education, by using orphans. One would see what would happen when, in their sixteenth or eighteenth year, they were presented with other boys or girls; one could verify whether, as Helvetius thought, anyone could learn anything; one would follow "the genealogy of every observable idea"; one could bring up different children according to different systems of thought, making certain children believe that two and two did not make four or that the moon is a cheese, then put them together when they are twenty or twenty-five years old; one would then have discussions that would be worth a great deal more than the sermons or lectures on which so much money is spent; one would have at least an opportunity of making discoveries in the domain of metaphysics.[73]

Hence, in these experiments one can make persons believe, say, that $2 + 2 = 5$. But this necessarily means something a bit different than that power = knowledge. (In other words, it's not $2 + 2 = 5$ in Orwell's sense.) That is, to the extent that such experiments issue in *discoveries* and not simply *tautologies*, this means something other than that "knowledge follows the advances of power."[74] The black box remains in place, in that it enters into how modern social systems work.

Another way of saying this is that the little games that Foucault here describes are games of strategy: the seeing-machine must deal with what the machine has already seen and already said, and take cognizance of that. In short, the seeing-machine, via its reflexive monitoring of action, is a black box to the very extent that the players see that too. Or as the narrator of Kazuo Ishiguro's 2005 novel *Never Let Me Go* puts it: "We lost ourselves completely in our game. . . . And yet, all the time, I think we must have had an idea of how precarious the foundations of our fantasy were, because we always avoided any confrontation"; and "we all played our part . . . in making it last as long as possible."[75]

The prolonging of the play in *Never Let Me Go* is a prolongation of knowing not knowing. (And Ishiguro is perhaps the great contemporary novelist of nonknowing, and the little social systems that make it up. It is, in that sense if no other, "Jamesian.") The novel is premised on ecologies of ignorance. More exactly, its social premises are the micro-institutions—game-like, sequestered, autistic—that realize the official world, and the forms of life and death proper to it.

The small worlds of the novel—working models both of the world and in it—are everywhere visible, and they are everywhere up and running. These little worlds include the playing field and the boarding school and the ubiquitous hospital. They include "the Sales" and "the Exchanges," with their autonomous "system of tokens as currency" (38)—which is "how we got hold of things from outside" (41). They include too, and not merely as one world among others, the art world and the system that determines what will count as art and what will not. The art system is in turn, and explicitly, "like a miniature version of one of our Exchanges." Each resembles the other in that each is self-determined, autonomous, self-evaluative—each is, as Ishiguro concisely puts it, a "smart cosy self-contained world" (157–158). Together these self-contained, self-similar, and discrete systems make up a world: they make up, that is, the indoor social life of the official world.

This also begins to bring into sharper focus the paradoxical situation of the work of art in relation to modern social systems. Here the sales and exchanges are how we get hold of things from outside. The art system is how we get hold of things from inside: "Your art will reveal your inner selves . . . what you were like inside" (254, 260). These systems between the inside and the outside provide the forms in which modern life comes to itself by staging itself—and thus allow the world to appear in the world.

The work of art—in this case, Ishiguro's *Never Let Me Go*—in its very formality performs its self-reflexive and self-contained, internalized and stand-alone character. In that, the work of art is both exceptional and exemplary today. It is *exceptional* in its autonomous relation to the outside world. It is *exemplary* in that it provides the very model of that autonomy of that world. This is, in short, the paradoxical status of the sui generis artwork in the company of social systems that realize what Durkheim—inaugurating modern sociology, and so indicating a society that had achieved self-description—described as the achievement of the almost sui generis society. The modern social system, like the modern work of art, performs its own unity. This is the character of a modern society trending on all fronts toward artificiality and toward autonomy—toward the autonomizaton of everything.[76] The modern work of art, that is, the work of art in modernity, rehearses and registers its relation to itself. The point not to be missed is that this does not distinguish the work of art from contemporary social systems. It epitomizes them. Reflexivity is not merely the philosophical and aesthetic predicament of the twentieth century but the defining attribute of the second modernization, and its forms of second life.

Another way of saying this is that the official world plays out, and registers, its own conditions, and in doing so becomes self-conditioning. In this way the form of the game, as Georg Simmel expressed it, models a self-modeling world and what he called "autonomous forms of sociation." He writes: "The more profound, double sense of 'social games' (*Gesellschaftsspiele*) is that not only the game is played in *a society* (as its external condition) but that, with its help, people actually 'play' society.'"[77] This does not distinguish game and life, but instead, as Wittgenstein expressed it, it indicates their resemblance to each other: a "game is not based on grounds. It is not reasonable (or unreasonable). It is there—like one's life."

Never Let Me Go sets this out from the ground up. In the self-reporting and captive, autotelic, and quarantined micro-worlds of *Never Let Me Go*, life itself is like one's life: life-like. These micro-systems are in turn the scenes of a *Bildungsroman* of sorts, scenes of the growing of persons. They are also the model institutions of a modern society and its form games.

The pedagogical experiments in the novel—centrally, the boarding school of sorts that centers it—each provide something of a limit case of persons brought up according to different systems of thought. The limit case in point resembles in part "playing in a sandpit," with all its sandbox elements. It resembles, alternatively, the playing of a "chess game," and the attempt to "teach . . . the game." (50). Here playing the game is there, like one's life, in that playing it out is not exactly a matter of knowing its rules. The chess game is played—and taught—without quite understanding the rules of the game; instead, one observes the play, or makes moves, and so makes things up from that (since rules, and following them, are not self-enforcing).

The novel thus proliferates maps and models of how to play its games, from "scaled down [and scaled up] versions" (66) to "life-size skeletons" (83) to "secret games" (90). It multiplies small worlds. In doing so, it proliferates scale models of a self-modeling world—and cases of defective knowledge.[78] The template of this game with unknown rules and reflexive ignorance is given early on by Henry Adams, in his account of the advent of a catastrophic modernity: "Had he been consulted, would he have cared to play the game at all, holding such cards as he held, and suspecting that the game was to be one of which neither he nor any one else back to the beginning of time knew the rules or the risks or the stakes?"[79] Today the rules, risks, and stakes are part of normal, everyday life, and death, in a game-like and second-life modernity.

The game-like and the life-like in *Never Let Me Go* turn out to "play their parts" in the official world in another sense, too. It turns out that these little institutions, and the persons who grow up in them, are literally the parts—or, we discover, "spare parts"—of a world. The pedagogical experiment as a limit case in making up persons according to different systems of thought is here literalized—in that it's not quite clear that these characters *are* exactly persons.

The schoolchildren are, we learn, or learn that we more or less already knew but deferred knowing, "clones—or *students*, as we preferred to call you" (261). They are grown for spare parts. These spare parts are the "donations" that will "complete" their lives and prolong the lives of others. The "first-person" narration is provided by one of the students, named "Kathy H." Hence she is named (without familial name) as if she were a real character in a fiction. Or in this case—in the crossing of artificial and real reality—in that she is an artificial person or clone: a fictional person with a real body. For this reason, the narrative mode of this "first-person" novel, its way of seeing and knowing, is in effect a way of *not* seeing and *not* knowing. And to use again one of the novel's code words, or terms of art, the mode of the narrative is a way of "deferring" that.

No doubt this coupling of species life and institutional forms of life lends itself to biopolitical analysis. No doubt too it epitomizes how processes of modernization posit the game-like and artificial character of a social order that nonetheless stipulates its biological characterization. But my interest here is a bit different. In *Never Let Me Go*, the problem of the artificial or biological character of persons and institutions is posed in terms of the character of the artwork itself. This makes it possible to redescribe the continuous transformation of life into forms of life that defines the second modernization.[80]

Never Let Me Go is a modern murder mystery of sorts. It is a story about making up and taking lives; and along those lines, it is about contemporary cultural techniques of life and death. The art world is one of the artificial small worlds of the novel, albeit not merely one among others: creating "your art," and then showing it on the market, "will reveal your inner selves" (175, 254). The artwork, in short, is what makes interiors available to perception and communication: it will tell us "what you were like inside" (260). The artwork, and the art scene and market that determine what works as art, thus betoken personhood, and its observation and self-observation. The work of art is an exchangeable, and collectible, token of personhood. But the internality of the artwork, and how it indexes the nature of inner selves, is a little more complicated here.

Consider, for example, the form of one character's artwork—his "imaginary animals" (the only student artwork detailed in the novel):

> That was when I first saw his animals. When he'd told me about them in Norfolk, I'd seen in my mind scaled-down versions of the sort of pictures we'd done when we were small. So I was taken aback at how densely detailed each one was. In fact, it took a moment to see they were animals at all. The first impression was like one you'd get if you took the back off a radio set: tiny canals, weaving tendons, miniature screws and wheels were all drawn with obsessive precision, and only when you held the page away could you see it was some kind of armadillo, say, or a bird. (187)

The body-machine complex in this scaled-down picture could not be more explicit. The drawing on the page indicates what this animal looks like; it seems, on "first impression," to indicate what these animals look like inside. They resemble "a radio set" and so a signaling device by which internal mechanisms, at one machinic and biological, communicate with what the novel insistently calls "the outside world." But the first impression is a bit misleading.

The whole point about these tiny "imaginary animals" is that "it's like they come to life by themselves" (178). They seem to come to life by themselves, they seem life-like, because their interior states are open to view: you can see inside them, and how they work inside. But more exactly, one doesn't quite see inside them in that there's no difference between what they are inside and what they are. The obsessive precision of the form of the work makes them one and the same. The form, the form of the work of art, seems to come to life by itself in the unity of its form and its contents. It is sui generis and autonomous, and it is autonomous and autogenic to the very extent that it stages its own internality, and depicts that.

What's crucial about their artworks, for the students, or clones, in the novel is that the work of art will show what they are inside—and so that what they are inside is not reducible to the parts inside them: "Art bares the soul of the artist" (254). But what's crucial about their artworks, for the novel, is not the difference between body and soul, matter and form, but their unity: the obsessive formality by which they seem to animate themselves.

"The more excited he got telling me about his animals, the more uneasy I was growing" (179). "Growing"—another of *Never Let Me Go*'s terms of art, in this novel about growing up posthuman—indicates that where animal life, or the life-like animal, comes from is itself a black box.

The work of art then seems to do what bodies do, in growing by itself and coming alive. But in doing so and recursively reflecting on it—in staging its own form—it has the self-propagating, autogenic, and magical properties of the black box, a little machine with a life of its own.

The problem of the artwork and the problem of the official world are in this way copied into each other. The autopoiesis of modern social systems and the autopoiesis of the work of art are here arranged like the two sides of a horseshoe, opposed on part of their surface but communicating on another level. "When man wants to learn about himself," as Stanislaw Lem's posthuman, and self-aware, machine Golem expresses it to his human students, "he must move circuitously, he must explore himself and penetrate from the outside, with instruments and hypotheses, for your genuinely immediate world is the outside."[81] As the cybernetics theorist Ross Ashby expresses it, "That homo has a brain no more entitles him to assume he knows how he thinks than possession of a liver entitles him to assume that he knows how he metabolises."[82]

If art, then, is the measure of interiority in *Never Let Me Go*, this is not exactly because it reveals that one has an interior of a particular kind, or even that there's a difference between interior states and bodily ones. The felt difference between having and knowing is the difference between self-reference and other-reference—between, say, having a body and knowing what it does, or how it grows. The work of art, like the body, seems to come to life on its own. The autopoiesis of the work of art does what a body does. (And of course the theory of the autopoiesis of social systems is derived directly from the account of the autopoiesis of biological systems.)[83] But unlike the body, the work of art not merely does that but depicts it: it records the experience in its own presence. It stages, via that circular detour, its own reflexivity. That conserves, or posits, the place value of an opacity and an ignorance—a black box—that makes it possible to keep going (and for parts of one body—say, a liver—to keep the life of another going.)

The continuous transformation of natural life into artificial forms of life, hetero-restrictions into self-restrictions, is not surprisingly most explicit in relation to the autonomization of sex in the novel:

We had to be extremely careful about having sex in the outside world, especially with people who weren't students, because out there sex meant all sorts of things. Out there people were even fighting and killing each other over who had sex with whom. And the reason it meant so much—so much more than, say, dancing or table-tennis—was because the people out there were different from us students: they could have babies from sex. That was why it was so important to them, this question of who did it with whom. And even though, as we knew, it was completely impossible for any of us to have babies, out there, we had to behave like them. We had to respect the rules, and treat sex as something pretty special. (84)

The world "out there" differs from the indoor world of the students, and so differs from the little game world, "say, dancing or table-tennis," in that the sex act can "mean all sorts of things"—killing, fighting, babies—that exceed the act itself. The rules out there, which make sex special, differ from the rules in here, in which bodies are no more than exchangeable tokens, or moves, in a game. But the larger point is, it will be seen, that whereas both the world out there and the world in here then both have rules to respect, the inside of the body has its own autonomy, as if it were part of what's outside of persons.[84]

In this way, the form of modern social systems and the form of the modern work of art—its reflexivity, its internality, its stand-alone and autogenic character—index each other, and precisely in terms of the form games of the official world. In short, whitening the black box turns out to be the same thing as taking the back off the artwork. And taking apart the work of art turns out to be the same thing as taking apart ourselves. It would be as if our insides could be turned inside out and opened to view, like the parts of a simple machine—one that turns inputs into outcomes with nothing changing in between. This is to posit an imaginary machine that works like a white box: a perpetual and immortal machine, an immortal body, one that runs on an endless loop. It is to posit, that is, something like the tape recording, the clone reproduction, of the song that gives the novel its title and refrain, "never let me go." That dream machine, or dream body, is one that runs with a perfect continence, since it loses nothing and gains nothing along the way. But if 2 + 2 = 4, the game—since there is no longer any reason to prolong the play—is over.

NOTES

An earlier version of this essay appeared in *Critical Inquiry* 36.1 (Autumn 2009), under the title "Parlor Games: The Apriorization of the Media." Forthcoming in *The Official World*.

1. On self-describing modernity, see, for example, Niklas Luhmann, "Deconstruction as Second-Order Observing," in *Theories of Distinction: Redescribing*

the *Descriptions of Modernity*, ed. William Rasch (Stanford: Stanford University Press, 2002), 94–112. The sentence from Lem is taken from Stanislaw Lem, *Imaginary Magnitude*, trans. Mark E. Heine (Orlando: Harcourt Brace Jovanovich, 1984), 131.

2. Patricia Highsmith, *Ripley's Game* (1974; London: Vintage, 1999), 5. Subsequent references are given parenthetically in the text.

3. This not merely, it will be seen, in that the observed scene of the crime—a demarcated and ruled zone of motive and act, outcome and information—looks like the scene of the game. I am here picking up from the postscript to my *True Crime: Observations on Violence and Modernity* (New York: Routledge, 2007).

4. Norbert Wiener, *Cybernetics: Or Control and Communication in the Animal and the Machine* (1961; Cambridge: MIT Press, 1965), 159. See Peter Galison, "The Ontology of the Enemy: Norbert Wiener and the Cybernetic Vision," *Critical Inquiry* 21 (Autumn 1994): 228–266.

5. Timothy Lenoir, "All but War Is Simulation: The Military-Entertainment Complex," *Configurations* 8 (2000): 289–335.

6. John von Neumann, "Zur Theorie der Gesellschaftsspiele," *Mathematische Annalen* 100 (1928): 295–320; for an English translation, see "On the Theory of Games of Strategy," in *Contributions to the Theory of Games*, vol. 4, ed. A. W. Tucker and R. D. Luce (Princeton: Princeton University Press, 1959), 13–42.

7. John von Neumann and Oskar Morgenstern, *Theory of Games and Economic Behavior* (1947; Princeton: Princeton University Press, 2007).

8. For a useful summary of game theory and its discontents, see William Poundstone, *Prisoner's Dilemma: John von Neumann, Game Theory, and the Puzzle of the Bomb* (New York: Anchor Books, 1992), 167–178. The popular understanding conserves a notion of rational intention that is itself intermittently revised in game theory. The capacity to forecast that future presents will look like present futures is premised on the sharing of those presumptions among other actors, that is, on their decision to behave as economic actors, or economists, are supposed to behave. But the point not to be missed is that the positing of rationality in game theory is thus nontrivial and reflexive too. As Oskar Morgenstern expresses it, "To determine optimal, or 'rational' behavior is precisely the task of the mathematical theory of games. *Rational behavior is not an assumption of that theory;* rather, its identification is one of its *outcomes.*" Oskar Morgenstern, "Game Theory," in *Dictionary of the History of Ideas*, ed. Philip P. Wiener (New York: Charles Scribner's Sons, 1968), 267. "Clearly, if more and more players act rationally," as Morgenstern elaborates it, "there will be shifts in actual behavior and in real events to be described. This is an interesting phenomenon worth pointing out. It has philosophical significance: progress in the natural sciences does not affect natural phenomena, but the spread of knowledge of the workable social sciences changes social phenomena via changed individual behavior from which fact there may be a feedback

into the social sciences." Cf. Morgenstern, "Vollkommene Voraussicht und Wirtschaftliches Gleichgewicht," *Zeitschrift für Nationalökonomie 6* (1935): 337–357. That is, one knows that social systems have emerged once there are sociologists. In systems-theoretical terms, one operates ongoingly on imperfect information—and only on that basis: a world that contains decisionmakers has an uncertain future, since it depends on what is decided in the present. Cf. Elena Esposito, "Probability and Fiction in Science and Economics," lecture, Facoltà di Scienze della Comunicazione. Università di Modena e Reggio Emilia, Italy, 21 June 2006. I return to this matter of feedback in a moment. For now, if this recursive rationality seems implausible, one might consider how the academic archipelago of disciplines—the sequestration and reciprocal ignorance on which the differentiation and mutual opacity of disciplines depends—keeps on going anyway. And not least by ongoingly reflecting on the fact that they do. These self-conditioned social microfields are premised on reciprocal *rules of irrelevance*—codes of *civil inattention* or *involvement shields*—by which self-generated and self-dispelled uncertainties can be processed with relative and "indoor" independence. I return to these rules of irrelevance, and the ignorance-management they enable, in what follows. (The italicized phrases are drawn from Erving Goffman's description of behavior in public places and its interaction rituals. In adapting them, I mean to suggest that such descriptions might be extended to the *relative continence* of the social microworlds that concern me here—to their self-conditioning and so to their ways of managing uncertainty and ignorance or nonknowing.)

9. See McKenzie Wark, *Gamer Theory* (Cambridge: Harvard University Press, 2007), [016]. Jesper Juul, *Half-Real: Video Games between Real Rules and Fictional Worlds* (Cambridge: MIT Press, 2005).

10. The games I am considering here are pathological games—"funny games" in the sense that Michael Haneke gives to violent play in his film of the same name. In a 1952 letter to Norbert Wiener, Gregory Bateson observed: "What applications of the theory of games do, is to reinforce the players' acceptance of the rules and competitive premises, and therefore make it more and more difficult for the players to conceive that there might be other ways of meeting and dealing with each other. . . . Von Neumann's 'players' differ profoundly from people and mammals in that those robots totally lack humor and are totally unable to 'play' (in the sense in which the word is applied to kittens and puppies)." Quoted in William Poundstone, *The Prisoner's Dilemma*, 198. Or, as Herbert Marcuse expressed it, RAND gamers "arrange games with death and disfiguration in which fun, team work, and strategic planning mix in rewarding social harmony. . . . [RAND] reports such games in a style of absolving cuteness." Herbert Marcuse, *One-Dimensional Man: Studies in the Ideology of Advanced Industrial Society* (Boston: Beacon Press, 1964), 80–81. Yes, no doubt. But it's not just that Highsmith and RAND are kitten-and-puppy-free zones. These pathological games (like Haneke's) are staged

for the sake of their observation, reported and recorded, with a psychodispassionate distance between the little planning world (and its models) and the larger planned one (with its working models too). The fun of that, as opposed to, say, the play-fighting of kittens, is a bit harder to locate, and not exactly my concern here. But it's joined in these cases to the self-exempting and self-administering and overlit micro-worlds, of, say, Sade or Bentham, Highsmith or Foucault—and hence bound to the differentiation and autonomous validity of modern social systems. It's linked to what training and measuring and comparing and assessing in these institutions come to look like, and feel like. And it depends on the apriorization of the media as condition of existence (the doubling of reality, via, e.g., the graphomanias of Sade or Highsmith; the observer-recorder worlds of Bentham or Foucault or Luhmann). That there are many disparate disciplinary approaches to explaining these links is a version of the same differentiation (here, of pleasure principles). As Roger Caillois notes, near the close of his *Man, Play, and Games* (trans. Meyer Barash [Chicago: University of Illinois Press, 2001]): "It is not merely [in defining the domain of play] a question of different approaches arising from the diversity of disciplines. The facts studied in the name of play are so heterogeneous that one is led to speculate that the word 'play' is perhaps merely a trap, encouraging by its seeming generality tenacious illusions as to the supposed kinship between disparate forms of behavior" (162). We might then take this "diversity" of self-observed capsule worlds into account as a component, or condition, of modern pathological games.

11. See Dirk Baecker, "The Reality of Motion Pictures," *MLN: Modern Language Notes* 111.3 (1996): 561.

12. For example, historical reality (singular persons and events that are real but accidental and inessential); and fictional reality (persons and events that are unreal but representative or essential); and real—that is, mathematical or statistical—reality (numbers are, of course, the first virtual reality). The co-emergence of the realistic novel (fictional reality) and the calculus of probabilities and statistics is well known; so too the collateral emergence of the fictional and the historical turns (not least in the rise of historical fiction). As Luhmann concisely puts it: "Modernity has invented probability calculations just in time to maintain a fictionally created, dual reality. . . . [W]hat are we to make of the fact that the world is now divided into two kinds of reality—a world of singular events and a world of statistics (or of inductive references), a reality out there and a fictional reality?" Niklas Luhmann, *Art as a Social System*, trans. Eva Knodt (Stanford: Stanford University Press, 1995), 70, 175.

13. In that the player commenting on the game is also its designer, the distinction between game and world reenters the game on that score too: the arbiter of the game enters into it. And how can the game player play the arbiter? On such a becoming-medial as a cultural technique (tacitly on the model of Deleuze's "becoming-machine"), see Joseph Vogl's superb "Becoming Media:

Galileo's Telescope," *Grey Room* 29 (Winter 2007): 14–25, to which I am here indebted.

14. See Dirk Baecker, "The Form Game," in *Problems of Form*, ed. Dirk Baecker, trans. Michael Irmscher with Leah Edwards (Stanford: Stanford University Press, 1999), 99–106. On the contingent as that which is neither necessary nor impossible, see Niklas Luhmann, *Observations on Modernity*, trans. William Whobrey (Stanford: Stanford University Press, 1998): "Anything is contingent that is neither necessary nor impossible. The concept is therefore defined by the negation of necessity and impossibility" (45). On the implications of a contingency defined by that simultaneous double negation, see Mary Ann Doane, *The Emergence of Cinematic Time: Modernity, Contingency, the Archive* (Cambridge: MIT Press, 2002), 231–232.

15. Caillois, *Man, Play, and Games,* 29

16. Erving Goffman, *The Presentation of Self in Everyday Life* (New York: Anchor Books, 1959), 244.

17. See Anthony Giddens, *Modernity and Self-Identity: Self and Society in the Late Modern Age* (Stanford: Stanford University Press, 1991), 144–180.

18. Luhmann, *Observations,* 17.

19. Ibid., 21; Luhmann, *Art,* 244, 312–313.

20. On the legal system, see Cornelia Vismann, *Files: Law and Media Technology,* trans. Geoffrey Winthrop-Young (Stanford: Stanford University Press, 2008), and Niklas Luhmann, *Law as a Social System,* trans. Klaus Ziegert (Oxford: Oxford University Press, 2008); on public opinion, see Elizabeth Noelle-Neumann, *The Spiral of Silence: Public Opinion, Our Second Skin* (Chicago: University of Chicago Press, 1993); on the economic system, see, for instance, Dirk Baecker, "The Form of the Firm," *Organization: The Critical Journal on Organization, Theory and Society* 13.1 (2006): 109–142; on crime as social system, see my essay "The Crime System," *Critical Inquiry* 30.3 (Spring 2004): 557–583; and centrally for this quick inventory, Luhmann, *Observations,* 16, 59–60.

21. I return in the next section to feedback and how the delay in recognizing feedback makes, for example, for the endless rehearsals of the "form and intent" paradox with respect to artificial (intentional) objects.

22. The affective turn today reproduces exactly this preference for affects that incorporate their self-reflection (or consist in it). I have in mind here the provocative recent work, for instance, of Brian Massumi, Rei Terada, and Sianne Ngai. I have in mind, too, work building in part on the earlier social-psychological work of Silvan Tomkins and Erving Goffman. Second-order affect theory trades in derivatives of feeling the same way that hedge funds trade in derivatives of financial products. See particularly Goffman's splendid account of the communicative structure of the "little social system" of embarrassment in Erving Goffman, "Embarrassment and Social Organization," in *Interaction Ritual: Essays on Face-to-Face Behavior* (New York: Anchor Books, 1967),

97–112. The current affective turn in academic criticism is on some fronts a re-turn to sensibility criticism, at times, arguably, via a methodologically concealed conservatism. (Hence the perpetual re-demonstration of the end of "the Carte-sian subject," its deconstruction playing on an endless loop.) It is, unarguably, a retrofitting to the world-systems of second-order observation. Such a retrofitting is embedded in the very notion of "the turn"—the linguistic turn, the cultural turn, the affective turn—as a way of marking historical epochs. This is an extra-ordinary vehicle of periodization: what amounts not merely to the modalization of history but to its self-observation. I take up "the turn," its observation, and its media in a moment.

23. Erving Goffman, *Encounters: Two Studies in the Sociology of Interaction* (1961; New York: Penguin, 1972), 19.

24. And, in the early 1840s, the first scheduled oceanic steamship service; the first railway hotel (in New York), along with railway station bookshops; the earliest department stores; the first modern urban system for the separate circulation of water and sewage (Chadwick in Britain); the first "package" tour—Thomas Cook's, between Leicester and Loughborough. And so on. For a useful summary of these systems tending toward total mobilization, see John Urry, *Mobilities* (Cambridge: Polity, 2007), 3–16. See also James R. Beniger, *The Control Revolution: Technological and Economic Origins of the Information Society* (Cambridge: Harvard University Press, 1986). It should be clear that 1839 is then a relay point, not a point of origin, what I take up as the apriorization of the media as ground of existence, a self-referential (self-observed) media union.

25. See Joel Snyder, "Res Ipsa Loquitur," in *Things That Talk: Object Lessons from Art and Science*, ed. Lorraine Daston (New York: Zone Books, 2004), 403.

26. I am indebted here to Bernhard Siegert, *Relays: Literature as an Epoch of the Postal System*, trans. Kevin Repp (Stanford: Stanford University Press, 1999), 110, 109, and passim.

27. The second chapter of *Ripley's Game* opens by italicizing precisely this shift from meaning and sense to pattern and code: "So it was that some ten days later, on 22 March, Jonathan . . . received a curious letter from his good friend Alan McNear. . . . Jonathan had expected—or rather not expected—a sort of thank-you letter from Alan for the send-off party" (13). We might read this as a little lesson in the rudiments of information theory. "So it was" is then the renovated idiom of a now postally sponsored fate, keeping its appointed rounds. The postal friend, then—one who is near but also far ("mcnear")—is less a subject than a position, a position in the communicative circuit. And what then makes possible the paradoxical equivalence of the *expected* and the *not expected* here is the pattern of expectations that yields the sort-of thank-you letter, its technical conditions of possibility: "The more probable the message, the less information it gives. . . . The transmission of information is impossible save as

a transmission of alternatives. If only one contingency is to be transmitted, then it may be sent most efficiently and with the least trouble by sending no message at all." Norbert Wiener, *The Human Use of Human Beings: Cybernetics and Society* (New York: Doubleday, 1950), 12. The epistolary novel and the detective/ crime novel are the two basic forms of narrative fiction. Here they are braided together: in Highsmith's crime novels there is a proliferation of letters, copied into the narrative. The love letter (which communicates the incommunicable) and the thank-you note (which says what goes without saying) approach the minimal trouble of the greeting card. In that curvature toward standardized values and the efficient regulation of mutual involvement, the channel represents itself in the channel. A typology of the post-epistolary (the postal squared) novel might be set out from, say, Stoker's *Dracula* (1897) and James's *Turn of the Screw* (1898), both gothicized epistolary novels, to Highsmith's Ripley novels—criminalized ones.

28. Claude Shannon, "Communication Theory of Secrecy Systems," in *Claude Elwood Shannon: Collected Papers*, ed. N. J. A. Sloane and Aaron D. Wyner (New York: IEEE Press, 1992), 113. See also Wiener, *Human Use*, chap. 7, "Communication, Secrecy, and Social Policy."

29. See Paul N. Edwards, *The Closed World: Computers and the Politics of Discourse in Cold War America* (Cambridge: MIT Press, 1996), 201.

30. Consider, to take two obvious fictional examples, the rehearsals of that coupling in Thomas Pynchon's novel of war and information, *Gravity's Rainbow*, or Neil Stephenson's about war games and Turing machines, *Cryptonomicon*. My concern in this essay is with what this looks like in parlor games like the murder novel.

31. Siegert, *Relays*, 262. See also note 27.

32. Claude Shannon and Warren Weaver, *The Mathematical Theory of Communication* (Urbana: University of Illinois Press, 1949), 95.

33. For Wiener, predicting the future in the coming together in space of a missile and a target is like playing poker: "If the action were completely at the disposal of the pilot, and the pilot were to make the sort of intelligent use of his chances that we anticipate in a good poker player, for example, he has so much opportunity to modify his expected position before the arrival of a shell that should not reckon the chances of hitting him to be very good. . . . On the other hand, the pilot does *not* have a completely free chance to maneuver at his will" (Wiener, *Cybernetics*, 5). Hence for Wiener, as for von Neumann, God does not play dice with the universe; he plays poker with it. See my essay "The Art of the Collision," in *Speed Limits*, ed. Jeffrey T. Schnapp (Miami Beach: Wolfsonian-Florida International University, 2009), 84–92.

34. I am here invoking the incisive account of Susan Stewart, *On Longing: Narratives of the Miniature, the Gigantic, the Souvenir, the Collection* (Durham: Duke University Press, 1993), 57, 58, 151, 159, 158, 152.

35. In systems-theoretical terms, it turns to second-order observation—the observation of observation—and so to a second order of vision.

36. See Barbara Rose, "Blow Up—the Problem of Scale in Sculpture," *Art in America* 56 (1968): 83. As Michael North has reminded me, the notion of the photograph as scale-free network is misleading, voiding its material conditions. The blow-up instead makes visible the distinction between medium and form. On the problems with assumptions of scale-free systems, see Evelyn Fox Keller, "Revisiting 'Scale-Free' Networks," in *BioEssays* 27 (2005): 1060–68. See also, on the microfilmic, Jonathan Auerbach and Lisa Gitelman, "Microfilm, Containment, and the Cold War," *American Literary History* 19.3 (2007): 745–768.

37. See Vogl, "Becoming-Media"; and Bernhard Siegert, "Cacography or Communication? Cultural Techniques in German Media Studies," *Grey Room* 29 (Winter 2007): 26–47. On the mechanized doubling of act and observation that is the condition and technique of motion pictures, see Baecker, "The Reality of Motion Pictures."

38. See Jack Goody and Ian Watt, "The Consequences of Literacy," in *Literacy in Traditional Societies*, ed. Jack Goody (Cambridge: Cambridge University Press, 1968), 27–68; and Elizabeth L. Eisenstein, *The Printing Revolution in Early Modern Europe* (Cambridge: Cambridge University Press, 1993).

39. Gregory Bateson, *Mind and Nature: A Necessary Unity* (New York: Bantam, 1980), 120–121.

40. Michel Serres, *The Parasite*, trans. Lawrence R. Schehr (Minneapolis: University of Minnesota Press, 2007), 79.

41. On this deconstructive *Leerlaufen*—empty-running: an idling engine—with respect to media-cultural techniques, see my essay, "The Daily Planet" forthcoming in *Post45*. For the moment I am concerned with the materialities of communication, technologies of reference, and the apriorization of the media as condition of existence in these literary-pathological games, that is, with the cultural techniques that become so completely coterminous with the events that they at once record and comprise that they become imperceptible.

42. See my *True Crime*, 57–90.

43. Elena Esposito, "The Arts of Contingency," *Critical Inquiry* 32 (2004): 11. On the media/form distinction in systems theory on which Esposito's lucid account draws, see Niklas Luhmann, *Die Gesellschaft der Gesellschaft*, 2 vols. (Frankfurt am Main: Suhrkamp, 1997), 1:1, 190–201.

44. That "terminological indifference" (see Vismann, *Files*, xii) is the crux of a series of media studies that center on cultural techniques—for example, file, post, index—which are at once object and act: they say what they do and, in doing so, do what they say. These relations (to adapt Deleuze's phrase) are real but abstract—in effect, living diagrams. I am concerned here with the conditions that magnetize these transferential relations—and lend to administration the feel of the performative.

45. Wiener, *Human Use*, 20. Peter Galison provides an extraordinarily detailed and lucid account of the "great modernisms of physics"—the scale-shifting histories of light, time, and space, and the material techniques for

measuring and mapping them—in *Einstein's Clocks, Poincaré's Maps: Empires of Time* (New York: W. W. Norton, 2003). See also Martin Jay, "Astronomical Hindsight: The Speed of Light and Virtual Reality," in *Refractions of Violence* (New York: Routledge, 2003), 119–132.

46. I touch on Ripley's mediality in *True Crime*, 113–116.

47. Wiener, *Human Use*, 20. For Wiener, it may be noted, this is "returning the emphasis of physics to a quasi-Liebnitzian [*sic*] state, whose tendency is once again optical" (20). That baroque turn (via Deleuze) is well marked in recent media studies. So too is the systems theory turn to matters of first-order and second-order observation. One finds in a range of "Kittlerian" media studies—on which account the "media determine our situation"—something of a migration to a systems theory outlook. I have in mind, for example, Siegert's "Cacography or Communication?"—with its emphasis on observation, recursivity, and contingency, and on how media "process distinctions"; or Vogl's "Becoming Media," with its emphasis on "a relativized observer who observes him- or herself as an observer." (I draw directly on both here.) The turn would in part seem to be from a history of media objects (gramophone, film, or typewriter, say) to medial operations. But these "objects" themselves are already (in von Foerster's formulation) "tokens for Eigenbehaviors"—recursively stabilized and so self-referential processes. See Heinz von Foerster, "Objects: Tokens for [Eigen]Behaviors," in *Observing Systems* (Seaside, Calif.: Intersystems Publications, 1981), 273–285.

48. The italicized phrase is drawn from Giorgio Agamben, *The Man without Content*, trans. Georgia Albert (Stanford: Stanford University Press, 1999).

49. David Riesman, *The Lonely Crowd* (1961; New Haven: Yale University Press, 1989), 16. The gyroscope is, however, already quasi-outmoded, for Riesman, as a model for persons. What Riesman traces is a shifting from the inner-directed to the "outer-directed" person; for the second, "the control equipment, instead of being like a gyroscope, is like a radar" (25). On radar and on the black boxes of a "radar philosophy," see the final section of this essay.

50. See Beniger, *The Control Revolution*, 302–307.

51. See Hans Sachs, "The Delay of the Machine Age," *Psychoanalytic Quarterly* 2.137 (1933): 404–424. The problem of that delay involves, in part, why, for example, the Greeks, adept at making little devices like toy steam engines, never thought of adapting these toys to do real work. On the delay of the second machine age—the delay in recognizing feedback, that is, the "idea that circular causation is of very great importance"—there is Bateson's useful summary: "Many self-corrective systems were also already known. That is, individual cases were known, but the *principle* remained unknown. Indeed, occidental man's repeated discovery of instances and inability to perceive the underlying principle demonstrate the rigidity of his epistemology. Discoveries and rediscoveries of the principle include Lamarck's transformism (1809), James Watt's invention of the governor for the steam engine (late eighteenth century), Alfred

Russel [sic] Wallace's perception of natural selection (1856), Clark [sic] Maxwell's mathematical analysis of the steam engine with a governor (1868), Claude Bernard's *milieu interne*, Hegelian and Marxian analyses of social process ... and the various mutually independent steps in the development of cybernetics and systems theory during and immediately after World War II" (Bateson, *Mind and Nature*, 117). See also Otto Mayr, *The Origins of Feedback Control* (Cambridge: MIT Press, 1970). One can add to this list the preadaptive advance that modern literature (or literature from the standpoint of modernity) represents, a matter to which I turn in a moment. On the ties between the visual arts and systems theory, see Pamela Lee, *Chronophobia: On Time in the Art of the 1960s* (Cambridge: MIT Press, 2004); and Andrew Galloway, *Protocol: How Control Exists after Decentralization* (Cambridge: MIT Press, 2004).

52. See Wiener, *Human Use*, 151, 24; Bateson, *Mind and Nature*, 116. These self-steering mechanisms (Wiener's term "cybernetics" is, of course, derived from the Greek word for steersman) involve "a method of controlling a system by reinserting into it the results of its past performance"—the feeding back of outcomes into input. It involves, that is, "the unpurposeful random mechanism which seeks for its own purpose through a process of learning" (Wiener, *Human Use*, 61, 38).

53. On that short circuit, see Siegert, *Relays*. There is a return to phenomenology in new media studies. And there is a tendency in that work toward something of an uneven adjectival drift, an entailment drift, from materiality to body to embodiment to experience: that is, the materialities of reflexivity become embodied reflection, which becomes human embodiment, which becomes "richly embodied human experience." On the presumptions at work in a range of such returns, one might consider Bruno Latour's critique of such tendencies: "Most often inspired by phenomenology, these reform movements have inherited all its defects: they are unable to imagine a metaphysics in which there would be other real agencies than those with intentional humans, or worse, they oppose human action with the mere 'material effect' of natural objects which, as they say, have 'no agency' but only 'behavior.' But an 'interpretative' sociology is just as much a sociology of the social than [sic] any of the 'objectivist' or 'positivist' versions it wishes to replace. It believes that certain types of agencies—persons, intention, feeling, work, face-to-face interaction—will *automatically* bring life, riches, and 'humanity.'" Bruno Latour, *Reassembling the Social: An Introduction to Actor-Network-Theory* (New York: Oxford University Press, 2007), 61.

54. See Ranulph Glanville, "A (Cybernetic) Musing: Ashby and the Black Box," *Cybernetics and Human Knowing* 14.2–3 (2007): 189–196.

55. The cold war think tank, the operations center of contemporary war gaming, is of course the RAND Corporation, and RAND of course—in what Marcuse called our administrative "syntax of abbreviation"—is an acronym for "research and development."

56. Malcolm Gladwell, *Blink: The Power of Thinking without Thinking*

(New York: Little, Brown, 2005), 99. Subsequent references are given parenthetically in the text. It's of course the case that the popularization of styles of systems thinking—from pop psychology and self-help to ecological/planetary studies to loose couplings of world-systems theory and transworldliness in recent literary history—is extensive and extending. My momentary focus on Gladwell here—at the risk of overburdening that account—is opportunistic: to rehearse, inventory, and take the measure of that spreading of a systems outlook, and the notion of "art" that goes with it. One might compare Gladwell's account with one of its primary sources, the incisive work of Gerd Gigerenzer, particularly *Gut Feelings: The Intelligence of the Unconscious* (London: Viking Adult, 2007).

57. On the war computer, see http://www.time.com/time/covers/0,16641,19 500123,00.html. On Charcot, see Anson Rabinbach, *The Human Motor: Energy, Fatigue, and the Origins of Modernity* (New York: Basic Books, 1990), 160. I examine these pathologies of agency and maladies of will in *Serial Killers: Death and Life in America's Wound Culture* (New York: Routledge, 1998), 74–81. The point not to be missed is that the reentry of observation into act is the real innovation of the managerial/control revolution: the observation and registration of the work process enter into the work process, or, better, emerge as the work process itself (the transference between the act and its registration, combining the symbolic and the real). There is, it may be noted, a direct tie between media studies and American studies by way of these communicative systems. The newly expanded field of American studies, for example—the enterprise: to boldly go where no Americanist has gone before—is not just one case among others. Americanization and a media a priori indicate each other from the start (from the democratic print public sphere on). Now transcultural, transatlantic, transnational—fields with the names of airlines, each new field, or funding object, setting thousands of keyboards in motion, forms of message and body transport in a culture premised on marketing the contingency that defines it. What has emerged, *via media*, is a notion of *America sans frontières*—unbound, always and everywhere. One finds here a transworldliness that is at the same time something else: for example, literary deep time or genre space as the space-time of the Dewey decimal system (library synchrony). After all, such technologies of recording, storing, and reference—files, index cards, the ring binder, and so on, the cascade of control technologies that proliferate with the second industrial revolution—rank with the plow and the stirrup as epoch-making cultural techniques, and so merit some description in this context too. See, e.g., Vismann, *Files;* Markus Krajewski, *ZettelWirtschaft* (Berlin: Kadmos, 2002). I take up some of the links between American studies and the apriorization of the media in "Die freie Natur," *Archiv für Mediengeschichte* 9 (2009): 127–138.

58. That is, the "gee-whiz" effect in these reality games is—*Believe it or not!*—constitutive: the construction of reality and the reality of construction are contin-

ually differentiated, and go on in and through each other. The connection between the name Ripley and the reality show is explicit in *The Talented Mr. Ripley*.

59. Or, in the terms of *Ripley's Game*, "How much did the enemy know?" (167). And "Was it even a game?" (189).

60. Sharon Ghamari-Tabrizi, *The Worlds of Herman Kahn: The Intuitive Science of Thermonuclear War* (Cambridge: Harvard University Press, 2005), 170; see also Ghamari-Tabrizi, "Simulating the Unthinkable: Gaming Future War in the 1950s and 1960s," *Social Studies of Science* 30.2 (April 2000): 190–213.

61. I am here referencing Paul de Man's unfolding of the premises of American New Critical formalism in his *Blindness and Insight: Essays in the Rhetoric of Contemporary Criticism* (Minneapolis: University of Minnesota Press, 1983), 20–35.

62. It goes without saying that such arguments will convince no one for whom the aesthetic difference is precisely abiding in ambiguity—or, better, living through undecidability.

63. Edgar Allan Poe, "The Mystery of Marie Roget," in *Tales and Sketches*, vol. 2, *1843–1848*, ed. Thomas Oliver Mabbott (Urbana: University of Illinois, 2000), 752; Poe, "The Imp of the Perverse," in *The Complete Tales and Poems of Edgar Allan Poe* (New York: Vintage, 1975), 281. See my essay "The Crime System"; and the version that appears in *True Crime*, 61–74.

64. Luhmann, *Art*, 68, 309.

65. Ibid., 309. The point not to be missed is that this is to raise the question of art "as" social system, not to posit their identity. For Luhmann, society consists in communications and nothing else. But the notion that art "makes perception available for communication" and the notion of art as social system (and so distinct from perceptual systems) remain in paradox in Luhmann's account.

66. Ibid., 312–313.

67. See Glanville, "(Cybernetic) Musing," 189.

68. Ross Ashby, *Introduction to Cybernetics* (London: Chapman and Hall, 1956), 86.

69. See Friedrich Kittler, *Discourse Networks, 1800/1900*, trans. Michael Metteer and Chris Cullens (Stanford: Stanford University Press, 1990); and Galloway, *Protocol*, 18, 22.

70. The law of distribution, across the equals sign, is inadequate to negative feedback systems. There is (as Bruno Latour has it) no transportation without translation (Latour, *Reassembling the Social*, 215). Or as Michel Serres expresses it: "A discourse with no jokers is even conceivable. This universe would reduce to an identity principle. Thus the universe in question is undervalued by a = a" (Serres, *The Parasite*, 163). On the concept of the black box, see Wiener, *Cybernetics*, xi, 27, 108; and Glanville, "(Cybernetic) Musing," 189–196. The earliest use of the term in this sense is attributed to James Clerk Maxwell in his

Theory of Heat (1871). Peter Galison points out that the term became popular in "radar philosophy" during the Second World War, via the use of common black-speckled boxes to encase radar equipment (Galison, "Ontology," 247). If the gyroscope anticipates such equipment, I have noted that the gyroscopic model of personhood—the "inner-directed" person—gives way in the cold war period to another model: the "control equipment" of the "other-directed person," a radar (Riesman, *The Lonely Crowd*, 25). On all counts, black boxes are "boxes with unspecified interiors," which report back "their *performed* action on the outer world, and not merely their *intended* action" (Wiener, *Human Use*, 27).

71. On modernity's "ecology of ignorance," see Luhmann, *Observations*, 75–112. See also Lars Qvortrup, "Luhmann Applied to the Knowledge Society: Religion as Fourth-Order Knowledge," in *Cybernetics and Human Knowing* 14 (2008): 11–27.

72. The belated recognition of the links between deconstructive and cybernetic accounts is now under way. Consider, for example, on Foucault, David Wellbery, "The General Enters the Library: A Note on Disciplines and Complexity," *Critical Inquiry* 35.4 (2009): 982–994; on Lacan, Lydia Liu, "The Cybernetic Unconscious: Rethinking Lacan, Poe, and French Theory," *Critical Inquiry* 36.2 (2010): 288–320; on Derrida, a scanning *Of Grammatology* (albeit the links are largely occulted in the subsequent generalization of deconstruction as the default position of a culture trending toward difference and diversity).

73. Michel Foucault, *Discipline and Punish: The Birth of the Prison*, trans. Alan Sheridan (New York: Vintage, 1977), 204.

74. Ibid.

75. Kazuo Ishiguro, *Never Let Me Go* (New York: Knopf, 2005), 47, 52. Subsequent references are given parenthetically in the text. What's overcondensed in the closing pages of this chapter is set out more extensively in my essay "The Official World," *Critical Inquiry* 37.4 (Summer 2011): 724–753.

76. On the "autonomization of everything" in modern social systems, and its aesthetic implications, see my essay "The Official World."

77. Georg Simmel, *The Sociology of Georg Simmel*, trans. and ed. Kurt H. Wolff (Glencoe: University of Illinois Press, 1950), 50.

78. The novel thus tacks closely to the genre of the *Bildungsroman*, with its secluded micro-societies—and their "miniaturization" in the "aesthetic harmony of the individual." See Franco Moretti, *The Way of the World: The Bildungsroman in European Culture*, trans. Albert Sbragia (New York: Verso, 1987), 36. It tacks closely to its history of a self-modeling on a model-picture *(Bild)*, with the difference that the genre here epitomizes itself: it is a *Bildungsroman* told from the standpoint of a clone or picture-model. The microsociety of the novel is a society that sees itself as self-constituting and, therefore, self-observing, via career "carers" and "donor" figures—death and life thus making up the dark side of a career. In short, the novel continues to play out the semantic vocation

of the *Bildungsroman* after its story of social and individual harmonization has been officially abandoned.

79. Henry Adams, *The Education of Henry Adams* (1907; Boston: Houghton Mifflin, 1918), 4.

80. It makes it possible, too, to redescribe why the fixation on large abstractions like "social construction" or "agency" leads thinking in a circle, and does so in fields that appeal to forms of art to map social forms of life. In short, inhabiting that circle, and rehearsing it, defines interpretive fields that model the reflexivity they describe, and hence consist, more and more, in defining and redefining what they are, or were. That institutionally prolongs the irresolution—or, in Ishiguro's terms, the "deferrals"—that sponsors them. And as I have set out (note 8), these archipelagoes of self-conditioned micro-fields thus make it possible for ecologies of ignorance—like those of *Never Let Me Go*—to prolong institutional play, in the good sense. That's why, too, every question asked after a talk really is "a great question."

81. Lem, *Imaginary Magnitude*, 175.

82. Ross Ashby, *Aphorisms* (2004), http://www.cybsoc.org/ross.htm (accessed 25 September 2012).

83. Niklas Luhmann's theorization of autopoietic social systems explicitly relies on the theorization of the autopoiesis and autonomy, the self-observing form, of biological systems in the work of Humberto Maturana and Francisco Varela. See, for instance, Humberto R. Maturana and Francisco J. Varela, *Autopoiesis and Cognition: The Realization of the Living* (Dordecht: D. Reidel, 1980), and *The Tree of Knowledge: The Biological Roots of Human Understanding* (Boston: Shambala Publications, 1987).

84. And of course the whole reason why the clones exist in the first place is to substitute artificial for natural conditions, and to eliminate what is "pretty special" about bodies that exceed intentions, and work like black boxes, for, or at the expense of, those who have, or are, them.

WORKS CITED

Adams, Henry. *The Education of Henry Adams.* Boston: Houghton Mifflin, 1918.
Agamben, Giorgio. *The Man without Content.* Trans. Georgia Albert. Stanford: Stanford University Press, 1999.
Ashby, Ross. *Aphorisms.* The Cybernetics Society. 2004. http://*www.*cybsoc.org (accessed 25 September 2012).
———. *Introduction to Cybernetics.* London: Chapman and Hall, 1956.
Auerbach, Jonathan, and Lisa Gitelman. "Microfilm, Containment, and the Cold War." *American Literary History* 19.3 (2007): 745–768.
Baecker, Dirk. "The Form of the Firm." *Organization: The Critical Journal on Organization, Theory and Society* 13.1 (2006): 109–42.

──. "The Form Game." In *Problems of Form*, ed. Dirk Baecker, trans. Michael Irmscher with Leah Edwards. Stanford: Stanford University Press, 1999. 99–106.

──. "The Reality of Motion Pictures." *MLN: Modern Language Notes* 111.3 (1996): 560–577.

Bateson, Gregory. *Mind and Nature: A Necessary Unity*. New York: Bantam, 1980.

Beniger, James R. *The Control Revolution: Technological and Economic Origins of the Information Society*. Cambridge: Harvard University Press, 1986.

Caillois, Roger. *Man, Play, and Games*. Trans. Meyer Barash. Chicago: University of Illinois Press, 2001.

De Man, Paul. *Blindness and Insight: Essays in the Rhetoric of Contemporary Criticism*. Minneapolis: University of Minnesota Press, 1983.

Doane, Mary Ann. *The Emergence of Cinematic Time: Modernity, Contingency, the Archive*. Cambridge: MIT Press, 2002.

Edwards, Paul N. *The Closed World: Computers and the Politics of Discourse in Cold War America*. Cambridge: MIT Press, 1996.

Eisenstein, Elizabeth L. *The Printing Revolution in Early Modern Europe*. Cambridge: Cambridge University Press, 1993.

Esposito, Elena. "The Arts of Contingency." *Critical Inquiry* 32 (2004): 7–25.

──. "Probability and Fiction in Science and Economics." Lecture at the Facoltà di Scienze della Comunicazione. Università di Modena e Reggio Emilia, Italy, 21 June 2006.

Foucault, Michel. *Discipline and Punish: The Birth of the Prison*. Trans. Alan Sheridan. New York: Vintage, 1977.

Galison, Peter. *Einstein's Clocks, Poincaré's Maps: Empires of Time*. New York: W. W. Norton & Company, 2003.

──. "The Ontology of the Enemy: Norbert Wiener and the Cybernetic Vision." *Critical Inquiry* 21 (Autumn 1994): 228–266.

Galloway, Andrew. *Protocol: How Control Exists after Decentralization*. Cambridge: MIT Press, 2004.

Ghamari-Tabrizi, Sharon. "Simulating the Unthinkable: Gaming Future War in the 1950s and 1960s." *Social Studies of Science* 30.2 (2000): 190–213.

──. *The Worlds of Herman Kahn: The Intuitive Science of Thermonuclear War*. Cambridge: Harvard University Press, 2005.

Giddens, Anthony. *Modernity and Self-Identity: Self and Society in the Late Modern Age*. Stanford: Stanford University Press, 1991.

Gigerenzer, Gerd. *Gut Feelings: The Intelligence of the Unconscious*. London: Viking Adult, 2007.

Gladwell, Malcolm. *Blink: The Power of Thinking without Thinking*. New York: Little, Brown, 2005.

Glanville, Ranulph. "A (Cybernetic) Musing: Ashby and the Black Box." *Cybernetics and Human Knowing* 14.2–3 (2007): 189–196.

Goffman, Erving. "Embarrassment and Social Organization." In *Interaction Ritual: Essays on Face-to-Face Behavior*. New York: Anchor Books, 1967. 97–112.

———. *Encounters: Two Studies in the Sociology of Interaction*. New York: Penguin, 1961.

———. *The Presentation of Self in Everyday Life*. New York: Anchor Books, 1959.

Goody, Jack, and Ian Watt. "The Consequences of Literacy." In *Literacy in Traditional Societies*, ed. Jack Goody. Cambridge: Cambridge University Press, 1968. 27–68.

Highsmith, Patricia. *Ripley's Game* [1974]. London: Vintage, 1999.

Ishiguro, Kazuo. *Never Let Me Go*. New York: Knopf, 2005.

Jay, Martin. "Astronomical Hindsight: The Speed of Light and Virtual Reality." In *Refractions of Violence*. New York: Routledge, 2003. 119–132.

Juul, Jesper. *Half-Real: Video Games between Real Rules and Fictional Worlds*. Cambridge: MIT Press, 2005.

Keller, Evelyn Fox. "Revisiting 'Scale-Free' Networks." *BioEssays* 27 (2005): 1060–68.

Kittler, Friedrich. *Discourse Networks, 1800/1900*. Trans. Michael Metteer and Chris Cullens. Stanford: Stanford University Press, 1990.

Krajewski, Markus. *ZettelWirtschaft*. Berlin: Kadmos, 2002.

Latour, Bruno. *Reassembling the Social: An Introduction to Actor-Network-Theory*. New York: Oxford University Press, 2007.

Lee, Pamela. *Chronophobia: On Time in the Art of the 1960s*. Cambridge: MIT Press, 2004.

Lem, Stanislaw. *Imaginary Magnitude*. Trans. Mark E. Heine. Orlando: Harcourt Brace Jovanovich, 1984.

Lenoir, Timothy. "All but War Is Simulation: The Military-Entertainment Complex." *Configurations* 8 (2000): 289–335.

Liu, Lydia. "The Cybernetic Unconscious: Rethinking Lacan, Poe, and French Theory." *Critical Inquiry* 36.2 (2010): 288–320.

Luhmann, Niklas. *Art as a Social System*. Trans. Eva Knodt. Stanford: Stanford University Press, 1995.

———. "Deconstruction as Second-Order Observing." In *Theories of Distinction: Redescribing the Descriptions of Modernity*. Ed. William Rasch. Stanford: Stanford University Press, 2002. 94–112.

———. *Die Gesellschaft der Gesellschaft*. Vols. 1 and 2. Frankfurt am Main: Suhrkamp, 1997.

———. *Law as a Social System*. Trans. Klaus Ziegert. Oxford: Oxford University Press, 2008.

———. *Observations on Modernity*. Trans. William Whobrey. Stanford: Stanford University Press, 1998.

Marcuse, Herbert. *One-Dimensional Man: Studies in the Ideology of Advanced Industrial Society*. Boston: Beacon Press, 1964.

Maturana, Humberto R., and Francisco J. Varela. *Autopoiesis and Cognition: The Realization of the Living*. Dordecht: D. Reidel, 1980.

———. *The Tree of Knowledge: The Biological Roots of Human Understanding*. Boston: Shambala Publications, 1987.

Mayr, Otto. *The Origins of Feedback Control*. Cambridge: MIT Press, 1970.

Moretti, Franco. *The Way of the World: The Bildungsroman in European Culture*. Trans. Albert Sbragia. New York: Verso, 1987.

Morgenstern, Oskar. "Game Theory." In *Dictionary of the History of Ideas*, ed. Philip P. Wiener. New York: Charles Scribner's Sons, 1968. 267.

———. "Vollkommene Voraussicht und Wirtschaftliches Gleichgewicht." *Zeitschrift für Nationalökonomie* 6 (1935): 337–57.

Noelle-Neumann, Elizabeth. *The Spiral of Silence: Public Opinion, Our Second Skin*. Chicago: University of Chicago Press, 1993.

Poundstone, William. *Prisoner's Dilemma: John von Neumann, Game Theory, and the Puzzle of the Bomb*. New York: Anchor Books, 1992.

Qvortrup, Lars. "Luhmann Applied to the Knowledge Society: Religion as Fourth-Order Knowledge." *Cybernetics and Human Knowing* 14 (2008): 11–27.

Rabinbach, Anson. *The Human Motor: Energy, Fatigue, and the Origins of Modernity*. New York: Basic Books, 1990.

Riesman, David. *The Lonely Crowd* [1961]. New Haven: Yale University Press, 1989.

Rose, Barbara. "Blow Up: The Problem of Scale in Sculpture." *Art in America* 56 (1968): 80–91.

Sachs, Hans. "The Delay of the Machine Age." *Psychoanalytic Quarterly* 137.2 (1933): 404–424.

Seltzer, Mark. "The Art of the Collision." In *Speed Limits*, ed. Jeffrey T. Schnapp. Miami Beach: Wolfsonian–Florida International University, 2009, 84–92.

———. "The Crime System." *Critical Inquiry* 30.3 (Spring 2004): 557–83.

———. "Die freie Natur." *Gefahrensinn: Archiv für Mediengeschichte* 9 (2009): 127–138.

———. "The Official World." *Critical Inquiry* 37.4 (2011): 724–753.

———. "Parlor Games: The Apriorization of the Media." *Critical Inquiry* 36.1 (Autumn 2009): 100–133.

———. *Serial Killers: Death and Life in America's Wound Culture*. New York: Routledge, 1998.

———. *True Crime: Observations on Violence and Modernity*. New York: Routledge, 2007.

Serres, Michel. *The Parasite*. Trans. Lawrence R. Schehr. Minneapolis: University of Minnesota Press, 2007.

Shannon, Claude Elwood. "Communication Theory of Secrecy Systems." In *Claude Elwood Shannon: Collected Papers*. Ed. N. J. A. Sloane and Aaron D. Wyner. New York: IEEE Press, 1992. 84–143.

Shannon, Claude Elwood, and Warren Weaver. *The Mathematical Theory of Communication.* Urbana: University of Illinois Press, 1949.

Siegert, Bernhard. "Cacography or Communication? Cultural Techniques in German Media Studies." *Grey Room* 29 (Winter 2007): 26–47.

———. *Relays: Literature as an Epoch of the Postal System.* Trans. Kevin Repp. Stanford: Stanford University Press, 1999.

Snyder, Joel. "Res Ipsa Loquitur." In *Things That Talk: Object Lessons from Art and Science*, ed. Lorraine Daston. New York: Zone Books, 2004. 195–221.

Stewart, Susan. *On Longing: Narratives of the Miniature, the Gigantic, the Souvenir, the Collection.* Durham: Duke University Press, 1993.

Urry, John. *Mobilities.* Cambridge: Polity, 2007.

Vismann, Cornelia. *Files: Law and Media Technology.* Trans. Geoffrey Winthrop-Young. Stanford: Stanford University Press, 2008.

Vogl, Joseph. "Becoming Media: Galileo's Telescope." *Grey Room* 29 (Winter 2007): 14–25.

von Foerster, Heinz. "Objects: Tokens for [Eigen]Behaviors." In *Observing Systems*. Seaside, Calif.: Intersystems Publications, 1981. 273–285.

von Neumann, John. "On the Theory of Games of Strategy." In *Contributions to the Theory of Games.* Vol. 4. Ed. A. W. Tucker and R. D. Luce. Princeton: Princeton University Press, 1959. 13–42.

———. "Zur Theorie der Gesellschaftsspiele." *Mathematische Annalen* 100 (1928): 295–320.

Wark, McKenzie. *Gamer Theory.* Cambridge: Harvard University Press, 2007.

Wellbery, David. "The General Enters the Library: A Note on Disciplines and Complexity." *Critical Inquiry* 35.4 (2009): 982–994.

Wiener, Norbert. *Cybernetics: Or Control and Communication in the Animal and the Machine* [1961]. Cambridge: MIT Press, 1965.

———. *The Human Use of Human Beings: Cybernetics and Society.* New York: Doubleday, 1950.

PART III

POLITICAL IMAGINARIES

8 Real Toads

The real toads of my title are first and foremost the ones invented by Marianne Moore in her poem "Poetry," living in "imaginary gardens" and, eventually, abandoned there by Moore when she cut the poem to three lines: "Poetry / I too dislike it / Reading it, however, with a perfect contempt for it, one discovers in it, after all, a place for the genuine" (Moore). Real toads are obviously aligned here with the "genuine," but the point of the poem is not, of course, to choose between them and the imaginary gardens; we might more plausibly say that we have no way of thinking about the real except in terms of its relation to the imaginary, and therefore to imagine that we could simply choose the real over the imaginary would be to make a very foolish mistake. Indeed, because of what Winfried Fluck has rightly called "the crucial role of the imaginary in social arrangements and social visions" (447), we cannot understand the reality of the real without locating it in the imaginary. So if, for example, I were to offer you as an example of a real toad the "Volcker shock" of 1979—sometimes called the "founding act of neoliberalism" (Panitch and Gindin) since it raised interest rates and drove the United States into a recession that emptied factories and broke unions—I could not possibly begin to account for its reality without locating it in its imaginary garden, even if the function of that garden was to enable me to situate myself in a way that made the toad invisible to me (that camouflaged the toad). And I don't mean by this just the fact that there are no great Volcker shock novels. I mean that neoliberalism itself has played almost no visible role in our cultural imaginary, and that the garden we literary critics have been most interested in has been largely, at least in our construction of it, inhabited not by real but by imaginary toads.

Indeed it is only within the last year that the concept of neoliberalism has begun to make its impression on Americans and in particular on American literary historians, mainly because the current worldwide recession can at least be imagined to foreshadow an end to it, thus making clear that for over thirty years we have been living in a historical period rather than a state of nature. And from this standpoint, just as the title of my talk is adapted from a famous poem, its subtitle ought to be an adaptation of another, almost equally famous (at least in our little garden) essay. But whereas Fredric Jameson's essay was called "Periodizing the 60s," mine should be called "Periodizing Everything since the Sixties." Jameson, of course, wrote in 1984, a year that, at the time, had the double advantage of still naming a horrifying but increasingly unlikely (Orwellian) future and of looking back at what seemed recently but definitively past—the 1960s themselves. The year 2009 makes no Orwellian threats (except to those who see in Barack Obama the threat of the gulag rather than the savior of the market—and I would remind you that as an exemplary neoliberal, Obama has posed no threat to markets; indeed one of his first economic appointments was Paul Volcker of the Volcker shock). But the events of what we might call fiscal 2009—especially if we begin it a few months early—very clearly brought about the end of the boom. And even if we are inclined toward the market's self-diagnosis (that this is essentially a financial crisis, caused by and thus curable by new forms of regulation) rather than toward a more structural account (that the various forms of speculative abuses we have witnessed are themselves only a response to the more fundamental problem of a falling rate of profit), we can nonetheless see that the self-descriptions we ourselves have preferred are no longer convincing, and that, whatever the true meaning of the crisis in the economy turns out to be, the crisis in culture makes it possible for us to imagine the end of the intellectual world that we ourselves have created and thus to periodize it.

At any rate, that's the methodological fantasy of this essay—that neoliberalism is ending. And the non-methodological and not so fantastic desire of this essay is that even if neoliberalism does not disappear (even if, as seems more than likely, Obama and Geithner and the rest succeed in rescuing it), the culture of neoliberalism will. So that even if we don't get a more just society, we'll at least get better books.

For the books we've had have not been so good. Some of you may remember that when, back in 1989, Francis Fukuyama announced what we can now see to be the arrival of neoliberalism—he called it the end of history—he did so with mixed feelings. The good news, he thought, was that the ideological supremacy of free markets and of the political arrangement most suited to them (liberal democracy) had been established; even communists were talking about the importance of being competitive in the marketplace. The bad news was that without "the worldwide ideological struggle" between capitalism and socialism to inspire us, we were in for "a very sad time." In the "post-historical period," he wrote, "there will be neither art nor philosophy, just the perpetual caretaking of the museum of human history" (124). The end of history would be good for markets, bad for art.

Right now, of course, it's not so clear how the good-for-markets thing is working out. But it's still true that we don't have any socialists. What the Obama administration wants, as I've already noted, is to rescue market competition, not restrain it. And, led by the kind of liberals even (or especially) bankers love, it may well succeed. But—this is my methodological fantasy—what if it doesn't? What if what we're seeing now is not just the end of a boom but the beginning of a new period of "ideological struggle"? If good for markets was bad for art, will bad for markets be good for art?

For, as I've suggested with respect to at least one art form, market triumphalism hasn't been so great. The past twenty-five years or so have been a pretty sad time for the American novel, and a lot of the best ones have indeed been committed to historical caretaking. It's no accident that Toni Morrison's *Beloved* was proclaimed the best work of American fiction over the period by the *New York Times* or that prominent also-rans included *Blood Meridian, Underworld,* and *The Plot against America.* Even younger writers like Michael Chabon and Colson Whitehead have rushed to take up the burden of the past. And it's not hard to see why. For although it's true that books about slavery and the Middle Passage, the Holocaust and the extermination of Native Americans, are more or less definitionally sad, it's also true that the logic by which they are produced and that makes them so attractive is an optimistic one.

Why? Because trying to overcome, say, the lingering effects of slavery doesn't involve criticizing the primacy of markets; it just involves making sure that everyone has equal access to them. So when *Beloved* reminds us that we are a nation divided by race and racism (and, in case we start to forget, *A Mercy* reminds us again), we're effectively being told that our problem is lingering racism—not burgeoning capitalism. And when Morrison wins the Nobel Prize and Obama is elected president, we're being reassured that we are headed in the right direction, even if we're not there yet.

Indeed, Morrison is such an icon of liberal culture that her very existence serves to register both the financial success and the moral superiority of those to whom the boom was good. When, for example, Drew Faust was sworn in as the new president of Harvard (endowment in 1987, the year *Beloved* was published, $3.85 billion; endowment at Faust's inauguration in 2007, $34.9 billion), Morrison was on hand to read from the not yet published *A Mercy* and to help attest to the fact that "even a few short years ago," as Faust put it, people like them could not have been on that platform and thus to the fact that universities over the last half century have served as "engines of the expansion of citizenship, equality and opportunity—to blacks, women, Jews, immigrants, and others who would have been subjected to quotas or excluded altogether in an earlier era." Thus "ours," she said, "is a different and far better world" (Faust).

But for whom? If you look at the economic data for the "few short years" Faust has in mind, what you see is not a society in which there is greater equality but one in which there is less. In fact, in his *Brief History of Neoliberalism*, David Harvey says that "redistributive effects [from poor to rich] and increasing social inequality have . . . been such a persistent feature of neoliberalization as to be regarded as structural to the whole project" (16). Thus, for example, in 1987 the top tenth of the American population made about 38 percent of the nation's income. (The bottom fifth made about 3.8 percent.) That top figure was substantially up from the relatively egalitarian numbers that prevailed from the end of World War II until the beginning of neoliberalism around 1980, but the really big jump is the one that has taken place since. In 2006, according to the economists Thomas Piketty and Emmanuel Saez, the top tenth earned about *half* of all the money made in America, more even than in 1928, till then the highest figure since the beginning of the twentieth century. The bottom quintile got 3.4 percent. And of course, if you look at universities like Harvard, what you see is that the welcome they've extended to racialized minorities has been withheld from the vast economic majority: "74 percent of students at the nation's top 146 colleges come from the richest socioeconomic quartile," the Century Foundation reported in 2004, "and just 3 percent come from the poorest quartile" (Kahlenberg, *America's Untapped Resource*).

The account of Faust's inauguration in the *Harvard Crimson* includes an interview with an enthusiastic undergraduate claiming (and who would doubt her?) to have read *Beloved* twelve times. But you only have to read it once to understand the ways in which "our" world is better, and even reading it twelve times, you won't get the slightest sense of the ways in which it's worse.

Which is just to say that increasing inequality—less social justice rather than more—is not something that American culture, even (or especially) liberal culture, has had much to say about. Rather, the more unjust and unequal American society has become, the more we have heard about how bad, say, the Holocaust was. And as the success of our cultural and economic elites at separating themselves from everyone else has grown more pronounced and as the actual Holocaust has begun to show the first signs of brand fatigue, enterprising writers like Philip Roth (in *The Plot against America*) and Chabon (in *The Yiddish Policemen's Union*) have boldly moved beyond condemning bad things that happened in the past to condemning bad things that didn't happen in the past: a Nazi takeover of the United States and the exile of a whole society of eastern European Jews to Alaska.

Today, however, things have finally gotten so bad that not just poor people but relatively rich people—till 2008 the boom's beneficiaries—have begun to feel the pain. (Even Harvard's endowment is only about six times what it was in 1987, not ten times as much.) And disapproval of holocausts is getting serious competition from fear of poverty. Which is just what the vast majority—the victims of the boom—have been worrying about all along. So maybe it's time for us to forget about the Holocaust and focus on the free market instead, to stop congratulating ourselves on being against genocide and to start questioning what it means to be for free trade. Although it doesn't appear anywhere on the *Times*'s best American fiction list, Bret Easton Ellis's *American Psycho* is a much better novel than most of the ones that do, and the Psycho's self-consoling reminder—"I am rich—millions are not" (392)—has the merit of problematizing the upper middle class's sense of its virtue rather than, like Roth and Morrison, pandering to it.

American Psycho, in other words, is an anti-liberal novel, committed to the idea that the wealth of the rich is extracted from the poor and therefore to the idea that there is a structural antagonism between them. That's the meaning of all those descriptions of what the rich people wear—"a suit by Lubiam, a great-looking striped spread-collar cotton shirt from Burberry, a silk tie by Resikeio and a belt from Ralph Lauren" (87). Or, to take a more recent example, that's the meaning of the notes the call girl Chelsea keeps on what she wears to each job ("a Michael Kors dress and shoes and La Perla lingerie underneath") in Stephen Soderbergh's film *The Girlfriend Experience*. The movie is set in November 2008 as Obama is about to win the election, and you can see the political point of Chelsea's clothes (and of the Psycho's description of everyone's clothes) by fast-forwarding two months and comparing them to the clothes worn to the inauguration by the novelist, essayist (*Bad Mother*), and passionate Obama supporter Ayelet Waldman. When Obama won the South Carolina primary, Waldman had predicted she'd see her readers "on the Mall in January," promising, "I'll be the one in the Women for Obama T-shirt" ("South Carolina"). By the time January came around, however (as she recounts in another blog post, "President Barack Obama"), a "fabulous Vera Wang gown" (a "loaner" from a friend) had replaced the T-shirt, supplemented by "five-inch Chloe boots" (also "fabulous," but her own), to be worn to the concert on the Mall. Unfortunately, the Chloes weren't so great for "dancing madly to U2," but they, along with the Vera Wang and a cocktail dress by Lanvin and a dinner catered by Daniel Boulud, nonetheless managed to convey what is essentially the same message as the Women for Obama T-shirt.

And that message is the exact opposite of the one conveyed by Chelsea's Michael Kors, or for that matter by the suede Yves Saint Laurent the Psycho's girlfriend wears, also to a U2 concert (maybe a depression will at least get us better rock and roll). For the meaning of the Saint Laurent is that the wealth of the rich comes at the expense of the poor, and *American Psycho*'s anti-liberalism consists in its recognition of their fundamentally opposed interests. As the Psycho says to a bum he's about to murder: "I'm sorry. It's just that . . . I don't have anything in common with you" (131). But the fantasy of Waldman's Chloe boots is that the things dividing us have nothing to do with money, and therefore we needn't be divided at all. When Waldman describes "white people and black people, Latinos and Asians," all "chanting 'Race Doesn't Matter, Race Doesn't Matter'" ("South Carolina"), she is describing a liberalism that replaces the antagonism between the rich and the poor with the alliance of the black and the white: "United. Not divided." After all, black women can have hot shoes too (Oprah was wearing Louboutins). "Race Doesn't Matter" is both an alternative to and a version of a slogan that can't quite be chanted at rallies but is nonetheless what's always being said: "Wealth Doesn't Matter." It can't be chanted at rallies because, once you put the point in those terms, it might occur to someone that wealth actually does matter. But it's being said anyway because the political vision of our liberalism is of the poor helping the rich to make a better America rather than, say, of the poor making a better America by taking away the rich's money.

And Waldman's autobiographical essays about being and having a mom essentially do the same political work as her Chloe boots and her husband's (it turns out she's married to Michael Chabon) alternative Holocaust history. For if historicist novels have been one literary way to make the reality of our social arrangements invisible, they haven't been the only one. It was also in 1987 that Margaret Thatcher, as canny a cultural critic as Toni Morrison, pronounced herself tired of hearing about society's problems and, in the wake of her triumph over the National Union of Mineworkers, took a stand not just against the idea that we should worry about social problems but against the idea of society itself, proclaiming: "There is no such thing as society. There are individual men and women, and there are families" (Thatcher).

Anybody looking to explain the increasing appeal of the memoir in contemporary writing need look no further. In this context, all the debates about whether memoirs really count as literature and about whether it matters if they aren't altogether true are completely irrelevant. Every sentence in every one of them, true or false, literary or non-, tells us that there are only individuals and (most of them add) their families. Thus, for example, the proper way for workers to see themselves is not as members of political collectives (like, say, the union) or even as workers but as entrepreneurs and as husbands and wives and fathers and mothers. And if you want some sense of the absolutely contemporary relevance of Thatcher's analysis, you can go beyond the memoir to the extraordinary success of the Broadway musical *Billy Elliot* (ten Tony Awards). It is, as its promotional materials say, "set against the backdrop" of the strike Thatcher broke, but what it's really about is Billy's grizzled old miner dad learning to respect his son's desire to become not a miner but a ballet dancer, and about Billy learning to respect his best friend's desire to cross-dress, and about all the miners learning that the union is irrelevant, and, most upliftingly, about everyone learning that, as the song says, "What we need is individuality": "If you wanna be a dancer, dance / If you wanna be a miner, mine, if you want to dress like somebody else, / Fine!" (John and Hall).

The point here is not that memoirists or the makers of *Billy Elliot* think of themselves as cheerleaders for the free market. The point is rather that in the memoir, society (like the miner's strike) is the "backdrop" against which—as the human capital economists who definitely *do* think of themselves as cheerleaders for the free market like to say—we either make or fail to make good choices. If you wanna be a miner, mine—but when it doesn't work out, it's because you made a bad choice. And if you wanna dress like somebody else, fine. . . . It's no accident that compared to, say, card check (the Employee Free Choice Act, intended to make it easier for workers to unionize), same-sex marriage has emerged as a centerpiece of American cultural liberalism. Card check, despite its euphemistically Thatcherite name, is not about the need for individual choice. Just the opposite: it's about escaping your individuality, and about the power of collective bargaining. Same-sex marriage, by contrast, is all about the rights of individuals, and especially, of course, their right to make families.

And the exemplary attraction of same-sex marriage emerges even more vividly when, as in California, it's an alternative to domestic partnership, when, in other words, the economic issues (the only issues that matter in card check) have largely been factored out. For here, as the suit recently filed by the Republican Ted Olson and the Democrat David Boies (opposing attorneys in *Bush v. Gore* but united in *Perry v. Schwarzenegger*) asserts, the harm in not being allowed to marry is "severe humiliation, emotional distress, pain, suffering, psychological harm, and stigma" (Boies and Olson 8). And of course, once you've described the problems as ones that have virtually nothing to do with the redistribution of wealth, you've also described the solution as one that has nothing to do with the redistribution of wealth. It's these problems, described in this way, that American liberalism (and American culture more generally) loves—hence the popularity of the memoir, more or less defined, like *Perry v. Schwarzenegger*, by its commitment to the primacy of emotional distress and psychological harm.

And hence also the opportunity to get rid of it. For when many people's jobs and everybody's investments begin to disappear, the idea that we'll be better off if we just stop stigmatizing one another and make better choices can begin to look a little less plausible. Maybe at that moment, capitalism starts to look like a problem for which human capital does not look like a solution, and the economic arrangements of the society you live in begin to seem more important than how your parents felt about you, how you feel about your kids, or even how you feel about yourself. So maybe another upside of the collapse of a Thatcherite economy will be the disappearance of this entirely Thatcherite genre. Maybe people will lose all interest in the moving stories of the struggles of other people to overcome destructive (though sometimes seductive) parents and seductive (though always destructive) addictions, and no one will want to read memoirs. Maybe people will even lose interest in their own struggles, thus conceived, and no one will want to write them, either.

So—no memoirs, no historicist novels. What else? Actually a lot of non-historicist novels will have to go too. For sure, no more books like *The Corrections* or *Light in August*, or any of Oprah's other choices. And no more stories about the children of immigrants trying to figure out whether or where they fit in American culture. Ethnic identity is just the family writ large, and no move is more characteristic of the neoliberal novel than the substitution of cultural difference for (one of the things Thatcher meant to deny) class difference. What the neoliberal novel likes about cultural difference is that it sentimentalizes social conflict, hopefully presenting us with an imagined world where people care more about respect for their otherness than about money for their mortgages. But you get a better sense of the actual structure of American society even from Waldman's boots than you do from all the accounts of people reclaiming, refusing, or repurposing their cultural identities. Just think of what it means for Touré (in the *Times*) to hail Colson Whitehead's novel about upper-middle-class black kids, *Sag Harbor*, as a contribution toward "reshaping the iconography of blackness" (Touré). As if the crucial thing about rich black people is that they offer new ways of performing race rather than the old way of embodying class.

But it's not just particular kinds of novels that make their contribution to the current misrepresentation of life under neoliberalism; it's some of the things that we take to be central to the very idea of the novel. In *How Fiction Works*, James Wood approvingly quotes Osip Mandelstam's claim that "the novel was perfected and strengthened over an extremely long period of time as the art form to interest the reader in the fate of the individual" (148–49), and he goes on to emphasize the importance of "psychological motivation" in producing this interest. Thus Wood himself understands "character"—the novel's primary technology of individuality—as crucial: "to deny character," he says, "is essentially to deny the novel" (105). It's one thing, however, to insist on the importance of character and individuality in Russia in the 1920s, quite another in the present-day United States, where liberals and conservatives both—let's call them neoliberals of the left and neoliberals of the right—are as unanimous in their enthusiasm for individuality as book reviewers are in their enthusiasm for character.

Thus when Michiko Kakutani (writing for the *New York Times*) attacks Jonathan Littell's controversial novel *The Kindly Ones* because its central character, the Nazi Dr. Aue, is a "cartoonish" "monster" we can neither "sympathize" with nor "understand" ("Unrepentant"), and when she applauds the "appealing" central character in Chabon's *Yiddish Policeman's Union*, in whose "plight" the reader becomes completely "absorbed" ("Looking"), we should understand that she is invoking simultaneously literary and political criteria of evaluation: good novels are defined by their interest in character, neoliberal politics by their respect for individuality. And we can go on to get some sense of what's at stake here for ambitious fiction just by sketching out some of the similarities and differences between the novels themselves. They both, for example, come equipped with glossaries: Chabon's explains the meaning of Yiddish terms like *luftmensh* (dreamer) and *sheygets* (non-Jewish male); Littell's gives you helpful explanations of the bureaucratic responsibilities of organizations like the *Hauptamt Ordnungspolizei* or "Main Office of the Order Police." If the point of Littell's glossary is that it familiarizes you with the institutional structure of the militarized society the book depicts, the point of Chabon's is that it replaces a society with an ethnicity; the novel's world is that of Detective Landsman "and his people." And the novel's major stylistic achievement is emblemized in the way it manages to use the ordinarily very pejorative term "yid" in the same tone and with the same inside pleasure that hip-hop culture has used the term "nigga." You don't exactly get "Whussup my yidz," but you do get lots of sentences like "Seems like I've known a lot of chess-playing yids who used smack" (5). If the Yiddish word that is Landsman's name had appeared in the glossary, the most plausible current translation would be "homie." Individuals, their families, and their "people": this is the way Chabon does neoliberalism.

By contrast, Dr. Aue's family is almost literally the House of Atreus; *The Kindly Ones*, of course, are what the Furies become in the third play in Aeschylus's trilogy, and Aue's domestic life, to the extent that he has one, is all incest and matricide, without the slightest effort to achieve "psychological plausibility." And the attraction of ethnicity—of "a people"—is reduced to nothing but the utility of racism: anti-Semites need Jews. Even more to the point, Kakutani is right: Aue himself is not at all sympathetic, and there's a certain sense in which he is indeed a monster—not so much an unappealing character as not really a character at all. Indeed, in one of the few really smart and serious American reviews of *The Kindly Ones*, Daniel Mendelsohn describes him instead as "ideology in action" ("Transgression"), and it's this that makes him seem monstrous—to a literary culture that wants characters instead of ideologies and to a political culture that wants the same thing.

Thus although, with respect to its subject matter, Littell's book belongs to the genre of neoliberal historicism, it doesn't quite deliver the desired dose of self-congratulation. Alternately a figure from Greek tragedy and a scrupulous Nazi bureaucrat, Aue images a society where individual character—good or bad—is largely beside the point, and his opening address to the reader, "Frères humains" (from Villon's *Ballade des pendus*), suggests that we might better understand ourselves as creatures like him—entirely structured by ideology—than as the psychologically complex and morally autonomous individuals our literature exists to tell us we are. Or, to put the point more precisely, we might understand our attachment to our psychological complexity and moral autonomy as itself a kind of ideological commitment, our way of imagining our world as nothing but individuals and families, markets and identities.

From this standpoint, *The Kindly Ones*, like *American Psycho*, would count as a kind of resistance to, if not as the end of, the "sad" time for art announced by Fukuyama—a return to ideology. And it would not be alone. The completely homegrown version of the American-born Littell living in Spain and writing in French would be the Baltimore-based David Simon, whose TV series *The Wire* is the most serious and ambitious American fiction of the twenty-first century so far. Unlike its more widely watched competitor *The Sopranos* (which really was about what David Chase always said it was about: "family"), *The Wire* is about institutions— unions, schools, political parties, gangs. It's about the world that neoliberalism has actually produced rather than the world our literature pretends it's produced. If a book like *American Psycho* looks back to the great novels of Edith Wharton—novels of manners in which what's always at stake are the hierarchies of the social order—*The Wire* is like a way of reinventing Zola or Dreiser for a world in which the deification of the market is going out rather than coming in.

But of course the idea that the deification of the market is on the way out is no doubt false. Unemployment may have reached 9.4 percent in May 2011, but May 2011 was also the best month for hedge funds since 2000; HFR's hedge fund index was up 5.23 percent. And, as I began by noting, it's not as if the goal of the Obama administration was to oppose neoliberalism. Indeed, it would be more accurate to say that its goal—and the goal of American liberalism more generally—is to perfect it, to get us back to the days of the booming economy, but without the pointless and expensive foreign wars, the waterboarding, the anti-immigration racism, the gay-bashing, and the propensity to appoint mainly straight white men to the Supreme Court. None of these things is good for business; some of them (the anti-immigration stuff) may even be bad for business. And American liberalism likes things that are bad for business even less than American conservatism does. That's why when it comes, say, to reforming health care, a socialized system—not just bad but fatal for business—was not even on the agenda.

But my point here has not been to imagine ways we could get a better society; it's just been to imagine ways we could get better fiction, and more generally, better art. Which we could still do even if the increasing inequality of the last thirty years goes back to increasing. For while it's more or less inevitably true that aesthetically ambitious books and TV shows are made by relatively rich people for an audience of other relatively rich people, it's not inevitable that these books and TV shows must be about how virtuous (antiracist, anti-sexist, anti-homophobic) rich people are.

It probably is inevitable, however, that we can't expect much of a cultural contribution from people like me: professors. Both our teaching responsibilities, which Andrew Ross has described as "grooming radicals" but which might more plausibly be called transforming the entitled children of the upper middle class into the credentialed children of the upper middle class (if we are trying to groom radicals, we are the worst teachers ever), and our research responsibilities, which consist primarily in articulating the fundamental values of neoliberalism in a tone of voice that suggests we are deeply hostile to the current political economic order when actually our deepest desire is to imagine ourselves as its moral exemplars, require loyalty to neoliberalism so complete and so sincere that expecting something better from us would be utterly unfair.

And indeed we can see an exemplary display of this loyalty in the very small professional world of American studies, first in the overwhelming success of the race and gender research project and more recently in the proclamations about internationalizing American studies and about the status of American exceptionalism. A mobile and hence multicultural workforce is as much a structural feature of neoliberalism as increasing economic inequality is, and so it's not surprising that, as Larry Griffin and Maria Tempenis report in "Class, Multiculturalism, and the *American Quarterly*," in 1965 (the year of the Immigration Act that explicitly repudiated the racism of the 1924 law and greatly expanded Asian immigration in particular), about 20 percent of *American Quarterly* was devoted to what they call "multicultural themes" and the "diversity debate," and that· by the mid-seventies that number had doubled, and by the late nineties it had doubled again—to 80 percent. Indeed we might say not only that the growing focus on race and gender has helped to provide the intellectual and ethical tools needed to understand and manage the multicultural labor force, but also that the comparative disappearance of class has helped us to understand its members in exactly the terms that neoliberalism finds congenial—as individuals whose identities need to be respected.

And just as neoliberal economies require mobile workforces, they also require mobile capital. It is for this reason that markets are faster than intellectuals to lose interest in, say, the idea of an American empire.

What American studies scholars try to portray as an effort to "contest the universalism of American exceptionalism" (Kaplan 16) can be more elegantly, economically, and accurately understood if juxtaposed with what the *New York Times* described as the increasing market share of Swiss, German, British, and Japanese banks in the business of "taking companies public, underwriting new bonds and advising corporations on mergers and acquisitions" (Bowley). It's one thing, in other words, to see American exceptionalism as the problem; it's something else to see capitalism as the problem. And it's yet another thing, when we *do* make the occasional effort to talk about capitalism, to lament the regional inequalities it has produced, as if a world where there were more poor people in the United States but fewer in, say, Ecuador would therefore be a more just world.

In both these cases—when we talk about it and when we don't—we treat neoliberalism as if it were only and inevitably the garden in which we and our toads live rather than itself one of the toads. As if, in other words, economic inequality were the world in which our injustices took place rather than itself the major injustice. And for the reasons I have suggested, it can't really make sense to count on American studies scholars to produce an alternative. But if we remind ourselves of what doctors (rather than professors) are supposed to do—above all, no harm—we might with at least some plausibility imagine a future in which, perhaps by repudiating the effort to do politically meaningful work and engaging instead in merely antiquarian historical projects, we might at least diminish the contribution we currently make to providing the neoliberal imaginary with the terms in which it happily produces its enviably good conscience.

NOTE

This is the slightly revised text of a talk I gave at the "Imagining Culture: Norms and Forms of Public Discourse in America" conference at the John-F.-Kennedy-Institut in Berlin in June 2009. A much earlier and much shorter version of it appeared in *Bookforum*, and a quite different version was published in *The Baffler*.

WORKS CITED

Boies, David, and Theodore B. Olson. "Complaint for Declaratory, Injunctive, or Other Relief." Filed 22 May 2009. United States District Court, Northern District of California.

Bowley, Graham. "Stalking a Weaker Wall Street." *New York Times*, 17 June 2009.

Chabon, Michael. *The Yiddish Policemen's Union*. New York: HarperCollins, 2007.

Cohn, Alexander B., and Bonnie J. Kavoussi. "Morrison Recites Passage for Faust." *Harvard Crimson*, 12 October 2007.

Ellis, Brett Easton. *American Psycho*. New York: Vintage, 1991.

Faust, Drew. "Installation Address: Unleashing Our Most Ambitious Imaginings." 12 October 2007. http://president.harvard.edu (accessed 18 April 2009).

Fluck, Winfried. "'The American Romance' and the Changing Functions of the Imaginary." *New Literary History* 27.3 (1996): 415–457.

Fukuyama, Francis. "The End of History?" In *The Geopolitics Reader*, ed. Gearoid O. Tuathail, Simon Dalby, and Paul Routledge. London: Routledge, 1998. 114–125.

Griffin, Larry, and Maria Tempenis. "Class, Multiculturalism, and the *American Quarterly*." *American Quarterly* 54.1 (March 2002): 67–99.

Harvey, David. *A Brief History of Neoliberalism*. New York: Oxford University Press, 2005.

John, Elton, and Lee Hall. "Expressing Yourself." From *Billy Elliot*. 2004. http://www.eltonography.com/songs/expressing_yourself.html.

Kahlenberg, Richard D., ed. *America's Untapped Resource: Low-Income Students in Higher Education*. New York: Century Foundation Press, 2004.

———. "Five Myths about College Admissions." *Washington Post*, 23 May 2010.

Kakutani, Michiko. "Looking for a Home in the Limbo of Alaska." *New York Times*, 1 May 2007.

———. "Unrepentant and Telling of Horrors Untellable." *New York Times*, 23 February 2009.

Kaplan, Amy. "Violent Belongings and the Question of American Empire Today: Presidential Address to the American Studies Association, October 17, 2003." *American Quarterly* 56.1 (March 2004): 1–18.

Littell, Jonathan. *The Kindly Ones*. Trans. Charlotte Mandell. New York: HarperCollins, 2009.

Mendelsohn, David. "Transgression." *New York Review of Books*, 26 March 2009.

Moore, Marianne. "Poetry." In *The Norton Anthology of Poetry*. http://www.wwnorton.com/college/english/nap/Poetry_Moore.htm.

Panitch, Leo, and Sam Gindin. "The Current Crisis: A Socialist Perspective." Countercurrents. 30 September 2008. http://www.countercurrents.org/gindin300908.htm (accessed 4 April 2008.)

Ross, Andrew. "Forum on Radical Teaching Now." *Radical Teacher* 83 (2008): 18.

Saez, Emmanuel. "Striking It Richer: The Evolution of Top Incomes in the

United States." 15 March 2008. http://elsa.berkeley.edu/~saez/saez-UStopin comes-2006prel.pdf (accessed 3 April 2008).

Soderbergh, Stephen. *The Girlfriend Experience*. Magnolia Pictures. 2009.

Thatcher, Margaret. "Interview for *Women's Own*." 23 September 1987. http://www.margaretthatcher.org/document/106689 (accessed 4 February 2008).

Touré. "Visible Young Man." *New York Times*, 1 May 2009.

Waldman, Ayelet. "South Carolina." 28 January 2008. http://my.barackobama.com/page/community/blog/ayeletwaldman (accessed 10 April 2009).

———. "President Barack Obama." 22 January 2009. http://www.ayeletwald man.com/archives/2009/01/president_barac.html (accessed 10 April 2009.)

Wood, James. *How Fiction Works*. New York: Farrar, Straus and Giroux, 2008.

9 Obama Unwound

*The Romanticism of Victory and the Defeat
of Compromise*

Barack Obama's 2008 mandate was crushed by the midterm elections of
2010, in which his party lost control of the House of Representatives and
of state legislatures and governorships all over the country. This reversal
did not prevent his re-election in 2012, but he did not win decisively or
broadly enough for a renewed mandate to be assumed. Obama's margin
of victory was smaller than in 2008—down from 7 to 2 percent of the
popular vote. His share of white voters fell from 43 percent to 39 percent,
and he owes his victory to turnout by African American, Latino, and
Asian American voters, whose supermajority voting for him may have
finally defeated the Republican's long-time "Southern Strategy" based on
appeals to white racial resentment. For Obama to regain his 2008 place
as the leader of a transformative coalition, winning the presidential election would need to be followed by a readoption of the progressive positions that during his first term he regularly compromised away.

   In 2008, Democrats had won a larger percentage of House of Representatives votes in the thirty-six non-southern states than at any previous time in recent history and held a solid majority in both chambers of
Congress to go with their new control of the executive branch. In 2010,
the national vote was almost the reverse, and the Republicans picked
up sixty-three seats in the House of Representatives (out of 435). One
analyst pointed out, "That's similar to 1994, and you have to go back
to 1946 and 1928 to find years when Republicans did better" (Barone).
Outside of Washington, D.C., Republicans gained about 675 seats in
statehouses, also their best showing since 1928, took nineteen state leg-
islative houses from the Democrats, and added five new governorships
(to hold twenty-nine of fifty) ("Election 2010"). Obama ruefully quipped
that while he had learned from the election results, "I'm not recommend-

ing for every future president that they take a shellacking like I did last night" ("Obama on Midterm Shellacking").

But how did the most celebrated presidential victory in nearly thirty years lose all of its power in only half a term?

American Political Romanticism

The November 2008 election was driven by an upwelling of classic American political *romanticism*. By that I mean most simply the feeling that a vision of a better world can actually be embodied in the American nation. In such a moment, the United States becomes for a majority of its various publics the vehicle of an elevated state of social being. The Democrats' two successful post-1980 presidential candidates called this "hope." Bill Clinton found some power in a pun on the name of his hometown, Hope, Arkansas, in his references to "a place called hope." Obama got closer to the real spirit of this with his slogan "Yes We Can." In these moments of romantic *break* with a given recent degraded political history, a transformed shared or *collective* world becomes possible: *Yes we can* enter this elevated social world together. There's a clear source for this feeling in the African American Christianity that has been so important to Obama himself. Although the term *romanticism* often suggests something unrealistic, in fact it is close to Benedict Anderson's notion of the imagined community, here with an emphasis on a freedom of collaborative construction.

This romanticism helped Obama win nearly two-thirds of voters under the age of thirty. This romanticism helped Obama produce the most important demographic shift in the election, which was that young white voters without a college education—the blue-collar workers who in the 1980s, in 1994, and again in 2000 voted as "Reagan Democrats" and Bush Republicans—broke with their parents and went for Obama rather than the Republican John McCain. The central desire of this political romanticism is that one's individual experiences and views will be seen in the political world as *legitimate*. One's views may not prevail, but they *will* be openly acknowledged as part of and shared and mainstream public life. Their possessor will be held to be a full and undamaged member of a common world, one at least transiently represented by national politics.

U.S. political romanticism, then, has several features. The first is the belief that a far better world can be incarnated by the nation. Second, this romanticism is not very specific about actual policies. Much research has shown that highly popular politicians stay vague enough to serve as screens on which a range of desires can be projected. They are like movie stars. They are like first loves. Freud once said, "Love is the overestimation of the object." This is true in politics as well, where the mass political leader tries not to exclude possibilities that are being projected onto him or her. This is easier to do in a campaign than in office, but politicians like Franklin Delano Roosevelt managed to do it by continuing to articulate higher inclusive hopes. The serious point here is that American political romanticism focuses less on good policy than on the affects, both individual and collective, that make good policy possible.[1]

The third feature of political romanticism is the desire to reimagine the country as an undamaged national group. Marx famously described the person as "an animal which can individuate itself only in the midst of society" (83–84), and this is indeed close to the popular intuition behind the desire for political renewal that was widespread in the United States during the 2008 campaign. The restored national group also requires a new leader or leaders, and also, most important, a new relation to leadership on the part of the public. I come back to this later on.

The fourth feature concerns the positive individual affect that would emerge from renewed political life. The group psychological conditions for this renewal were analyzed as a *political* problem with particular depth and clarity by C. Fred Alford in the 1990s. He described them as occurring when "members reclaim lost and alienated parts of themselves that they have previously devoted to the group" (Alford 71). Loss and alienation are not distinctive features of American political life, but there is special pain connected to the contrast between elevated expectations in a country that claims to be the best of all possible democracies and that country's actual practice. The bitterness of American political discourse is distinctive, and much has been written on this and related symptoms such as low voter turnout,[2] without, in my view, truly grasping the widespread animus toward national politics or its sources in the systemic failings of the American system.[3] What this meant in the 2008 campaign was an imagined *end of suffering*—an end of personal suffering from experiencing the government as a negative, oppressive, offensive, or violent force. This hoped for end of suffering from a terrible public world was arguably the central feature of anti-Bush Americans' response to the Bush II era. It wasn't just that he was too right wing: *it was that he had defiled the country.* George W. Bush created a flat contradiction between most people's sense of belonging in or to the country and the operating principles of the government of the United States. This contradiction meant that much of the country *suffered* Bush rather than merely endured him.

This suffering crossed political lines. One example of this phenomenon comes from my own family. My parents are classic working-class children of New Deal Democrats who were the first in their respective families to go to college—and my father, assisted by massive educational momentum in California in the 1950s, went on to medical school. The political companion to their economic mobility, as for so many whites of their "silent generation," was a shift toward Eisenhower Republicanism. My father voted for Reagan many times, and then for Bush in 2000. But in November 2003, about six months after the U.S. invasion of Iraq, while he and I were having lunch, we got on to politics, and he suddenly exclaimed, "I hate Bush."

I was surprised and asked: "Why, Dad? You voted for him, and he cut your taxes, like you wanted him to." My father replied, "Because he kills people, for no reason."

Things were never the same after that. My father was done with Bush, and also with the Republican Party. He voted for the Democratic candidate, John Kerry, in 2004, and he voted for Obama in 2008. In the process he generated a continuous discourse of what I would call *political suffering*—a state in which, even when one is not being persecuted or economically destroyed, one is in a state of alienation in which a part of one's own identity—national identity—is contradicted and offended by collective politics, embodied in the leader.

Obama's initial political power came from his apparent ability to offer an alternative to the political rules of the Bush era and thus to alleviate cross-spectrum political suffering. Obama's power was not only to address the offended progressives who had wandered for years in the Bushian wilderness, but also to promise to end the suffering of many conservatives as well. This meant that Obama's popularity did not rest on his ability to look and act "center-right." It rested on his ability to address the country's half-unexpressed wounded romanticism. Obama was not speaking to a fantasy of a utopian America but was addressing a felt desire to build a world in which personal desire could be *realized*, not rejected, in a *shared* polis that would be called the United States. In his best moments, Obama built not a coalition of the center-right with progressive rhetoric to fool people, but a coalition of political sufferers who imagined a non-agonizing common world constituted by political life.

Obama's Promise

How is it that Obama could do something enormous like this? In fact he couldn't, but we can identify the *means* by which he occasionally seemed to reconcile people's lives with their political system so that they could imagine life in common. The means were simple: he could tell the truth *in public* about ordinary—though politically charged—*individual* experience.

This is what Obama did in his great campaign speeches, particularly the one in Philadelphia in March 2008 that made him the front-runner. This was the speech in which he broke with his pastor, Jeremiah Wright, and there were crucial moments in which Obama showed his now dominant capacity for inhibiting inclusive honesty by patronizing Wright and falsifying civil rights history. And yet the core of the speech was to tell the truth *in public* about people's real thoughts and feelings about race.

> Like other predominantly black churches across the country, [Reverend Wright's] Trinity embodies the black community in its entirety—the doctor and the welfare mom, the model student and the former gang-banger. Like other black churches, Trinity's services are full of raucous laughter and sometimes-bawdy humor. They are full of dancing, clapping, screaming and shouting that may seem jarring to the untrained ear. The church contains in full the kindness and cruelty, the fierce intelligence and the shocking ignorance, the struggles and successes, the love and yes, the bitterness and bias that make up the black experience in America.
>
> And this helps explain, perhaps, my relationship with Reverend Wright. As imperfect as he may be, he has been like family to me. He strengthened my faith, officiated my wedding, and baptized my children. Not once in my conversations with him have I heard him talk about any ethnic group in derogatory terms, or treat whites with whom he interacted with anything but courtesy and respect. He contains within him the contradictions—the good and the bad—of the community that he has served diligently for so many years.
>
> I can no more disown him than I can disown the black community. I can no more disown him than I can my white grandmother—a woman who helped raise me, a woman who sacrificed again and again for me, a woman who loves me as much as she loves anything in this world, but a woman who once confessed her fear of black men who passed by her on the street, and who on more than one occasion has uttered racial or ethnic stereotypes that made me cringe.
>
> These people are a part of me. And they are a part of America, this country that I love. (Obama, "More Perfect Union")

This passage modeled the possibility of finding the truth of individual experience in the shared political world. Obama's portrait of the black community was not subtle, but he described its range and greatness in a way unknown in mainstream politics and then embraced *all* of that range. Obama's description of his white grandmother included his love for her, her love for him, her racial anxiety about black people, and his divided response to her anxiety, which included understanding, feeling rejected, and rejecting her. If this man won, he would not lead the country to redemption, but he would lead many millions of voters out of the "pharaoh's land" where all regular people need to hide their real beliefs from the political world, a hiding that makes them suffer.

Obama in this moment offered an instance of a leader who speaks as a fully aware member of his or her group. He displayed himself as a "good leader," one who is willing and able to "help citizens reclaim lost parts of themselves alienated in the group and so foster individual and group development" (Alford 155).[4] The ability to bring lost, repressed, denied, or rejected parts of oneself into the open leads to a crucial moment in group psychology in which the individual is able to bring previously rejected aspects of herself into the group and not just the partial self that includes only those features acceptable to the group's most aggressive, most dominant members. The pandemic bullying, shunning, exclusion, and denunciation typical of American political culture keeps most individuals from participating in group self-governance for the obvious reason that participation poses a threat to the self, and particularly to the most heterodox and thus creative parts of the self.[5] A group consisting of largely self-concealed individuals is a group whose members will look to leaders to perform all of the governance that they feel too threatened and too weak to perform themselves. This "regressed" group cannot be democratic. When Obama spoke in public to the generally hidden parts of brown, black, yellow, red, and white selves, he at least for a moment welcomed normally unauthorized or unspeakable parts of each listener back into the national community. This is the psychological precondition for democratic activity—a "good enough equality" in which the leader makes it clear that no member of the group will be allowed to exclude or subordinate another specifically on the basis of his or her divergence from a group norm.

Reviving the Basis of Participation

The correct question for Obama after the midterm defeat was not, How can you now become more center-right, or even more bipartisan, or engage in a still more complete compromising of your party's core positions? Obama's familar calculation in 2012 appeared to be that the election would be decided by the swing voters, who could go for either main candidate, and that these people would be especially impressed by the candidate who seemed most like a swing voter himself. This would mean, in practice, that the candidate would display "nonideological" maturity grounded in ambivalence. Obama was seeking the votes of people who admire compromise as such. The political math was fundamentally flawed for the cultural and group-psychological reasons I have discussed. The correct—and victory-oriented—question for Obama after the midterms was, How can you take the romantic hope for a positive shared world and link it to collective *deliberation?*

There is a theoretical question here, which is, What is *romantic deliberation?* We know a decent amount about this, as already noted: it occurs when lost parts of selves are able to come forward, no desires are excluded in advance, and egalitarian relations among peers are more powerful than the relation to the leader.[6] With his grassroots Internet campaign in 2008, and, most important, with his major moments of personal truth telling, Obama made it seem that the dull procedures of political life could lead to a common world in which most people could provisionally feel at home. Obama's only hope for reelection depended on distinguishing between romantic-inclusive group formation based on modeling full disclosure and his doomed substitute for that compromise.

After taking office, Obama steadily sacrificed disclosure to expediency in the specific sense of conforming policy to the wishes of exactly those established powers that had made the majority of the electorate feel unsafe in the first place. His compromise banking policy opened a split between Wall Street and Main Street that has been more polarized than anything I've seen in my lifetime. The bank bailout helped destroy the earlier sense of incipient common life by making politics seem—once again—like a way to favor a tiny elite over everyone else. Obama thus reverted to the political history with which he was expected to produce a break. The bailout involved his team in the kinds of concealments (of who got the bailout money) and exaggerations (of the recovery) that he had denounced during the 2008 campaign. If one widely discussed account is correct, Obama's banking policy was in part the result of his being bullied and excluded by several of his own top economic officials (Suskind).

Obama made similar concessions in foreign policy, military strategy, civil liberties, and other areas where a pivotal issue for democratic theory and experience is the high proportion of the public that is excluded from knowledge and authority. A seemingly minor episode, his reference in a national press conference to the arrest of the prominent literary and cultural scholar Henry Louis Gates Jr. in his own Cambridge home, was a turning point in Obama's general approach to controversial issues, and his mistake occurred not when he said that the police had behaved "stupidly," but when he retreated from that candid statement into a staged sit-down between the disputants in which they were supposed to work out a compromise, one that put compromise ahead of dealing with the anger and accusations at the heart of the episode.[7] Equality, disclosure, and accountability are all essential to the intragroup functionality that makes self-rule possible. Obama's retreat from these betrayed the political romanticism—the democratic imagination—that had made so many otherwise skeptical people flock to him in the first place.

From Disappointment to Anger

After the November 2010 election, the intensity of the disappointment in Obama went from bad to worse. Observers have been particularly baffled by his apparent love of the premature compromise, the ready capitulation, even the apparent sacrifice of core principles. Jane Hamsher, founder of the political blog *Fire Dog Lake*, focused on two features of the Obama administration's negotiating strategy: its hostility to the left wing, in contrast to the Republicans' cultivation of their Tea Party right wing, and Obama's weakness as a negotiator. In a piece about his acceptance of Republican demands to extend tax cuts for the wealthy and his failure at the G20 meetings in 2010, Hamsher wrote: "The need for credit, the desire to be seen as a 'winner' and the anger at lack of perceived support from those he thinks should be on his side are things that are consistently being exploited by everyone who negotiates with Obama. Moreover, his willingness to call anything a 'win'—no matter how badly he gets cleaned out—sends a signal that stagecraft rather than substance will always be his focus." She noted Obama's tendency toward sudden reversals, too, which can also be exploited by adversaries. At the G20 meetings, held not long after the election, he criticized the Chinese for currency manipulation, wrote Hamsher, "and then patronizingly told the Chinese they needed to be 'a responsible partner.'" She went on: "Okay, so he wants to get tough with the Chinese. No doubt they are watching his actions closely. So what does he do? After 'getting tough' and making bold public statements at the G20 insisting he would not budge on the Bush tax cuts, in front of every major world power, he returns home—and does just that" (Hamsher, "Barack Obama").

Obama's reversals became so confusing that allies and opponents alike had a hard time understanding what he really believed himself. In a *New York Times* column observing that Obama was on the verge of a destructive, unnecessary capitulation to Republican desires to cut Medicare, Paul Krugman concluded by saying: "Of course, it's possible that the reason the president is offering to undermine Medicare is that he genuinely believes that this would be a good idea. And that possibility, I have to say, is what really scares me" (Krugman, "Messing with Medicare"). The fear rests in part on simply not being able to establish the core beliefs of the man who is the national Democratic Party leader and U.S. president.

By mid-summer of 2011 Obama appeared to lack the political muscle and the stable beliefs required to negotiate a lifting of the debt ceiling with congressional Republicans. He had given up so many core Democratic positions in the pursuit of an apparent non-deal that he had alienated a large percentage of his base, at a moment when the Republicans had consolidated theirs. Commentary on Obamanomics from the center and left went from exasperated to apoplectic. Leading finance blogger Yves Smith was among the mildest in remarking, "The fact that Obama is regularly being compared to Herbert Hoover and now Nixon should give him pause" (Smith).[8] Krugman wrote multiple columns arguing that Obama's economic policies were creating a "Lesser Depression," and argued in July 2011 that the structure of Obama's negotiations ensured decline either way: "If either of the current debt negotiations fails, we could be about to replay 1931, the global banking collapse that made the Great Depression great. But, if the negotiations succeed, we will be set to replay the great mistake of 1937: the premature turn to fiscal contraction that derailed economic recovery and ensured that the Depression would last until World War II finally provided the boost the economy needed" (Krugman, "The Lesser Depression").

And yet in the summer of 2011, likening Obama to Hoover was relatively tame. In an interview, the economics professor Michael Hudson called the debt negotiations a "good-cop-bad-cop charade." The Republicans were calling for more tax cuts, tax loopholes, tax holidays, and no prosecutions for tax fraud, Hudson observed, and continued:

> Mr. Obama can turn around and pretend to be the good cop. "Hey, boys, let me at least do something. I'm willing to cut back Social Security. I'm willing to take over what was George Bush's program. I share your worries about the budget deficit. We have to balance it, and I've already appointed a Deficit Reduction Commission to prepare public opinion for my cutbacks in the

most popular programs. But you have to let me get a little bit of revenue somewhere."

In the end the Republicans will make some small token concessions, but they'll get their basic program. Mr. Obama will have sold out his constituency.

The problem is, how can Mr. Obama move to the right of where George Bush stood? The only way he can do this is for the Republicans to move even further to the right. So the Republicans are accommodating him by pushing the crazy wing of their party forward, the Tea Party. Michelle Bachman, Eric Cantor and their colleagues are coming with such an extremist, right-wing attitude that it gives Mr. Obama room to move way to the right as he triangulates, depicting himself as the less crazy alternative: "Look. I'm better than these guys are." (Hudson)

Hudson argued that Obama was not being forced into a compromise that sold out his party's core value of government-insured decent retirement income and health coverage, but rather that he *wanted* to sell out his party. He went on to suggest that Obama agreed with Wall Street that the country needed a depression "in order to cut living standards and labor by 30 percent" (Hudson). Around the same time another pundit remarked: "I guess the Democratic Party just disappeared last week. Do they care? Will anyone miss them?" (Elliott).

Lest it seem that these are just the comments of angry—albeit well-established—intellectuals, polling data suggested a similar collapse in Obama's stature among ordinary voters. His job approval rating hovered between 40 and 45 percent—"higher than you'd expect," given massive dissatisfaction with the economy (McMorris-Santoro). But more negative evidence emerged from an in-depth study in July 2011 that asked, among other things, whether a series of statements fit Obama well or not very well. Obama's rating was slightly positive only on "Offers a hopeful vision for the future." His scores on the others were as follows, with the number indicating the spread on "well" over "not very well."

Strong leader: −5
On your side: −8
Trust to make the right choices for the country: −11

Perhaps the most remarkable finding here is that only a minority of voters (44 percent) thought that Obama was "on their side" (Greenberg and Seifert). It's possible that some people disagreed with Obama's policies but still gave him credit for wanting to help them. But in fact, all of Obama's rhetoric of good intentions and acting responsibly to reach compromise had failed to convince a majority that the president *was* on their side, as opposed to the side of Wall Street or somebody else. The lack of trust was remarkable in relation to someone whose public persona—the deep voice, the crisp, assured delivery, and the candor about at least some important emotional realities—had been so carefully constructed to inspire exactly that.

It's the Economy, as Usual

In trying to explain Obama's weak position with the public, most sympathetic commentators focused on his economic positions. His military policies, which extended and even intensified those of the Bush administration, had alienated much of his base (Greenwald), but the "Lesser Depression" in Krugman's term, had remained a top issue with the population as a whole. Here I categorize a range of responses into three types for the sake of simplicity:

1. Obama is a right-wing capitalist and tolerates or even seeks a controlled economic depression (Hudson).
2. Obama is a "New Economy" capitalist, seeking investment in infrastructure and research, but is intimidated by right-wing capitalists and feels they must be accomodated (Krugman, "The Lesser Depression")
3. Obama is (1) or (2) at different times, and is more fundamentally driven by a prior political outlook or framework.

The evidence for (2), Obama as a New Economy capitalist, is widespread. For his interest in the high-tech economy, one can point to his State of the Union message of January 2011, with its vision of America "winning the future" via innovation-oriented reinvestment in infrastructure and research (Obama, "Winning the Future"). For his intimidation by Wall Street and the circle of advocates for the finance industry whom he himself appointed as his leading economic advisers, one has the testimony of Sheila Bair, the head of the Federal Deposit Insurance Corporation from 2006 to 2011, who corroborated many other descriptions of Obama as believing that if he didn't accept all the demands of the bankers, they would wreck the economy. Obama's positions placed him squarely to the right of Bair, a Bob Dole Republican, who wanted tougher bank regulation and modifications for mortgage holders facing eviction during the subprime lending crisis, only to see Obama and his advisers defeat her on these points (Nocera, Bair). The fact that Obama seemed not to see (or react to) the conflict between helping Wall Street, which had recovered nicely, and helping Main Street, which had not, provided further evidence that, whether out of fear or confusion, he sticks to a muddled capitalist center that, to be fair to him, has pervaded national Democratic policy thinking for two generations.

Obama's support of the finance industry brings us back to thesis (1), which is more plausible than it at first appears. Obama does not want to destroy the economy or the middle class as such. Yet a hallmark of New Economy Democrats is their preference for Schumpeter over Keynes, that is, for "creative destruction" over the mass distribution of resources. A classic stimulus, in their view, props up ordinary activities and a large number of economic losers who will in effect "waste" capital on consumption that could be plowed into productive investment. Note, too, that when this investment does occur, it is often in other countries where production costs are lower. So although we might reject Hudson's formulation in (1) to the effect that Obama consciously *wants* the American working and middle classes to take a 30 percent haircut while blaming Republicans for it, Hudson may be close to the likely *outcome* of an innovation-oriented Democratic theory of economic "trickle down," which is to let big investors with their expertise make all the relevant decisions on the allocation of capital, resulting, if the recent past is any guide, in job loss, concentration of wealth at the top, and reduced living standards for the majority of society. A year after Hudson's interview, the Federal Reserve reported that between 2007 and 2010 the median American family's net worth had fallen by about 39 percent (Appelbaum).

Theses (1) and (2) also converge around the fact that it doesn't matter in practice whether Obama is right or center, is in favor of concentrated wealth and weak social investment or merely held at bay by those who are. The result was the same: a failed economic recovery juxtaposed with a complete financial recovery for bank and corporate profits and salaries, the continued widening of record-setting levels of inequality, and historic lows in tax burdens.[9] Obama's economic policies did enormous damage to his political standing, since they offered little help for the bottom 90 percent or so of the population who form both the working and middle classes—and the Democratic Party's entire natural constituency.

This brings us back to the question of Obama's rapid political decline between 2008 and 2010. He is not an economist, but he had been an extremely successful politician. How could he have let his economic policies sabotage his political future?

Observers have proposed various explanations for his poor performance. A year into Obama's presidency, one could find a growing consensus that his advisers were center-right and that Obama himself must be as well.[10] Bush was far right, while Obama was a moderate conservative. He was, for instance, far more interested in using American military force to confront Islamic militants than he was in removing the causes of their grievances, such as the constant use of American military force in the Islamic world. At the same time, he embraced Islamic traditions in a speech in Cairo that could never have been given by George W. Bush. Obama may not have believed that markets were self-regulating, but he never made a statement about regulation that did not include a moment when he said, "I believe in the power of the free market," by which he meant that markets and companies are the sole sources of real economic value (Obama, "Speech on Financial Reform"). Another example: Obama initially favored gay civil unions but not gay marriage. And another: earlier in his career he said he'd favor single-payer national health care like Canada's, but his actual bill forced everyone without existing coverage to buy health care insurance with public money from the current private system. There are long lists of these mixed positions that could be used to show that Obama is not center-left or progressive but is center-right, so he was bound to disappoint everyone left of center. It would thus be perfectly logical for him to try to synthesize thesis (1) (trickle-down right-wing capitalist) with thesis (2) (New Economy public-investment capitalist) to continue the moderate-to-liberal Republican tradition of post-Clinton Democratic economics that he honored by appointing so many figures from the Clinton administration.

But if Obama is a center-right politician in a conservative country dominated by a combination of center-right and far-right views, he should have been doing better politically than he was. In reality, the country was not simply center-right as the financial crisis became a general economic crisis. For example, solid majorities of Americans actually wanted a "public option" in health care, but this was too radical for Washington. Similarly, the Democratic candidates who performed the most poorly in the 2010 election were the pro-corporate Blue Dogs. As one post-election report noted: "The Blue Dog caucus was cut in half, going from fifty-four to twenty-six. At the same time, the seventy-nine-member Progressive Caucus lost about four members." As a result, an underappreciated effect of the 2010 election was that "progressives [made] up a notably higher percentage of Democratic House members in the 112th Congress" (Goodman). While conventional wisdom says that victory lies in the center, in fact voters punished the center in 2010, in the form of Democrats who displayed the economic and other priorities of Republicans.

• • •

And indeed Obama was repeatedly warned by commentators that things were not going as planned. High-profile mainstream economists like Joseph Stiglitz and Paul Krugman wrote detailed critiques coupled with suggestions for alternative courses of action. Progressive activists warned that when Obama let Rahm Emanuel, his chief of staff at the time, marginalize the president's Left, he was weakening his base, eliminating valuable political thinking, and even helping to create the Tea Party as the only populist alternative (Hamsher, "Rahm"). In addition, in the summer of 2010 a leading Democratic polling firm released a policy "alert" tied to a detailed study showing that Obama's "go forward" campaign framework would fail, and that he needed to shift to an explicitly pro–middle class anti–Wall Street campaign (Carville and Greenberg). In short, a wide range of commentators predicted that Obama's right-of-center economic muddle would cost the Democrats the 2010 election. He stuck to it anyway, and proved his critics to be correct.

We need to continue with this question of *why* Obama would hold economic beliefs that damaged him politically. To do this, we will need to look at thesis (3).

Centrism and Compromise

The guiding impulse is deeper than Obama's policy convictions. It has appeared repeatedly throughout his career, surfaced in the press conference after the 2010 election, and was a staple of his negotiations with the relentless Republicans in the summer of 2011. Speaking in March 2011 to a "bi-partisan group of college students" active in politics, Obama said:

> If you're only talking to people who you agree with, then politics is always going to disappoint you. Politics will always disappoint you. You think about some of the issues we've worked on over the last couple of years. I think that the college Republicans here would say that I was a pretty liberal president. But if you read the *Huffington Post*, you'd think I was some right-wing tool of Wall Street. Both things can't be true. What it has to do with is this sense that we have a position and we can't compromise on it. And so one of the challenges of this generation is I think to understand that the nature of our democracy and the nature of our politics is to marry principle to a political

process that means you don't get 100% of what you want. You don't get it if you're in the majority. You don't get it if you're in the minority. And you can be honorable in politics understanding that you're not going to get 100% of what you want. And that's been our history.

(Think of Abraham Lincoln and the Emancipation Proclamation not emancipating slaves in allied states and regions.)

Here you got a wartime president who's making a compromise around probably the greatest moral issue that the country ever faced, because he understood that right now my job is to win the war and to maintain the union. Well can you imagine how the *Huffington Post* would have reported on that. It would have been blistering. Think of it. "Lincoln sells out slavery [*sic*]." There'd be protests. They'd run a third party guy. And so I think as you guys talk to your friends about getting involved civically, don't set up a situation where you're guaranteed to be disappointed. That's part of the process of growing up. And that doesn't mean that you're not principled. . . . It means that you're pushing the boulder up the hill, and you get it a certain way, and other people are pushing, and sometimes it's going to slip back—right? (Obama, "The President Speaks")

The overt theme of this statement is compromise, and the subtheme is disappointment. Obama says that compromise is the nature of American democracy and the nature of American politics. Compromise is the essential element, and failure to compromise ensures disappointment. He also claims that compromise is the essential element of accurate political understanding: confusion about who he is stems from the fact that both the Republicans and the *Huffington Post* take uncompromising positions. Obama also insists that compromise is compatible with principle, and uses Lincoln, an American icon of steady principle, to mock the idea that the Emancipation "compromise" meant that Lincoln had sold out his antislavery principles. Obama aligns himself with Lincoln as another great compromiser, presenting compromise as the great principle and, indeed, the principal greatness of American politics. Obama is in effect telling these students that *his* core political value is not market economics or racial equality or tax fairness or democracy abroad but *compromise itself.*

Compromise also has a vexed relation to the theme of disappointment. Obama's stated claim, simplified, is:

1. If you don't compromise, politics will always disappoint you.

He implies that the inverse of this statement is true:

2. If you do compromise, politics will not disappoint you.

But in both logic and political life, (2) is false. Obama had to know that he had disappointed tens of millions of people. He had to know that he had disappointed them precisely through his compromises. Obama was justifying compromise as the central mode of political life, but not really as what he said it was, a way of *avoiding* disappointment, but as a form of politics that is *always disappointing*. His real message to the students was to learn to accept disappointment: it is "part of the process of growing up." Obama's deeper message was thus

3. Politics is disappointing.

And the less conscious message hiding in this unspoken statement was:

3a. My politics are disappointing.

And yet we're not quite finished. Obama also implicitly offered an *explanation* for why he was so disappointing:

3b. My politics are disappointing because my core value is compromise.

I am suggesting that this is the dominant psychological driver behind Obama's policy positions. He always compromises. He often compromises too soon, when it seems strategically foolish for his side. This leads to what his supporters can regard as a *bad* compromise. The psychological value of the bad compromise is that it guarantees disappointment in one's own supporters and, more important, in oneself. Obama's administration has been a spectacular disappointment—to Obama's supporters, to Obama's opponents, and to Obama himself. An explanation of Obama's unconscious preference for disapointment over hard-fought, unambiguous victory while *governing* (rather than while campaigning) is beyond my scope. The result for the Democratic Party was straightforward, and it was to cement its reputation as the party of disappointment. Obama's reference to "running a third party guy" alluded to a growing sentiment in the country that the two-party system is unable to solve our obvious problems. Occupy Wall Street and similar movements elsewhere had become by September 2011 symptoms of the depth of the country's disappointment in the Obama presidency and in the compromising that, with him presiding, constituted the political system as such. In economic policy, the practical effect of Obama's incessant compromising has been to install at the summit of the Democratic Party exactly that hybrid that

Obama told the students is impossible, the *liberal capitalist tool* who subjects government agency and New Deal traditions to the private-sector agenda to which they were meant to serve as an alternative. Compromise and its inevitable disappointment blocked Obama's ability to articulate the creative powers of the public sector.[11] Obama failed to adapt to new conditions, and replaced development with disappointment as the primary deliverable of his enfeebled party.

Obama finally racked up such a purely disappointing performance—in the first presidential debate on October 3, 2012—that he was compelled, throughout the final weeks of his campaign, to push the progressive positions that had created his mass base in 2008.

A Less Disappointing Politics

There have been enormous institutional pressures on Obama, and I don't want to be mistaken as minimizing these. But he just as fundamentally undermined his own potential by abandoning his earlier apparent commitment to what I've called political romanticism. In that tradition, to repeat, the public disclosure of the refused truths of private experience allows individuals to return lost or alienated parts of themselves to politics with diminished fear of retribution. In contrast, Obama's politics of compromise avoids candor and its attendent potential for the psychological safety of the general public. It ensures personal disappointment, translated as the triumph of the great powers that damaged the psychological well-being of the individual in the first place. Compromise and its resulting disappointment induce general individual withdrawal from participation in public life. "Growing up" in politics then means unending efforts to protect the self from disappointment, which leads to the regressed group formation of standard politics, which leads to constant disappointment.

I use a final example, however, to suggest a road to recovery. This comes from the language in a study I mentioned earlier—a series of opinion experiments that Democracy Corps ran with four thousand voters in July 2011 (Greenberg and Seifert). Participants were presented with two fixed Republican messages and then a variety of Democratic messages. They were then asked to rate Obama and the Democrats on various points. The outcomes were complicated, but one clear finding was that Obama would likely shift opinion most strongly in his direction through two sets of messages in particular. One of them invoked "Change," and a second was called "Middle Class." The most striking thing about the messages used in the experiment is the directness of their texts, which I quote here in order of their effectiveness:

> We have to start by changing Washington. It is dominated by big banks, big donors and corporate lobbyists. So politicians rush to bailout [sic] Wall Street. Big oil keeps its tax breaks and companies still get breaks for outsourcing jobs. The middle class won't catch a break until we confront the power of money and the lobbyists. Expose their meetings, clean out tax loopholes, and limit donations. Getting the economy back for the middle class starts with changing Washington.

> The biggest problem we face is the decline of the middle class. The middle class has been smashed and struggles to keep up with the rising costs of gasoline, college education and health care. We need to help small businesses, help people who work hard with education and training and protect critical middle class programs like Medicare for the elderly. We need to invest in innovation and new energy to create the middle class jobs of the future. (Greenberg and Seifert)[12]

Obama's innovation economy appears at the end of the second discursive option, and it was relatively attractive to voters, but less so when it was part of a sequence called "Progress-Compete," in which the focus was on economic "reforms" and "winning in the global economy."[13] Both "reform" and "economic competition" have been associated with deindustrialization, the sending of blue- and white-collar jobs offshore, and stagnating or declining incomes for the great majority of American workers. The most successful sequence—as noted earlier—calls for innovation, but only in a framework that begins by stating the need for an attack on the banks and their lobbyists, a cleaning out of Washington, and "getting the economy back for the middle class" through adversarial confrontation with economic elites. Voters in this sequence shifted to Obama in part because they liked the second paragraph, which proposed education and training for people who work hard, *after* the proverbial playing field has been leveled with some vigorous class warfare on the rich. In a country mythically opposed to socialism and solidarity in general, it is striking to see potential voters shift strongly in favor of a candidate who would tell the truth about the predatory role of the finance industry in both creating an economic crisis and blocking recovery for the majority of the population.[14]

A variety of polling data suggests that a majority of Americans view themselves and their children as excluded from whatever wealth the United States continues to generate. It appeared that Obama could survive in this climate only if he started to speak openly about this fear and the only way in which it could be realistically addressed—through openly egalitarian policies that put more resources back into the hands of the ordinary people who have never stopped working to create that wealth. If, however, he continued instead to compromise with the military, with Congress, and especially with Wall Street, and to disappoint everyone else, as in his catastrophic performance during the first presidential debate, he would have ensured that 2012 repeated the debacle of 2010, pushing recovery for both the United States and the world economy further out of reach. Having avoided that fate in the November 2012 elections, Obama has a chance to recover inclusion *and* equality as the guiding principles of his second term.

NOTES

An earlier version of the discussion of American Political Romanticism appeared in Christopher Newfield, "American Political Romanticism and the Psychological Impacts of Obama's Presidency," *South Atlantic Quarterly* (Winter 2011): 243–251.

1. American studies has generated an important literature on political feelings to which I cannot do justice here. See in particular the valuable analyses of political affect in Laurent Berlant, *The Queen of America Goes to Washington City: Essays on Sex and Citizenship* (Durham: Duke University Press, 1997); and Ann Cvetkovich, *An Archive of Feelings: Trauma, Sexuality, and Lesbian Public Cultures* (Durham: Duke University Press, 2003).

2. For an older but standard (and still relevant) comparison of voter turnout, see G. Bingham Powell, "American Voter Turnout in Comparative Perspective," *American Political Science Review*, 80.1 (March 1986): 17–43.

3. For an intelligent skirting of the issue, see E. J. Dionne, *Why Americans Hate Politics* (New York: Simon & Schuster, 2004). In contrast, for tireless exposition of Americans' hostility to their political leaders across the political spectrum, see Glenn Greenwald's blog at Salon.com, for example, "Why Do Voters Hate Incumbents?" Salon.com, 19 May 2010 (accessed 2 June 2010).

4. Alford describes the normal collective state in terms of a "regressed group," in which each member exists in a "schizoid compromise" with the following three features: "1. One part of the self sees itself as instrument of the other's malevolent or careless will. The other may be group or leader; generally . . . the primary fear is of the group, displaced onto the leader. 2. Another part of the self imagines itself to be in an ideal relationship with the other, so that the other's

power, beauty, and so forth becomes an extension of one's own. 3. Still a third part of the self is isolated and withdrawn, a result of not being able to fully invest the self in any real relationship" (Alford 52). In my view, this describes standard, repetitive features of American political life, with its frequent loathing for some major portion of the national group, erratic love-hate relationships to leaders, and a continuous failure to create democratic self-management based on egalitarian respect for peers. For analyses of this issue's permutations in classic American literature, see, for example, my essays "The Politics of Male Suffering: Masochism and Hegemony in the American Renaissance," *differences* 1.3 (Winter 1989): 55–87; "Democracy and Male Homoeroticism," *Yale Journal of Criticism* 6.2 (Fall 1993): 29–62; and, with Melissa Solomon, "'Few of our seeds ever came up at all': A Dialogue on Hawthorne, Delany, and the Work of Affect in Visionary Utopias," in *No More Separate Spheres*, ed. Cathy N. Davidson and Jessamyn Hatcher (Durham: Duke University Press, 2002), 377–408, and "The Culture of Force," *South Atlantic Quarterly* (Winter 2006): 241–263. Regression and group regression are complex concepts in themselves, with complicated ties to related concepts, particularly the intimate public sphere (Lauren Berlant), mixed feelings (Ann Cvetkovich), identification (e.g., Diana Fuss), subjection (Judith Butler), wound culture (Mark Seltzer), and cruel optimism (Berlant), among others. Consideration of these relationships is beyond my present scope.

5. On bully culture, see Roddey Reid, "The American Culture of Public Bullying," *Black Renaissance Noire* (2010): 174–187.

6. On this last point I part company with Alford, who is most interested in overturning what he sees as a stigmatization of leadership as such in political theory, and in calling for the recognition of good leaders who encourage people to become aware of their projections onto leaders, a move that leads him to see constitutional liberalism as the most developed state of public life (Alford 74).

7. I make the case that this episode was a turning point for Obama's relation to the public in "American Political Romanticism."

8. See also Scarecrow, "President Barack Herbert Hoover Obama."

9. For a set of charts on low U.S. taxation rates, see Philip Davis, "Tempting Tuesday: Murdochs Testify to Parliament," *Seeking Alpha*, 18 July 2011. One summary reads: "Not surprisingly, Wall Street and the top of corporate America are doing extremely well as of June 2011. For example, in Q1 of 2011, America's top corporations reported 31% profit growth and a 31% reduction in taxes, the latter due to profit outsourcing to low tax rate countries. Somewhere around 40% of the profits in the S&P 500 come from overseas and stay overseas, with about half of these 500 top corporations having their headquarters in tax havens. If the corporations don't repatriate their profits, they pay no U.S. taxes. The year 2010 was a record year for compensation on Wall Street, while corporate CEO compensation rose by over 30%, most Americans struggled. In 2010 a dozen major companies, including GE, Verizon, Boeing, Wells Fargo, and Fed Ex paid U.S. tax rates between –0.7% and –9.2%. Production, employ-

ment, profits, and taxes have all been outsourced. Major U.S. corporations are currently lobbying to have another "tax-repatriation" window like that in 2004 where they can bring back corporate profits at a 5.25% tax rate versus the usual 35% U.S. corporate tax rate. Ordinary working citizens with the lowest incomes are taxed at 10%." "An Investment Manager's View on the Top 1%," Who Rules America, July 2011, http://sociology.ucsc.edu/whorulesamerica/power/investment_manager.html.

10. See, for example, Edward Luce, "America: A Fearsome Foursome," *Financial Times*, 3 February 2010; Steve Clemons, "Core Chicago Team Sinking Obama Presidency," *Huffington Post*, 9 February 2010; and Nate Silver, "What Killed Obama's Approval Numbers," FiveThirtyEight.com, 29 January 2010 (accessed 24 July 2011).

11. For a discussion of this problem in the context of California's Democratic Party, see Christopher Newfield, "Jerry Brown's Budget: A Danger to Himself and Others," *Huffington Post*, 21 January 2011.

12. This is Split E in the study.

13. This is Split C in the study.

14. The other top sequence for Democrats was Split G, "No Blame Game—Crisis-Then-Change" (my modified title). It reads: "Half the country blames George Bush for the state of the economy and the other half blames Barack Obama. But that blame game will not help create new jobs. We face immense economic problems that will take years to solve. We need to start working together to reduce spending and the deficit and ask the richest to pay their fair share of taxes. We need to support education, innovation and new American industries. When Obama took office, the deficit was surging, homes and stocks lost value and we were losing 750,000 jobs a month. The auto industry went bankrupt. Not everything Obama did was popular, and it has taken 4 years to get back to a place where people can breathe, but barely. Now, the economic focus has to be on changing our economy—on getting new American jobs, raising working and middle class incomes, cutting wasteful spending and getting the deficit down, while asking the wealthiest to contribute." This sequence embeds demands on the rich in a language of bipartisanship designed not to alienate moderates (Greenberg and Seifert).

WORKS CITED

Alford, C. Fred. *Group Psychology and Political Theory*. New Haven: Yale University Press, 1994.
Appelbaum, Binyamin. "Family Net Worth Drops to Level of Early '90s, Fed Says." *New York Times*, 11 June 2012.
Bair, Shelia. *Bull by the Horns: Fighting to Save Main Street from Wall Street and Wall Street from Itself*. New York: Free Press, 2012.

Barone, Michael. "The Depth and Breadth of GOP Victories." *Real Clear Politics.* 8 November 2010. http://www.realclearpolitics.com.

Carville, James, and Stan Greenberg. "AN ALERT: Changing the Framework and Outcome in 2010." Greenberg Quinlan Rosner Research. *Democracy Corps.* 20 September 2010. http://www.democracycorps.com (accessed 19 July 2011).

"Election 2010: Governor Final Results." *Real Clear Politics.* November 2010. http://www.realclearpolitics.com.

Elliott. "Sunday Talking Heads: July 24, 2011." *Fire Dog Lake.* 24 July 2011. http://www.firedoglake.com (accessed 24 July 2011).

Goodman, Amy. "As Right-Leaning 'Blue Dogs' Lose Seats, Democrats' Progressive Caucus Increases Plurality in Next Congress." *Democracy Now.* 4 November 2011. http://www.democracynow.org.

Greenberg, Stan and Erica Seifert. "Winning on a Losing Economy." *Democracy Corps,* Greenberg Quinlan Rosner Research. 18 July 2011. http://www.democracycorps.com (accessed 3 August 2011).

Greenwald, Glenn. "Barack Obama Is Gutting the Core Principles of the Democratic Party." *The Guardian.* 21 July 2011.

Hamsher, Jane. "Barack Obama and the Art of Negotiation." *Fire Dog Lake.* 20 December 2010. http://www.firedoglake.com.

———. "Rahm Goes Apeshit on Liberals in the Veal Pen." *Fire Dog Lake.* 7 August 2009. http://www.firedoglake.com.

Hudson, Michael. "Wall Street's Euthanasia of Industry." Interview on *Guns and Butter.* KPFA Radio, Berkeley, Calif. 16 July 2011.

Krugman, Paul. "The Lesser Depression." *New York Times.* 21 July 2011.

———. "Messing with Medicare." *New York Times.* 24 July 2011.

Marx, Karl. *Grundrisse.* Trans. Martin Nicolaus. New York: Penguin Press. 1973.

McMorris-Santoro, Evan. "Gallup Pollster: Obama's Ratings Higher Than You'd Expect." *Talking Points Memo.* 21 July 2011. http://www.talkingpointsmemo.com.

Nocera, Joe. "Sheila Bair's Exit Interview." *New York Times.* 9 July 2011.

Obama, Barack. "A More Perfect Union." Constitution Center, Philadelphia, Pennsylvania, 18 March 2008. http://www.huffingtonpost.com (accessed 15 October 2012).

———. "Obama on Midterm Shellacking: 'It Feels Bad.'" Press Conference. *PBS News Hour.* 3 November 2010.

———. "Obama's Speech on Financial Reform." Cooper Union, New York. 22 April 2010. http://www.whitehouse. gov.

———. "The President Speaks to a Bipartisan Group of College Students." Tech Boston Academy. 8 March 2011. http://www.whitehouse.gov.

———. "Winning the Future." State of the Union Address. United States House of Representatives, Washington, D.C. 25 January 2011. http://www.whitehouse.gov.

Scarecrow. "President Barack Herbert Hoover Obama Explains How to Avoid a Depression." *Fire Dog Lake.* 23 July 2011. http://www.firedoglake.com.

Smith, Yves. "Get Ready for TARP 2.0." *Naked Capitalism.* 23 July 2011. http://www.nakedcapitalism.com (accessed 24 July 2011).

Suskind, Ron. *Confidence Men: Wall Street, Washington, and the Education of a President.* New York: Harper, 2011.

DONALD E. PEASE

10 Barack Obama's Orphic Mysteries

This essay constitutes an effort to explain the state fantasy with which Barack Obama hegemonized an alternative to the biopolitical settlement normalizing George W. Bush's global war on terror. In what follows, I argue that Obama has not displaced but presupposed Bush's homeland state of exception as the political imaginary through which he transformed national and international politics. I am interested in particular in Obama's usage of the racial fantasies that he found condensed in the figure and the film *Black Orpheus* to achieve his geopolitical aims.

Named after *orphasias*, the dark one, Orpheus is the historical figure credited with teaching Greeks their foundational myths and sacred rites. Orpheus's lyre is said to have permitted the Argonauts to elude the Sirens. In the most famous of the Greek myths associated with his name, Orpheus descended into the underworld after the death of his beloved Eurydice to plead with its rulers for her release. According to Ovid, Orpheus's eloquent entreaty on her behalf brought the underworld to a standstill.[1] The arcane rituals associated with Orpheus's name have entered contemporary political theory to explain the transformation of bare life (*zoē*) into sovereign citizens of the body politic (*bios*).[2] *Black Orpheus* is also the name of a prizewinning 1959 film made in Brazil by the French director Marcel Camus. Camus's musical retelling of the Greek legend of Orpheus and Eurydice is set in a Rio de Janeiro favela during Carnival.

In this passage in his 1995 autobiography *Dreams from My Father: A Story of Race and Inheritance*, Barack Obama recalled his mother's reaction to the film *Black Orpheus* to exemplify the racial fantasies he entered political life to supplant:

> The story line was simple: the myth of the ill-fated lovers Orpheus and Eurydice set in the favelas of Rio during Carnival. In Technicolor splendor, set against scenic green hills, the black and brown Brazilians sang and danced and strummed guitars like carefree birds in colorful plumage. About halfway

marcel Camus (1959)

through the movie, I decided that I'd seen enough, and turned to my mother to see if she might be ready to go. But her face, lit by the blue glow of the screen, was set in a wistful gaze. At that moment, I felt as if I were being given a window into her heart, the unreflective heart of her youth. I suddenly realized that the depiction of childlike blacks I was now seeing on the screen, the reverse image of Conrad's dark savages, was what my mother had carried with her to Hawaii all those years before, a reflection of the simple fantasies that had been forbidden to a white middle-class girl from Kansas, the promise of another life: warm, sensual, exotic, different.[3]

This revelation took place in 1982, when his mother, while visiting Obama during his student years at Columbia University, asked him to accompany her to a showing of the movie at a theater in Greenwich Village. Rather than sharing his mother's enchantment with *Black Orpheus*, her twenty-year-old son discerned in the film's depiction of blacks the racial fantasy underpinning his mother's over-idealizations of African Americans. In his mother's eyes, "every black man was Thurgood Marshall or Sidney Poitier; every black woman Fannie Lou Hamer or Lena Horne. To be black was to be the beneficiary of a great inheritance, a special destiny, glorious burdens that only we were strong enough to bear."[4] After isolating the image repertoire that *Black Orpheus* projected in his mother's political unconscious, Obama tacitly designated his mother's elevation of black Americans into political messiahs and Camus's representations of them as childlike colonial savages as recto and verso images coined in the same foundational racial fantasy.

Obama described his mother, Stanley Ann Dunham Soetoro—"a lonely witness for secular humanism, a soldier for New Deal, Peace Corps, position-paper liberalism"—as representative of the 1960s American Left.[5] In *Dreams from My Father*, Obama diagnosed the antithetical, let's call them orphic, racialized images populating his mother's gaze as having resulted from contrary but interdependent tendencies informing the political imaginaries of the majority of U.S. citizens. He thought that his mother's exalted images of African American civil rights leaders presupposed opprobrious images of African Americans as an unacknowledged rationale. In *The Audacity of Hope* (2006), Obama identified this recalcitrant complex of contradictory self-representations as responsible as well for the constraints that African Americans imposed on their own social and political ambitions.

Obama grounded this diagnosis on his belief that when African American civil rights leaders internalized the American Left's quasi-messianic images of their political movement, they indirectly legitimated demonizing representations of American blacks. As exceptions to these degrading representations, such ennobling images of civil rights leaders only proved the rule of the oppressive imaginary. This structural racial antinomy animated a viciously circular social logic: African Americans who felt oppressed by such humiliating images needed to idealize civil rights leaders as the emancipators from the social imaginary that these civil rights leaders also required as the justification for their rule.

Obama discerned the black messiah/black devil complex as the racist antinomy that underpinned the history of race relations in the United States. This complex of antithetical representations also regulated what was considered possible and impossible for African American political leaders to desire. To transform the orphic machinery that saturated the United States' social imaginary, Obama added a scenario to the national political drama through which he persuaded the majority of American voters to act on a desire that should have been impossible for an African American leader to realize.

Although many of his followers described him as a black messiah, Barack Obama did not aspire to become the civil rights leader of oppressed African Americans. And despite the fact that his political enemies assaulted him with racist stereotypes, Obama never described himself as the victim of such efforts. Instead of repudiating this structuring antinomy, Obama's presidential campaign presupposed the system of racialized images he found depicted in *Black Orpheus*. Unlike the protagonist of Marcel Camus's film, however, Obama ran as at once the effect of and the limit to these structuring antitheses.

Obama considered the black messiah/black demon complex a structural racist antinomy that could not be historically surpassed. As the horizon that embraced and held the new rules and norms that Obama produced from within its framework, this structuring antinomy constituted the non-progressive backdrop for the changes Obama aspired to introduce into the political order.

An event that took place during the 2008 Democratic primaries supplied then senator Barack Obama with the occasion to turn the black messiah/black terrorist complex into a "teachable moment." From January through March 2008, right-wing political commentators published selected passages from sermons delivered by Jeremiah Wright, Obama's pastor at Chicago's Trinity United Church of Christ, as proof that the man whose sermons had inspired Obama to write *The Audacity of Hope* was in fact an anti-American terrorist. Rather than defending Reverend

Wright or castigating his opponents, Obama delivered a speech on March 18, 2008, at the National Constitution Center in Philadelphia, titled "A More Perfect Union."[6]

In his national address, Obama refused to represent his political campaign as an effort to get out of this racial divide. Observing that he had never been "so naïve as to believe that we can get beyond our racial divisions in a single election cycle, or with a single candidacy," Obama described the controversy as a "racial stalemate" that represented the "complexities of race in this country that we've never really worked through—a part of our union that we have yet to perfect." Upon locating the basis for the nation's racial division in the United States Constitution, Obama gave expression to the desire to achieve "a more perfect union." Having resituated the racial antagonism within the context of the constitutive gap separating our founding ideals from lived political reality, Obama reasserted the "impossible" desire animating his presidential run as undergirded by the conviction that in "working together we can move beyond some of our old racial wounds, and that in fact we have no choice if we are to continue on the path of a more perfect union."[7]

This speech permitted Obama to point to a flaw within the social symbolic order—the rift in its perfectible union—that enabled him to represent his extraordinary desire as if it were a universal political responsibility. Instead of remaining subject to these antithetical images, President Obama suspended their rule by positioning himself within the breach in between these antagonistic representations and expressing his intention to achieve a "more perfect union" through them.

Obama first inhabited this rift at the 2004 Democratic National Convention when he refused to identify as either a member of the red states or the blue states so as to declare himself a representative of the United States of America. Obama also ran his presidential campaign from this unprecedented political space. In aspiring to make a more perfectible union out of resolutely antagonistic partisans, Obama could not wholly identify with either one of the parties to the dispute. He occupied the strange position of being simultaneously more than and less than the antagonists. He was more than one because he could not perform as one of the factions he aspired to unify and render their union *more* perfectible; less than one because that act had to be subtracted from the political order whose union he would render more *perfectible*.

Once he took office as president, representations of Obama's governance oscillated between the opposite poles of the aforementioned racial antinomy. Following Obama's election in 2008, the members of the Tea

Party movement represented Obama as a figure who lacked the state-authorized long-form birth certificate required to certify his status as a legitimate United States citizen and reimagined him as a Muslim terrorist intent on convoking "death panels" to endanger the American people's biopolitical welfare. Contrarily, "progressive" liberals represented Obama's election as the birth of a postracial nation. While each of these fantasies drew upon two of the primordial conditions of belonging—birthright citizenship and civil death—inherent to what I have called a neo-orphic political imaginary, each fantasy transposed these elements into utterly antithetical characterizations of Obama's mode of national belonging.

At the one extreme, Obama's political supporters characterized him as the most inspired of the nation's sovereign leaders; at the other extreme, his political opponents cast him as one of mankind's accursed. In these antithetical formulations, the extimate belonging of President Obama as the sovereign head of state sat in uncanny proximity to the intimate non-belonging of President Obama as what Giorgio Agamben has called *homo sacer*.[8]

Obama took up his position within the rift through which he would render the union more perfectible by representing both the faction who extolled him as a postracial messiah as well as the people who had been cast in the role of *homines sacri*. As *homo sacer*, Obama belonged to the order by not belonging to it. But in order to exercise the power to render the union more perfect, Obama took up a position within the order as a figure who exceeded existing ordinations. Obama's oscillation between the positions of the sovereign and the *homo sacer* enabled him to deploy both of the positions within the structuring racist antinomy—the venerated racial prophet/the demonized terrorist—to his political advantage. Obama reworked the seemingly endless alternation of these antagonistic images into the energies animating the momentum of his political movement.[9]

Although Obama's historical project has been translated into Christological terms,[10] it operates according to a temporal logic that disconfirms the *telos* of redemptive historiography. Upon representing the desire for change in terms of his effort to achieve a "more perfect union," Obama ratified an understanding of history as a series of impasses. Obama may have represented his presidential campaign as a truly "transformative moment," a change whose time had come, but he invariably situated the change that has indeed come within the context of the never-ending effort to achieve a "more perfect union."

The transformative moment of Obama's election and the structuring racist antinomy that should have rendered it impossible did not converge to form a postracial American society. They instead collided into each other. Every moment of Obama's presidential movement also reestablished the antagonism that reimposed the racial divide. The past produced within the grasp of this complex, as he made clear in his 2008 address at the National Constitution Center, "isn't dead and buried. In fact, it isn't even past."[11] In occupying this rift in between antagonistic positions and permanently striving for a more perfect union, Obama took up a site that envisioned American history as an accumulation of stalemates. And he characterized the project he undertook from within this location as making "a way out of no way."[12]

I have chosen the term "orphic" to describe the structuring antinomy underpinning the United States' racial imaginary because Obama discerned this recalcitrant structure during a viewing of *Black Orpheus*. Barack Obama's election to the presidency did not displace the structural antinomy that he found illuminated in *Black Orpheus* as a twenty-year-old. But twenty-eight years later, Obama represented the changes he had effected in the United States' social imaginary within the context of *Black Orpheus*.

In this passage from an address he delivered on March 20, 2011, in the Teatro Municipal where *Black Orpheus* was set, Obama represented himself as a figure who would have been unimaginable to his mother, and to the film's director as well as its audience:

> Now, one of my earliest impressions of Brazil was a movie I saw with my mother as a very young child, a movie called *Black Orpheus*, that is set in the favelas of Rio during Carnival. And my mother loved that movie, with its singing and dancing against the backdrop of the beautiful green hills. And it first premiered as a play right here in Teatro Municipal. That's my understanding.
>
> And my mother is gone now, but she would have never imagined that her son's first trip to Brazil would be as President of the United States. She would have never imagined that. And I never imagined that this country would be even more beautiful than it was in the movie.[13]

During his presidential campaign, Obama converted the idealized child/savage colonial orphic machine into the precondition for the emergence of this previously unimaginable figuration. By occupying the rift in between them, Obama created a figuration of (and as) Black Orpheus that would have been unimaginable to the racial imaginary this antinomy regulated.

I examine the historic occasion for Obama's Rio address as well as the efficacy of Obama's orphic fantasy at the conclusion of this essay.

I hope to specify the changes Barack Obama effected within the U.S. political imaginary by briefly considering a montage of scenarios—the New Orleans Superdome in the wake of Hurricane Katrina, the Tea Party movement's town hall meetings, the memorial service for the Americans gunned down in Tucson in January 2011, the underside of Bush's homeland security state, the Teatro Municipal through which Obama's iteration of *Black Orpheus* accomplished this transformation.

Hurricane Katrina: Awakening Black Orpheus

Barack Obama located the origins of his movement in the sudden revelation of a nonsynchronizable now-time. This moment took place during a memorial service President George Herbert Walker Bush led to commemorate the life of the great civil rights leader Rosa Parks. While listening to President George W. Bush's father celebrate her memory, Barack Obama recalled the abandoned and homeless people of New Orleans after Hurricane Katrina as the memory that this memorial service had foreclosed from recognition.

> As I sat and listened to the former President . . . , my mind kept wandering
> back to the scenes of devastation . . . , when Hurricane Katrina struck the
> Gulf Coast and New Orleans was submerged. I recalled images of teenage
> mothers weeping or cursing in front of the New Orleans Superdome, their
> listless infants exposed hoisted to their hips, and old women in wheelchairs,
> heads lolled back from the heat, their withered legs under soiled dresses. . . .
> Listening to people's stories, it was clear that many of Katrina's survivors
> had been abandoned long before the hurricane struck. They were the faces
> of any inner-city neighborhood in any American city, the faces of black
> poverty—the jobless and almost jobless, the sick and soon to be sick, the
> frail and the elderly.[14]

President Bush's memorialization of this great civil rights leader from the past coincided with the state's abandonment of the African Americans who had been forced to take up residence in the New Orleans Superdome. Their abject impoverishment and homelessness had not received the state's notice before Hurricane Katrina, and their hopeless economic condition did not receive representation in the remarks with which the former president commemorated Rosa Parks. Rather than remaining fully absorbed within Bush's commemoration of Rosa Parks's historic accomplishments, Obama recalled a constellation of images—of slaves beaten by their masters, of migrant laborers forced into transfer centers, of Indians slaughtered by the thousands, of Vietnamese families dragged from their huts and shot and burned—that disrupted the commemorative ritual. It was in this eventful moment that Obama resolved to transform the desire for a different America into the object cause of a presidential campaign rather than a contemporary civil rights movement. Obama seized the revolutionary moment that surged up in this space when he linked the image of Katrina with this series of associated images to inaugurate his movement.

The tidal shift in the national self-regard that Barack Obama's fantasy enabled was not the result of the restriction of his identification to the homeless people of New Orleans. His "movement" was grounded in a much more pervasive sense of dispossession—of citizens stripped of their constitutional rights by the Patriot Act, of parents separated from their children by war, of families forced from their homes by the subprime mortgage crisis—that was already inscribed and awaiting enactment in the script responsible for the production of the Bush homeland security state.

Desire takes off when its object cause embodies or gives positive existence to the void that animates desire. Obama stood in the place of all of the figures who, in having been removed from their mandated positions within the social order, now lacked a place. The odd man in, Obama embodied the excess of confusion and need introduced by the desire for an alternative into objective reality. As the placeholder for all who could not be constitutively included within the social order, Obama became the object cause for those disparate desires, and the object cause as well of the missing America through which those desires became imaginable.[15]

The mirrors that Obama added to the U.S. political culture did not merely reconfigure the existing field. They also took the ground out from under the already positioned field, and they brought an entirely different field into view. In the acceptance speech that Obama delivered at the Democratic National Convention on August 29, 2008, the third anniversary of Hurricane Katrina, he associated his presidential campaign with the audacious hope for this alternative future. In his victory address at Grant Park, he associated that hope with the encompassing aspiration to achieve a more perfect union.

The Tea Party Captivity

Obama's standing as a transformational object, his capacity to produce what could be called a surplus effect of potential change, constituted the genius of his presidential campaign. It also organized the profound sense of loss that emerged once the movement for change was supplanted by specific presidential policies. Obama's policies necessarily alienated particular constituencies even as they gratified the desires of others. His election brought audacious hope into intimate relationship with radical despair.

Despite the apocalyptic pitch surrounding Obama's run against John McCain, McCain had been gathering strength every week until an event took place that utterly changed the political terrain. After the financial meltdown, Obama became the beneficiary of a whole set of desperate needs and demands. The turning point in the campaign took place when Obama exploited the subprime mortgage crisis to persuade the majority of Americans to divest their credibility in Bush's global war on terror and reinvest it in the ambition to make a transgenerational dream come true.

The 9/11 of the economic order also incited the emergence of a populist movement that embroiled Obama's presidency. One month after his inauguration, powerful Republican lobbies and Fox News began to promote the Tea Party movement. The movement included financiers and cynical politicians as well as members who had suffered real economic and emotional losses in the wake of 9/11 and the financial meltdown.

Obama organized his presidential campaign as a populist grassroots movement that cohered around two aims: to bring an end to President George W. Bush's unconstitutional state policies—abridgment of civil rights, preemptive strikes, renditions, internment of detainees at Guantánamo Bay—and to oppose the war in Iraq. The Tea Party movement produced a mirror image of Obama's grassroots populist movement, which had as one of its purposes the mimetic redescription of what Obama's campaign had called audacious hope as the achievement of a terrifying reality. In the contest that ensued, the architects of the Tea Party appropriated the organizing components of Obama's successful grassroots campaign—its antiwar initiative and its status as a constitutional movement—as models and targets.

Just as Obama overwhelmed opposition to his presidential campaign by building on the fantasy of a new, as yet unimaginable America, so too did the Tea Partiers build their own fantasy. After the trauma of the financial collapse, the Tea Party constructed the fantasy of an autonomous political sphere—reimagined within the representational matrix of the post-Reconstruction South—whose members were organized around a Contract from America. Whereas President Obama governed through the propagation of the desire to achieve a "more perfect union," the Tea Party members construed themselves as having seceded from Obama's union and forged an alternative.

The primary context for the Tea Party's interpretation of the economic collapse was the global war on terror. Its effectiveness as a political bloc depended on two basic factors: the extent to which the weakening of the global war on terror's conventional articulations led social elements to enter a "crisis" state of unfixity, and the extent to which the Tea Party's new articulations borrowed from and reworked traditional frameworks. The participants in the Tea Party movement identified their opposition to Obama's changes in financial and health care policies with the Boston patriots' iconic revolutionary act of dumping crates of tea overboard to protest the British tyrant George III's unfair taxation. But Tea Partisans redeployed figures instituted to conduct George W. Bush's global war on terror—illegal aliens, detainees, U.S. intelligence interrogators, terrorists— as the underpinning for lurid fantasies that supplied imaginary explanations for real economic and emotional distress.

In calling the Tea Party a fantasy, I do not mean that we need only to expose its phantasmic myth about the cause of the financial collapse to reveal the underlying truth. Following Slavoj Žižek, I would argue that instead of offering an escape from reality, fantasies actively construct social reality itself as an escape from some traumatic dimension.[16] Fantasies produce a figure, the subject who is supposed to believe in them, as the precondition of their credibility. Political commentators who believe they can dismantle the power of the fantasy by exposing its factual inaccuracies believe that credibility rises and falls with the truth of the factual state of affairs. Racism proliferates through its exponents' contempt for factual accuracy.

Because state fantasies construct a perfect order, they are always accompanied by symptom figures onto whom all the imperfections of the existing order must be projected. There would be no system without the symptom as the element that stitches up the inconsistencies of its ideology and gives consistency to being. But the symptom figure does not exist in the social symbolic order. As the embodiment of elements that cannot be integrated within that order, it demarcates that order's limits of tolerance and coherence. After 9/11 the terrorist was a symptom figure who facilitated the stitching up of inconsistencies in the entire ideological system. "The terrorist" summed up, gave coherence to, and offered a solution to a range of popular concerns.

When President Obama redescribed the global war on terror as "overseas contingency operations," he dismantled the most powerful consolidating framework invented since the cold war. After he removed the figure of the symptomal element—the universal terrorist—that had brought into coherence a whole range of internal political forces, the entire system of managed fear that this symptomal element had organized began to come apart. In the wake of the financial disaster in 2008, the Tea Party movement put Obama into the place of the symptom figure he had removed. For Tea Partiers, Obama was the most visible symptom of the loss of the American way of life. Obama was thereafter made to occupy the position of the figure that he had eradicated.

In the wake of the Obama administration's dismantling of Bush's state fantasy, the paramilitary movements and the Christian fundamentalists that President Bush had aligned with the imperatives of the homeland security state have reemerged with collective fantasies of their own. The Tea Partiers who disrupted town hall meetings, demanded that Obama give proof of his U.S. citizenship, propagated rumors of death panels, plotted the "teabagging" of Obama, demanded state secession, declared Obama the Antichrist, issued ultimatums, refused to permit their children to listen to the president's schoolroom address, and brought their guns to anti-Obama rallies have refused to give up their psychic attachments to the global war on terror.

The Tea Party movement was constructing fantasies associated with birth and death at a moment when the social contract, partially as a result of the financial meltdown, was undergoing a complete redescription. Obama's bailout of financial institutions and his proposed changes in the health care contract quite literally affected Americans' most intimate sense of secure belonging—jobs, health, and home. The Tea Partisans produced a retroactive relation between Obama's changes in health care policies and the financial crisis. Exercising a retroactive causality, they represented Obama's health care legislation as the definitive cause of the financial catastrophe.[17]

The deep psychic hold—the haptic uptake—of the birther/deather fantasies derives from their working at the most intimate level of both the body and the psyche of those who are taken up by them. Both fantasies are underpinned by a logic of psychic reversal for which revenge supplies the rationale. If Barack Obama's election constituted reparation for the wrongs performed against minoritized populations in the historical past, then, this fantasy has it, he intended to do to the majority of United States citizens what had been done to the historically oppressed. These beliefs cannot be answered by fact because they have inscribed persons within an order made in the image of fears that have become their reality.

The birthers' propagation of the belief that Obama lacks a valid birth certificate reimagined him as an illegal immigrant. The deathers conjuring of scenarios in which President Obama convoked death panels to decide on their continued viability identified U.S. citizens as equivalent to the detainees targeted for coercive interrogation in the war on terror. These conjoined fantasies tacitly constructed President Obama as himself a "terrorist," an enemy of the state whose health care policy threatened the biopolitical security of the homeland. That fantasy began to experience uptake when the town hall meetings in which Obamacare was discussed became sites for the acting out of the fear and the rage.

By dissociating their project from Obama's "now," the Tea Party undermined his strategic use of the collective desire to form a more perfect union as the basis for "change." Obama could not answer the explicit racism that was built into the Tea Party movement's imagined secession without identifying himself as the leader of a civil rights faction. It took an event that reawakened a series of past events from within the United States' transgenerational trauma to undermine the Tea Party movement's stalemate.

On January 8, 2011, a lone gunman shot Congresswoman Gabrielle Giffords and eighteen of her associates and constituents in a political rally in Tucson, Arizona, fatally wounding six of them. This traumatizing moment recalled a series of assassinations—of presidents and presidential candidates and charismatic civil rights leaders: Jack and Bobby Kennedy, Martin Luther King Jr., and Malcolm X.[18]

President Obama's memorial service in Tucson recalled the "transformative moment" of his campaign when memories of the helpless figures huddled in the New Orleans Superdome overtook his consciousness during the memorial service for Rosa Parks. When President Barack Obama traveled to Tucson on January 12, 2011, however, he did not do so as a representative of the civil rights movement or to commemorate the achievements of a dead black leader. This time a scene of catastrophic political violence became the occasion for an African American president to serve as the nation's designated mourner. The persons who had been shot in Tucson were neither presidents nor civil rights leaders. They were mostly white Americans performing everyday political activities. Obama's Tucson address produced an answer within the real world to the Tea Party's fantasies about death panels and Obama's un-Americanness.

The town hall meetings that members of the Tea Party members had turned into shouting matches over Obama's health care policies supplied the scene with its biopolitical unconscious. The lone gunman's rage, his violent hatred, his taking the law into his own hands—all of this recalled the modus operandi of the Tea Party movement. President Obama could not directly assign the movement responsibility for the shootings without reducing himself to one of its political antagonists, but his commemorative remarks conjured Tea Party demonstrations as their phantasmic context.

In Tucson, Obama turned the Tea Party into the spectral accomplices within a scenario in which he executed two significant acts of dissociation: of his movement from that of the Tea Party and of his biopolitics from an armed terrorist's thanato-politics. The memorial service also enabled Obama to use the images with which the Tea Party movement had demonized him to recover the position in between irreconcilable antagonists. Holding the space of the rift in between the Tea Party and its victims, Obama characterized the Tucson shootings as symptomatic of the need for a "more perfect union":

> That process of reflection, of making sure we align our values with our actions—that, I believe, is what a tragedy like this requires. For those who were harmed, those who were killed—they are part of our family, an American family 300 million strong. We may not have known them personally, but we surely see ourselves in them. In George and Dot, in Dorwan and Mavy, we sense the abiding love we have for our own husbands, our own wives, our own life partners. Phyllis—she's our mom or grandma; Gabe our brother or son. In Judge Roll, we recognize not only a man who prized his family and did his job well, but also a man who embodied America's fidelity to the law. In Gabby, we see a reflection of our public spiritedness, that desire to participate in that sometimes frustrating, sometimes contentious, but always necessary and never-ending process to form a more perfect union.[19]

As the representative of what it means to be alive within a vital body politic, Obama fashioned his address to rejoin the order of facts with the order of feelings in a now restored political order. The phrases from his memorial address quite literally displayed Obama's care. They removed each of the persons Obama commemorated from the oblivion of a mass shooting, celebrated each as part of a national family, as a representative of the nation's shared need for political forms of life, and as deserving of our collective memory.

In attending to Americans who had been attacked while participating in a collective form of political life, President Obama renewed the state's relationship to the health and welfare of the national body politic. Each time he restored a wounded form of civic life, he separated it from the Tea Party's violence. By turning this "quintessential American scene" into the dialectical image that brought back to memory all those other scenes of political violence, Obama also disclosed the nonsynchronous temporalities that haunted our contemporary moment.

The Real State of Exception: Obama's Orphic Mysteries in Bush's Underworld

The biohistorical event that took place in Tucson provided President Obama with an actually existing space in which he could remediate the rift in the body politic. The care he showed for the wounded in Tucson gave him access to the most intimate levels of biopolitical life—where the *zoē* of ontologically vulnerable individuals was conjoined with the *bios* of the body politic.

Obama's commemorative remarks drew a tacit parallel between the U.S. citizens who lost their lives in New York and Washington, D.C., on September 11, 2001, and the citizens who were subjected to a comparably senseless violence in Tucson. But comprehending the significance of this moment to Obama's political imaginary requires drawing a distinction from the events on which his predecessor had legitimated his biopolitics.

When he inaugurated the emergency measures of the homeland security state, Bush cited the traumatic power of the events that took place on 9/11 as justification. The homeland security legislation turned the state of exception into a juridical political apparatus that inscribed the body of the people within a quasi-permanent biopolitical settlement. This biopolitical arrangement first subtracted the population from the forms of civic life through which they recognized themselves as a free and equal citizenry and then positioned these life forms—the people, their constitutional rights and liberties—into nonsynchronous zones of protection.[20]

President Bush's emergency measures set the citizens whose rights and liberties the homeland security state protected in an antithetical relationship with the detainees and illegal combatants whom it reduced to the condition of sheer naked biological life (*homo sacer*). Stripped of the rights of citizens *and* prisoners of war, these persons were reduced to the status of unprotected flesh (*zoē*) whose lives the state could terminate according to decisions that were outside juridical regulation. In order to protect the entirety of the law against attack, the state subordinated its own laws to this urgent eschatological mission. The vacuum opened up by the vanishing of objective reality into this singularity was filled in by the mythologized reality in which the emergency state erected its eschatological version of *Realpolitik*.

The citizens who had been shot and killed in Tucson held a biopolitical status equivalent to that of the figures whose radical dislocation had been normalized by President Bush's state of exception. They had suffered the loss of the social textures of the biopolitical lifeworlds into which they were born. Outside the protection of all particular laws, their bodies were abandoned to a field of violence. At the most intimate level of their being, they had been given over to a terrorizing power that conditioned them absolutely.

The distinction between Barack Obama's mode of governance and George Bush's turned on their different relationship to the state of exception. In *Theses on the Philosophy of History*, Walter Benjamin asserted that when the state of exception becomes the rule, "we must arrive at a concept of history that corresponds to this fact. Then we will have the production of a real state of exception before us as a task."[21] During his presidential campaign, Obama connected his perception that under the Bush administration the state of exception had indeed become the rule with the imperative to undertake the production of an alternative.

The presidential campaign correlated the real state of exception with the revolutionary potential of Obama's movement. At the level of the law, movement personified the sheer anomic or constituent power—neither constituted by nor constituting state power—of what Benjamin referred to as pure or revolutionary violence. The revolutionary violence animating Obama's movement supplied its members with a warrant for undermining Bush's state of exception in the name of an alternative order of legality that Obama's election as president would bring into existence.

But after his election, Obama did not abolish the state of exception that George Bush had normalized. He instead used the Bush state of exception as the backdrop for his restoration of the normal constitutional democracy. In so doing, President Obama restricted his production of the "real" state of exception with the restoration of the constitutional rights and liberties from which President Bush's homeland security legislation had dissociated United States citizens.

Earlier I described the use to which Obama put the nation's structural racist antinomy in generating the momentum of his political movement. During his term as president, Obama turned this racist antinomy into the dynamic jointure through which he reconnected the body politic with their constitutional rights and liberties. Rather than supplanting this racist structure, Obama positioned himself in a rift between its antagonistic representations so as to represent two dialectically opposed iterations of the people—its sovereign citizens as well as its *homines sacri*. In his Tucson address, Obama turned the torsion produced by his oscillation between the two poles of this racist antinomy—sovereign leader, *homo sacer*—into the dynamic jointure through which he reconnected the body politic with its constitutional rights and liberties. This structural antinomy became the vital portal through which Obama's rules and norms inhabited the U.S. body politic.

In Tucson, Obama entered a site of generalized violence in which the exception had become the rule. But the Real state of exception he inaugurated at this site entailed his reperforming the constitutive rites on which the United States was founded. At this Real state of exception in between the nation and the state, Obama reaffirmed the foundational premises of the United States' social contract at the very site on which a terrorist had forcibly removed U.S. citizens from the condition of national belonging. In reinstituting the power of the state as the guarantor of their rights, Obama first reinstated the wounded within the condition of common humanity, then he brought them out of the realm of civic death and reconnected them with their constitutional rights and liberties.

In an effort to elucidate the role that fantasy played at this event, permit me to recast the symbolically efficacious action President Obama performed in Tucson as the prototypical mystery that Black Orpheus enacted within Bush's underworld. When Barack Obama traveled to this devastated place, he acted on the attributes of the figure mythologized as Black Orpheus. Standing in between the state and persons whom a terrorizing assassin had reduced to precariously vulnerable biological life, Obama's Black Orpheus, as the plenipotentiary of the U.S. body politic's vital political energies, performed the state's foundational orphic mystery. In the rift between these vulnerable mortalized biological life forms (what Giorgio Agamben calls *zoē*) and the immortal citizen-bios, Orpheus acted on the charismatic dimension of the state, the extralegality (*lex animata*) animating the law's effectivity. Oscillating between speaking as the sovereign and as representative of the *homines sacri* threatened by a gunman's terrorizing violence, Black Orpheus personified the jointure between natural life and the law through which they became once again entwined with the Constitution. No longer bare life, the wounded recovered their participant capacities at the jointure of life and law through the intercession of Black Orpheus.

Losing Eurydice: The Gaze of Orpheus

In this essay I have tried to elucidate the state fantasy Barack Obama instituted to replace George W. Bush's homeland security state. The "Black Orpheus" fantasy has enabled me to explain how Obama dissociated his biopolitical initiatives from the Tea Party's and differentiated his governmental rule from Bush's homeland security state. But in representing President Obama's biopolitical imaginary primarily in terms of the Black Orpheus fantasy responsible for hegemonizing it, I have risked a dual mystification—of the particulars of President Obama's mode of governance as well as of an analysis of its workings. Obama may have wanted us to envision his administration through the visage of Black Orpheus. I cannot conclude this discussion of Barack Obama's state fantasy, however, without asking what this fantasy mystifies.

I can begin to answer this question by returning to the Teatro Municipal that was the point of departure for this excursus and reading the opening phrases of President Obama's address from a slightly different perspective:

> Now, one of my earliest impressions of Brazil was a movie I saw with my mother as a very young child, a movie called *Black Orpheus*, that is set in the favelas of Rio during Carnival. And my mother loved that movie, with its singing and dancing against the backdrop of the beautiful green hills. And it first premiered as a play right here in Teatro Municipal. That's my understanding.
>
> And my mother is gone now, but she would have never imagined that her son's first trip to Brazil would be as President of the United States. She would have never imagined that. And I never imagined that this country would be even more beautiful than it was in the movie.

At the outset of these remarks, I described Barack Obama as having become unimaginable to *Black Orpheus*'s repertoire of racist representations, and I interpreted Obama's recollection of his dead mother as a reprise of Orpheus's efforts to call Eurydice back from the underworld. But if these lines do indeed refer to the Black Orpheus Obama personified in achieving the presidency, the Eurydice to which they now allude cannot be restricted to Obama's mother. Eurydice would necessarily include the members of the grassroots political movement that Black Orpheus's eloquence persuaded to elect Barack Obama. In the ancient myth, Orpheus discloses his hubris when he disobeys Hades's order not to look back as his song releases Eurydice from the underworld. When he looks back at the political movement Black Orpheus promised to lead out of President Bush's underworld, it is President Barack Obama who has now become unimaginable to Eurydice. The chief reason he has become unimaginable to Eurydice now has less to do with Black Orpheus's breach of the racial imaginary than with President Barack Obama's failure to realize the transformative change he promised.

During the presidential campaign, participants in Obama's movement bombarded President Bush with demands that he end state policies that violated the United States Constitution—preemptive strikes, the opening of the detention center at Guantánamo Bay, unauthorized domestic surveillance—and would undermine the legislation spelled out in Bush's Homeland Security Act.[22] Rather than moving the nation out of Bush's underworld, President Obama renewed the surveillance provisions of the Patriot Act, ordered his attorney general to initiate juridical proceedings against persons illegally detained at Guantánamo Bay, and increased the use of preemptive strikes abroad.

President Obama signed an executive order authorizing the bombing of military bases in Libya on March 19, 2011, the anniversary of the exact day when George W. Bush had initiated his campaign against Saddam Hussein. He enunciated the rationale for the bombing in the same March 20 speech in which he recalled his initial viewing of *Black Orpheus*. In his address at Teatro Municipal, President Obama placed the mask of Black Orpheus over foreign policies that the members of his political movement would never have imagined him undertaking.

In the body of his address President Obama constructed a series of dubious rhetorical analogies—correlating the "universal" human aspirations for freedom and socioeconomic justice informing the "Arab Spring" with his own grassroots movement, with his "humanitarian" intervention in Libya, as well as with his neoliberal trade agreements with Brazil—that would have been comparably unimaginable. President Obama's efforts to transpose the truly revolutionary movement taking place in the Middle East into a mirror image of his disbanded grassroots political movement rivaled the cynicism evidenced in the Tea Party's appropriative maneuvers. President Obama named his military campaign in Libya "Odyssey Dawn" so as to draw it into the imaginary orbit of the "Arab Spring," and he deployed technologies—drone missiles and special ops units—to remove those who were killed or disfigured from the field of visibility. But after the visage of Orpheus is removed, Eurydice discovers that she still remains in Bush's underworld.

During his campaign, Barack Obama took pride in his ability to take up positions in between hostile factions so as to negotiate the desire of each for a "more perfect Union." But President Obama's rifts solidified into recalcitrant political deadlocks. I concluded my book *The New American Exceptionalism* with the observation that I did not know whether the audacity of hope Barack Obama had aroused was a sign of political renewal or a symptom of radical despair.[23] It may be that we have entered a now-time in which radical hope and audacious despair have achieved a more perfect union.

NOTES

This essay is a significantly revised version of "Black Orpheus: Barack Obama's Governmentality," which appeared in *States of Emergency—States of Crisis*, ed. Winfried Fluck, Katharina Motyl, Donald E. Pease, and Christoph Raetzsch, *REAL: Yearbook of Research in English and American Literature*, vol. 27 (Tübingen: Gunter Narr Verlag, 2011): 57–72. For an analysis of the relationship between state fantasy and governmental rule, see Donald E. Pease, *The New American Exceptionalism* (Minneapolis: University of Minnesota Press, 2009).

1. The speculative claim that the civic religion of modern states derives from the transformational rituals sedimented within the Orphic movement was broached initially in what remains the best scholarly treaties on the Orphic mysteries: W. K. C. [William Keith Chambers] Guthrie, *Orpheus and Greek Religion: A Study of the Orphic Movement* (London: Methuen, 1935).

2. In *Homo Sacer: Sovereign Power and Bare Life*, trans. Daniel Heller-Roazen (Stanford: Stanford University Press, 1998), Giorgio Agamben derives *homo sacer* as a term of art from Roman law that can be translated as the "sacred" or the "accursed" man. In Roman law, *homo sacer* describes a person who is banned, may be killed by anybody, but may not be sacrificed in a religious ritual. The *homo sacer* was banned from society and denied all rights and all functions in civil religion. The genealogy of Agamben's *homo sacer* can be traced back to the Orphic mysteries, whose ceremonies rested on a crucial distinction in Greek between "bare life" (*zoē*) and a qualified mode of life (*bios*).

3. Barack Obama, *Dreams from My Father: A Story of Race and Inheritance* (1995; New York: Three Rivers Press, 2004), 123–124.

4. Ibid., 51.

5. Ibid., 50.

6. For the full text of Obama's speech, see http://blogs.wsj.com/washwire/2008/03/18/ (accessed 28 May 2011).

7. Obama, "Perfect Union."

8. For a brilliant description of the role the proximity of the sublime and

desecrated bodies of the sovereign played in fashioning the fiction of the "king's two bodies," see Eric Santner's remarkable volume *The Royal Remains: The People's Two Bodies and the Endgames of Sovereignty* (Chicago: University of Chicago Press, 2011).

9. Anthony Bogues called my attention to the ways in which the oscillation between the position of the sovereign and that of *homo sacer* could become the means of understanding the formation of a subaltern political movement. This dynamic underpins his analyses of the ethics of living together in his magisterial book *Empire of Liberty: Power, Desire, and Freedom* (Hanover: Dartmouth College Press/University Press of New England, 2010). For an analysis of the relationship between state fantasy and governmental rule, see Donald E. Pease, *The New American Exceptionalism* (Minneapolis: University of Minnesota Press, 2009).

10. Hortense Spillers spelled out the troubling political consequences of Christological readings of Obama's campaign in a talk she delivered at Brown University on April 4, 2011, published as "Destiny's Child: Obama and Election '08," *boundary 2* 39.2 (2012): 3–32.

11. Obama, "Perfect Union."

12. Ibid.

13. For this address, see http://www.whitehouse.gov/ (accessed 28 May 2011).

14. Barack Obama, *The Audacity of Hope: Thoughts on Reclaiming the American Dream* (New York: Crown Publishers, 2006), 295.

15. I elaborate on Obama as the object cause of postnational desire and the related notion of "transnational Haunting" in *The New American Exceptionalism*, 198–213.

16. I elaborate on the central claims in this portion of my argument in "States of Fantasy: Barack Obama and the Tea Party Movement," *boundary 2* 37.2 (2010): 89–105. Throughout this analysis Žižek's Lacanian reading of state fantasy has supplied the interpretive context for my understanding of the role state fantasy plays in the Tea Party movement. See Slavoj Žižek, *First as Tragedy, Then as Farce* (New York: Verso, 2009), especially 43–56.

17. The fantasy work that the Tea Party performed was evidenced on October 30, 2009, when Representative Virginia Foxx, a Republican member of the House of Representatives from North Carolina, articulated her opposition to "Obamacare" by explicitly linking health care legislation to the war on terror: "I believe we have more to fear from the potential of that bill passing than we do from any terrorist right now in any country." See http://thinkprogress.org/politics/ (accessed 11 February 2010).

18. When I first heard that a political figure had been critically wounded in a political rally in Arizona, a stronghold of the Tea Party movement, I immediately feared that the president had been shot.

19. For the transcript of Obama's Tucson speech, see http://www.washingtonpost.com/ (accessed 28 May 2011).

20. I elaborate on this account of Bush's biopolitical settlement in mythopo-

etical construction in "The Mythological Foundations of the Homeland Security State," in *The New American Exceptionalism*, 162–179. For an unparalleled analysis of the role the Bush administration's policies played in skewing the entire intellectual field, see Paul Bové, *A More Conservative Place: Intellectual Culture in the Bush Era* (Hanover: Dartmouth College Press/University Press of New England, 2013).

21. Walter Benjamin, "Theses of the Philosophy of History," in *Illuminations*, ed. and intro. Hannah Arendt, trans. Harry Zohn (New York: Schocken Books, 1988), 257.

22. For an analysis of the relationship between pure revolution and constituent power, see my discussion in *The New American Exceptionalism*, 207.

23. "Whether that state of fantasy is a sign of the audacity of hope or a symptom of cultural despair is a question that remains to be answered." Pease, *The New American Exceptionalism*, 213.

WORKS CITED

Agamben, Giorgio. *Homo Sacer: Sovereign Power and Bare Life*. Trans. Daniel Heller Roazen. Stanford: Stanford University Press, 1998.

Benjamin, Walter. "Theses of the Philosophy of History." In *Illuminations*. Ed. Hannah Arendt. Trans. Harry Zohn. New York: Schocken Books, 1988. 253–264.

Bogues, Anthony. *Empire of Liberty: Power, Desire, and Freedom*. Hanover: Dartmouth College Press/University Press of New England, 2010.

Bové, Paul. *A More Conservative Place: Intellectual Culture in the Bush Era*. Hanover: Dartmouth College Press/University Press of New England, 2013.

Guthrie, W. K. C. [William Keith Chambers]. *Orpheus and Greek Religion: A Study of the Orphic Movement*. London: Methuen, 1935.

Obama, Barack. Address at the Memorial Service, Tucson. 13 January 2011. http://www.washingtonpost.com (accessed 28 May 2011).

———. "President Obama Speaks to the People of Brazil." Address at the Teatro Municipal, Rio de Janeiro, 20 March 2011. http://www.whitehouse.gov/ (accessed 28 May 2011).

———. "A More Perfect Union." Keynote Address at the National Constitution Center, Philadelphia, 18 March 2008. http://blogs.wsj.com (accessed 28 May 2011).

———. *The Audacity of Hope: Thoughts on Reclaiming the American Dream*. New York: Crown Publishers, 2006.

———. *Dreams from My Father: A Story of Race and Inheritance* [1995]. New York: Three Rivers Press, 2004.

Pease, Donald E. "Black Orpheus: Barack Obama's Governmentality." In *States of Emergency—States of Crisis*, ed. Winfried Fluck, Katharina Motyl,

Donald E. Pease, and Christoph Raetzsch. *REAL: Yearbook of Research in English and American Literature.* Vol. 27. Tübingen: Gunter Narr Verlag, 2011. 57–72.

———. "States of Fantasy: Barack Obama and the Tea Party Movement." *boundary 2* 37.2 (2010): 89–105.

———. *The New American Exceptionalism.* Minneapolis: University of Minnesota Press, 2009.

Santner, Eric. *The Royal Remains: The People's Two Bodies and the Endgames of Sovereignty.* Chicago: University of Chicago Press, 2011.

Shakir, Faiz. "Rep. Foxx: Health Care Reform Is a Bigger Threat Than 'Any Terrorist Right Now in Any Country.'" *Think Progress.* 2009. http://www .thinkprogress.org (accessed 11 February 2010).

Žižek, Slavoj. *First as Tragedy, Then as Farce.* New York: Verso, 2009.

CODA The Imaginary and the Second Narrative

Reading as Transfer

The Conflict of Interpretations

One of the most puzzling aspects about literary criticism and literary scholarship is that critics and scholars never seem to be able to agree on the meaning and significance of a literary text. This strange phenomenon is by no means restricted to notoriously difficult, ambiguous, or enigmatic texts like *Hamlet* or *The Turn of the Screw*. It can be observed throughout literary studies, and includes such apparently transparent modes of representation as realism, naturalism, and even documentary texts. The same conflict of interpretations can also be observed in other fields of the humanities, such as, for example, cultural studies, film studies, or art history, where the interpretation of fictional texts and other aesthetic objects stands at the center.[1] These disagreements over meaning and value never seem to subside and are rekindled with every new interpretation. This is even more puzzling in view of the fact that the academic institutionalization of literary studies promised to put the interpretation of literary texts and aesthetic objects on more professional and "objective" grounds. Yet the professionalization of literary and cultural studies has led not to a reduction of interpretive conflicts but, quite on the contrary, to their proliferation.

One answer to the problem of never-ending interpretive conflicts has been surveys of competing approaches or "literary methods," often in the form of an introduction to major theories and methods of the field. Until the arrival of poststructuralism, these surveys were based on the assumption that literary and cultural studies are still in need of more rigorous methods and that a comparison of approaches would lead to a distinction between true and false, better or worse. Recently a more pluralistic view has come to prevail in which every method has a potential of its own, so that different approaches can happily complement one another: formalist approaches focus on form, ideological analyses on the text's ideology, gender studies on the role of gender in identity construction, and so on. Such a well-intentioned pluralism, however, merely obscures the problem. Two Marxist or two feminist critics may be in complete agreement about the desirability of a Marxist or a feminist approach, and they may even agree about what it consists of, and yet they may nevertheless offer different interpretations of one and the same text. Similarly, a reader's views (and interpretations) of texts can change, although his or her theoretical position and methods are still the same.

Another frequent response to the challenge of interpretive conflicts is the call for historical contextualization. Meaning undergoes changes in history, and thus it seems reasonable to argue that the best way of getting at the "true" meaning of a text is to reconstruct the historical context in which it was produced and by which it was shaped. This is the starting point of a variety of society- and history-focused approaches, ranging from Marxism and the sociology of art to (new) historicism and even systems theory. Indeed it is reasonable to insist that we should know as much as possible about the historical context of a text and the social and political factors that shaped its meaning and form. In the final analysis, however, such historical reconstructions cannot be sufficient, because they cannot explain the fact that literary texts and aesthetic objects can continue to provide an aesthetic experience although the historical situation has changed. What historical contextualizations (of whatever kind) cannot explain is why texts like *Huckleberry Finn* can still affect us, although we live in different times and circumstances. Yet it is reasonable to assume that the way in which they affect or interest us today will influence our interpretation decisively. Thus, even if we may agree on the interpretation of the historical context itself (by no means a given), we have not yet explained the conflict of interpretations, because, depending on different views of the text, the historical context will also be interpreted differently. To "always historicize" thus cannot solve the problem of interpretive conflicts.

One reason for never-ending disagreements about the interpretation of literary texts and other aesthetic objects is that critics hold different views about their political, social, and aesthetic functions and uses. At first sight, the term *function* may raise the suspicion of a throwback to sociological functionalism, or, if the term is narrowed down to political function, to a search for direct political consequences of literature. In this sense, the term appears ill-applied to literature, however, because it will hardly ever be possible to establish causal links between a literary text and concrete social or political effects. And yet I want to claim that the term *function* is useful nevertheless and, in effect, indispensable for literary and cultural studies.[2] Since any interpretation of a literary text or aesthetic object must go beyond a mere replication of the object, we must make decisions about what we consider important or unimportant in a text. But on what grounds do we decide what is important? The only way in which we can make sense of a text that has a "fictive" referent is to assume that texts are designed to do something and that their textual elements have been arranged in the way they are in order to achieve this goal.[3] In other words, we can make sense of the texts' elements only by postulating that they are "functional" with regard to a particular effect we ascribe to them. Or to put it differently: it is our hypothesis about the text's (political and/or aesthetic) function that makes a text's structure "readable." A structure is meaningless if it is not seen as being created for a reason (or as following a certain logic, for example, that of language). As interpreters, we do not encounter a fictional text first and then try to determine its function. On the contrary, we cannot interpret a fictional text without already implying a function. To use the term *function* in this sense thus means to use it as a heuristic category, not as a word for directly traceable social or political effects.[4]

Even if the concept of function is used heuristically, however, and not in naïve sociological fashion, two objections may still be raised. Is it not reductive to work on the assumption of a single function when any literary text can obviously have several different functions at the same time? And even more pertinently, is literature, in its inherent referential ambiguity, rhetoricity of language, and imaginary surplus of meaning, not exactly the opposite of a text that is "functional" in its organization, so that any heuristic assumption of an implied function must unduly homogenize the text? The argument is valid, but it conflates two levels that should be kept apart logically. To employ the term *function* as a heuristic category does not yet determine whether my hypothesis entails homogenization or heterogenization. It all depends on the function implied. If I assume the function to be a deconstruction of logocentrism, then my attention will be drawn to those operations of the text that are "functional" for the purpose of deconstruction, such as constant slippages in signification, but this will by no means homogenize the text in the "functionalist" sense of one unifying principle. Similarly, the contrast between mono- and multi-functionality confuses two levels. If we speak about historical functions of a particular text, then we may indeed encounter a variety of functions. But this is different from employing the term as a heuristic category, because in terms of interpretation, hypotheses about several functions will not work differently from hypotheses about a single function. They, too, will become the foundation for interpretive choices based on the hypothesis that certain textual features are designed to achieve certain effects.

Even those approaches that position themselves in open opposition to "functionalism" and value literature as counter-realm to the iron grip of rationality cannot escape this logic. Formalists, for example, who insist that the special value of literature lies precisely in its potential to be "without function" can attribute special significance to this functionless dimension of *Zweckfreiheit* (disinterestedness) only because it promises to serve an important function on another level, namely, the liberation of culture from the alienating effects of materialism and instrumental reason. Similarly, the poststructuralist valorization of heterogeneity and difference is generated by a belief in their social, cultural, and political desirability. The disseminative power of language would not be considered important—so much so, in fact, that all interpretive energy is spent on demonstrating it—if it did not play a crucial role in the social theories of the Paris May by which deconstruction was strongly inspired. As a power analysis that no longer posits any "outside" from which the system could still be critiqued, deconstruction remains one of the few options of resistance. Again, it is precisely the resistance to being "functionalized" by invisible power effects that opens up a new function for literature and shapes all subsequent methodological decisions. No matter what we think of these claims, in each case a hypothesis about the function that literature has within a larger system will determine the interpretive choices the interpreter makes.

A Theory of Aesthetic Experience

Questions about the function of literature are posed in almost all of Wolfgang Iser's work in literary studies, including his seminal contributions to reception theory, *The Implied Reader* and *The Act of Reading*. Doggedly he returns to the question why human beings expose themselves to fictional texts again and again, although as a rule they are well aware of the fact that these texts are invented and in most cases practically useless. Iser has coined the term *Fiktionsbedürftigkeit* (a need for fictions) to describe this phenomenon, and the development of his own work in three major stages—a modernist aesthetics of negation, reception aesthetics, and the project of a literary anthropology—can be seen as a renewed attempt to find a convincing explanation.[5] These three stages of his work are linked by a basic starting point: trying to find out why human beings need fiction means having to focus on the specific potential that fiction has as a form of communication. We search out fictional texts not primarily for information or documentation but for a special experience with the text or aesthetic object. We read not "for meaning" but in order to have the kind of experience we call an *aesthetic experience*. Seen this way, the aesthetic function of the text is the basis for the realization of other functions, because political or social functions of fictional texts can be realized only through an aesthetic experience.[6] How can we define *aesthetic experience*, however?

When a text or an object is considered as fiction, we cannot regard the object as simply referential, because when we read a fictional text, even a realistic novel, reality is created anew. Since we have never met a character named Hamlet and in fact know that he never existed, we have to come up with our own mental image of him. Inevitably this mental construct will draw on our own feelings and associations, or, to use a broader, more comprehensive term, on our imaginary. These imaginary elements can gain a *Gestalt*, however, only if they are connected with discourses of the real. As Iser has argued, literary representation is thus not a form of mimesis but a performative act. The double reference of fiction creates an object that is never stable and identical with itself. And it is this non-identity that can be seen as an important source of aesthetic experience, because it allows us to do two things at the same time: to articulate imaginary elements and to look at them from the outside. As a result of the doubling structure of fictionality, we are, in Iser's words, "both ourselves and someone else at the same time." Iser writes:

> In this respect the required activity of the recipient resembles that of an actor, who in order to perform his role must use his thoughts, his feelings, and even his body as an analogue for representing something he is not. In order to produce the determinate form of an unreal character, the actor must allow his own reality to fade out. At the same time, however, he does not know precisely who, say, Hamlet is, for one cannot properly identify a character who has never existed. Thus role-playing endows a figment with a sense of reality in spite of its impenetrability which defies total determination. . . . Staging oneself as someone else is a source of aesthetic pleasure; it is also the means whereby representation is transferred from text to reader. (Iser 1989b, 244)[7]

It is important to note that this transfer is not to be confused with a mere projection of our own desire into the text. Our reading experience remains tied to the text and depends on what the text offers. When the text provides a characterization of Hamlet or Huck Finn, our imagining them will be shaped by the description. Critics do not disagree that Huck Finn is about twelve years old, illiterate, and speaks a colorful colloquial vernacular. Nevertheless, despite this factual basis, the Huck Finn imagined by Wolfgang Iser will be different from the Huck Finn imagined by Winfried Fluck, because both of these readers will draw on different imaginary resources in order to endow, as Iser puts it, "a figment with a sense of reality." Or as Rita Felski reminds us, "The work only comes to life in being read, and what it signifies cannot be separated from what readers make of it" (Felski 87).[8]

The basic point about fictional texts and aesthetic objects is, then, that in order to acquire significance and to provide an aesthetic experience, they have to be brought to life by means of an imaginary transfer on the side of the reader. When we start reading a book, we are confronted with abstract letters on a page. Structuralism has taught us that the words formed by these letters are arbitrary in their reference. Moreover, in the case of fictional material, the represented world is invented, at least in the particular form in which we encounter it in the text. Without any investment from our side, this invented world would not take on any degree of reality and would thus not make any sense. Bärbel Tischleder has provided a number of simple but helpful illustrations for the indispensability of such transfers when she says, "When a figure in a film rubs against a cat's fur, or burns herself, or simply walks in the snow, or carries a heavy suitcase, this representation can take on meaning for us only if we draw on our own experiences and memories in order to imagine what it means to be in such a situation" (Tischleder 78; my translation).

No matter how well crafted a literary text is, it cannot solely determine its meaning. It always needs a reader in order to become actualized (and thus "meaningful"); the reader, however, can actualize a literary text whose reference is "fictionalized" only by drawing on his or her own associations, mental images, and feelings as an analogue. Since, as a result of the doubling structure of fictionality, we are, in Iser's words, "both ourselves and someone else at the same time," we can be inside and outside a character at once.[9] On the one hand, the fictional text allows us to enter another character's perspective and perhaps even his or her body; on the other hand, we cannot and do not want to give up our own identity completely. In reading, we thus create other, more expressive versions of ourselves. This is achieved, however, in a much more complex way than is suggested by the term *identification*. One may assume, for the sake of the argument, that it may be possible to "identify" with a character, but one cannot identify with a whole text. It is the text, however, that provides an aesthetic experience, not just single characters in it. Clearly, in actualizing the text in the act of reading, the reader has to bring all characters to life by means of a transfer, not merely the good or sympathetic ones.[10] The "more expressive version of ourselves" is thus not a simple case of self-aggrandizement through wish fulfillment but an extension of our own interiority over a whole (made-up) world.

Iser's "performative" theory of aesthetic experience is supported by a number of works on the psychology of reading and the transaction between reader and text. In *Becoming a Reader*, J. A. Appleyard argues that in reading, we experience a double state of mind: "We both identify ourselves with the characters, incidents, and themes of the work, but also keep them at a safe distance." We can simultaneously enact and observe certain experiences; we can indulge in a temporary "abandonment to the invented occurrences" and yet also take up "the evaluative attitude of the onlooker" (Appleyard 39, 53–54). We become observer and partici-pant at the same time. In similar fashion, Catherine Gallagher and Ste-phen Greenblatt write in their *Practicing New Historicism*, "In a mean-ingful encounter with a text that reaches us powerfully, we feel at once pulled out of our own world and plunged back with redoubled force into it" (Gallagher and Greenblatt 17). In her study *Reading Cultures: The Construction of Readers in the Twentieth Century*, Molly Travis conceives of reading as a process of going "in-and-out" and emphasizes the compulsive dimension of the act: "I conceive of agency in reading as compulsive, reiterative role-playing in which individuals attempt to find themselves by going outside the self, engaging in literary perfor-mance in the hope of fully and finally identifying the self through self-differentiation. Such finality is never achieved, for the self is perpetu-ally in process" (Travis 6). And Gabriele Schwab, a student of Iser's, has pointed out: "Literature requires a specific dynamic between familiarity and otherness, or closeness and distance, in order to affect readers. The old cliché that we 'find ourselves' in literature refers to the fact that un-less literature resonates with us we remain cold to it. On the other hand, complete familiarity would never engage our interest but leave us equally indifferent" (Schwab 10). Literature enables readers to enter other worlds that are different from their own but remain, strangely enough, their own worlds at the same time.[11]

The Articulation Effect of Fiction

In aesthetic experience, then, the transfer needed to give meaning and significance to the text in the act of reception allows us to give expression to associations, feelings, moods, impulses, desires, or corporeal sensations that otherwise have not yet found any satisfactory expression—either because of censorship, or social or cultural taboos, or simply because society has not been interested so far. I call this the "articulation effect" of fiction.[12] Because of fiction's status as a made-up world that can transcend reality claims, fictional texts and aesthetic objects can employ "official" discourses of the real as a host for the expression of as yet unformulated and possibly "unsayable" things. The conceptualization of this articulation effect should not be restricted to narratives of transgression or negation, however, or to the idea of a liminal state (Schwellenerfahrung).[13] For example, the popularity of the sentimental novel in the mode of Richardson may be explained by its skillful evocation of the "guilty pleasures" of illicit affairs, and thus by the articulation of socially tabooed associations.[14] We could, in this case, apply categories such as desire or the unconscious for that which is articulated. Nevertheless, as a name for the flow of diffuse, decontextualized, and protean associations, sensations, and sentiments that are always a part of us, but at the same time "unrepresentable" because these elements possess no inherent structure, the phenomenological concept of the imaginary goes beyond definitions of the unformulated or unsayable as the culturally tabooed. The unformulated dimension that fictional texts articulate should thus be sought not primarily or even exclusively in a repressed, other side of ourselves, cut off from consciousness and self-awareness, but in the more fundamental fact that there exists a dimension of interiority—ranging from psychic structures and diffuse affects to bodily sensations—that can never be fully represented and expressed. Because fictional texts require a transfer in order to be actualized, they can provide the gratification of articulating something radically subjective while at the same time representing this dimension in a "public" version that appears to provide recognition.

Literature gives a determinate shape to imaginary dimensions, ranging from fantasy elements to affective dimensions, by linking these elements with a semblance of the real. The fictional text emerges out of the combination of the two. Without imaginary elements, the text would be a mere duplicate of discourses of the real; without semblance of the real, the imaginary would not have any form and thus would not be able to appear in representation. As Iser writes:

> The act of fictionalizing is therefore not identical to the imaginary with its protean potential. For the fictionalizing act is a guided act. It aims at something that in turn endows the imaginary with an articulate *gestalt*—a *gestalt* that differs from the fantasies, projections, daydreams, and other reveries that ordinarily give the imaginary expression in our day-to-day experience. . . . Just as the fictionalizing act outstrips the determinacy of the real, so it provides the imaginary with the determinacy that it would not otherwise possess. In so doing, it enables the imaginary to take on an essential quality of the real, for determinacy is a minimal definition of reality. This is not, of course, to say that the imaginary *is* real, although it certainly assumes an appearance of reality in the way it intrudes into and acts upon the given world (Iser 1993, 3).

As a representation of yet unformulated and indeterminate imaginary elements, the fictional text goes beyond discourses of the real; as a form of representation drawing on a semblance of the real, it is more than a mere fantasy or daydream; as a combination of the two elements, it places the reader in a position "in between." This creates the need for a constant movement between the real and the imaginary elements of the text. Iser writes elsewhere:

> A piece of fiction devoid of any connection with known reality would be incomprehensible. Consequently, if we are to attempt a description of what is fictional in fiction, the time-honored opposition between fiction and reality has to be discarded and replaced by a triad: the real, the fictional and the imaginary. It is out of this triadic relation that I see the literary text arising. Within this context, the act of fictionalizing is seen as a constant crossing of boundaries between the real and the imaginary. By transforming reality into something which is not part of the world reproduced, reality's determinacy is outstripped; by endowing the imaginary with a determinate gestalt, its diffuseness is transformed (Iser 1986, 5).

This "duplicity" can explain fiction's usefulness for an articulation of the imaginary: "As an agglomerate of diffuse feelings, images, associations, and visions, the imaginary needs fiction to be translated into a coherent, comprehensible, and culturally meaningful expression" (Fluck 1996, 423).[15] Fictional texts are especially useful, for they can link the subjective and the social by means of an analogue.[16] Because readers have to draw on their own associations, feelings, and bodily sensations in the transfer process, the actualization of the text establishes analogies between elements that may be far apart historically but linked by unforeseen and often surprising resemblances. This articulation effect is, I think, one of the major gratifications that fictional texts and aesthetic objects provide, and it can be seen as one of the reasons for the increasing role that fictional texts and aesthetic experience have come to play in modern societies. For modern society, this articulation effect serves an important purpose, because it contributes new elements to the ongoing conversation of a culture and thus functions as a source of constant redescription and reconfiguration. For the individual, the articulation effect is welcome, because it can provide a cultural recognition of her own interiority. Again, however, this "empowerment" through fiction should not be falsely construed as self-aggrandizement, or as a fantasy of imaginary strength, but should be seen as a form of imaginary self-extension.

Another way of describing this phenomenon is to say that literary texts or aesthetic objects function as a host for readers who use them in parasitical fashion.[17] After reunification in Germany, for example, there was a brief moment when some East Germans compared themselves to the American South after the Civil War. In both cases, a "better" world seemed to have been conquered by an inferior civilization with primarily materialistic values. Let us imagine for the sake of the argument that such an East German ran across the novel *Gone with the Wind* at the time. This East German had never been to the American South, in fact knew hardly anything about it, except that it was racist. Had she still read the novel in the communist German Democratic Republic, this might have been her major focus. All of a sudden, however, she sees something else in the book, namely, an analogy between what she considers the cruel fate of two superior civilizations. The imaginary and emotional elements she invests in the transfer that actualizes the novel may now be dominated no longer by feelings of superiority but by the theme of how to deal with humiliation and defeat. This potential of the fictional text to function as host for the articulation of hidden, perhaps only half-conscious or unconscious emotional and imaginary dimensions of the self provides the only plausible explanation for me of why we read fictive texts about people who never existed.

The important point here is that the transfer between two worlds that are far apart—that of a southern belle of the nineteenth century and that of a late-twentieth-century reader in Leipzig—becomes possible by way of analogy: "In the image consciousness," writes Jean Paul Sartre in his study of the imaginary, "we apprehend an object as an analogon for an-other object" (Sartre 52). This analogy can be constituted by different points of reference, ranging from structural similarities to affective af-finities. In principle, any element of the text—word, image, figure, scene, event, deictic references, descriptions of space, narrative perspective—can become a point of departure for establishing an analogy, often in en-tirely unexpected and unforeseen ways.[18] To acknowledge this key role of analogizing means to grasp an important aspect of the act of reading, namely, that as a rule, it takes place in segmented form. Although we may faithfully read every line of the text, we nevertheless read selectively by focusing on certain segments and skipping or disregarding others. The imaginary that seeks analogies for the purpose of articulation can take its point of departure from any aspect of the text and zoom in on any seg-ment without considering the larger context.

For example, we can attach imaginary links to the heroic dimension of a gangster or outlaw figure (Bonnie and Clyde dying in slow motion) while ignoring the criminal context. This, in effect, is the reason why one and the same text can be praised as either subversive or ideologically af-firmative, depending on the segment to which the imaginary is attached. Even in the ideologically most conformist text, such as, for example, a do-mestic novel of the American antebellum period, there may be rebellious acts by characters that the reader can activate for a transfer, although these characters may in the end submit to the patriarchal order. The effect of the novel may thus be the opposite of its ideological project. This can provide one of the explanations for the gratifications of popular culture and the striking, seemingly contradictory phenomenon that popular cul-ture is regularly criticized for its ideological nature and at the same time praised for its subversive force.[19] The ongoing debate in feminist criticism about whether the domestic novel is deeply compromised by a Victorian gender ideology or whether it can be seen as a cunning form of female self-empowerment can be attributed to the fact that these arguments take different segments of the text as their point of departure for the establish-ment of analogies. The possibilities for discovering analogies in the act of reading are indeed unlimited. Analogies between text and reader can be established on every level of the text. They can be established between the recipient and potentially all characters in the text (not only the ego-ideal; villains can also offer aspects that invite a transfer, such as strength or stances of rebellion), between the reader and single traits of a character, between kinetic, haptic, and other sensuous dimensions of the text and the reader's body schemata, and even between a setting and an inner mood of the reader.[20] Analogies can be established between parallel feelings or moods or sensations,[21] but they can also be based on associations created by language.[22]

This potential of fictional texts and aesthetic objects to suggest ever new, potentially unlimited imaginary analogies can explain major aspects of literary and cultural studies to which I drew attention at the beginning of this essay. For one thing, it can provide an explanation for the fact that texts offer gratification for readers who live in worlds that are entirely different from the world of the text and its historical context. Taking into account the possibilities of segmentation and analogizing, we can understand not only why a text like *Gone with the Wind* is still popular in contemporary America, although this contemporary America is far removed from the plantation wonderland of the text, but also that it is popular in other countries where southern plantations have never been part of the cultural imaginary.[23] Second, the key role of imaginary analogies in the transfer process can provide an explanation for the fact that different readers can read one and the same text differently: at a closer look, it turns out that they take their point of departure from different segments of the text, so that their readings are based on different analogies. Finally, the fact that aesthetic experience is constituted by a transfer based on imaginary analogies that emerge in the act of reading can explain why we may read one and the same text differently at different times: simply put, the difference is produced by the discovery of new analogies in the transfer process.[24] Ambiguous or enigmatic texts produce a larger number of disagreements, because they also open up new, increased possibilities for analogizing. Moreover, since establishing analogies by means of a transfer often happens spontaneously and in unforeseen ways in the act of reading because of the diffuse and "creative" nature of the imaginary, aesthetic objects are often seen as exemplary models of creativity, for what is creativity other than finding unforeseen linkages? Seen this way, it is not only avant-garde texts that may be considered as manifestations of the experimental but also fictional texts and aesthetic objects in general, because their realization in the act of reception will have a "creative" dimension of unpredictability.

By representing reality in a fictional mode, the literary text restructures reality. This doubling is repeated by the reader in the act of reading. In this reception, the reader produces a second narrative that constitutes, in fact, a second text. In the Gilded Age, Mark Twain faced the problem of racial relations, and one of his responses was to redefine the issue in terms of the moral struggle in chapter 31 of his novel *Adventures of Huckle-*

berry Finn. In his famous interpretation of the novel, Lionel Trilling in turn experienced this scene as especially meaningful because he saw it in (and transformed it into) categories that reflected his own struggle for independence against a Stalinist Left.[25] Such a redescription should not be seen as solipsism. On the contrary, it is the beginning of an act of articulation that makes Trilling's experiences intersubjectively accessible. The prospect that fictional texts can enable us to express and authorize our own need for articulation drives us back, again and again, to literature and other aesthetic phenomena.

Interpellation, Identification, Transfer

An analysis of aesthetic experience by means of a transfer may appear plausible in the case of reading, but it seems counterintuitive in the case of visual material in the media, because the characters we encounter there have an immediate physical presence. Before we can even begin to think about who Hamlet might be, we have already seen him in the shape of, say, Laurence Olivier. We no longer have to imagine him and need not come up with our own image of what Hamlet looked like. This does not free us, however, from the need to bring this person to life by drawing on our own store of memories, feelings, bodily sensations, and bodily memory. If the person on the screen suffers, we can only imagine what suffering is and what it may mean for him on the basis of our own experiences and memories of suffering. Clearly, the perception of a picture involves an imaginary activity too. No less than literature, although with different modalities, the aesthetic experience of the image, including pictures and motion pictures, is one for which non-identity and doubleness are constitutive. One may claim, in fact, that the art of a movie consists of the way in which it manages to engage us sufficiently to draw on such imaginary associations.

One of the reasons for the popularity of the modern mass media can be attributed to the fact that they have entirely new means at their disposal for engaging the viewer—for example, by fast editing, close-ups, montage, and by a combination of image and sound. Visual images are especially effective in drawing us into transfers without our even being aware of it. The development from print to the visual media and on to recorded music can be described as a story in which our involvement as recipients has become more and more direct, unmediated, body-centered, and sensuously intense. In this context it is important to recall again that the transfer through which we constitute an aesthetic object does not merely apply to characters. It pertains to every aspect of the text or object. We also have to bring to life the villains, emotional conflicts, spatial references, even the November fog, by means of our own imagination, our feelings, and our own bodily sensations. Since the visual image comes so quickly and so directly at us, this often happens without any awareness on our side, which in turn means that visual images are also especially effective in triggering imaginary transfers. A theory of aesthetic experience developed in the analysis of the reading process is thus not restricted to literary studies but can be useful for cultural studies at large.

These considerations are confirmed by recent theoretical work on the image.[26] A photograph even in a documentary mode is not just a representation of an object but is crucially determined by the idea the photographer has about the object. In that sense it is also a representation of the interiority of the photographer. This picture collides with another interiority in the act of reception, that of the viewer whose interiority is in itself already defined by a whole range of images, because otherwise the self could not develop any sense of itself. We do not encounter an image "for the first time" in the act of reception, then. Rather we see it in the context of a cultural imaginary that plays a crucial part in determining what different viewers actually see in looking at one and the same picture. The image always already precedes the picture. It is the virtual background for the actualization of the meaning of the picture. Images are already there as part of the imagination before we "see" them in representation. Or, more precisely, what we actually see is shaped by our cultural imaginary, the storehouse of images in our imagination with which we approach the pictures. The transfer through which aesthetic experience is brought about thus entails a screening of the picture in terms of the images with which we approach it. In this process, we "de-corporealize" the image in order to be able to link it with new experiences and meanings, so that we can make it "our own."[27] The result is the construction of an image we may all share as a picture on the pictorial surface, but which is nevertheless individualized in the act of reception because of the imaginary transfer it stimulates.

What these observations all add up to is that a subject positioning by interpellation or a discursively produced reader or spectator position cannot determine the second narrative produced by the reader or spectator in the act of reception. In the transfer process that constitutes aesthetic experience, we can take up multiple identificatory positions. There is the possibility of "identification based on difference and identification based on similarity" (Stacey 171). While there are masculine and feminine spectator positions, viewers do not have to assume these positions according to their assigned genders. Moreover, we may identify with characters at one point but distance ourselves at the next when they act against our expectations. Filmic apparatus theory implies a far-ranging power of interpellation over the spectator, while the actual experience of watching movies is one of moving in and out of characters, switching sides and sympathies, getting angry or disappointed with characters or plots (which we usually express by calling a film "unrealistic"), of unexpected crossover identifications, and, altogether, a constant readjustment in response to the film and the way it affects us. As a result, we can be both object and subject of the act of seeing at the same time. The pleasure of the imagination, and also of the movies, is that we do not "necessarily identify in any fixed way with a character, a gaze, or a particular position, but rather with a series of oscillating positions" so that "the pleasures of watching a movie are also the pleasures of mobility, of moving around among a range of different desiring positions" (Williams 57). This is possible because in the transfer model our relation to the aesthetic object is established not by identification with a particular figure but by analogies between a potentially wide range of textual elements and the recipient's imaginary. If identification were the main mode of reception, then responses to fictional texts and aesthetic objects should be fairly predictable. Yet the history of reception of any fictional text reveals ever new possibilities for analogies. In consequence, there will always be new readings emerging.

The Imaginary and the Inadequacy of Interpretation

It is important in this context to be clear about the source and function of the fictional articulation effect. It should by no means be conceptualized as driven by a prediscursive, "authentic" residue of experience, nor should the transgressive potential of avant-garde texts be seen as its privileged manifestation.[28] The reason for a constantly renewed drive for articulation is not a prediscursive desire or unconscious drive but an inherent inadequacy of representation. We can speak only through the signs and cultural patterns that are available to us, but these will never completely express the full range of associations, feelings, and bodily sensations that seek articulation. Hence our imaginary perpetually exceeds the cultural script. We can articulate our interior states only through language, and yet we are constantly striving for new expressions of this interiority, because the imaginary that we articulate by attaching it to conventional signs is no longer identical with the imaginary that strove for expression.[29] On the one hand, the imaginary has found a possibility for articulation, but on the other hand, this articulation is possible only at the cost of reduction. We may articulate our desire by saying "I love you," but by attaching our feeling to such a conventional formulation that seems "safe" from misunderstanding, we also reduce the imaginary and full emotional dimension that may be connected with the experience of love. Paradoxically, then, articulation by means of fiction constantly refuels our need for articulation; this, in effect, provides another reason why we return to fictional texts again and again, although we are well aware of their practical "uselessness."

Fictional texts are ideal means for the articulation of an interiority that seeks representation. What makes them so wonderfully effective for this purpose, however—their ability to link imaginary elements with a semblance of the real—is at the same time also the reason for the insufficiency of representation and, consequently, for ever newer attempts to fill the gap. Since articulation can be achieved only by analogy, it remains indirect, provisional, and temporary, and since it can never fully express an interior state, it must stimulate an ongoing search for analogies that promise a fuller expression. Thus one analogy will be quickly replaced by another, often from one sentence to the next or from one image to the next. Barbara Maria Stafford captures this inherently provisional dimension when she says: "Analogy, born of the human desire to achieve union with that which one does not possess, is also a passionate process marked by fluid oscillations. Perceiving the lack of something—whether physical, emotional, spiritual, or intellectual—inspires us to search for an approximating resemblance to fill its place" (Stafford 2).

And yet what may appear as weakness from the perspective of adequate representation is also something that can provide the act of reading with special interest. On the one hand, the reader is driven to a search for ever-newer analogies because of the failure of representation to articulate the imaginary fully. On the other hand, it is precisely this shortcoming that may lead to the discovery of surprising, unexpected new affinities. Reading can be an adventure because it always holds the promise of unexpected encounters and discoveries. This, in effect, may explain the phenomenon of a hunger for fiction (*Lesehunger*), including the amazing fact that we expose ourselves again and again to fictional texts although we are aware that the fictional world is "unreal." The reason for our constant desire for articulation lies in the inability of representation to articulate our imaginary and express our interior states fully. Fictional texts and aesthetic objects can provide the illusion of fulfilling our wishes for articulation, but they can do so only by stimulating our desire for articulation ever anew.

But why do we experience the limits of representation as frustrating and as a challenge to try again? Once more, Iser's work can be taken as a point of departure. Ultimately, all hypotheses about the function of aesthetic experience must postulate an anthropological need. Iser's phenomenological approach in *The Act of Reading*, developed to give an account of aesthetic experience that would not be restricted to an experimental, modernist mode, is insufficient to deal with this question. Thus it made sense for Iser to return to a reconsideration of the function of literature and, by doing so, to move from reception aesthetics to the project of a literary anthropology. Iser's anthropological turn addresses two problems in particular: it helps to do away with a still lingering modernist bias of reception aesthetics by shifting the point of emphasis, more consistently than before, from the category of literature to that of fictionality as a mode of representation characterized by doubleness. And it does this by reconceptualizing the basic interplay that constitutes the "in-between" state of aesthetic experience through a new set of concepts, the real and the imaginary, the latter defined not in psychoanalytical terms as the source of an illusion of wholeness, but phenomenologically, as an indeterminate, diffuse, and protean flow of impressions and sensations.[30]

A significant problem remains, however. In Iser's reception aesthetics, the doubling structures of literary fictionality can be described only as potential, that is, in terms of their various doubling operations, because any attribution of a more specific meaning or function would arrest the ceaseless play of negativity.[31] And although Iser's anthropological turn promised to provide a more concrete description of the function of literary texts, it does not really enlarge the descriptive range, because the anthropological reason given for why we need fiction is another version of the experience of non-identity, namely, the "unknowability" of the self and the "inexperienceability" of the end (Iser 1989b). But do we really seek out fictional texts again and again in order to be confronted with the unknowability of the self? Are all our aesthetic experiences reenacting the same diffuse search for knowledge of an inaccessible origin or end? Even if this were the case, this diffuse longing for articulation and self-awareness is obviously articulated in historically, culturally, and psychologically different and diverse ways. Why so many different genres and media, then? Why comedy, tragedy, romance, and melodrama, historical novel and realistic novel, why literature, film, comics, and painting?

I want to suggest a different explanation and postulate a different anthropological need that can link my argument with an important recent development in critical theory, namely, a shift in criteria of social justice from distribution to recognition.[32] For American studies, Alexis de Tocqueville's *Democracy in America* is especially suggestive in this respect. What limited Tocqueville's analysis of American democracy, the Olympian perspective of a French aristocrat, can also be regarded as a major strength of his analysis, because it allowed him to grasp a fundamental transformation that the new political system of democracy brought about, which he subsumes under the term "equality." From the large-scale perspective of a comparison between aristocratic and democratic society, Tocqueville's understanding of equality refers not to ideals of social or economic justice but to the (then revolutionary) idea of an equality of rank. Equality of rank means that in principle, nobody can claim to be better or more worthy than anybody else in a democratic society. This, however, puts social and cultural life on an entirely new basis, for it creates a need to find new sources of recognition. As Amy Gutman has summarized the challenge in her introduction to Charles Taylor's "Politics of Recognition": "In the ancient regime, when a minority could count on being honored (as 'Ladies' and 'Lords') and the majority could not realistically aspire to public recognition, the demand for recognition was unnecessary for the few and futile for the many. Only with the collapse of stable social hierarchies does the demand for public recognition become commonplace, along with the idea of the dignity of all individuals. Everyone is an equal—a Mr., Mrs., or Ms.—and we all expect to be recognized as such" (Gutman 6).

In his own plea for a politics of recognition, Taylor uses this point of departure to argue for a multicultural politics of recognition. For Taylor, recognition means acknowledgment of the other person's dignity and leads to a demand for mutual respect. My reading of Tocqueville (who actually does not use the term *recognition*) points in another direction and starts on a more basic level: since rank no longer indicates the worth of a person, the individual is forced to take it upon herself to demonstrate her worth to others, because nobody else will do it for her. This is especially true in a society of immigrants with great cultural diversity and great mobility, because this mobility will increase the frequency of encounters with strangers and will create a need on the side of the individual to develop commonly understandable forms of self-presentation.

This new condition created by democracy must also affect the role of the aesthetic. One consequence of Tocqueville's starting premise, in contrast to Taylor, is that the problem of recognition is discussed not as an issue of moral philosophy but as a problem of identity formation under new social conditions. If everybody is considered an equal, then the problem must arise for the individual how to distinguish oneself from all the others who are equally equal: "They have swept away the privileges of some of their fellow creatures which stood in their way, but they have opened the door to universal competition: the barrier has changed its shape rather than its position. When men are nearly alike, and all follow the same track, it is very difficult for any one individual to walk quick and cleave away through the dense throng which surrounds and presses them" (Tocqueville 537).

In an essay on changing perceptions of America in Europe, called "American Studies and the Romance with America" (Fluck 2009), I offer a new version of the history of American studies: no longer as the response to knowledge gaps but as a sequence of changing imaginary attachments to objects of desire that pose a special imaginary attraction. In literary American studies in Germany this sequence is easy to trace: the attraction first to American modernists (a strong alternative to a discredited German culture) and then postmodernists (for a while the new avant-garde in international literature). Then, earlier than in other disciplines in the humanities, popular culture and the media (above all film) became preferred objects of analysis and pushed American studies in the direction of an extension into cultural studies. Finally, and most important for understanding the present situation, it was ethnic and African American literature that proved especially attractive and, paradoxically enough, continued the romance with an America in which these groups are, or had been, marginalized.

Why that special focus? What is the attraction that steers students and younger faculty in the direction of ethnic and African American studies? For most commentators, it seems that the phenomenon can be best explained, on the one hand, as a search for recognition on the part of the ethnic or racial groups themselves, and on the other hand, as a gesture of loyal political support on the part of those white middle-class Americanists who live in Bamberg or Braunschweig and may be far removed from the political struggles of ethnic or racial minorities in the United States. If, however, the main motive for focusing on this literature is a politics of recognition in Taylor's sense, how can that motive explain the fascination ("desire") of readers in Bamberg or Braunschweig who are not part of the group and thus cannot use this literature for their own search for recognition? Or can they?

At this point it is useful to recall that aesthetic experience does not rest on direct identification but that it is based on a transfer that can open up a field of analogies. The question would then be what analogies ethnic and African American literature offer to white readers outside the group. If one looks at it from the perspective of reading as transfer, a major point is that this literature takes its departure from experiences of misrecognition or the denial of recognition (as in Ralph Ellison's *Invisible Man*) and that the ensuing narrative is that of a transformation of inferiority into (moral) superiority, of discrimination into empowerment. Or to put it differently, ethnic and African American literatures can be especially attractive because they dramatize exemplary scenes of misrecognition. And since, as we have seen, reading by means of a transfer is selective and therefore segmented, these scenes of misrecognition can be taken out of their context and can function as an analogy for readers who consider lack of attention and recognition the major injustice they are experiencing under democratic conditions. In this case the ethnic and/or racial groups' search for recognition would become the host for articulating the reader's own imaginary longings for increased recognition in a politically correct manner. For a critical analysis of interpretations, such a reading would have consequences: it would mean having to look at competing interpretations in terms of the analogies on which these interpretations are based.

Transfer as Narrative Reconfiguration

But if it is one of the major functions of literary texts to provide individuals with an opportunity to inscribe themselves into cultural discourses in their own, highly subjective way, how can we say anything meaningful about this process at all? How is it possible to discuss a reading, if this reading acquires meaning only by means of a transfer in which an "invisible" imaginary dimension is articulated? We can characterize the structure of the transfer that constitutes aesthetic experience, but we cannot come up with a ready-made formula to describe its content or psychic function. The whole point about aesthetic experience is that it goes beyond such formulas and particularizes them in entirely unpredictable ways. The obvious problem is, however, that we have no direct access to that which is added in transfer. Strictly speaking, aesthetic experience is untranslatable. The only "document" we have is the reader's or interpreter's redescription of the aesthetic object that has functioned as host. In this redescription, the interpreter produces a second narrative that provides clues for that reader's encounter with the fictional text. For reasons discussed at the beginning of this essay, none of these readings or interpretations will ever be identical. But the difference can be instructive where certain patterns of reception emerge. The cultural history of literary texts thus cannot be separated from their varying uses in the act of reception; it is a history of second narratives. Literary history and the history of reception cannot be separated. As articulation of an imaginary that seeks articulation, the second narratives through which the literary text is actualized have their own historically distinct patterns, and a history of the second narratives through which literary texts are actualized and appropriated at different times is therefore one of the logical follow-up projects of any attempt to understand the changing functions of fiction. Seen from this perspective, the phenomenon of interpretive disagreement and conflict, which provided the point of departure for this essay, is no longer an irritating problem but, quite the contrary, an indispensable resource.

NOTES

1. In this chapter, literature and the literary text are thus taken as paradigms for aesthetic objects.

2. This argument has been developed in a number of my publications; see *Das kulturelle Imaginäre*; "The Role of the Reader and the Changing Functions of Literature: Reception Aesthetics, Literary Anthropology, *Funktionsgeschichte*"; "Aesthetic Experience of the Image"; "Playing Indian: Media Reception as Transfer."

3. The various approaches to literary interpretation are therefore based on different assumptions as to what provides the (minimum of) textual coherence that is the precondition for the possibility of interpretation. In New Criticism, for example, this coherence is provided by the text's structure, understood, however, not merely as a set of rules for the production of texts but as an innertextual pattern that transforms everyday language into the language of art—and thereby creates the aesthetic experience of an object without "extrinsic" purpose. Inevitably, interpretations based on these premises will focus on the identification of this pattern. But even in poststructuralist approaches, in spite of the valorization of heterogeneity and difference, the single sign is of interest only if it can be shown to be part of a disseminative trace, for only in this way can its deconstructive function be demonstrated. Again, a hypothesis about what function literature has—in the case of American deconstruction, for example, to provide telling instances of rhetorical self-deconstruction—determines the direction interpretation will take.

4. Iser confirms the logical priority of function over structure, but on different grounds. In the literary text, he writes, "the order and the formation of structures depend on the function that the text has to fulfill" (Iser 1979, 11). Such a formulation still seems to imply that we can determine the "real" function first and then explain the text's structure. Clearly, however, just as critics will differ on the text's meaning, so will they hold different hypotheses about the text's function. To introduce the term *function* as a heuristic category of analysis is thus an attempt not to anchor interpretation on "real" grounds but to draw attention to underlying assumptions that guide and govern every interpretation.

5. For a detailed analysis and discussion of the development of Iser's work, see my essay "The Search for Distance: Negation and Negativity in Wolfgang Iser's Literary Theory."

6. On this point, see my essay "Aesthetics and Cultural Studies."

7. See also Bruce Wilshire, *Role Playing and Identity*, from which Iser may have taken his Hamlet example: "It would follow, then, that the character Hamlet is real just insofar as we constitute ourselves by experiencing ourselves and speaking about ourselves through him—both as stage actors and as audience, or life actors; that is, when we experience ourselves and speak about ourselves through the proxy of Hamlet. The character's reality is a function of our own reality as playing, experimenting, self-knowing beings" (Wilshire 93).

8. On the role of images in this process, see Ellen Esrock's study *The Reader's Eye*.

9. This is the reason "why the identity constructed by the fictional text is actually more adequately described as a case of non-identity, since it puts the reader in a state *in-between* two identities, with neither of whom she is entirely identical" (Fluck 2007, 70).

10. As Carol J. Clover writes in her essay on horror movies, "We are both Red Riding Hood *and* the Wolf; the force of the experience, the horror, comes from 'knowing' both sides of the story" (Clover 1989, 95). The argument that fictional texts can dramatize and enact inner conflicts, for example, between the open expression of a desire and its disciplining, finds support here. In this respect, too, Clover offers an interesting comment: "Observers unanimously stress the readiness of the 'live' audience to switch sympathies in midstream, siding now with the killer and now, and finally, with the Final Girl" (Clover 1989, 113).

11. See also on this point Wilshire: "Together with the actors we alienate ourselves as characters so that we can return to ourselves as persons. Hamlet is ourselves speaking to ourselves about our essential possibilities" (Wilshire 99).

12. For this term and a more detailed version of my argument, see my history of the American novel, *Das kulturelle Imaginäre: Eine Funktionsgeschichte des amerikanischen Romans, 1790–1900*.

13. Thus my concept of aesthetic experience differs significantly from two

models that can be found in current debates: a concept of aesthetic experience as intensified experience, if not "epiphany" (Gumbrecht), and as a mode of experience that provides a liminal experience and can thus transform our perception (Fischer-Lichte). In both cases, aesthetic experience is rather conventionally equated with a modernist aesthetic. There are, however, many instances of aesthetic experience that do not have any dramatic effects of transformation; in fact our daily exposure to fictional texts and aesthetic objects (such as films or television series) that do not fit the transformative model is the rule and not the exception. But in this case, too, audiences seek these experiences again and again.

14. Famously, Ian Watt called Richardson's novel *Pamela* "a work that could be praised from the pulpit and yet attacked as pornography, a work that gratified the reading public with the combined attractions of a sermon and a striptease" (Watt 173).

15. See in this context Josué Harari's reference to the "duplicity" constituted by the imaginary: "The imaginary world is always with us, as a parallel world to our world; there is not a single moment of our existence which is not imbued with the imaginary. . . . In like manner, the real cannot be separated from the imaginary or the imaginary from the real" (Harari 57).

16. The recently renewed interest in the concept of the imaginary has put special emphasis on the social imaginary. See, for example, Charles Taylor's *Modern Social Imaginaries;* and Paula Moya and Ramón Saldívar, who provide a "transnational" reconsideration of the concept: "The trans-American imaginary is 'imaginary' to the extent that it figures a very real but fundamentally different syntax of codes, images, and icons, as well as the tacit assumptions, convictions, and beliefs that seek to bind together the varieties of American national discourses" (Moya and Saldívar 2). Cornelius Castoriadis calls the social imaginary "the radical instituting imaginary" (Castoriadis 1994, 136). It is important to note in this context that for Castoriadis the radical imaginary is the source of the self-creation of society ex nihilo and, hence, a counter-term to the idea of interpellation and subjection, whereas some recent uses of the term *social imaginary* seem to move the concept precisely in that direction.

17. This process must not take place consciously: "Our education, our upbringing, our social position predisposes us to certain cultural choices, yet there is often an unpredictability and surprise in the way that we feel ourselves claimed by some texts and left cold by others" (Felski 76).

18. As a basic form of literary representation, metaphor is already a form that works by analogy: "The essence of metaphor is understanding and experiencing one kind of thing in terms of another" (Lakoff and Johnson 5).

19. As Richard Slotkin has pointed out in his analysis of a composite heroic type in nineteenth-century American dime novels, in combining detectives with the style of outlaws and vice versa, popular culture derives its effectiveness at cultivating a seemingly contradictory range of choices: "This consensus, which

is national in its scope and in its concerns, finds its clearest and most pervasive expression in the mythology developed and purveyed by the media of mass culture. The commercial prosperity of those media depends on their power to incorporate a wide range of social and political referents and to entertain fantasies that express all sides of the public's contradictory desires and beliefs" (Slotkin 154).

20. See my essay on the aesthetic experience of space, "Imaginary Space; or, Space as Aesthetic Object."

21. Kuiken, Miall, and Sikora describe a case taken from their empirical reader research: "For example, one respondent reflecting on an orange colored patch was reminded of a medicine once taken and . . . was capable of fusing the emotional memory with the present color-impression. . . . In both cases, resonance occurs between explicitly recalled personal memories and some portion of the world of the aesthetic object" (Kuiken, Miall, and Sikora 181–182).

22. Rita Felski speaks of the possibility of an "emotional, even erotic cathexis onto the sound and surfaces of words" (Felski 63). A whole new field is opened up when we extend these considerations to images: "This brings me to the additional, novel claim that the visual arts are singularly suited to provide explanatory power for the nature and function of the analogical procedure" (Stafford 3).

23. On this point, see Stafford: "Since no form of organization, no matter how encyclopedic, can give complete access to the diversity of existing or imagined things, analogy provides opportunities to travel back into history, to spring forward in time, to leap across continents" (Stafford 11).

24. See the criticism of "classical" empirical reception studies by Kuiken, Miall, and Sikora: "Studies of reader personality . . . and gender . . . have examined the activities of actual readers to show how their sense of self influences the course of reading. However, they have been primarily concerned with the influence of enduring character traits—and less with the influence of fluctuations in the sense of self that occur during adult life. Moreover, because of their concern with stable personality characteristics, investigators in this tradition have seldom addressed changes in the sense of self . . . that may occur through literary reading" (Kuiken, Miall, and Sikora 174).

25. Lionel Trilling, introduction to *Adventures of Huckleberry Finn*. For an analysis of Trilling's reading, see Jonathan Arac's study *"Huckleberry Finn" as Idol and Target: The Functions of Criticism in Our Time*. For Arac, the "hypercanonization" of Twain's novel begins with Trilling's introduction.

26. Cf. Hans Belting, *Bild-Anthropologie;* Gottfried Boehm, ed., *Was ist ein Bild?;* Gernot Böhme, *Theorie des Bildes;* W. J. T. Mitchell, *Picture Theory: Essays on Verbal and Visual Representation;* Martin Schulz, *Ordnungen der Bilder;* Hans Belting, ed., *Bilderfragen: Die Bildwissenschaften im Aufbruch.*

27. This is Belting's term (Belting 2001, 21).

28. The assumption of an insatiable longing for the undifferentiated whole-

ness of the womb is one of the most problematic premises of Castoriadis's theory of the imaginary.

29. See Castoriadis's characterization of the, as he calls it, radical imagination of the singular human being in his essay "Radical Imagination and the Social Instituting Imaginary," where he writes: "This 'inside' is a perpetual, truly heraclitean, flux of representations *cum* affects *cum* intentions, in fact indissociable. . . . [F]or all we know, this stream of representations *cum* affects *cum* desires is absolutely singular for each singular human being" (Castoriadis 1994, 143–144).

30. The distinction between psychoanalytic and phenomenological definitions of the imaginary is important. For Lacan, the imaginary is the source of the subject's misrecognition and self-alienation; for Iser—as for Castoriadis in *The Imaginary Institution of Society*, a book that was influential in Iser's anthropological turn—the imaginary is the source of a creative energy that escapes the control of systemic power effects and can therefore function as a source of cultural and social change. Although Castoriadis took his point of departure from a psychoanalytic position and was influenced by Lacan, he broke with him in the 1960s and "wrote several critiques of Lacanian theory and practice. . . . According to Castoriadis, if the subject-to-be (mis)recognizes its reflected image in the 'mirror'—or mirroring other—it must already possess certain imaginary capacities for representation and identification" (Elliott 153–154). Thus Castoriadis can claim: "The imaginary does not come from the image in the mirror or from the gaze of the other. Instead, the 'mirror' itself and its possibility, and the other as mirror, are the works of the imaginary, which is creation *ex nihilo*" (Castoriadis 1987, 3).

31. Thus a shift of interpretive emphasis can be noted in Iser's transition from reception aesthetics to literary anthropology. While the former deals primarily with the phenomenology of text processing and highlights the role of textual blanks, the latter focuses on various manifestations of the text's doubling structures and their interaction. This "play of the text," however— exemplified, for instance, in Iser's book *Laurence Sterne's* Tristram Shandy—can only lead to a typology of play movements, because any further concretization would undermine the conceptualization of the play of the text as a manifestation of negativity. This, however, leaves only one route open, namely, "to grasp different modes of negativity that are in play with one another" (Iser 1989c, xiv). To me, this is the most sterile and disappointing aspect of Iser's approach.

32. See especially Charles Taylor, "The Politics of Recognition"; and Nancy Fraser and Axel Honneth, *Redistribution or Recognition? A Political-Philosophical Exchange*. Although varying in their philosophical premises and argumentative approaches, all three authors are primarily interested in the concept of recognition as a normative term in order to establish a new and more comprehensive criterion of justice than that of liberal rights or economic equality. All three are not interested in fictional texts and other aesthetic objects

(although Honneth has referred to Ralph Ellison's novel *Invisible Man* as an extreme case of misrecognition). For literary and cultural studies, these approaches therefore remain limited in their usefulness.

WORKS CITED

Adams, Suzi. "Interpreting Creation: Castoriadis and the Birth of Autonomy." *Thesis Eleven* 83 (2005): 25–41.
Appleyard, J. A. *Becoming a Reader: The Experience of Fiction from Childhood to Adulthood.* New York: Cambridge University Press, 1991.
Arac, Jonathan. *Huckleberry Finn as Idol and Target: The Functions of Criticism in Our Time.* Madison: University of Wisconsin Press, 1997.
Belting, Hans. *Bild-Anthropologie.* Munich: Fink, 2001.
———, ed. *Bilderfragen. Die Bildwissenschaften im Aufbruch.* Munich: Fink, 2007.
Boehm, Gottfried, ed. *Was ist ein Bild?* Munich: Fink, 1994.
Böhme, Gernot. *Theorie des Bildes.* Munich: Fink, 2006.
Brownstein, Rachel M. *Becoming a Heroine: Reading about Women in Novels.* New York: Penguin, 1982.
Castoriadis, Cornelius. *The Imaginary Institution of Society.* Cambridge: Polity Press, 1987.
———. "Radical Imagination and the Social Instituting Imaginary." In *Rethinking Imagination*, ed. Gillian Robinson and John Rundell. London: Routledge, 1994. 136–154.
Clover, Carol J. "Her Body. Himself. Gender in the Slasher Film." In *Fantasy and the Cinema*, ed. James Donald. London: BFI, 1989. 91–133.
Elliott, Anthony. "The Social Imaginary: A Critical Assessment of Castoriadis's Psychoanalytic Social Theory." *American Imago* 59.2 (2002): 141–170.
Esrock, Ellen J. *The Reader's Eye: Visual Imaging as Reader Response.* Baltimore: Johns Hopkins University Press, 1994.
Felski, Rita. *Uses of Literature.* Oxford: Blackwell, 2008.
Fischer-Lichte, Erika. "Ästhetische Erfahrung als Schwellenerfahrung." In *Dimensionen ästhetischer Erfahrung*, ed. Joachim Küpper and Christoph Menke. Frankfurt am Main: Suhrkamp, 2003. 138–161.
Fluck, Winfried. "'The American Romance' and the Changing Functions of the Imaginary." *New Literary History* 27.3 (1996): 415–457.
———. *Das kulturelle Imaginäre: Eine Funktionsgeschichte des amerikanischen Romans, 1790–1900.* Frankfurt am Main: Suhrkamp, 1997.
———. "The Search for Distance: Negation and Negativity in Wolfgang Iser's Literary Theory." *New Literary History* 31.1 (2000): 175–210.
———. "Aesthetics and Cultural Studies." In *Aesthetics in a Multicultural Age*, ed. Emory Elliott, Louis Freitas Caton, and Jeffrey Rhyne. New York: Oxford University Press, 2002. 79–103.

———. "The Role of the Reader and the Changing Functions of Literature: Reception Aesthetics, Literary Anthropology, *Funktionsgeschichte.*" *European Journal of English Studies* 6 (2002): 253–271.

———. "Aesthetic Experience of the Image." In *Iconographies of Power: The Politics and Poetics of Visual Representation*, ed. Ulla Haselstein, Berndt Ostendorf, and Peter Schneck. Heidelberg: Winter, 2003. 11–41.

———. "Imaginary Space; or, Space as Aesthetic Object." In *Space in America.* ed. Klaus Benesch and Kerstin Schmidt. Amsterdam, New York: Rodopi, 2005. 25–40.

———. "Playing Indian: Media Reception as Transfer." *Figurationen* 2 (2007): 67–86.

———. "American Studies and the Romance with America: Approaching America through Its Ideals." In *Romance with America? Essays on Culture, Literature, and American Studies*. Heidelberg: Winter, 2009. 87–104.

Fraser, Nancy, and Axel Honneth. *Redistribution or Recognition? A Political-Philosophical Exchange*. London: Verso, 2003.

Gallagher, Catherine, and Stephen Greenblatt. *Practicing New Historicism*. Chicago: University of Chicago Press, 2000.

Gumbrecht, Hans Ulrich. "Epiphanien." In *Dimensionen ästhetischer Erfahrung*, ed. Joachim Küpper and Christoph Menke. Frankfurt am Main: Suhrkamp, 2003. 203–222.

Gutman, Amy, ed. *Multiculturalism: Examining the Politics of Recognition*. Princeton: Princeton University Press, 1994.

Harari, Josué. *Scenarios of the Imaginary*. Ithaca: Cornell University Press, 1987.

Iser, Wolfgang. *Der Akt des Lesens: Theorie ästhetischer Wirkung*. Munich: UTB, 1976.

———. "The Current Situation of Literary Theory." *New Literary History* 11 (1979): 1–20.

———. "Fictionalizing Acts." *Amerikastudien/American Studies* 31 (1986): 5–15.

———. *Laurence Sterne's* Tristram Shandy. Munich: UTB, 1987.

———. "The Art of Failure: The Stifled Laugh in Beckett's Theater." In *Prospecting: From Reader Response to Literary Anthropology*. Baltimore: Johns Hopkins University Press, 1989a. 152–193.

———. "Representation: A Performative Act." In *Prospecting: From Reader Response to Literary Anthropology*. Baltimore: Johns Hopkins University Press, 1989b. 236–261.

———. "The Critical Turn: Toward 'Negativity' and the 'Unsayable.'" In *Languages of the Unsayable: The Play of Negativity in Literature and Literary Theory*, ed. Sanford Budick and Wolfgang Iser. New York: Columbia University Press, 1989c. xi–xx.

———. *The Fictive and the Imaginary: Charting Literary Anthropology*. Baltimore: Johns Hopkins University Press, 1993.

Kuiken, Don, David S. Miall, and Shelley Sikora. "Forms of Self-Implication in Literary Reading." *Poetics Today* 25.2 (2004): 171–203.

Lakoff, George, and Mark Johnson. *Metaphors We Live By.* Chicago: University of Chicago Press, 1980.

Mitchell, W. J. T. *Picture Theory: Essays on Verbal and Visual Representation.* Chicago: University of Chicago Press, 1994.

Moya, Paula M. L., and Ramón Saldívar. "Fictions of the Trans-American Imaginary." *Modern Fiction Studies* 49.1 (2003): 1–18.

Sartre, Jean Paul. *The Imaginary: A Phenomenological Psychology of Imagination.* London: Routledge, 2004.

Schulz, Martin. *Ordnungen der Bilder.* Munich: Fink, 2007.

Schwab, Gabriele. *The Mirror and the Killer-Queen.* Bloomington: Indiana University Press, 1996.

Slotkin, Richard. "Mythologies of Resistance: Outlaws, Detectives, and Dime-Novel Populism, 1873–1903." In *Gunfighter Nation: The Myth of the Frontier in Twentieth-Century America.* New York: Atheneum, 1992. 125–155.

Stacey, Jackie. "Feminine Fascinations: Forms of Identification in Star-Audience Relations." In *Stardom: Industry of Desire*, ed. Christine Gledhill. London: Routledge, 1991. 141–163.

Stafford, Barbara Maria. *Visual Analogy: Consciousness as the Art of Connecting.* Cambridge: MIT Press, 1999.

Taylor, Charles. "The Politics of Recognition." In *Multiculturalism: Examining the Politics of Recognition*, ed. Amy Gutman. Princeton: Princeton University Press, 1994. 25–73.

———. *Modern Social Imaginaries.* Durham: Duke University Press, 2004.

Tischleder, Bärbel. *"Body Trouble": Entkörperlichung, Whiteness und das amerikanische Gegenwartskino.* Frankfurt am Main: Strömfeld, 2000.

Tocqueville, Alexis de. *Democracy in America.* Garden City, N.Y.: Anchor Books, 1969.

Travis, Molly. *Reading Culture: The Construction of Readers in the Twentieth Century.* Carbondale: Southern Illinois University Press, 1998.

Trilling, Lionel. Introduction. In Samuel Langhorne Clemens, *Adventures of Huckleberry Finn.* Ed. Sculley Bradley, Richmond C. Beatty, and E. Hudson Long. Reprint. New York: W. W. Norton, 1948. 310–320.

Watt, Ian. *The Rise of the Novel.* Berkeley: University of California Press, 1967.

Williams, Linda. "Review of Judith Mayne, *Cinema and Spectatorship.*" *Film Quarterly* 48.2 (1994–95): 56–57.

Wilshire, Bruce. *Role Playing and Identity: The Limits of Theatre as Metaphor.* Bloomington: Indiana University Press, 1982.

Contributors

LAURA BIEGER is assistant professor/Juniorprofessorin of American culture at the John-F.-Kennedy-Institut for North American Studies, Freie Universität Berlin. She is the author of *Ästhetik der Immersion: Raum-Erleben zwischen Welt und Bild. Las Vegas, Washington und die White City* (2009), and *No Place Like Home: The Ontological Narrativity of Belonging and the American Novel* (forthcoming), and co-editor of several volumes of essays (on American studies, literature, and culture, on fashion as a critical paradigm for cultural studies, and, forthcoming, on space, place, and narrative).

LAWRENCE BUELL is Powell M. Cabot Research Professor of American Literature at Harvard University and author of numerous books including *Literary Transcendentalism* (1973), *New England Literary Culture* (1986), *Emerson* (2003), and three ecocritical books. He is a former Guggenheim and NEH Fellow and a member of the American Academy of Arts and Sciences. He is at work on two book projects: a cultural and critical history of the dream of the Great American Novel, and a study of the uses and abuses of environmental memory.

CHRISTA BUSCHENDORF is professor and chair of American literature and culture at Goethe-Universität Frankfurt am Main. She studied at Johannes-Gutenberg-Universität Mainz and Heinrich-Heine-Universität Düsseldorf, taught at Universität Bielefeld and Jena, and was a Visiting Fellow at Harvard in 2003–4, 2007–8, and 2011–12. Her scholarship focuses on transatlantic intellectual history, the reception of antiquity in America, and American poetry. In her current teaching and research she is exploring the approach of figurational and relational sociology to (African) American studies. Her latest book publications are *The High Priest of Pessimism: Zur Rezeption Schopenhauers in den USA* (2008) and *Civilizing and Decivilizing Processes: Figurational Approaches to American Culture*, edited with Astrid Franke and Johannes Voelz (2011).

WINFRIED FLUCK is professor and chair emeritus of American culture at the John-F.-Kennedy-Institut for North American Studies, Freie Universität Berlin. He is a founding member of the Graduate School for North American Studies at Freie Universität Berlin, a member of its Executive Board, and co-director of the Dartmouth Futures of American Studies Institute. His latest book publications are *Romance with America? Essays on Culture, Literature, and American Studies*, edited by Laura Bieger and Johannes Voelz (2009), *American Dream? Eine Weltmacht in der Krise*, edited with Andreas Etges (2011), and *Re-Framing the Transnational Turn in American Studies*, edited with Donald Pease and John Carlos Rowe (2011).

HERWIG FRIEDL is professor emeritus of American literature and history of ideas at Heinrich-Heine-Universität Düsseldorf. He studied American and German literatures and philosophy at the University of Heidelberg and at Cornell; he was a Postdoctoral Fellow at Yale in 1973–74, a Visiting Professor at the University of New Mexico in 1984, and a Visiting Scholar at Harvard in 2002, 2006, and 2007. His book publications include a study of Henry James's aesthetic theory (1972) and as editor essay collections on E. L. Doctorow (1986), on women's studies as cultural studies (2000), and on gender and conceptions of space (2006). His numerous essays focus on Transcendentalism, Pragmatism, modernism (Gertrude Stein), and American thinking in an international context.

HEINZ ICKSTADT is professor emeritus of American literature at the John-F.-Kennedy-Institut for North American Studies, Freie Universität Berlin. His publications include *Poetic Experience and the Structure of Metaphor: The Language of Hart Crane* (1975), *Der amerikanische Roman im 20. Jahrhundert: Transformationen des Mimetischen* (1998), and *Faces of Fiction: Essays on American Literature and Culture from the Jacksonian Age to Postmodernity*, edited by Susanne Rohr and Sabine Sielke. He also has edited and co-edited several books on American literature and culture, among them a bilingual anthology of American poetry, and is co-editing the first English-German edition of Pound's *Cantos*. He was president of the German Association of American Studies from 1990 until 1993, and president of the European Association of American Studies from 1996 to 2000.

LENE M. JOHANNESSEN is professor of American literature and culture in the Department of Foreign Languages at the University of Bergen, Norway. Her areas of research and teaching are generally focused on the ideological, cultural, social, and aesthetic manifestations and negotiations of the en-route as these are refracted in narratives, specifically in American and postcolonial literatures. She is the author of *Passage of Crisis: Threshold Time in Chicano Literature* (2008) and *Horizons of Enchantment: Essays in the American Imaginary* (2011), as well as the editor of several books in American and postcolonial studies.

CHRISTOPHER NEWFIELD is professor of English at the University of California, Santa Barbara. He is the author of *Unmaking the Public University: The Forty-Year Assault on the Middle Class* (2008), *Ivy and Industry: Business and the Making of the American University, 1880–1980* (2003), and *The Emerson Effect: Individualism and Submission in America* (1996), and he is a co-editor of *Mapping Multiculturalism* (1996) and *After Political Correctness: The Humanities and Society in the 1990s* (1995). He is also an active blogger and a regular contributor to the *Huffington Post*.

WALTER BENN MICHAELS is professor of English at the University of Illinois, Chicago. He is the author of several books on literary history and theory and is currently writing about the relation between aesthetic autonomy and political economy in the twenty-first century. The book will be called *The Beauty of a Social Problem*.

DONALD PEASE is the Ted and Helen Geisel Third Century Professor in the Humanities at Dartmouth College, chair of the Dartmouth Liberal Studies Program, and director of the Dartmouth Futures of American Studies Institute. He is the author of *Visionary Compacts: American Renaissance Writings in Cultural Context* (1987), *The New American Exceptionalism* (2009), and *Theodore Seuss Geisel* (2010), as well as editor and co-editor of numerous volumes, including *Reframing the Transnational Turn in American Studies* (2011), and general editor of *The New Americanists*, a series published by Duke University Press.

RAMÓN SALDÍVAR is professor of English and comparative literature and holds the Hoagland Family Professor of Humanities and Sciences chair at Stanford University. In 2007 he was the co-winner of the Modern Language Association Prize for best book in the area of U.S. Latina/Latino and Chicana/Chicano Literary and Cultural Studies for his book *The Borderlands of Culture: Américo Paredes and the Transnational Imaginary* (2006). In 2011 he was awarded the National Humanities Medal by President Barack Obama. He is currently working on a new project, tentatively titled "Race, Narrative Theory, and Contemporary American Fiction."

MARK SELTZER is Evan Frankel Professor of Literature at the University of California at Los Angeles. He has previously worked at Cornell and at the John-F.-Kennedy Institut, Freie Universität Berlin, and at the Humboldt Universität in Berlin. He has been a Visiting Fellow at the Stanford Humanities Center, the Center for Literary and Cultural Studies at Harvard, and the National Humanities Center, and Research Fellow at the Zentrum für Literatur-und Kulturforschung and the Max Planck Institut für Wissenschaftgeschichte in Berlin. He is the author of, among other works, *Serial Killers: Death and Life in America's Wound Culture* (1998), *True Crime: Observations on Violence and Modernity* (2007), and, forthcoming, of *The Official World* (from which the piece in this volume is adapted).

JOHANNES VOELZ is assistant professor of American studies at Goethe-Universität Frankfurt. He holds a Feodor Lynen Fellowship at Stanford University (2012–2014), awarded by the Alexander von Humboldt Foundation. He is the author of *Transcendental Resistance: The New Americanists and Emerson's Challenge* (University Press of New England, 2010) and has co-edited three essay collections. His articles have appeared in journals such as *American Literary History*, *Comparative American Studies*, and *Religion & Literature*.

Index

aesthetics, ix, xxv–xxvi, 27; aesthetic experience, 240–49; and the imaginary, 251–57; and interpretation, 237–40; modernist, 43, 49–54, 146–47; negative, 12, 15

affect, 134, 194, 210n1, 210–11n4, 244, 261n29; affective turn, 143, 160–61n22

Agamben, Giorgio, 219, 230, 233n2

Althusser, Louis, xiii–xv

Anderson, Benedict, xvi–xvii, xxii, 87, 193; "imagined communities," xiv–xv, 25, 84–86, 90, 103n4

Appadurai, Arjun, viii, 112

apparatus theory, 251

Appleyard, J. A., 243

area studies, 5, 112, 124

Armstrong, Nancy, 36–37

Ashby, Ross, 149, 155

autopoiesis, 155, 169n38

Bacigalupo, Massimo, 58

Bakhtin, Mikhail, 52, 108, 122

Behdad, Ali, 31

belonging, xi–xiii, 86–87, 90, 219

Bender, Thomas, 30

Benjamin, Walter, 229

Bercovitch, Sacvan, 27, 120

Bildungsroman, 5, 9, 32, 35–39, 152, 168–69n778

biopolitics, 153, 226–31

blackness: and identity politics, 180–85; black intellectuals 89–90; black nationalism 88–89, 103nn3–4; black studies, 28; blackface 43; "postblack" writers, 4. *See also* Du Bois, W. E. B.

borderlands, 16; post-borderlands, 3–4, 10–11

border studies, xvi. *See also* borderlands

Bourdieu, Pierre, 67–68, 85, 88, 102n1, 102–103n2

Bulosan, Carlos, 33, 35–36

Caillois, Roger, 131, 150–51n10

Camus, Marcel, 215–17

capitalism, 48, 54–55, 101, 179, 184–89, 202–12

Castoriadis, Cornelius, xvi–xix, 25, 44, 67–68, 73, 109, 259, 259n28, 260nn29–30; *The Imaginary Institution of Society*, xvi, 26. *See also* imaginary, the

Cather, Willa, 33–34, 36

Chabon, Michael, xxiv, 16, 179, 181–82, 185–86

Charcot, Jean-Martin, 145

Chatterjee, Partha, 26, 38

Cheah, Pheng, 36–37

colonialism, 6, 7, 15, 45, 117, 199, 216, 220

cosmopolitanism, 17, 44–45, 53–58, 92–93

crisis, 178, 202–204, 212n14, 222–25

Darío, Rubén, xxi, 46

DeKoven, Marianne, 43, 55

desire, 6, 14–15, 44, 58, 193–95, 217–33, 242–44, 251–55

Dewey, John, 54, 68

diaspora, viii, 5, 7–8, 14, 17–18, 25, 35

Díaz, Junot, xx–xxi, 4–10, 14–17

Douglass, Frederick, xxii, 90–96, 102, 103nn5–6

Du Bois, W. E. B., xxii, 89–102; "double consciousness," 89–90, 99

Durkheim, Émile, xxii, 67, 70, 74, 82n2, 127, 132, 151

Elias, Norbert, xxii, 84–88, 94–95, 102

Ellis, Bret Easton, 181

Welty, Eudora, 108, 110
West, Cornel, 88–89
Whitehead, Colson, xxiv, 4, 179, 185
whiteness, 36
Whitman, Walt, xxiii, 43, 45, 60n8, 78,
    110–26
Wiener, Norbert, 137, 142

Williams, William Carlos, xxii,
    47–48, 52–54, 56–58
Wood, James, 185
Wuthnow, Robert, 31, 37

Žižek, Slavoj, 16, 20n21, 224,
    234n16